Malcolm D. Mc Lean

Publication of Volume V

was made possible

by

THE UNIVERSITY OF TEXAS

AT ARLINGTON

PREVIOUS VOLUMES

*The editing of these volumes was financed by a $20,000
grant from the J. M. West Texas Corporation
combined with research leave from
Texas Christian University*

Volume

I. 1788-1822. THE TEXAS ASSOCIATION.

Publication made possible by a grant of $10,000 from
the Kathryn O'Connor Foundation. This volume won
both the Coral Horton Tullis Memorial Prize, offered
by The Texas State Historical Association "for the
most important contribution to Texas history in 1974,"
and the Summerfield G. Roberts Award, offered by the
Sons of the Republic of Texas.

II. 1823 through September, 1826. LEFTWICH'S GRANT.

Published with a grant of $6,000 from the Kathryn
O'Connor Foundation and $5,000 from the Alice Sneed West
Foundation. On the basis of Volumes I and II, Dr. McLean
received an Award of Merit on September 19, 1976, from
the American Association for State and Local History,
"for his contribution to the study of Texas history in
Papers Concerning Robertson's Colony in Texas."

III. October, 1826, through April, 1830. THE
NASHVILLE COLONY.

The Publications Committee of the Texas Historical
Foundation honored this volume by choosing it as the
first to be sponsored by that group, and it advanced
a Bicentennial Grant of $15,000 to facilitate its
publication.

IV. May through October 10, 1830. TENOXTITLAN,
DREAM CAPITAL OF TEXAS.

With this volume The University of Texas at Arlington
assumed the financial responsibility for publishing
the remainder of the series.

*All of these volumes can be purchased
from the UTA Press, Box 19929,
The University of Texas at Arlington
Arlington, Texas 76019*

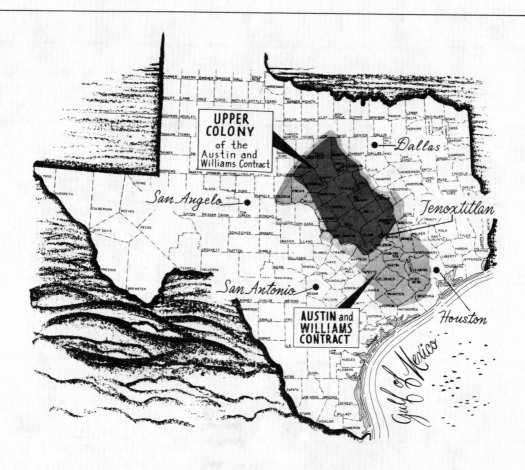

Map showing how Austin designed the boundaries of the Austin & Williams Contract so as to include all of his earlier colonies, and, in addition, to swallow up Leftwich's Grant, later known as the Upper Colony.

These boundaries, which have never been properly defined on any previous map, were as follows: "The said measurement shall begin on the left bank of the Lavaca River, withdrawing ten leagues from the coast, following said River upstream to its westernmost headwaters; from thence a straight line shall be drawn to the Northwest until it touches the road that goes from Béxar to Nacogdoches, known with the name of the Upper Road, and following this in a Northeasterly direction to the Colorado River, ascending the right bank of said river to the mouth of the Salt or Red Fork, which enters about fifteen leagues above the mouth of the Pecan or Nueces River; from the said Salt Fork a straight line shall be drawn to the Northeast to the heights which divide the waters of the Brazos and Trinity Rivers; following the said heights toward the Southeast to the principal headwaters of the San Jacinto and, descending this River to the line of the ten littoral leagues, the said line shall continue toward the West to the point where the present demarcation began."

— Map originally published in *Texas Parade*, Austin, August, 1949, page 11.

PAPERS CONCERNING
ROBERTSON'S COLONY
IN TEXAS

COMPILED AND EDITED

BY

MALCOLM D. McLEAN

VOLUME V

October 11, 1830, through
March 5, 1831

THE UPPER COLONY

The UTA Press

Box 19929

THE UNIVERSITY OF TEXAS AT ARLINGTON

ARLINGTON, TEXAS 76019

1978

FIRST PRINTING
Copyright© 1978 by The University of Texas at Arlington
All rights reserved
for material not previously published elsewhere.

Library of Congress Catalogue Card No. 73-78014
Manufactured in the United States of America

ISBN 0-932408-05-2

The translations of Béxar Archives documents that appear in this
volume have been made by Dr. Malcolm D. McLean of UT Arlington,
with the permission of Mr. Harold W. Billings, Director of General
Libraries, UT Austin, and, in return for this courtesy, UT Arlington is
happy to grant permission to UT Austin to incorporate Dr. McLean's
translations into its long-term project to translate the Béxar Archives,
and to deposit such translations with the Béxar County Commissioners
Court, the owner of the original documents.

Affectionately Dedicated

to my wife,

MARGARET STONER McLEAN,

who is completing her fortieth year

of work on these *Papers*

without pay.

M. D. M.

PREFACE

We want to begin this preface by giving the complete details concerning the copyrights covering the volumes in this series — something we have never seen done before in a preface. In that connection we wish to express our deep appreciation to Dr. James Newcomer, Director of the TCU Press, who transferred the copyright to Volumes I, II, and III of the *Papers Concerning Robertson's Colony in Texas* to Dr. Malcolm D. McLean, 409 Baylor Drive, Arlington, Texas 76010, on November 4, 1977. These transfers were recorded on November 14, 1977, in the Copyright Office of the United States of America, The Library of Congress, Washington, D.C. 20559, as follows:

Volume I, Class A Registration No. A 579746, recorded in Volume 1644 on Page 260.

Volume II, Class A Registration No. A 685339, recorded in Volume 1644, Page 261.

Volume III, Class A Registration No. A 799763, recorded in Volume 1644, Page 262.

The application for copyright to Volume IV, in the name of The University of Texas at Arlington, UTA Box 19929, Arlington, Texas 76019, was filed on October 26, 1977, under Class A Registration No. A 905074.

Next we want to give proper credit to various individuals who had an integral part in preparing the copy for Volume V. Jennifer Jiles, who had typed many of the documents for this volume, resigned, effective February 14, 1978, to move on to a better position in the UTA Library, and her position as Research Associate for the Robertson Colony Collection was filled on March 1, 1978, by Mrs. Laura Braddy, who came to UTA after gaining more than thirteen years of experience with the Texas Christian University Press.

In order to bridge the gap and provide for a smooth transition in making this change, John A. Hudson, UTA Librarian, took the initiative in applying to Dr. Bob F. Perkins, Dean of the Graduate School, for additional funds, and, on January 31, 1978, Dean Perkins made a grant from the Organized Research Fund for assistance in editing the Robertson Colony Papers.

On March 14, 1977, Mr. Hudson assigned Miss Terri Diane Hiller, a part-time Clerical Assistant in the Library, to help with the very exhausting task of making Xerox copies of the entire Robertson Colony Collection. This work was completed on August 31 of that same year.

J. C. Martin, Director of Special Collections, made it possible for us to proceed more rapidly with our research in the future by ordering Segments Two and Three of the Béxar Archives on microfilm, thus giving the UTA Library a complete set of this invaluable research tool, which contains the official records of Texas from 1717 through 1836.

Most of the photographic illustrations for this volume were made by Bruce A. Austin, Clerk Assistant in the Audio Visual Technical Services of the UTA Library.

On May 12, 1978, Dr. Wendel H. Nedderman, President of The University of Texas at Arlington, gave his permission for us to use The UTA Press imprint on Volume V, just as we had done on Volume IV.

Mr. Dudley Wetsel, UTA Vice President for Business Affairs, and Dr. Willie A. Baker, Vice President for Academic Affairs, are still working on the plans for the promised special quarters for housing the Robertson Colony Collection, and, although the actual construction has not been started as we go to press, there is a possibility that the Robertson Colony Room could be finished and ready for dedication by the time that this volume is published.

Mr. Larry D. Minor, Manager of the UTA University Bookstore, and Mrs. Margaret Roberts, Sales Clerk, have continued to handle the sale of all volumes through the Bookstore.

Turning now to the friends off campus who have given us special assistance, we wish to thank Dr. Paul Parham, Librarian at Texas Christian University in Fort Worth, for his continued support of this research project, and we are particularly indebted to various members of his staff for keeping us supplied with rolls of microfilm from the Béxar Archives, which we have had to borrow through Inter-Library Loan while waiting for the UTA Library to receive their copies of this same film from The University of Texas at Austin. Also in Fort Worth we have continued to draw upon the Newspaper Microfilm Collection of the Amon Carter Museum of Western Art for copies of rare Tennessee, Louisiana, Arkansas, and Texas newspapers.

In Austin we received valuable assistance from the following individuals:

Sister M. Dolores, Catholic Archives of Texas, for helping us with religious terminology.

Miss Matilde S. Rosales, Spanish Translator in the General Land Office.

Dr. Dorman Winfrey, Director and Librarian, Texas State Library.

Miss Victoria Reed and Ralph Elder, in the Archives of The University of Texas at Austin.

Mrs. Betty B. Schmidt, Secretary, The General Libraries, The University of Texas at Austin, for completing all arrangements for providing UTA with a microfilm copy of the Béxar Archives.

In College Station, Texas, we wish to pause for a moment to thank Eleanor Hanover Nance (Mrs. Joseph Milton Nance) for drafting the maps showing the location of Fort Tenoxtitlan.

Down in Galveston Mr. Robert A. Nesbitt and The Rosenberg Library are to be thanked for furnishing a copy of the Samuel M. Williams portrait.

From Nashville, Tennessee, we received some very valuable new information from Mrs. W. F. Fullerton, genealogist, concerning Major Sterling C. Robertson's life before coming to Texas.

Finally, Dr. John Porter Bloom, of The National Archives, Washington, D.C., deserves special praise for the copious information he sent concerning Indian Peace Medals.

Malcolm D. McLean
Professor of History and Spanish
The University of Texas at Arlington

409 Baylor Drive
Arlington, Texas 76010

June 8, 1978

TABLE OF CONTENTS

PAPERS CONCERNING ROBERTSON'S COLONY IN TEXAS
Volume V: October 11, 1830, through March 5, 1831
THE UPPER COLONY

CALENDAR

October (continued), 1830

March, 1831

INTRODUCTION

Once again we must remind the reader that *this is a story of a piece of land and how it influenced the lives of men*. We made this statement in the "Proem" to Volume I, but some critics of the series apparently either never read it or missed the point completely. We are in no hurry to skip on over to the part they already know about: we are trying to find out what really happened in Texas in that vague and mysterious period before the Texas Revolution, and in the process we expect to contribute something new and different, based on the actual writings of the participants themselves.

Although the present volume is limited to a time span of less than five months (from October of 1830 to March of 1831), it covers a series of events that had a vast effect on the ownership of land in Texas today, and it reveals the decision which blasted Stephen F. Austin's political career. On the lighter side, it shows us how the lives of the Anglo-Americans, the Mexicans, and the Indians became intimately intertwined, in a more humane, sympathetic, and understanding atmosphere than the usual Texas histories would lead us to believe ever existed here.

"Four Little, Three Little, Two Little Indians"

For instance, in Volume IV we told how the Nicasio Sanches Expedition captured four little Indian boys and a Negro slave on the banks of the San Gabriel. In this volume we learn that the Negro was ordered "liberated" back into slavery by being returned to his owner down in Austin's Colony.

As for the little Indians, General Manuel de Mier y Terán, Commandant General of the Eastern Interior States, ordered that they should be sent to the Commissar in Monterrey. Before these orders could be carried out, however, one of the babies had died because it was too young to adapt to "civilized" food. The next two were so young that they had not been weaned, and the Mexican families, in the process of feeding and caring for them, became so fond of them that they filed an application for permission to go through all the legal formalities and adopt them as their own. General Mier y Terán approved the request, on the condition that Ramón Músquiz, the Political Chief, would assume the responsibility for their "preservation" and education. So — *¿Quién sabe?* — maybe the descendants of José Antonio Salinas and Juan Casanova, the two men who adopted these little fellows, can point with pride and affection to a Tawakoni Indian somewhere in their family tree.

On the other hand, the descendants of Damacio Galván or Manuel de Luna can point with equal pride to the fact that their ancestor received a special citation from the Vice President of Mexico for distinguished service as a scout on that same expedition.

That brings us down to "one little Indian boy," as the song concludes. That fourth little Indian was forwarded from Béxar to Laredo, and from there to Monterrey, and, furthermore, he was furnished with travel expenses and a military escort — to protect him from the Indians, naturally.

Somehow we have a feeling that these benevolent results may not have been exactly what Colonel Elosúa had in mind when he ordered Captain Sanches "to pursue the Tawakonis to their village and punish them severely."

Lo, the Westering Indian

In the first few pages of this volume we also come across a highly symbolic scene which cries out for the attention of some aspiring Texas artist. It shows Bracisco, a Waco Indian chief, standing on the east bank of the Brazos River at the San Antonio Crossing.

Around his neck he is wearing a large silver peace medal. On one side it shows a miniature of James Madison, President of the United States, and on the other side it depicts the hands of an Indian and a white man, joined, with a tomahawk and peace pipe and the words: "PEACE AND FRIENDSHIP."

These medals had been struck off in solid silver in 1814 and 1815, and obviously they must have been distributed some time before President Madison went out of office in 1817, to Indians in or near the United States. Then why did Chief Bracisco turn up some thirteen years later on the Brazos River, in Mexican territory, wearing one of these medals? This placed him far west of the Sabine, which then marked the United States-Mexican boundary.

The answer lies in a letter that Peter Ellis Bean, the Mexican Indian Agent in Nacogdoches, wrote to Colonel Antonio Elosúa, the Military Commandant in Béxar, on October 12, 1830, reporting that the United States Congress had appropriated money to move over 100,000 Indians to lands west of the Mississippi, and that some of them were bound to infiltrate into Texas. Colonel Bean recommended that Mexico should take some countermeasures. Specifically, he proposed another campaign against the Wacos and Tawakonis. He went to San Antonio for a conference with Elosúa, and a call for civilian volunteers was sent out to Austin's and DeWitt's colonies, but the whole plan fell through when Elosúa discovered that nobody knew where the Indians were. When these facts were reported to General Mier y Terán, he ordered Elosúa to limit himself to providing safety for the new establishment at Tenoxtitlan.

Colonel Bean did accomplish two other things on that trip to Béxar, though. He filed a formal request to be allowed to defend his honor against a charge of bigamy, and, on his return journey, he carried the payroll from Béxar to the troops at Tenoxtitlan.

The Permanent Site of Tenoxtitlan

Now that we have mentioned Fort Tenoxtitlan, we should bring the reader up to date on what has happened concerning that project since the end of Volume IV. The reader will recall that the temporary encampment had been located on the east bank of the Brazos River and below the Béxar-Nacogdoches Road, in Austin's Colony. That was in July of 1830. It was not until some three months later, on October 17, 1830, that Lieutenant Colonel Francisco Ruiz marched his troops up the Brazos into the area that had been assigned to the Nashville Company and camped at the place which he had selected for the permanent site of Fort Tenoxtitlan.

It was described by Stephen F. Austin as being on the west bank of the Brazos, about twelve miles below the mouth of the San Andrés (Little River) and about one hundred miles above San Felipe de Austin. It was beautifully situated and abundantly supplied "with large and pure fountains of water." The country around it was very fertile and pleasant, and the Brazos River was said to be navigable above that point in time of freshets (i.e., when the river was on a rise).

Today the site can be reached by going northeast from Caldwell, Texas, on Highway 21, then turning left on Highway 1362 to the vicinity of the Teal Prairie School. From this point the site is off the road to the right, in a pasture on private property. Near the site stands a marker erected during the 1936 Texas Centennial Celebration. However, in order to save the reader the trouble of tramping through high weeds, getting himself covered with ticks and redbugs, opening and closing about four gates or gaps, exposing himself to poison ivy, or being chased by a bull, we are going to reproduce the inscription on the marker here. It reads as follows:

2000 FEET SOUTH
SITE OF

FORT TENOXTITLAN

ESTABLISHED BY THE MEXICAN GOVERN-
MENT IN JULY, 1830, IN AN ATTEMPT
TO STEM ANGLO-AMERICAN SETTLEMENT.
NAMED IN HONOR OF THE AZTEC
CAPITAL, NOW MEXICO CITY. ABANDONED
BY MEXICAN TROOPS IN 1832. IN THE
TOWN WHICH GREW UP AFTER 1834
MANY PROMINENT TEXANS LIVED. THE
PLACE PASSED FROM THE MAP AFTER 1860

[Near Caldwell][1]

As we have already pointed out, the date of July, 1830, refers to the establishment of the temporary site below the Béxar-Nacogdoches Road, but this marker is actually near the permanent site above the road, which was established on October 17, 1830.

A much longer inscription is found on the marker erected by the Burleson County Historical Survey Committee and dedicated at 4:00 p.m. on July 19, 1970. Located five miles east of Caldwell on Highway 21 in a roadside park, it reads as follows:

MARKER INSCRIPTION

"DREAM CAPITAL OF TEXAS"

FORT TENOXTITLAN

(SITE ABOUT 8 MILES NORTHEAST)

FOUNDED BY MEXICO AS A BULWARK AGAINST ANGLO-AMERICAN IMMIGRATION, THIS FORT AND ITS NEARBY CITY WERE TWICE PROPOSED FOR THE CAPITAL OF TEXAS.

ALARMED BY THE INFLUX OF ANGLO SETTLERS INTO TEXAS, MEXICO IN 1830 SOUGHT TO ERECT A LINE OF FORTS TO KEEP OUT THE INTRUDERS. THE ANCIENT AZTEC NAME FOR MEXICO CITY (ORIGINALLY PRONOUNCED "TEN-OX-TEET-LAN") WAS GIVEN THIS SITE; IT MEANS "PRICKLY PEAR PLACE". SO HOPEFUL OF THE FORT'S SUCCESS WAS THE MILITARY COMMANDANT OF THE REGION THAT HE ENVISIONED IT AS THE CAPITAL OF TEXAS. BUT ANGLO IMMIGRATION DID NOT CEASE. INSTEAD IT THRIVED ON THE FRIENDSHIP OF THE LOCAL SOLDIERS AND INCOMING PIONEERS. THE COLONIZER STERLING C. ROBERTSON INTRODUCED SCORES OF SETTLERS.

IN 1832 THE SOLDIERS WERE WITHDRAWN AND THE FORT FINALLY DEFAULTED TO THE ANGLOS. SUBSEQUENTLY IT WAS A SUPPLY CENTER AND MUSTERING POINT FOR EXPEDITIONS AGAINST THE INDIANS. DURING ITS BRIEF LIFE MANY TEXAS PATRIOTS LIVED HERE, INCLUDING 5 SIGNERS OF THE TEXAS DECLARATION OF INDEPENDENCE, A MARTYR OF THE ALAMO SIEGE, AND 7 SOLDIERS OF THE BATTLE OF SAN JACINTO.

TENOXTITLAN WAS AGAIN SUGGESTED FOR THE CAPITAL OF TEXAS DURING THE REPUBLIC, BUT AUSTIN WON OUT. IN 1841, AFTER MANY INDIAN RAIDS, THE SITE WAS ABANDONED. (1970)

Marker Awarded by Texas State Historical Survey Committee

Dr. Malcolm D. McLean presenting a copy of
his article and talk on Tenoxtitlan to Mrs.
D. L. Alford, Jr., Chairman of the Burleson
County Historical Survey Committee, for preservation in their splendid museum in the
basement of the Burleson County Court House,
Caldwell, Texas. This presentation was made
after the unveiling of the marker on July 19,
1970. The text of the inscription on the opposite page is a facsimile reproduction from
the program distributed on that occasion.

Since I had read a paper on Tenoxtitlan at the annual meeting of the Texas State Historical Association on April 26, 1963, and it had been published serially in *The Burleson County Citizen and The Caldwell News* and reprinted in *The Southwestern Historical Quarterly*,[2] I was awarded the honor of making the dedicatory address at the unveiling of this marker in July of 1970. Shouting to make my voice heard above the deafening roar of traffic along the nearby highway, I found the setting quite a contrast to the somnolent silence which must have prevailed in those Brazos River bottoms one hundred and forty years earlier, when one lonely, lumbering oxcart made its creaking, complaining way to the banks of that stream, laden with the cannon, the cannon balls, and the blacksmith's anvil and forge for that tiny outpost in the wilderness. If I had realized that on the day of the dedication we would experience the same sweltering heat that must have greeted Colonel Francisco Ruiz when he pitched camp at the temporary site in July, 1830, I would have suggested that we postpone the dedication until October 17, 1970, the anniversary of the date Ruiz arrived at the permanent location. In any event, that helps to explain why I chose October 17, 1978, as the publication date for this volume.

Let us return now to the plans for building the fort.

The Plans for the Fort

On October 12, 1830, General Mier y Terán, writing from his headquarters in Matamoros, notified Colonel Elosúa that on that same date he was sending a model and a plan for a fort to Rafael Chowell, who was to make a copy of the specifications to use in building Fort Anáhuac. Then he was to forward them to Elosúa for the building of Fort Tenoxtitlan. Chowell did not forward the little box containing the model to Béxar until November 8, 1830, but Elosúa sent it on to Francisco Ruiz almost immediately (on November 13, 1830). It was the day after Christmas, though, before Ruiz sent both the plan and the model down to San Felipe to get the specifications translated into English because the Anglo-Americans who were going to bid on furnishing the materials for the fort did not know any Spanish. (There is a touch of irony here, in that the materials for the fort to keep out Anglo-Americans were to be supplied by Anglo-Americans.) By the end of January, 1831, Ruiz had decided that he did not have anybody available with enough experience to direct the construction of the fort, so he sent all the documents back to Elosúa in Béxar, with a suggestion that he request professional assistance from General Mier y Terán.

The Cost of Materials and Labor
(and Groceries)

Finally, however, on February 20, 1831, Santiago Navayra, the official who had been commissioned to superintend the construction of the fort, did submit to Colonel Elosúa two estimates of the cost of building the fort, either out of lumber or out of bricks. These estimates had been made by an architect down in San Felipe, to whom Navayra had been introduced for that purpose by Samuel M. Williams, but Navayra forgot that expert's name immediately, so the credit will have to go to that ever growing list of Architects Anonymous whose buildings we pass on the streets every day.

Some of the specifications are hard to figure out or visualize, but it appears that, if they built the structures of wood, they would need about 65,000 feet of logs of one size or another, plus 12,300 feet of boards, 3,850 shakes, 90,600 shingles, 49,000 bricks, and 1,500 pounds of nails, as well as door latches and locks. There was to be a *noria*, or well, equipped with a series of buckets for raising water to the surface, and around the outside there was to be a moat. The outside walls would be two feet thick and the inside walls one foot. It would take 66 men and 13 officials 100 days, and they would need 4 crosscut saws, 2 handsaws, 60 axes, 10 broad-axes, the corresponding number of picks and shovels, 30 oxen, and 10 oxcarts. To feed the crew it would take 15,000 pounds of meat, 316 bushels of corn, 500 pounds of coffee, 500 pounds of sugar, and 300 pounds of salt. According to the way we read the figures, it looks like it would have cost about 22,750 pesos to build the fort of wood.

The estimate for building the fort out of bricks was much more systematic. They calculated that, if they employed 80 workmen, they could mold and stack 16,000 bricks a day, and, if they worked 26 days a month for six months, they would produce 2,496,000 bricks. However, they conceded that, if the workmen were skillful or fast, they could knock off two months. It would take an additional 50 workmen to burn the bricks and furnish the bricklayers with mortar, plus another 15 workmen to burn the necessary amount of lime. Add to this 15,000 feet of boards, 20 quintals of iron, 400 pounds of nails, 3 wagons and oxen to pull them, the salaries of bricklayers, carpenters, blacksmiths, the cost of putting a wooden stockade on the wall of the moat, and that would run to a total of about 20,000 pesos. For the outside walls of the moat, terrapleining the bulwarks and esplanades, the wall of the patio, and for the stables, the powder magazine, the *azoteas* (flat roofs) of the stables, terrapleining the patio, and the *noria*, it would take a total of 2,416,500 bricks and 7,731 bushels of lime. For beams they would need 100,000 feet of lumber, 10,000 feet of boards, 2,000 pounds of iron, and 400 pounds of nails.

So it looks like it would have cost about 2,750 pesos more to build the fort of wood, but they could have finished it sooner, taking about four months, whereas it might have taken as much as six months if they had built it of brick. However, it probably would have cost more to build the brick version than we have indicated, since we notice that they did not figure in the cost of food with the brick estimate. Obviously the estimates of the two versions are not strictly comparable, to put it mildly.

This question of cost may turn out to be academic anyway, since, despite the fact that the Commissar in Béxar had been ordered to give first priority to disbursements for the construction of Fort Tenoxtitlan, up to the end of this volume he had earmarked only 2,000 pesos for that purpose — whenever they came in — but Mexican customs receipts had dropped off so drastically that there was very little money to send to Tenoxtitlan. A little later on in this "Introduction" we shall find out what was causing that drop in receipts at the Mexican customs.

The People at Tenoxtitlan

The payroll for the Álamo de Parras Presidial Company shows that there were 64 members of that unit on duty in Tenoxtitlan on January 1, 1831, and to this number we must add the picket of 40 men from the Béxar Company who had arrived at the permanent site of Tenoxtitlan on October 23, 1830, to reinforce that garrison. Three days later an oxcart, a mule train, and an escort were dispatched from Tenoxtitlan to Béxar to bring out the families of nine men in the Álamo Company. Those nine families left Béxar for Tenoxtitlan on November 5, 1830, carrying all their worldly possessions in *one* oxcart. It had also been suggested that some of the old folks might be able to ride in the cart. The scene depicting their arrival in Tenoxtitlan would require the talents of an entirely different kind of artist from the one we suggested for painting the portrait of Chief Bracisco on the Brazos.

The Catholic Parish of Tenoxtitlan

For several months the Álamo Company had been carrying the position of Chaplain on its payroll, but that post had been shown as vacant. Now, however, with the arrival of these Mexican families in Tenoxtitlan, there was an increased need for a Catholic priest. Consequently on October 30, 1830, General Mier y Terán ordered Colonel Elosúa to send Presbyter Juan Nepomuceno Ayala from Béxar to serve as priest for the Parish of Tenoxtitlan. At first Father Ayala objected to the assignment, complaining that he was suffering from "the French infirmity" (venereal disease) and therefore could not ride on horseback. To this Colonel Elosúa replied that he had no authority to *change* General Mier y Terán's orders, only to *enforce* them, and therefore, (to couch the story in Biblical language) he had better get *on* his ass and ride! So that is why Father Ayala rode tall in the saddle.

Before he left Béxar, however, Father Ayala asked Father Refugio de la Garza, the priest in charge there, to supply him with the following ornaments and vessels that he would need in officiating at Mass in his new Parish of Tenoxtitlan:

1 white chasuble, one flesh-colored, and one mulberry-colored
1 black cape
1 alb (priest's white linen robe)
1 altar cloth
1 missal (Mass book)
1 altar
1 hand bell
1 very small vial for the holy oil for the sick
1 ditto for the oil of the catechumens (those who are being taught the Catechism) and holy chrism

A Peaceful (?) Indian Mission

On the morning of November 16, 1830, three Keechi Indians were in Tenoxtitlan on what they thought was a peaceful mission, when suddenly, for no apparent reason, an Anglo-American aimed his carbine at one of them and tried to kill him, but the gun hung fire, and he only succeeded in breaking the Indian's thumb. The Indian immediately ran to Colonel Francisco Ruiz, the commanding officer, held up his dangling right thumb, and demanded protection.

On investigating the matter, Ruiz learned that the shot had been fired by James Cooper, whose brother, William, had been killed by Indians down in Austin's Colony on Caney Creek only a few days earlier. James had come up to Tenoxtitlan with a band of civic militia under the command of Captain Abner Kuykendall, and, believing that he recognized the Indian as a member of the band that had murdered his brother, he had fired the shot and then run away to hide in the brush. He skulked for several hours in the thickets about the post, trying to get in a better shot and finish the job, until finally Colonel Ruiz had his soldiers to mount up and escort the Indian out of town.

We can readily imagine the indignation of the Anglo-Americans when they saw the Mexican troops being used to protect an Indian they were convinced was a murderer.

Smuggling in the Shadow of Sanctity

Mexican troops were being used for other unusual purposes, too, as we shall soon see. The first inkling that something might be amiss came in a letter from General Mier y Téran to Colonel Elosúa, dated November 22, 1830, transmitting an order from the

Secretary of War and Navy to put a stop to smuggling. Two days later he wrote Elosúa another letter, admonishing him to make absolutely sure that the soldiers under his jurisdiction actually received cash for their services instead of being forced by the paymaster to accept merchandise at exorbitant prices. On January 6, 1831, Severo Ruiz, Captain of the Álamo Company, acknowledged receipt of a circular concerning the pursuit and apprehension of smugglers, but he did not promise to obey it. Next day Colonel Francisco Ruiz, the Military Commandant of Tenoxtitlan, likewise acknowledged receipt of orders concerning pursuit of contraband.

The case finally broke on January 19, 1831, when Colonel Elosúa sent Francisco Ruiz an indictment drawn up against Lieutenant Francisco Castañeda because of a shortage of funds in the Álamo Company. Captain Severo Ruiz was also implicated and relieved of his command of the Álamo Company. That meant that, due to a shortage of officers in the area, Francisco Ruiz would have to assume the additional duties of Captain of the Álamo de Parras Presidial Company while still serving as Military Commandant of Fort Tenoxtitlan.

Let us turn now to Captain Severo Ruiz, who eventually becomes the key figure in the case. According to his record of service, which will be published in full in Volume VI of these *Papers*, Severo Ruiz was 32 years old, a native of Santa Bárbara, an important mining center in the Mexican state of Chihuahua. He was married to María del Refugio Sánchez, but she had remained behind in Monterrey, where she was drawing her monthly living allowance of 30 pesos from the Commissar there. Severo had entered military service as a Cadet on May 1, 1812, and been promoted to Second *Alférez* in 1813, First *Alférez* in 1817, Lieutenant in 1818, and Captain in 1821. After serving successively with the Flying Company of Tamaulipas, the Lampazos Company, and the First Permanent Company of Tamaulipas, he had been assigned to his present post with the Álamo Company on April 1, 1828. He had participated in five actions of war and various sorties against the wild Indians, in one of which he was "bruised by a bullet." He had taken the Oath of Independence at the proper time and sworn allegiance to the Plan of True Liberty in Monterrey on March 6, 1823. Furthermore he was said to be "addicted to the Established Form of Government." Curiously enough, though, when Colonel Francisco Ruiz made a copy of Severo's record in March of 1831, he left a blank opposite the entries for Valor, Application, Capacity, Instruction in Ordinances, In Exercises, in Maneuvers, Military Conduct, Civil Ditto, and Health. There was a reason.

This case, which stretched out over a period of nineteen months and filled some 500 pages of tedious testimony, is important to our story primarily because Francisco Ruiz, the Military Commandant at Tenoxtitlan, was put in charge of hearing the depositions, and because the Captain of the Álamo Company, the Paymaster, and the former Paymaster all became implicated and consequently were either confined to prison or kept busy giving testimony. Therefore it greatly delayed the construction of Fort Tenoxtitlan.

Piecing together the bits of evidence, we finally discover that Severo Ruiz was actually using his Mexican Government pack mules to carry his smuggled merchandise, with a military escort to protect it from the Indians. Most of the smuggling was done while the Álamo de Parras Presidial Company was still stationed within the grounds of what we now know as the Alamo, the shrine of Texas liberty, a former mission which was later converted for military use.

The chief item being smuggled was tobacco, which was brought into the country at Brazoria, down in Austin's colony, and transported inland for sale in Goliad, San Felipe, Gonzales, Béxar, Laredo, and even beyond the Rio Grande, to Revilla, Mier, El Pilón, Cadereita, and Gualeguas. Shipments were unloaded on a lot behind the Alamo

Chapel and carried on foot to a store operated by a civilian named Pedro del Toro.

One subterfuge frequently used was to dispatch the government pack mules on an official mission, for instance, to carry supplies from Béxar to Laredo, and then add civilian pack mules to the convoy. The point of rendezvous on the Béxar-Laredo run was a mesquite thicket near the Espada Mission, from which the mules, loaded with mysterious bales wrapped in buffalo hides, would silently emerge to join the caravan. Sometimes those bales contained tobacco; on other occasions they were filled with chamois skins, which were exchanged beyond the Rio Grande for a return load of *piloncillo* (brown sugar in cones).

There were fringe benefits, too. Sometimes Severo Ruiz, who could be easily recognized even in the darkness because he had "a torrent of a voice" that was clearly audible at a great distance, would meet a rival smuggler on the trail. The competitor would leave the trail and fade discreetly into the brush, thus avoiding the official scrutiny of Captain Severo, but a little farther on the said captain would find a pack mule tied to a tree, loaded with tobacco, which the smuggler had apparently "abandoned." Severo would confiscate both the mule and the tobacco, of course, but he had such a poor memory that neither item would be entered on his company books.

On these trips Severo was accused of either renting these mules to private citizens or selling them outright and pocketing the proceeds. In the latter instance the mule would be entered on the books as "strayed away," "lost," "died," or "stolen by Indians." At other times he would report a "mule lost" and a "mule purchased," which turned out to be the same mule, which had never been out of the corral.

There were still other charges: that he operated a private store in his home and made his soldiers accept items of merchandise at ridiculously high prices instead of paying them their salaries in cash. Such items included corn, men and women's shoes, soap, flour, castrated young goats, muttons, chile, ribbons, silk, ornamental combs, and liquor.

When this military investigation expanded to implicate Lieutenant Francisco de Castañeda, it was revealed that Castañeda was a brother-in-law of Ramón Músquiz, the Political Chief, who also operated a general merchandise store on the side, and that some of these questionable bills had found their way to the Músquiz store. Thereupon Castañeda filed a counter suit through civil channels, before the Béxar Ayuntamiento, and so it went. If the reader desires to pursue the subject further, he will find complete details in this volume, under January 19, 1831.

Sterling C. Robertson Arrives in Tenoxtitlan

Now that we have given the reader a general idea of some of the things that were happening in and around Tenoxtitlan shortly after it was founded, let us return to that tiny settlement just eight days after the Mexican soldiers reached the permanent site for the fort. On that Monday, October 25, 1830, Major Sterling C. Robertson and six other individuals presented themselves before Colonel Francisco Ruiz, Military Commandant of that post, and Robertson showed him the contract which the Nashville Company had made with the State Government of Coahuila and Texas on April 15, 1825, for the introduction of foreign families to settle on the Brazos above the Béxar-Nacogdoches Road, explaining that they had come to select a place to establish their principal settlement, either on Little River or the Brazos.

Ruiz replied that Tenoxtitlan had been occupied for the purpose of establishing a military post, whereupon Robertson expressed great pleasure, adding that he wished it were even closer to the settlement they were going to establish.

Five days later Ruiz reported Robertson's arrival to Colonel Elosúa in Béxar, pointing out that these foreign families might occupy lands that would be suitable for the Mexican families that were going to be settled around Tenoxtitlan. He added that Robertson and the other members of his party had conducted themselves very harmoniously with the Mexicans, and a doctor who came with the group even cured some of the sick soldiers without charging them anything. (This was probably Dr. Thomas J. Wootton, of Bedford County, Tennessee, who had signed a colonization contract with Robertson & Thomson on September 15, 1830, promising to "practice phisick in the sd. Grant," in return for which he was to be given a town lot in the town they were planning to lay off. — see McLean, *Papers*, III, 527.)

Elosúa forwarded the Ruiz letter to General Mier y Terán in Matamoros on November 9, 1830, asking for a decision in the matter, and he wrote him again on the same subject on November 19, but Mier y Terán did not answer until December 20, and that reply did not reach Ruiz until the middle of February of the following year. While we are waiting for that reply, though, we have other developments to report.

Thomson's Clandestine Passage Around Nacogdoches

Meanwhile, on October 28, 1830, just three days after Robertson had made his appearance in Tenoxtitlan, Alexander Thomson, his partner, had arrived in Nacogdoches with the first nine families en route to settle in the Nashville Colony. He was immediately ordered, by Vicente Córdova, the alcalde, to collect all his families and present them, which he did, and the group contained a total of fifty "souls" (the term used for measuring population in those days).

It is important here for the reader to make a mental note that there were fifty people in that first group, and we will add that this figure was clearly stated in a letter that Alexander Thomson wrote to Stephen F. Austin on November 13, 1830, for later we shall find Austin reporting to the Mexican authorities that the Nashville Company "had not taken the first step" toward settling its colony. Robertson also reported that there were *fifty* persons in the group, in a letter that he wrote to Ramón Músquiz, the Political Chief, on that same date, so it should have been perfectly obvious to everybody concerned that they had taken the first step, especially since these fifty persons were collected and marched into the Alcalde's office in Nacogdoches.

Then Colonel José de las Piedras, the Military Commandant of the Frontier at Nacogdoches, sent for Thomson and informed him that on the preceding Saturday (October 23, 1830) he had received an order from General Mier y Terán not to let anyone enter unless he had a valid passport from the Mexican Consul in New Orleans, or unless he belonged to the colony of Stephen F. Austin. Since Thomson and his party had already set out from Tennessee more than eight weeks before Piedras received that order, they naturally did not have any passports.

Piedras made the nine families go back five miles on the road to Natchitoches and camp at the Rancho del Carrizo, but he did allow Thomson and four companions (Everton Kennerly, James Ledbetter, Thomas Sherman, and Thomas J. Wootton) to go on to San Felipe because he had told them that, if they could get permits from Stephen F. Austin to settle in his colony, he would let them pass through Nacogdoches. If they failed to get the permits, they were to return to Nacogdoches within twenty days and begin their return journey to the United States.

When the families who had been left at the Rancho del Carrizo began to reflect upon their situation, however, they concluded that they had a valid colonization contract which had been made with the State Government of Coahuila and Texas long before the law restricting immigration had been passed, that this contract was still in force, and that, as a matter of fact, it had been Stephen F. Austin himself who had secured the confirmation of the contract for the Nashville Company on October 15, 1827. (See Volume III, pp. 292-303 of these *Papers*.) Furthermore, they had given up their homes in Tennessee, had spent a great deal of their money, and were much fatigued from having been on the road for more than eight weeks, so they decided that, if Piedras would not let them pass *through* Nacogdoches, they would go *around* the town.

The next day (which would have been on October 19, 1830), they cut a road around Nacogdoches, which required comparatively little work, since all that they had to do was to open a connecting road, from the place where they were camped, north to another road which paralleled their original route but passed about a mile north of Nacogdoches. After they had reached a point several miles northwest of Nacogdoches, they turned almost due south and returned to the road from Nacogdoches to Béxar. The road which they had opened became known as "The Tennesseans' Road," and was used by many subsequent immigrants who were not provided with passports or permits.

On the night of November 12, 1830, they reached the Brazos River and camped below the road, on the land claimed by the squatter locally known among the Mexicans as "Yonny" (Johnny) Williams, taking shelter, ironically enough, in the same barracks that had been built by the soldiers sent to keep out the Anglo-Americans, on the first or temporary site of Tenoxtitlan, which had been vacated by the Álamo Company only four weeks earlier.

Robertson and Thomson Visit Tenoxtitlan

Meanwhile, earlier that same day, Major Robertson had ridden up to Tenoxtitlan with two companions to tell Colonel Francisco Ruiz about the impending arrival of the families en route to the Nashville Colony. Nine had stopped on the land first occupied by the Álamo Company, and many more were due to arrive at the same place within a few days. Since Robertson's first visit, however, Ruiz had received an official letter from Colonel Elosúa dated October 26, 1830, instructing him not to permit the introduction of North American families. Therefore Ruiz told Robertson that he would have to detain the families until he could get a ruling from Elosúa.

Next day Ruiz wrote to Elosúa, stressing the damages that would result for Robertson if he were delayed for a long time, after such a long journey, and the expenditures that it would be necessary for him to make in order to support the families in their temporary camp.

Ruiz also drafted a letter in Spanish, for Robertson's signature, addressed to Ramón Músquiz, the Political Chief in Béxar, in which Robertson traced the history of the colonization project from the original grant to Robert Leftwich down through the transfer to the Nashville Company, the appointment of Hosea H. League as their agent, and the confirmation of the contract through the intercession of Stephen F. Austin. Robertson explained that he had been one of the original stockholders and that for the past three years he had been trying to get the Nashville Company to let him establish 200 families, and that finally, in June of 1830, they had consented to do so. He said that he had contracted with 200 families, and that he had already arrived with the first 10. Part of the balance were on their way, and the rest would arrive during the coming winter and next spring (which would put him within the six-year deadline of April 15, 1831). He stressed the fact that the families who had just arrived were extremely poor, due to the expenses they had incurred on a journey of 900 miles, over a period of 63 days. Furthermore, Robertson said that he needed to return to Tennessee by January 1 in order to bring out the rest of the families, who had sacrificed everything "for the laudable desire to emigrate and establish themselves in the Nashville Colony, and, with these developments, there can be no doubt that both those families as well as those who are here with me, will all be enveloped in ruin."

While Robertson and Ruiz were working on that letter, Alexander Thomson was drafting another one to Stephen F. Austin, saying that, according to Colonel Piedras, Austin was authorized to give passports to the Nashville Company families. He enclosed a letter that Frost Thorn had written to Austin, recommending that he appoint an agent in Nacogdoches and offering to serve in that capacity. Thomson added that he expected to see Austin in a few days, at which time he implied that he would be asking him for the passports.

As another gesture of good will, Ruiz wrote an informal letter to his good friend Samuel M. Williams down in San Felipe, asking him to get Stephen F. Austin to write something in favor of these Nashville Colony families, concluding that, "as far as I am concerned, the ones I have seen look like very good people. . . ."

And he dispatched the letter by special courier. Obviously Colonel Ruiz was trying to do everything he could to help these unfortunate families, for, after serving so long on the Texas frontier, he had reached the conclusion that "what this country needs is honest, hardworking people — even if they come from Hell itself."

Later he joined the Texans and signed their Declaration of Independence along with Robertson, as we shall see in a future volume.

The Piedras Repercussions

Meanwhile Colonel Peter Ellis Bean, after delivering the payroll from Béxar to Tenoxtitlan, had continued on his way back to Nacogdoches, and he met the Nashville Company families west of the Trinity. They told him they were headed for San Felipe, so he reported that fact to Colonel Piedras as soon as he arrived in Nacogdoches.

Piedras flew into a rage and dashed off a letter to Elosúa, charging that "aided by the darkness of the night, they took roundabout roads in order to hide themselves from this post, and they continued their journey toward [San Felipe de] Austin, according to the news I have, thus mocking the authorities of the country and the laws which prohibit their entry." He demanded that an all-points bulletin be sent out for the families to be forced to leave the country.

Next he wrote a letter to Stephen F. Austin, asking him to notify Alexander Thomson and his nine families to leave the country immediately. He also sent the same information to the Political Chief.

As an afterthought on the letter to Austin he commented: "They will endeavor I suppose to obtain permission as Settlers in your Colony, but as they have come into this Country contrary to law, and have disrespected the Authorities of this Town, and treated them with contempt, I think they ought not to be admitted."

However, on comparing the Robertson & Thomson colonization contracts reproduced in these *Papers* and the list of grantees shown in Virginia H. Taylor's volume on *The Spanish Archives of the General Land Office of Texas*, we find that, in direct violation of these orders, Austin did take at least four of these Nashville Company colonists, admit them into his own colonies, and claim the corresponding premium lands for them. Their names are as follows:

CURD, ISAIAH, October 12, 1835, 1 league in Austin's Fifth Colony, in present Brazos County.

FORD, WILLIAM W., October 17, 1832, ¼ league in Austin's Second Colony, in present Montgomery County.

THOMSON, ALEXANDER, June 20, 1832, 1 league in Austin's Second Colony, in present Fayette County.

WALKER, TANDY, April 27, 1831, 1 league in Austin's Second Colony, in present Grimes County.

Other similar cases will be reported in future volumes.

Robertson Returns to Tennessee

As we mentioned earlier, it was the middle of February, 1831, before Colonel Francisco Ruiz received a definitive reply from General Mier y Terán, and, when he did, it was negative. The Mexican authorities in Texas were ordered to round up Robertson and Thomson, plus all of their colonists, and escort them forthwith to the east bank of the Sabine. Ruiz blandly replied that he would do so, "as soon as the said Robertson, whose whereabouts is unknown to me, presents himself." That was on February 16, 1831.

Meanwhile Robertson, learning that Stephen F. Austin had been elected as the sole Deputy to represent Texas in the Congress of Coahuila and Texas, and that he was preparing to set out for the state capital, went to see Austin, who promised him, "on his word of honor, to secure the appointment of a commissioner for the Nashville Company to put the families belonging to same in legal possession of their lands," and also to solicit an extension of time to fulfill their contract, on account of the obstacles and difficulties placed in their way by the Mexican authorities.[3]

In that interview with Austin he must have also learned more about the way that lands were granted by the Mexican Government, for on November 28, 1830, he had the nine heads of families who had come to Texas in that first group to sign an agreement that, in case they should receive title to more land than Robertson & Thomson had promised them, they would convey the excess to Robertson & Thomson. The signers of that document were Isaiah Curd, Quintin Dines, James Farmer, Everton Kennerly, George A. Kerr, Henry J. Pair, Jeremiah Tinnin, John Wilson, and Thomas J. Wootton. Robertson also had them to confirm their individual contracts along about this same time, with the last ones signing on December 2, 1830.

On the latter date he signed up two more colonists: William W. Ford, of Marengo County, Alabama, and Tandy Walker, formerly from Perry County, Alabama, but then an inhabitant of the State of Coahuila and Texas. Clues as to the whereabouts of Robertson during the next few weeks are meager, and those that we do have may be misleading. For instance, we know that on December 9, 1830, he sold 101½ acres of his land in Giles County, Tennessee, to John Luker, for fifty dollars, and the next day he sold 2½ acres on Brown's Creek, adjoining the Nashville Grave Yard, to Peyton Robertson, for six hundred and twenty-five dollars, but the documents do not reveal where the transaction took place. We do know that this second sale was handled by Robertson's brother, Eldridge B. Robertson, through a power of attorney.

One month later (on January 11, 1831) we find Robertson in the Atascosito District of Texas (near present Liberty, Texas) signing a contract with Hannah (Pride) Allen, formerly of Louisiana but now a resident of the Atascosito District, and her son-in-law, George A. Pattillo, who had also come to Texas from Louisiana.

A few days more, and we discover him entering into an agreement with Joseph Peveto, of Louisiana. In the last few contracts we notice that Robertson was signing both for himself and for Alexander Thomson, and that he referred to both himself and Thomson as being from Tennessee, whereas by March 25, 1831, Robertson was signing for himself only, with no mention of Thomson, and he said that he was from the State of Coahuila and Texas.

However, all these activities directed toward the colonization of Central Texas were abruptly interrupted when the Tennessee State Supreme Court of Errors and Appeals set the case of Sterling C. Robertson, charged with the murder of Edward

Randolph, for a hearing on the third Thursday of February, 1831. (The reader will remember that, in Volume III of these *Papers*, pp. 63-65, Robertson had been convicted of manslaughter but had filed an appeal, on a writ of error.) On March 10, 1831, though, the judge denied Robertson's appeal and ordered that he be imprisoned for nine calendar months.

For the moment, therefore, it looks as if all is lost, so far as Robertson's activities in the colonization of Texas are concerned, but such was not the case, as we shall learn in a future volume. Meanwhile let us return to Stephen F. Austin to see how he carried out his promise to Robertson.

The Law of April 6, 1830

Before we do that, though, we need to review, briefly, the Law of April 6, 1830, which is usually referred to in Texas history as "having put a stop to immigration from the United States into Texas." Actually that is a dramatic over-simplification of what happened. We reproduced the complete text of this law in Volume III, pp. 494-500, but we need to analyze and interpret it here so that the reader will understand what is to follow.

First of all, the law sought to increase the Mexican Government's income by relaxing import restrictions so that more duties would be collected in the Customs, but we have already seen (in Volume IV, p. 41) how graft became so widespread in that department that those receipts decreased instead of increasing.

Secondly, the duties collected were to be expended in sustaining the integrity of Mexican territory by building forts and arsenals.

Settlers were to come from three sources: (1) Mexican criminals who had been convicted of the worst crimes were to be transported coastwise from Veracruz and other points to Matamoros, and then taken inland to such places as Tenoxtitlan, where they were to be used as a labor force in building those forts and arsenals. If their families wanted to accompany them, they were to be transported and supported at government expense, and, after the convicts had served out their terms, to make sure that they did not return to the interior of Mexico, they were to be given land and agricultural implements and support for a year so that they would remain in Texas. (2) Mexican civilian families would be transported to Texas at government expense, and given land and agricultural implements, and support for one year. (3) Certain foreign families were to be allowed to come in, provided they had a valid passport "issued by the agent of the Republic at the place from where they came."

The big jolt, however, came in Article 11, which we are going to quote here, both in the Spanish original and in our own translation because we believe that it will be clearer than the one on file in the General Land Office. The Spanish original reads thus:

11. En uso de la facultad que se reservó el congreso general en el art.° 7.° de la ley de 18 de agosto de 1824, se prohibe colonizar a los estrangeros limítrofes en aquellos estados y territorios de la federación que colindan con sus naciones. En consecuencia se suspenderán las contratas que no hayan tenido su cumplimiento y sean opuestas á esta ley.[4]

We would translate this article to read as follows:

11. In use of the faculty which the General Congress reserved for itself in Article 7 of the Law of August 18, 1824, it is prohibited to settle foreigners from adjoining countries, in those states and territories of the Federation which have a common border with their nations. Consequently the contracts which have not

been complied with, and which are opposed to this law, shall be suspended.

Finding a Loophole in the Law

When Austin saw a copy of this law, he became greatly alarmed because he knew that, if it were rigidly enforced, his entire project for settling his colonies with settlers from the United States would come to an end because he had never *completely* complied with any of his contracts. That is to say, he had never brought in the total number of families for which he had contracted. This may come as quite a shock to many Austin fans, but here are the facts as reported by Virginia H. Taylor in her book on *The Spanish Archives of the General Land Office of Texas*, on pp. 32-46:

Austin's Colonies	Families Contracted	Titles Issued	Short
FIRST	300	297	3
SECOND	500	460	40
THIRD	100	59	41
FOURTH	300	175	125
FIFTH	800	152	648
TOTALS:	2,000	1,143	857

Therefore, before publishing a translation of the law in San Felipe, Austin stalled for time until he could figure out some way to interpret this law so that it would not apply to his colony, and then get his interpretation approved by the Mexican authorities. Noticing that Article 10 said: "No variation will be made with respect to the colonies already established," Austin wrote General Mier y Terán and asked him to rule that his colony was already "established," and to issue instructions for no obstacles to be placed in the way of colonists immigrating to his colony.[5]

"Established" could have been interpreted as meaning that, in compliance with Article 40 of that law, the *empresario* had brought in at least 40 families, secured the appointment of a Land Commissioner, had them all swear to support the General Constitution and the Constitution of the State, and held an election to choose the officers for the municipality.

Or, since Article 12 provided for rewarding the *Empresario* with five leagues and five labors of premium land for each 100 families that he brought in, it could have been argued that the makers of the law had already anticipated the possibility that the contractor might not be able to bring in the maximum number so they would reward him in installments for each 100 families that he did succeed in introducing.

This latter interpretation is the one that eventually came to be accepted as the measure of compliance, as we shall see in later volumes.

Apparently Austin succeeded in convincing General Mier y Terán to accept his colony as "established," and to instruct Mexican officials not to place any obstacles in the way of immigrants coming to his colony, for on November 12, 1830, we find Colonel Piedras writing Colonel Elosúa that he has received superior orders not to permit the entry of any Americans at Nacogdoches without a valid passport from the Mexican Consul in New Orleans, *"or unless they belong to the Colony of Stephen F. Austin."*[6]

A couple of weeks earlier, when Alexander Thomson had encountered his difficulty with Colonel Piedras, Frost Thorn, a resident of Nacogdoches, had sent a letter by Thomson to Stephen F. Austin, recommending that Austin provide Piedras with a list of the people who were coming to Austin's Colony, thus saving each immigrant the trouble of having to ride to San Felipe and get an individual permit to take back to Piedras before he could officially enter Texas.

Thomson also wrote to Austin, recommending that he appoint somebody to act as his agent in Nacogdoches, and reporting that Frost Thorn had expressed a willingness to perform that function, but that, unfortunately, he was leaving for New Orleans and would be gone for two months, whereas Austin needed to have an agent in Nacogdoches immediately.

Meanwhile Austin had asked Thomas F. McKinney to recommend somebody, and McKinney had suggested Michel Branamour Menard, a French Canadian Indian Chief who had arrived in Nacogdoches as a trader less than a year earlier — on November 28, 1829. Austin wrote out Menard's appointment on November 13, 1830, and dispatched it to him with a letter instructing him to admit "all who are honest, industrious and moral," but added that "I do not require that all should be rejected who bring no recommendations with them, for I know that many good men emigrate without providing themselves with recommendations, because they are not apprised of the necessity of doing so."

Austin authorized Chief Menard to collect half a dollar per certificate issued, but that amount was to be collected from the immigrant, not from Austin.

Menard received the letter and appointment on November 27, 1830, but, after showing it to Colonel Piedras, he was forced to write back to Austin in his best fractured Frenglish, that Piedras had said that

having the wright youself (to give Certificat) it was surpassing your faculty to Extend the wright to other . . . he said if you could furnish him with . . . a Certificat of your own Signature he has no objection to Let him pass, but upon no other term . . .

Slips That Pass in the Night

If all that Piedras wanted was a certificate bearing Austin's signature, that could be arranged. As soon as Austin arrived in Béxar on his way to the state capital, he obtained 200 sheets of blank paper, signed his name at the bottom of each one, and sent them to Samuel M. Williams in San Felipe, with the following instructions:

I send you two hundred signatures, have certificates printed over them verbatim like the others and fill them up, all except the name — give as many to R. Williamson as he wants and send some to McGuffin and some to Piedrass, and some to Col Thorn — Try and have them printed at night when no one is present, & take care that none of the blanks get into other hands. let none know any thing of this but Lesassier, & Williamson —

. . .

There can scarcely be a more difficult thing than to play a *double game*, it is dangerous, and it is at times, a nice point to draw the distinction between such a game, and dishonor —[7]

In suggesting that some of these certificates be sent to Colonel José de las Piedras, the Mexican Commandant of the Frontier at Nacogdoches, Austin should have known that he was treading on thin ice indeed. His father, Moses Austin, had been publicly denounced for a similar activity which was supposed to have occurred in his dealings with an official of the Spanish Government in Louisiana in 1803. Full details of that transaction are set forth in a letter which Moses Austin allegedly wrote from Mine au Burton on February 17, 1803, to Mons. P. Delassus de Luziers, a Spanish officer, offering to pay him one-fourth of the profits that might be made on a speculation, if a passport could be issued to permit Moses Austin to import flour through New Orleans, a closed port. The full text of this letter was reproduced in a communication which a person signing himself "Aristides" wrote to Moses Austin and published in the *Louisiana Gazette*, of St. Louis, in 1811. This "Aristides" went on to accuse Moses Austin of offering a bribe of five thousand dollars to Mr. Luziers, but he did not say whether the bribe was accepted.[8]

Now let us go back and have a closer look at that certificate Austin had printed in San Felipe. We have reproduced a facsimile copy of it, accompanied by an English translation, in this volume, under January 15, 1831. Does it meet the requirements of the State Colonization Law of March 24, 1825, which stipulated, in Article 5, that "the new settlers who present themselves to be admitted, will have to establish, by means of certificates from the authorities in the place from which they came, their Christianity, morality, and good customs"?

No. Austin's certificate did not meet any of these requirements: it was not issued by the authorities in the place from which the immigrant was coming, and it said nothing about his Christianity, or morality, or customs. Therefore, since the certificate did not meet the requirements of the law, we must conclude that it was illegal.

Austin Departs for Saltillo

On December 31, 1830, Austin set out from Béxar on his journey to Saltillo to serve as the only Deputy from Texas to the State Congress of Coahuila and Texas. He went at the taxpayers' expense and was provided with an official escort. This meant that ostensibly he was representing the interests of *all* Texans, a fact which should be kept in mind as we examine some of the things that he did while serving in that capacity.

Arriving at Río Grande on January 3, 1831, he wrote Samuel M. Williams, reassuring him that: "After my arrival at Saltillo I think I can get your petition granted, and if so you are more entitled to that League than any one else, and you shall have my support to get it—but keep this to yourself...."[9] As we shall see later, the importance of this statement lies in the fact that Austin said *your* petition, not *our* petition, and that this petition apparently concerned only *one* league of land.

Reaching Monclova on January 8, 1831, Austin was received into the home of Don Víctor Blanco "with great friendship and attention." Víctor Blanco was the brother-in-law of Ramón Músquiz, the Political Chief in Béxar. He had served as Governor of Coahuila and Texas from May 30, 1826, to January 27, 1827, and had helped to suppress the Fredonian Rebellion. He was elected as the first Vice-Governor under the Constitution of Coahuila and Texas.[10] In short, he was a very influential man.

Blanco told Austin that he wanted to get land in Texas for his ten children, and that he was going to appoint Samuel M. Williams as his attorney, to act as his agent, and also as the agent of many others. Don Víctor wanted the lands for his own family to be carefully selected on the lower Trinity, or on the San Jacinto. As for the other grants, they were of secondary consideration, since Blanco's friends wanted to acquire them "for speculation," to use Austin's own words.[11]

As we shall see in future volumes, many of these grants for Blanco's friends were eventually located above the Béxar-Nacogdoches Road, in what later became known as Robertson's Colony, so we can truthfully say that the night Austin spent with Víctor Blanco was one that would long be remembered in the annals of Texas jurisprudence because it exercised a tremendous influence on the ownership of land in Texas, and later, when those eleven-league grants were contested in the courts, they provided employment for lawyers for many, many years to come.

Austin Arrives at the State Capital

On the evening of January 12, 1831, Austin reached Leona Vicario (now known as Saltillo), after an unpleasant journey through the mountains, which were white with snow and ice, but it was early in February before he did anything that we need to add to the thread of our story.

Just before he left San Felipe, Austin had received an inquiry from the Governor concerning Texas lands that were being sought by the Villeveques, a French company, but he had postponed making a reply until he could consult the state archives in Saltillo. As soon as he was able to do that, though, he wrote the Governor, on February 3, 1831, that, among other things, the land sought by the Villeveques conflicted with the contracts of the Nashville Company and David G. Burnet, so he recommended that, instead, the Villeveques be granted other lands in East Texas.[12] Then next day he applied for the Nashville Company lands for himself and Samuel M. Williams.

Austin's Application for a Contract for Himself and Williams

Actually, what Austin did was neither as simple nor as straightforward as we have made it sound above. It must have been while he was doing the checking on the Villeveques' case that he also inquired about a petition which had supposedly been sent in by Samuel M. Williams, but it could not be found. That could have been either the petition we mentioned above—the one that appears to have concerned only one league of land—or it could have been the one which Williams had filed on April 6, 1830, for seven additional leagues of land, to complete his total of eleven. By referring to Volume III, pages 492-493, we notice that the seven-league petition was not approved by Ramón Músquiz until February 9, 1831, a week after Austin made his search, so that explains why he could not find it in Saltillo: it was still in Béxar.

At that moment—when the secretary in the state archives told him that he could not find the Williams petition — Austin may have made the fatal decision that was eventually to destroy his political career in Texas: he told the secretary that he would present another petition as Williams' agent.[13]

Producing a Power of Attorney

However, if Austin was going to present a petition as Williams' agent, he would first have to produce a document showing that he had been authorized to act for Williams. How could he do that if Williams was 270 leagues away in San Felipe, Texas, and this matter needed to be dispatched immediately?

First we need to point out that, according to Article 7 of a Mexican decree of October 6, 1823, powers of attorney were to be written on official paper bearing the Second Stamp, but this same type of paper was used for a wide range of other purposes, including "loose certified copies given by judges or notaries for the use of the interested parties...." Therefore it was very convenient to have this type of paper on hand for any number of contingencies that might arise. (See the complete text of this decree in Volume II, pp. 128-138, of these *Papers*.)

Secondly, as we have just seen above, Austin did not hesitate to sign documents in advance, with the date, place, and other information to be filled in later.

He did not hesitate to date documents back into the past either. See, for example, the letter he wrote his brother-in-law, James F. Perry, on September 22, 1830, reproduced in Volume IV, pp. 528-536, of these *Papers*. In that case he enclosed a power of attorney for Perry to sign, explaining that "it ought to have been signed when you were here and is dated then." Although James Franklin Perry and Emily Austin Bryan had been married since September 23, 1824, and therefore would normally have been entitled to receive only *one* league as a married couple, this power of attorney was used to get *eleven* leagues for them, listed separately as "James F. Perry & Emily M. Austin."

This practice of misdating documents also appears in a letter that Austin wrote Samuel M. Williams on March 21, 1832, concerning a document he was trying to get the Ayuntamiento of Béxar to sign in support of a memorial that had already been signed in San Felipe. His exact words were as follows:

> . . .I am told that the Ayto. here [in Béxar] will support the memorial, but they think that they ought to have been consulted first. and that even now if they do anything, it ought to bear a date anterior to the memorial from there [San Felipe], so as to make it appear that Bexar was the *Movil* [the one who originated the idea], and then the other Aytos. should follow in its wake.
>
> I have agreed to this idea and assured them that nothing should be said about it. you will therefore keep this part of the letter entirely to yourself.[14]

For an example of how Austin signed documents in advance on a truly large scale, however, see the following quotation from the letter he wrote James F. Perry from Mexico City on October 2, 1833:

> I left with Williams a great number of deeds signed by me so that he might furnish all the titles of the . . . colony. Take possession of them and of all of my papers. Should these blanks fall into bad hands they will make any use of them they please.[15]

Thirdly, we should mention that, due to the scarcity of people on the Texas frontier, it was the custom, in the land office of various *empresarios* — not just Austin alone — to keep on hand several copies of these official sheets bearing the "SECOND STAMP" already signed in advance by the "witnesses," in the same manner that Austin signed the deeds he left with Williams, so that they would be readily available for issuing certified copies of land titles to the grantees, with the originals being left on file in the land office.

These sheets were signed about half way down the page, at the point where the signatures would normally occur if the preceding space were used to copy in the field notes of a land grant. However, suppose that one of these pre-signed sheets was used to make a certified copy of some other kind of document that did not contain as much text as a land grant — a power of attorney, for instance. In that case the clerk would have to stretch the text in order to bring it down to the signatures and make it look natural. That could be done by leaving ample margins on both sides, and, if it still fell short, the clerk could stop before he got to the bottom of the page, fill in that space with curlicues, add some more at the top of the next page, leave even wider margins, and finally get the text down to the signatures.

The great advantage of using this so-called certified copy was that it did not have to contain the actual signature of the person who was supposed to have signed the original document.

Bearing the foregoing facts in mind, we can see how extremely fortunate it would have been if Austin had just happened to have had one of those pre-signed sheets of paper in his pocket when he realized that he would have to present, to the secretary in the state archives, a power of attorney authorizing him to act for Samuel M. Williams.

He did present just such a document, and it meets all the specifications that we have outlined above, as will be seen by consulting the facsimile copy that we have reproduced under December 17, 1830, in this volume. The only thing lacking is an admission, in Austin's own words, that this document was already in existence before Williams knew about it. That admission will be forthcoming shortly, but first let us see how Austin used the document.

On February 4, 1831, he drafted a petition addressed to the Governor of Coahuila and Texas, speaking both for himself and as agent for Samuel M. Williams, asking that they be granted a contract to establish 800 families in the interior of Texas within the following boundaries:

> Beginning the line on the left bank of the Lavaca River ten leagues from the coast, and following said river upstream to its westernmost headwaters, and from thence in a straight line toward the northwest to the road that goes from Béxar to Nacogdoches, known as the Upper Road, and following said road toward the northeast to the Colorado River, it will go up said river to the Salt or Red Fork which enters about fifteen leagues above the Pecan or Nueces River, and from the said Salt Fork a straight line shall be drawn toward the northeast to the heights that divide the waters of the Brazos and Trinity Rivers, and following the said heights toward the southeast to the principal headwaters of the San Jacinto River, and descending this river to the line of the ten litoral leagues along the coast, the said line shall continue toward the west to the point where the first line began on the Lavaca River.[16]

Austin pointed out that parts of the land within this area had already been designated for his colonization contracts of June 4, 1825, and November 20, 1827, and he admitted that it would also swallow up the area covered by the contract which Robert Leftwich had made on April 15, 1825, for the Texas Association (later known as the Nashville Company), and that the Leftwich Contract was not due to expire until April 15, 1831 — over two months *after* the date of this application — but he insisted that, "despite the fact that this new contract will not go into effect until the days indicated, I ask that it be celebrated now. . . ."

Thus we see that Austin failed to comply with his promise to Robertson to secure the appointment of a commissioner for the Nashville Company, to put their families in legal possession of their lands, and to solicit an extension of time to fulfill their contract.

The next day after Austin had drafted this application, he wrote Williams as follows:

> . . . The office has been searched for your petition, it cannot be found — This morning I told the secretary that I would present another petition as your agent, he said that he would look once more, and if the other could not be found that I could present a new one, and the Gov[erno]r has promised that it shall be *immediately* dispatched — So that you may consider the thing as certain —[17]

Austin no doubt hoped that Williams would notice the word *new*, and he underlined the word *immediately*, probably to convey the idea that Austin thought he could handle the situation without waiting for Williams to send a power of attorney from San Felipe.

The Austin & Williams Contract

The Austin & Williams Contract — the most gigantic of all the colonization contracts ever issued in Texas—was granted on February 25, 1831, but it never has been given full credit — or discredit — for the detrimental influence it exercised on the colonization of Texas. Dr. Barker and other Texas historians have criticized the Texas Association or the Nashville Company for making a speculation of their grant among non-resident stockholders, but, when Austin got control of the area, we might say that the situation was ten times as bad. We might say that, but it would sound like an undocumented exaggeration, or, to say the least, it would sound trite, but the truth is even more surprising.

On the one hand, the Nashville Company, speaking in terms of only one league per family, had been able to persuade actual settlers from the United States to come to Texas, but these families had been unable to obtain a legal title to the land because of obstacles placed in their way by the Mexican officials.

On the other hand, Austin & Williams allowed non-resident Mexican politicians to locate eleven-league grants in the area, and they were able to obtain legal titles, which kept others from settling on the land. The people who owned these eleven-league titles, however, were not there to protect their land from the Indians, or to put it into cultivation, or to develop it in any way. To make matters even worse, Austin & Williams, during the three years they had control of the area (from 1831 to 1834), were unable to get a land commissioner appointed, so the families who were actually in the area had to go elsewhere to get land with a legal title.

To sum it all up, therefore, the documentary evidence shows that speculation under Austin & Williams was eleven times as bad as it had been under the Nashville Company.

Furthermore, the area covered by the Austin & Williams Contract has never been properly shown on Texas maps. Most of these maps have been based on the 1835 edition of Austin's map of Texas, an excerpt of which is reproduced in this volume, under February 25, 1831. By comparing that excerpt with the map which we have drawn for the frontispiece of this volume, the reader will see that there is no line on the Austin map to show that the contract extended below the Béxar-Nacogdoches road to within 10 leagues of the coast. Also, when the line on Austin's map reaches the westernmost headwaters of the Lavaca River, it does not continue in a straight line *northwest*, as called for in the contract; Austin ran it due *north*. On reaching the mouth of the Salt or Red Fork of the Colorado River, Austin does not run his line *northeast*, as specified in the contract; he runs it *due north*, to a point above the Tahcajunova River, then follows what must have been an old Indian trail, veering first north and then south, in a generally easterly direction, to the Cross Timbers. At that point Austin's map makes no attempt to follow the watershed between the Brazos and Trinity Rivers, down to the headwaters of the San Jacinto. When the line does appear on the Austin map, it moves east from the headwaters of the San Jacinto, to follow the watershed between the San Jacinto and the Trinity. Only by referring to the frontispiece of this volume can the reader see the all-enveloping nature of the Austin & Williams Contract clearly depicted.

The Upper Colony

On the other hand, when we look at the excerpt from the 1835 Austin map, we see "Austin & Williams Grant" written across the area above the Béxar-Nacogdoches Road, in the region occupied by "Large droves of Wild Cattle and Horses." We do not realize that it also extended below the road to include the part marked "Austin's Colony." From this point forward this area above the road will be referred to as "The Upper Colony of the Austin & Williams Contract." Later it will become "Robertson's Colony."

It was not until March 5, 1831, that Austin dared reveal to Williams the magnitude of what he had done, and even then he spoke in guarded terms. He said:

> *Private*—I wrote by last mail that your petition was granted—since then I have recd the testimonio [certified copy] and will send it and all the others by Fernando Rodrigues who starts in a few days for Bexar.
>
> The power of attorney is effected in union with myself—the lower line is ten leagues from the coast—the upper on the heads of the Brazos and Colorado: I wish the [B]oss [Terán?], to take a part in this — if he will, all is safe. I am operating on a pritty large scale, for a taciturn and noisless man, but I have no other object in view than the genl prosperity of *us all*...Keep all this to yourself: The fate of Texas, in some respects depends on the month of *May* next — untill then look back and take council from the past a[nd keep] all quiet — you can shew [parts of?] the letter to Luke if you think prop[er but] to no one else and he must not mention or breathe it to anyone.[18]

A few days later Austin wrote Williams: "read over my letters by the last two mails more is meant there than is plainly expressed...."[19]

First of all, Austin was trying to tell Williams what was in the power of attorney that Williams was supposed to have issued.

Secondly, by giving the general location of boundary lines along the seacoast and above the headwaters of the Brazos and Colorado Rivers, he was trying to tell Williams that they had obtained a colonization contract, not a mere grant of one to seven leagues in the name of Williams alone, which was what Williams would have been expecting.

By hinting that he would have to bring somebody else into the plot to make everything safe, he implied that he had done something that might not be safe if they could not find somebody to cover it up. General Manuel de Mier y Terán, according to Dr. Barker's guess, would have been the logical official who could do that.

In referring to the general prosperity "of us all." he meant Luke Lesassier, Robert M. Williamson, Francis W. Johnson, and perhaps others—the group Austin referred to as *congress* — this again according to Dr. Barker's surmise, which seems to have been pretty accurate, since we shall encounter all of these characters in future volumes.

The fate of Texas depended to some extent on the month of May, 1831, because by that time the contract of the Nashville Company would have expired, and Austin & Williams could begin to act publicly in taking over the area, at which time there might be repercussions from Robertson.

By looking back and taking council from the past, Williams would remember that, in a similar situation in the fall of 1827, when Hosea H. League had asked Austin to intervene with the state government to get an extension of boundaries to the west for the Nashville Colony, Austin had neglected to do so, and, instead, had obtained that area for himself.

Yes, indeed, Williams and Lesassier would be wise not to mention or breathe it to anyone!

But despair not, gentle reader. Central Texas will be settled, but not by Austin & Williams, as we shall see in Volume VI.

NOTES

[1]*Monuments Erected by the State of Texas to Commemorate the Centenary of Texas Independence. The Report of the Commission of Control for Texas Centennial Celebrations. Compiled under the Direction of Pat M. Neff, Walter F. Woodul, L. W. Kemp, Publication Committee. Harold Schoen, Compiler* (Austin: Commission of Control for Texas Centennial Celebrations, 1938), p. 124.

[2]Malcolm D. McLean, "Tenoxtitlan, Dream Capital of Texas," *The Burleson County Citizen and The Caldwell News*, Caldwell, Texas, May 7, 21, 28, June 4, 11, 18, 25, and July 2, 1964; reprinted in *The Southwestern Historical Quarterly*, Austin, Texas, Vol. LXX, No. 1 (July, 1966), pp. [23]-43.

[3]Sterling C. Robertson to the Governor of Coahuila and Texas, April 2, 1834, in William Curry Harllee, *Kinfolks* . . . (4 vols.; New Orleans: Searcy & Pfaff, Ltd., 1934-1937), III, 2834-2835.

[4]Taken from an original 4-page folder, printed on the first [3] pages, made available on November 6, 1976, by J. P. Bryan, Jr., No. 3 Shadowlawn, Houston, Texas 77005.

[5]Stephen F. Austin to Manuel de Mier y Terán, May 18, 1830, in Barker, *Austin Papers*, II, 380-381.

[6]José de las Piedras to Antonio Elosúa, November 12, 1830, in this volume.

[7]Stephen F. Austin to Samuel M. Williams, December 28, 1830, in this volume.

[8]"Aristides" to Moses Austin, letter published in the *Louisiana Gazette*, St. Louis, August 1, 1811, page 3, columns 3-4.

[9]Stephen F. Austin to Samuel M. Williams, January 3, 1831, in Barker, *Austin Papers*, II, 571-572.

[10]Webb, *The Handbook of Texas*, I, 171-172.

[11]Stephen F. Austin to Samuel M. Williams, January 9, 1831, in this volume.

[12]Stephen F. Austin to the Governor of Coahuila and Texas, February 3, 1831, in this volume.

[13]Stephen F. Austin to Samuel M. Williams, February 5, 1831, in this volume.

[14]Stephen F. Austin to Samuel M. Williams, March 21, 1832, in Barker, *Austin Papers*, II, 758-761.

[15]Stephen F. Austin to James F. Perry, October 2, 1833, in Barker, *Austin Papers*, II, 1006-1007.

[16]See complete text in this volume, under February 4, 1831.

[17]Stephen F. Austin to Samuel M. Williams, February 5, 1831, in this volume.

[18]Stephen F. Austin to Samuel M. Williams, March 5, 1831, in this volume.

[19]Stephen F. Austin to Samuel M. Williams, March 12, 1831, in Barker, *Austin Papers*, II, 612.

PAPERS CONCERNING

ROBERTSON'S COLONY

IN TEXAS

Volume V

October 11, 1830, through
March 5, 1831

THE UPPER COLONY

MANUEL DE MIER Y TERÁN TO ANTONIO ELOSÚA[1]

[Translated from Spanish]

[October 11, 1830]

Office of the Commandant General and

Inspector of the Eastern Interior States.

With much satisfaction I have been informed, by Your Lordship's Official Letter No. 345, of the 24th of the month just past, and the attached documents, about the punishment that was given to the Tahuacano and Hueco Indians by Citizen Captain Nicasio Sanches with the First Permanent Company of Tamaulipas and the other volunteer troops and settlers from that city [Béxar] whom Your Lordship placed under his orders. The services of the said company and individuals are appreciable and of even more merit because of the scant resources with which they made the campaign. Your Lordship will give thanks in my name to the said captain and to those who accompanied him, and I hope that the expedition will not cease until it has entirely dislodged the tribes of Tahuacanos and Huecos from the points which they have occupied, retiring them toward the other side of the headwaters of the Trinity River, for from the place where they were located they have been a great threat to that city. I am making a report to the Supreme Government concerning what happened, with a recommendation of the merit which has been earned by the aforementioned Captain

Sanches, the Citizens Lieutenants Francisco Castañeda and Ignacio Rodríguez, and the troops and settlers who composed the party of Citizen Gaspar Flores, making special mention of Private Dámaso Galván and Settler Manuel Luna, who shall be rewarded with twenty-five pesos each for the important service which they performed as spies.[2]

By means of the newspapers of that Department and by means of the physical description of the negro apprehended, you will endeavor to locate his owner, to whom you will deliver him, after the owner has proved that the negro belongs to him, for which purpose I have had translations made of the papers in English that were found on the field of action. Meanwhile the negro shall remain at Lavaca as a prisoner. Your Lordship will order that the children who were taken prisoners shall be forwarded to Monterrey and placed at the disposal of the commissar there for such purposes as shall be indicated to him, the expenses of their trip to that city being paid by that commissariat. I am saying this to you by way of reply for your information.

God and Liberty, Matamoros, October 11, 1830.

M. Mier y Terán

[rubric]

To the Citizen Principal Commandant)
)
of Coahuiltejas.   )

[*Enclosures:*]

No. 1.=According to what I think, this is an account of
what has been given to a negro from Austin's Colony, such
as a knife, etc., and it is signed by James Bird and D. B.
White.=Translated.=Alejandro Yhary.
A Copy. Matamoros, October 11, 1830.

Guerra [rubric]

Office of the Commandant General and
Inspector of the Eastern Interior States.
No. 2=Translation.=April 30, 1830.=To all the Americans.=
San Antonio Crossing of the Brazos.=Today there arrived in
this place a Hueco captain named Bracisco who was wearing a
silver medal around his neck, with the miniature of James
Madison, President of the United States, on the obverse,
and, on the reverse, the hands of an Indian and an American
joined, with the tomahawk and pipe, with the date 1809.[3]
They profess friendship for the Americans. If any American
finds this paper and does not know them, he should be very
careful.=Signed: James Courts [?], Clerk of Halsbury [?].
=Translated.=Alejandro Yhary.
A Copy. Matamoros, October 11, 1830.

Guerra [rubric]

---

[1]BA 135, Frames 0185-0192. On this same date Mier

y Terán sent a copy of this letter to the Citizen Commissar of Béxar.

[2]At this point in the original manuscript a note has been inserted in the lefthand margin which reads as follows: "Order of the 20th to the 21st of October of 1830. This is being copied in the general order of the day for the satisfaction of all the individuals of this garrison, and especially for those who took part in the expedition. [Signed:] Elosúa [rubric]."

[3]For a possible explanation of what may have happened to Chief Bracisco and his silver medal, see the following note which was appended to Colonel John Henry Moore's account of his battle with the Comanches on the upper Colorado River on October 24, 1840:

"In the late battle, a silver medal, about the eighth of an inch in thickness and two and a half inches in diameter, was taken from an old Indian, supposed to have been upwards of 100 years of age, who was killed, one side of which presents a profile, in relief, of James Madison, with the words *James Madison President, of the United States. 1809.* The reverse presents clasped hands with the calumet and tomahawk, and the words *Peace and Friendship.*

--John Henry Moore to Branch Tanner Archer, Secretary of War, November 7, 1840, published in the *Austin Gazette*, and reprinted in *The Brazos Courier*, Brazoria, Texas, on November 24, 1840. There is a microfilm copy of this newspaper in the Microfilm Room of The University of Texas at Arlington Library, labeled as follows: "Pre-Civil War & Republic of Texas Newspapers, Set No. 1, Reel 3."

--Photo by BRUCE AUSTIN, *Audio-Visual
Technical Services, UTA Library*

Reverse:
PEACE AND FRIENDSHIP

Two hands clasped in token of amity;
on the cuff of the left wrist three
stripes and as many buttons; the
other wrist is bare; above the hands,
a pipe of peace and a tomahawk
crossed.

By John Reich.

Obverse:
JAMES MADISON
PRESIDENT OF THE U.S.
A.D. 1809

Bust of the President.

THE JAMES MADISON PEACE AND FRIENDSHIP MEDAL

Above are shown the designs that were used on the James
Madison Peace and Friendship Medal. The originals were struck
off in solid silver, in three different sizes (76 mm, 62 mm, and
51 mm), in 1814 and 1815. Later a small hole was made through
the medal exactly over the head of the President, so as to suspend the medal erect when worn by the Chiefs.

An excellent account of the creation of these medals can
be found in Francis Paul Prucha, *Indian Peace Medals in American*

History (Madison: The State Historical Society of Wisconsin, 1971), pp. 95-98.

We found a much briefer description in *Medals of the United States Mint*, prepared under the direction of the Honorable Eva Adams, Director of the Mint, by Captain Kenneth M. Failor, USNR, Consultant to the Director of the Mint, and Eleanora Hayden, Bureau of the Mint (Washington, D. C.: U. S. Government Printing Office, [1969]), pp. 11-13.

In the back of this book there was a statement that bronze replicas of these medals could be ordered from the United States Mint, Philadelphia, Pennsylvania, for three dollars each, but, when we sent in our order, it was returned with the statement that these medals are now on sale through the Bureau of the Mint, 55 Mint Street, San Francisco, Ca. 94175, and that the price had gone up to $5.25.

The medal shown here is the largest size, measuring 76 mm in diameter. The two smaller sizes (62 mm and 51 mm) did not have the fur cloak, or robe, draped around the bust below the shoulders, according to Bauman L. Belden, *Indian Peace Medals Issued in the United States* (New Milford, Connecticut: M. Flayderman & Co., 1966), p. 29.

James Madison, fourth President of the United States, served from March 4, 1809, to March 3, 1817. How this medal made its way into the Southwest and turned up on the Brazos River in Mexican Texas, thirteen years after Madison went out of office, would make a challenging topic for somebody to investigate.

ANTONIO ELOSÚA TO CASIMIRO LEÓN[1]

[Translated from Spanish]

To Lieutenant Colonel Citizen Casimiro León.

Béxar, October 11, 1830.

Esteemed friend: By your much appreciated letter of September 24 last I have been informed of everything you tell me concerning your infirmities affecting your vision, which I regret very much.

The expedition which went out in the month of August against the Tahuacanos [Tawakonis] and Huecos, [Wacos], and returned to this city in September just past, succeeded in attacking a village of the former on the San Xavier [San Gabriel] River, killing three and taking as prisoners four children and a negro who had run away from Austin's Colony. They took 10 rifles, five lances, one hundred and ninety-five animals [horses], and all their plunder, without any loss of any kind on our side.[2]

That's all there is for now to communicate to you. I hope that you will get better, and call on me whenever you need to. Your friend,

[Antonio Elosúa][3]

---

[1]The Béxar Archives at the University of Texas Archives, Austin; Texas Christian University Library, Fort Worth, Texas 76129, MICROFILM 3, Roll 134, Frame 0659. The "Béxar Archives" will be cited hereinafter simply as "BA." The word "Béxar" should carry a written accent on the first syllable, so we plan to show it consistently with an accent throughout this volume regardless of how it may have

occurred in the original manuscripts.

[2]For further details concerning the expedition
against the Tawakonis and Wacos, see the *Papers Concerning
Robertson's Colony in Texas, compiled and edited by Malcolm
D. McLean, Volume IV, May through October 10, 1830. Tenox-
titlan, Dream Capital of Texas* (The UTA Press, Box 19929,
The University of Texas at Arlington, Arlington, Texas
76019, 1977), pp. 498-527. Cited hereinafter as McLean,
Papers.

[3]Since there is no article on Antonio Elosúa in the
Handbook of Texas, and since he is playing such a prominent
part in these *Papers*, we have translated the following biographical note from Vito Alessio Robles, *Coahuila y Texas
desde la consumación de la Independencia hasta el Tratado
de Paz de Guadalupe Hidalgo* (2 vols.; México: Talleres
Gráficos de la Nación, 1945-1946), I, 65-66:

"Elosúa was born in Havana about the year 1778. He
came to New Spain in 1802, and that same year he enlisted
as a cadet in the Mexico City Infantry Regiment. Later he
served in the Veracruz Infantry Regiment. On March 13,
1813, he marched to the Colony of Nuevo Santander [modern
Tamaulipas] under the orders of Colonel Joaquín de Arre-
dondo, participating in the military activities at Aguayo,
Juamave, Palmillas, and Tula, and extending his activities
to the Province of San Luis Potosí. He took part in the
Battle of Medina, Texas, on August 18, 1813. In 1817 he
took part in the seige and storming of Soto la Marina. On
March 9, 1818, he was appointed Adjutant Inspector of Coahuila and Texas, and on November 25, 1820, he was named
Political and Military Governor of the Province of Coahuila,
a post which he filled until March 21, 1822, the date on
which he began to function as Deputy from Coahuila in the
First Constituent Congress, the sessions of which were prolonged to October 31, 1823. As Governor of Coahuila he
announced his support of the Plan of Iguala on July 6,
1821, in the City of Monclova. Later he occupied the post
of Adjutant Inspector of Coahuila and Texas from May 30,
1826, until October 9, 1833, the date on which he obtained
his retirement. He died on November 17 of the same year
in San Antonio, Texas, and his body was buried in the
Valero Chapel. Elosúa substituted as Governor of Coahuila
in place of Colonel Manuel Pardo, who was born in Santander [Spain] about the year 1774 and took part in the war
with France in 1795, with Portugal in 1801, in the expedition to Aranjuez in March of 1802, and in the action in
Madrid on May 2 of the same year. He assumed the governor-
ship of Coahuila on the death of Governor Antonio García de
Texada on March 9, 1818. Elosúa in turn was replaced on

March 22, 1822, by Colonel Antonio Crespo, who was born in
Havana in 1787, and he served in that position until September 13, 1824. (Archivo de la Secretaría de la Defensa
Nacional, Exps. XI/III-2-15/9598, XI/111/4/4749, XI/111/5/
1634."

MANUEL DE MIER Y TERÁN TO ANTONIO ELOSÚA[1]

[Translated from Spanish]

[October 12, 1830]

Office of the Commandant General and

Inspector of the Eastern Interior States.

Under this same date I am writing Citizen Rafael
Choubel [Chowell] as follows:

"In a wooden box I am sending you the model and
plan which is to serve for the construction of the fort.
Please note that the thickness of the walls has not been
drawn to scale, and they should have the same thickness as
any ordinary house, in proportion to the material with
which they are constructed. Around this building, for a
distance of 400 varas [about 1110 feet] no building shall
be permitted, for it is to serve as the citadel in the
settlement which is to be formed in the course of time.
Also you should try to clear the ground of brush and any
other objects which might tend to limit the effectiveness
of firearms.

"As soon as you have taken down the information
furnished by the model, you will forward it to Colonel Don
Antonio Elosúa so that he may use it in the construction at
Tenoxtitlan, and please do so as soon as possible, adding
such explanations as one usually makes when the objects
which are designated by plans or models are actually constructed. In conclusion I have the pleasure of assuring

you of my highest esteem."

And I am sending you this copy for your information and guidance.

God and Liberty.   Matamoros, October 12, 1830.

Manuel de Mier

y Terán

To Colonel Antonio Elosúa

---

[1]Volume 53, pp. 116 and 116 verso, Spanish Archives, General Land Office, Austin, Texas.

ANTONIO ELOSÚA TO MANUEL DE MIER Y TERÁN[1]

[Translated from Spanish]

[October 12, 1830]

Office of the Principal Commandant)   No. 366
)
of Coahuila and Texas.   )

Most Excellent Sir:

In compliance with the superior order from Your Excellency

dated September 2nd last, this very day forty men from the

Béxar Company have marched to reenforce the Tenoxtitlan

Garrison.[2] I have the honor of reporting this to Your

Excellency by way of reply, and to enclose for you the

original official letter from the captain of said company

showing the extent to which they have been supplied, and

the scarcity of resources from which it is suffering, in

order to assist them in the future, since I do not have a

single *real* in the cash box, so that Your Excellency may

see fit to take all this for your superior consideration.

God and Liberty. Béxar, October 12, 1830.

[Antonio Elosúa]

To the Most Excellent Commandant General.

He replies that forty men from the Béxar Company

have marched to reenforce the Tenoxtitlan Garrison, and he

encloses an official letter from the captain of said com-

pany concerning the extent to which they have been sup-

plied, and the hardships under which it is suffering, in

order to assist them in the future.

_____

[1]BA Roll 135, Frames 0332-0333.

[2]By referring to McLean, *Papers*, III, 440, the reader will notice that Mier y Terán had ordered Elosúa to send 58 men, not 40, but Elosúa makes no explanation as to why he did not send the other 18 men. We might infer, however, that it was because he could not find any funds with which to supply them.

ANTONIO ELOSÚA TO FRANCISCO RUIZ[1]

[Translated from Spanish]

[October 12, 1830]

Office of the Principal Commandant of Coahuila and Texas.

With your official letter dated the 2nd of the present month I received the list of the individuals of the Álamo Company who were not present at the reading of the report on the subsistence which has been furnished to them during the present year, and I shall take care to see that that ceremony shall be carried out in this city [Béxar]. I am reporting this to you by way of reply.

God and Liberty. October 12, 1830.

[Antonio Elosúa]

To the Military Commandant of Tenoxtitlan,)
)
Citizen Lieutenant Colonel Francisco Ruiz.)

_____

[1]BA Roll 135, Frame 0334. For the list of individuals referred to above, see McLean, *Papers*, IV, 558.

ANTONIO ELOSÚA TO SEVERO RUIZ[1]

[Translated from Spanish]

[October 12, 1830]

Office of the Principal Commandant of Coahuila and Texas.

By your official letter dated the 25th of the past month, I have been informed of the desertion of the privates from that company under your command, Felipe Hernández and Eduardo Treviño, whose apprehension I have ordered, all of which I am reporting to you by way of reply.

God and Liberty. Béxar, October 12, 1830.

[Antonio Elosúa]

To Captain Citizen Severo Ruiz.

---

[1]BA Roll 135, Frame 0335.

ANTONIO ELOSÚA TO SEVERO RUIZ[1]

[Translated from Spanish]

[October 12, 1830]

Office of the Principal Commandant of Coahuila and Texas.

I am forwarding to you the private who deserted
from that company under your command, José María Vidal, and
I am enclosing for you the file of the case started against
him here so that, after adding to it his personal description, you can continue the investigation at the point, and,
when it has been concluded, with your legal opinion there-
on, you can return it to me for the purpose of justice.

God and Liberty. Béxar, October 12, 1830.

[Antonio Elosúa]

To the Commandant of the Álamo Company.

---

[1]BA Roll 135, Frame 0345.

ANTONIO ELOSÚA TO ALEXANDRO TREVIÑO[1]

[Translated from Spanish]

[October 12, 1830]

Office of the Principal Commandant of Coahuila and Texas.

The Captain of the Álamo de Parras Company, in an official letter dated the 25th of September last, writes me as follows:

"Privates Felipe Hernández and Eduardo Treviño" etc.

And I am forwarding it to you so that you can seek their apprehension, if they should happen to come into this city.

God and Liberty. Béxar, October 12, 1830.

[Antonio Elosúa]

To the Major of the Plaza,   )
)
Citizen Captain Alexandro Treviño.)

---

[1]BA Roll 135, Frame 0341.

PETER ELLIS BEAN TO ANTONIO ELOSÚA[1]

[Translated from Spanish]

[October 12, 1830]

I have observed in the newspaper from Washington that the Congress of the United States has placed at the disposal of the President of that Republic the sum of five hundred thousand pesos [dollars] for the purpose of buying the lands possessed by the Indians listed below, and moving said Indians to the west of the Mississippi River from the states where they are now residing.=The state of Ojayú [Ohio], 2,407 Indians. The State of Alebamú [Alabama], 17,000. Tenací [Tennessee], 20,000. Norcarolina [North Carolina], 8,000. Misisipi [Mississippi], 28,625. In the Florida Territory, 5,000. Mechiguin [Michigan] Territory, 28,380. Which amounts to a total of 109,412.=And there is no doubt that, when these [tribes] cross the Mississippi River, many of them are bound to come and infiltrate through our frontiers, and this is a threat which we should take measures to avoid and keep them from coming in. I am communicating this to Your Lordship in order that the corresponding measures can be taken toward such an interesting objective.=God and Liberty. Béxar, October 22, 1830.=Pedro Elías Bean.=To the Principal Commandant, Colonel Don Antonio Elosúa.   A Copy.

---

[1]BA Roll 135, Frames 0614-0615.

ANTONIO ELOSÚA TO JOSÉ DE LAS PIEDRAS[1]

[Translated from Spanish]

[October 13, 1830]

Office of the Principal Commandant of Coahuila and Texas.

I have been informed of everything Your Lordship was pleased to report to me in your official letter of the 28th of September last relative to the fact that it would be appropriate to prepare a combined expedition against the Tahuacanos and the Huecos who are threatening us.

It seems to me that such an expedition would be a very good idea, and I desire it. I am only waiting for the arrival in this city, as Your Lordship reports to me, of Colonel Don Pedro Elías [Peter Ellis] Bean, in order to make the proper arrangements concerning the matter. I am reporting this to Your Lordship by way of reply, with the understanding that I will give you, at the proper time, the necessary information for your guidance.

God and Liberty. Béxar, October 13, 1830.

[Antonio Elosúa]

To the Commandant of the Frontier at Nacogdoches.

---

[1]BA Roll 135, Frames 0399-0400.

ANTONIO ELOSÚA TO ALEXANDRO TREVIÑO[1]

[Translated from Spanish]

[October 13, 1830]

Office of the Principal Commandant of Coahuila and Texas.

I have reported to the Most Excellent Commandant General, with your official letter of the 6th of the present month, in which you report to me the need, of that company under your command, for an officer to command the forty men who marched to reinforce the Tenoxtitlan Garrison, and for which reason you ask that Lieutenant Citizen Manuel Lafuente, who is now at Lampazos, be incorporated into same. I am reporting this to you by way of reply.

God and Liberty. Béxar, October 13, 1830.

[Antonio Elosúa]

To Captain Don Alejandro Treviño

----

[1]BA Roll 135, Frame 0401.

ANTONIO ELOSÚA TO ALEXANDRO TREVIÑO[1]

[Translated from Spanish]

[October 13, 1830]

Office of the Principal Commandant of Coahuila and Texas.

I received the proceedings drawn up against the private who deserted from the Álamo de Parras Company, José María Vidal, which you sent me with your official letter of the 10th of the present month, which I am now answering.

God and Liberty. Béxar, October 13, 1830.

[Antonio Elosúa]

To the Major of the Plaza.

---

[1]BA Roll 135, Frame 0402.

ANTONIO ELOSÚA TO ALEXANDRO TREVIÑO[1]

[Translated from Spanish]

[October 13, 1830]

Office of the Principal Commandant of Coahuila and Texas.

I received, with your official letter dated the 10th of the present month, the deposition taken from the private who deserted from the Second Permanent Company of Tamaulipas, Remigio Garza. I am reporting this to you in reply.

God and Liberty. Béxar, October 13, 1830.

[Antonio Elosúa]

To the Major of the Plaza.

---

[1]BA Roll 135, Frame 0403.

For the background of this case, see McLean, *Papers*, IV, 447, 466, 470, 475, and 562.

RAMÓN MÚSQUIZ TO THE AYUNTAMIENTOS OF

GOLIAD AND SAN FELIPE DE AUSTIN[1]

[Translated from Spanish]

[October 14, 1830]

Office of the Political Chief

of the Department

War having been declared against the Tahuacano
[Tawakoni] Indians for the various assassinations and frequent robberies of *caballadas* which they have committed,
after every exertion dictated by compassion has been used
to procure their friendship by costly presents, the Principal Military Commandant of this Department has manifested
to me the urgent necessity for a new expedition against
these feeble enemies, to correct their insolence or exter-
minate them, in order by this means to preserve the lives
and property of the inhabitants of the different towns
which, for such a long time, have suffered from them enor-
mous harm. For this purpose he is counting on the influence of this Headquarters and the cooperation of the worthy
citizens under its jurisdiction, and for this reason I am
reporting this fact to Your Lordship in order that you may
invite the inhabitants of your municipality who voluntarily
may wish to make themselves available to the country for
such an important service, being persuaded that in this
manner they will secure their own happiness and that of

future generations. I hope that, within the shortest possible time, Your Lordship will communicate to me the result
of this measure so that I can plan the said expedition with
the aforementioned Chief in such a way that it will produce
the success which we are hoping for.=God, etc. Béxar,
October 14, 1830.=To the Ayuntamientos of Goliad and the
Villa of [San Felipe de] Austin.[2]

---

[1]BA Roll 135, Frames 0433-0434. The copy that was
sent to San Felipe was translated and published in *The
Texas Gazette*, [San Felipe de] Austin, Texas, on October
30, 1830, on page 3, columns 2-3, with the following head-
ing and introduction:

TRANSLATION

Of a letter addressed to the Ayuntamiento of this
jurisdiction, by the chief of the department, calling on
the inhabitants of the Jurisdiction, to volunteer in an
expedition against the Tahuacana Indians.

[Here they inserted the text of the letter. Then
the following was added:]

In communicating the above notice to the inhabitants of this municipality, the Ayuntamiento flatters
itself with the hope that a sufficient number will be found
anxious and ready to cooperate with the inhabitants of the
department, in so desirable and laudable a wish, as that of
punishing these insolent and thievish Indians.
[San Felipe de] Austin, October 30, 1830.
By order of the Ayuntamiento
THOS. BARNETT, pres't.
S. M. Williams,
   Secretary pro tem.

[2]There is another copy of the Músquiz letter on BA
Roll 135, Frame 0998.

RAMÓN MÚSQUIZ TO JOSÉ DE LAS PIEDRAS[1]

[Translated from Spanish]

[October 14, 1830]

By some depositions that I ordered taken in the court of this city concerning the designs of Don Juan Antonio Padilla when he ordered Preciliano Fuentes assassinated, and by the case drawn up by the military attorney against Private Antonio Coy, following the orders of Your Lordship, a copy of which was forwarded to the alcalde of that town, and which, because of its contents, was sent on to me, I have been persuaded, by the evidence itself, that Don Juan Antonio Padilla has been the author of the death of Fuentes perpetrated by Coy, and in view thereof this man, under no reason or pretext, should be allowed to leave prison under bond, as he is reported to have done.

I beg Your Lordship, out of consideration for the fact that in that town this Headquarters does not have any person from whom to obtain information concerning the proceedings and management of the Alcalde in the home of Padilla, and therefore I beg you, for the sake of justice and the public interest, which is concerned about the punishment of crime, to be so good as to inform me, by whatever method you consider to be most appropriate, concerning all the news that you may be able to gather concerning this subject, and whether it is true that Padilla, when his preparatory deposition was taken, made out the questions himself, and while at the same time the proprietary alcalde was present in that town, the First Regidor, pretending, improperly, that he was the one in authority, was the one who issued the order to the commander of the guard for Padilla to be placed at liberty, and that Justo Liendc, an accomplice in the assassination of Fuentes, is directing the Alcalde, so that, in view thereof, if it turns out that said report justifies it, Your Lordship can take such measures as will be most conducive to remedying such scandalous abuses and malfeasances in office which tend to delay the better government which fortunately we have been enjoying, and the justice which must be administered promptly and completely. Meanwhile please accept the manifestations of my personal consideration and respect.=God, etc. Béxar, October 14, 1830.=R. M. [Ramón Músquiz]=To Colonel Don José de las Piedras, Commandant of the Frontier at Nacogdoches.

---

[1]BA Roll 135, Frames 0437-0438. For the background of the Padilla case, see McLean, *Papers*, III, 58-60.

ANTONIO ELOSÚA TO MANUEL DE MIER Y TERÁN[1]

[Translated from Spanish]

[October 15, 1830]

Office of the Principal Commandant   No. 369.

of Coahuila and Texas.

                    Most Excellent Sir:

The Plan for building the fortified house at Tenoxtitlan
did not come attached to the superior official letter from
Your Excellency dated September 20 last relative to this
matter.[2]

        I am informing Your Excellency of this fact so
that, if you see fit, you can order that it be forwarded to
me at the earliest opportunity so that I can send it to the
Lieutenant Colonel Commandant of that post, Citizen Francisco Ruiz.

        God and Liberty. Béxar, October 15, 1830.

                                [Antonio Elosúa]

To the Most Excellent Commandant General

[Manuel de Mier y Terán]

Reports that the plan which the Most Excellent Commandant
General said he was sending for the fort at Tenoxtitlan has
not come in, and consequently he asks for it.

---

[1]BA Roll 135, Frames 0562-0563.

[2]See McLean, *Papers*, IV, 486-487.

THE COMMISSAR GENERAL AT BÉXAR TO MANUEL

DE MIER Y TERÁN[1]

[Translated from Spanish]

[October 15, 1830]

Most Excellent Sir:

To the Satisfaction of the Citizen Principal Commandant of Coahuiltejas and my own, *Alférez* Don Santiago Navayra has been commissioned to undertake the work of the principal habitation or fortification that is to be constructed in Tenoxtitlan and under the intervention of Lieutenant Colonel Don Francisco Ruiz, according to what Your Excellency has ordered, and, with regard to paying the expenses of that work from the commissariat under my supervision, they will be made available as soon as I have the funds to do so, in preference to all other expenditures, and I am reporting this to Your Excellency in reply to your official letter of September 20 just past which deals with this matter.

God and Liberty. Béxar, October 15, 1830.

To the Most Excellent Commandant General)
)
of the Eastern Interior States,   )
)
Don Manuel de Mier y Terán.   )

---

[1]BA Roll 135, Frame 0221.

ANTONIO ELOSÚA TO THE MILITARY COMMANDANT

OF GOLIAD[1]

[Translated from Spanish]

Office of the Principal Commandant   [October 16, 1830]
of Coahuila and Texas.

A settler in that *Villa*, Onorato Moya, has in his possession a sword issued by the Government which belongs to Antonio Rodríguez, a Private who deserted from the Álamo de Parras Company. It was sold by Simón Treviño, of Laredo, to Moya several days ago when he was in this city.

Therefore you will please get in touch with the Alcalde of that Municipality concerning this matter, and, having recovered the said sword, you will forward it to me as soon as possible.

God and Liberty. Béxar, October 16, 1830.

[Antonio Elosúa]

To the Military Commandant of Goliad.

---

[1]BA Roll 135, Frames 0481-0482.

FRANCISCO RUIZ TO ANTONIO ELOSÚA[1]

[Translated from Spanish]

Office of the Military Commandant   [October 16, 1830]

of Tenoxtitlan.————————————   No. 21.

I am respectfully enclosing for Your Lordship the original

official letter which *Alférez* Don Santiago Navayra has

addressed to me in reply to the one I passed on to him[2]

notifying him of the appointment which Your Lordship was

pleased to give to the said officer for undertaking the

work which His Excellency has ordered to be constructed at

the new establishment [of Tenoxtitlan], which said reply it

has seemed to me appropriate to bring to the superior

attention of Your Lordship because the aforementioned offi-

cer asked me to do so, adding on my part that I am of the

opinion that there should be advanced to him something in

cash until the budget can be drawn up, in order to get

started on the work as soon as the plan is received.

God and Liberty. Tenoxtitlan, October 16, 1830.

To the Principal Commandant)   Francisco Ruiz
of Coahuila and Texas,   )
Colonel Don Antonio Elosúa.)   [rubric]

---

[1]BA Roll 135, Frames 0483-0484.

[2]See Santiago Navayra to Francisco Ruiz, October
10, 1830, in McLean, *Papers*, IV, 586-587.

FRANCISCO RUIZ TO SAMUEL M. WILLIAMS[1]

[Translated from Spanish]

Tenoxtitlan, October 16, 1830

Mr. Samuel M. Williams:

My most esteemed and fine friend: I hope that you and your family are enjoying the best of health and that our esteemed friend Don Stephen [F. Austin] is doing likewise .... I am taking advantage of this opportunity to trouble you. Therefore I am sending you by the bearer of this letter, whose name is Private Thomas [*sic*] de Lazo, ten pesos so that through him you may have purchased for me a reticule of a nature which will be described for you orally by the said bearer. Also please get me a blanket like the one I asked Don Stephen in the last mail to get, and I will send the money to pay for it as soon as you let me know how much it cost.

...

Your friend who loves you and kisses your hand,

Fran[cis]co Ruiz

[Rubric]

---

[1]Samuel May Williams Papers, Rosenberg Library, Galveston, Texas.

IRA INGRAM TO HOSEA H. LEAGUE[1]

Austin Oct=16th 1830--

My Dear Sir,

In conformity with your request, that I would give you my reasons in writing, for proposing a dissolution of the mercantile co=partnership existing between you & myself, I take this opportunity presented by a leisure moment, to comply with it.

And first; The connexion has long since ceased to be mutually beneficial, and I presume we shall both agree in the opinion, that there is not even a hope, of any change for the better.[2]

Secondly; The balance of your account is considerable, at *present*; must be increased more (or less), in winding up the concern; whether more than will ultimately fall to you on a dividend of the profits, I cannot foretell; but we both know this, that neither of us can claim any thing on the score of profits, till the debts are all paid--and we owe to Col. Fisher, a heavy debt, which must, and ought, to have the preference of all others. That he will look to, and call on me *personally*, for a settlement, past experience leaves no room to doubt-- The means of paying him, ought, therefore, to be at my disposal.--

Thirdly; You owed it to me, to have informed me frankly, the full extent of your private responsibilities, which have since become serious embarrassments, at the time we formed the connexion; and my feelings have been wounded whenever, I have reflected, that, on this subject, I was left in the dark. Were I able to meet, *ours*, mine, and *your* debts, I would advance for you as cheerfully as for my Brother--but I am not; and self preservation calls loudly for timely precaution

Fourthly; Perhaps it is not yet too late, if left to myself, by means of great exertions, to recover--but if I am not, it will hardly be worth my while to make an effort. Again--If disenthralled from all alliance, I *may* be fortunate enough, to place myself in a situation, during the winter, to render you double the aid that I could, if no change takes place.

I am informed that you have attributed this proposition to unfriendly feelings. I am truly sorry that you should have suffered yourself thus to weigh my motives. They merit a very different construction. I am not in the habit of prateing of my friendships, but if I were, the notoriety of my course of conduct towards you, for years past; would spare me the trouble, in this instance, of becoming my own commentator.--

I have no Cold--no unfriendly, no neutral feelings towards *you*, or *yours*.

No, Sir; if your happiness depended on my volition, you would soon forget your sufferings, and be surrounded by felicity, and carressed by those you love. I remain, Sir,

                                    Yours respectfully

                                        Ira Ingram

                                         [rubric]

Maj. H. H. League

        [Addressed:] H. H. League Esq Present

----

     [1]Benjamin C. Franklin Papers, The University of
Texas Archives, Austin.

     [2]League was in jail on a charge of being an accom-
plice in the murder of John G. Holtham. See McLean,
Papers, IV, 453.

SINCE FRANCISCO RUIZ WROTE ANTONIO
ELOSÚA ON OCTOBER 29, 1830, THAT "ON THE
17TH OF THE MONTH WHICH IS NOW ENDING,
THIS DETACHMENT WAS TRANSFERRED TO THE
NEWLY CHOSEN TERRAIN," WE ARE INSERTING,
ON THE NEXT TWO PAGES, SOME MAPS SHOWING
THE LOCATION OF THE PERMANENT SITE OF
FORT TENOXTITLAN.

THESE MAPS WERE ORIGINALLY DRAWN BY
ELEANOR HANOVER NANCE (MRS. JOSEPH MILTON
NANCE) AND PUBLISHED, IN A REDUCED FORM,
TO ACCOMPANY AN ARTICLE BY MALCOLM D.
McLEAN ENTITLED: "TENOXTITLAN, DREAM
CAPITAL OF TEXAS, " WHICH APPEARED IN THE
SOUTHWESTERN HISTORICAL QUARTERLY FOR
JULY, 1966 (VOL. LXX, NO. 1), pp. [23]-43.

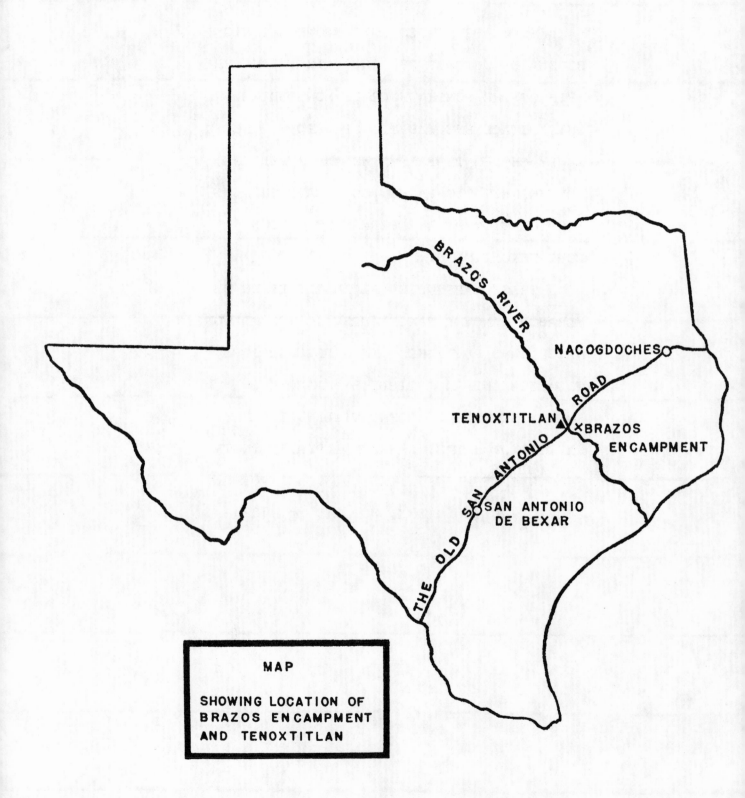

BRAZOS RIVER

NACOGDOCHES

ROAD

TENOXTITLAN ▲ ✕BRAZOS
ENCAMPMENT

THE OLD SAN ANTONIO

○SAN ANTONIO
DE BEXAR

MAP

SHOWING LOCATION OF
BRAZOS ENCAMPMENT
AND TENOXTITLAN

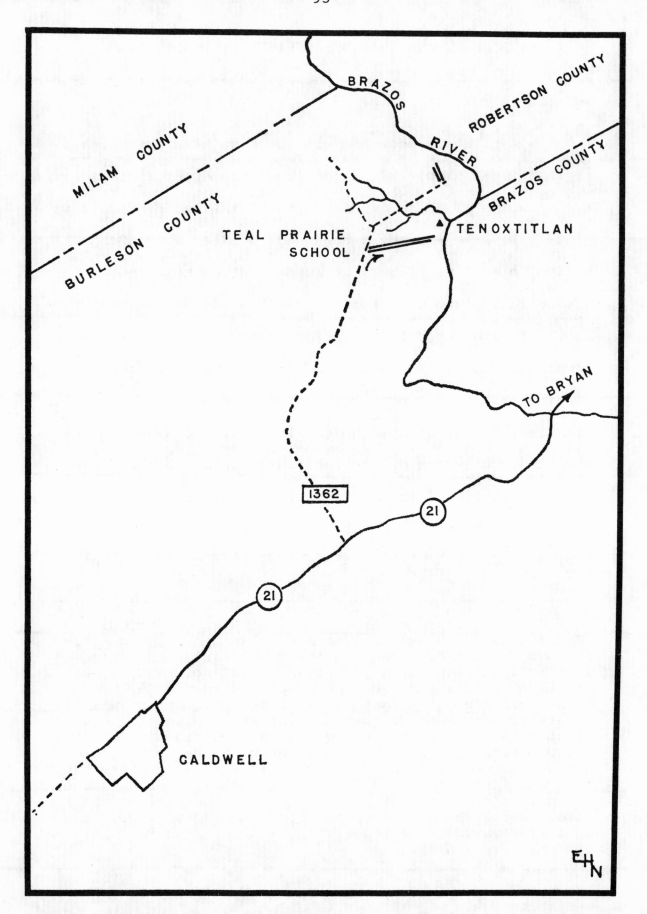

MAP SHOWING HOW TO REACH THE SITE OF TENOXTITLAN TODAY

STEPHEN F. AUSTIN'S DESCRIPTION OF TENOXTITLAN[1]

[Entered under October 17, 1830]

...

A military post and village have been established on the west bank of the Brazos above the upper road and about twelve miles below the mouth of the San Andress river [Little River], and about one hundred miles above San Felipe de Austin. This post is called Tenoxticlan [Tenoxtitlan] and is beautifully situated and abundantly supplied with large and pure fountains of water. It is understood to be the intention of government to keep up a considerable garrison at this place to protect the northern frontier of the colony from the Indians, and also to promote the settlement of the interior country on the Brazos. Tenoxticlan bids fair to become a considerable inland town. The country round it is very fertile and pleasant, and the Brazos river is navigable above this in time of freshets.
    ...

---

[1]This is an excerpt from an article entitled: "Descriptions of Texas by Stephen F. Austin ...," contributed by Eugene C. Barker to the *Southwestern Historical Quarterly*, Austin, Texas, October, 1924 (Vol. XXVIII, No. 2), pp. 98-121. The passage quoted appears on p. 109. Dr. Barker explains in a footnote that the description was apparently intended for publication in pamphlet form to be circulated in Europe. It appears in a subdivision of the article headed: "1831. Emigration to Texas from Europe," but we have moved it up to October 17, 1830, the date the site was first occupied, because the description has more to do with the topography and natural advantages of the site, than with the houses or people in the village, so what it says would be equally applicable, either in late 1830 or early in 1831.

ANTONIO ELOSÚA TO MANUEL DE MIER Y TERÁN[1]

[Translated from Spanish]

Office of the Principal Commandant   [October 22, 1830]

of Coahuila and Texas.   No. 384.

Most Excellent Sir:

Your Excellency has been pleased to warn me, with your
superior official letter of the 11th of the current month,
that the campaign against the Hueco and Tahuacano Indians
should not cease until they have been dislodged from the
points which they have occupied, from which they have been
such a great threat to this city, and made to withdraw to
the other side [east bank] of the headwaters of the Trinity
River, which I shall have to do.

Within the past few days Colonel [Peter Ellis] Bean
has arrived, sent by the Commandant of the Frontier at
Nacogdoches, proposing to me a combined expedition against
the said Indians, as Your Excellency will see from the
original official letter which I am attentively enclosing
for you.

As soon as I received the first communication from
the aforementioned colonel relative to this matter, I got
in touch with the Political Chief of this Department so
that he could request, in advance, the cooperation of the
settlers in Austin's Colony, and, as a matter of fact, he
has written to them, the results of which have not yet
been learned.[2]

As soon as Mr. Bean arrived, the two of us consulted the experts who have lived among the Huecos and Tahuacanos, and who are informed of their customs and their
territories; we examined the information which at present
they have concerning them, and we have gathered all the
information that we believe to be pertinent to the case.

The result of all this has been that the aforementioned Indians are not at present in the places which they
have occupied because during the winter they withdraw to
spend that time in the shelter of the forests and creeks
and to occupy themselves in hunting. For this reason we
do not know where they can be found. Earlier it had been
suspected that they had gone toward the Comanches, and the
Comanches themselves had confirmed that fact, and now,
after the blow that they suffered from the last expedition,
it is to be feared that they have become mixed with them,
which can be definitely confirmed the first time that they
come here.

Consequently it appears that the season or the
opportune moment for our expedition to go out has not
arrived yet, and that it is necessary to wait for same. I
shall be on the lookout for it in order to take advantage
of it, and meanwhile it will be possible for the horses
belonging to almost the entire garrison to recover, for
they are still in poor condition. It will be possible to
obtain better information and also to get resources with

which to supply the troops better, a point which is no less important.

And I have the honor of reporting all this to Your Excellency, reassuring you of my good will and respect.

God and Béxar. October 22, 1830.

[Antonio Elosúa]

Reports everything that has occurred to him concerning the fitting out of the new expedition that is being undertaken and which is to go out against the Huecos and Tahuacanos.

---

[1]BA Roll 135, Frames 0624-0625.

[2]See Ramón Músquiz to the Ayuntamientos of Goliad and San Felipe de Austin, October 14, 1830.

ANTONIO ELOSÚA TO MANUEL DE MIER Y TERÁN[1]

[Translated from Spanish]

Office of the Principal Commandant   [October 22, 1830]

of Coahuila and Texas.   No. 385.

Most Excellent Sir:

I am enclosing for Your Excellency the original official letter which has been passed on to me by Colonel Peter Ellis Bean concerning the news which he has seen in the newspaper from Washington concerning the Indians of the United States, from whom they are trying to buy the lands which they are occupying and move them to the west of the Mississippi, in which case they will come closer to our frontiers and may even penetrate them, so that, in view thereof, Your Excellency may be pleased to take such measures as may appear appropriate.

God, etc. Béxar, October 22, 1830.

Encloses an official letter from Colonel Bean which gives news about lands in the United States which they are trying to buy from the Indians and make them cross over to the west of the Mississippi.

---

[1]BA Roll 135, Frame 0626.

ANTONIO ELOSÚA TO THE MILITARY COMMANDANTS OF NACOGDOCHES,

LAVACA, TENOXTITLAN, AND LA BAHÍA[1]

[Translated from Spanish]

[October 22, 1830]

Office of the Principal Commandant of Coahuila and Texas.

His Excellency the Commandant General Inspector of these States, in an official superior letter dated the 8th of the present month, has been pleased to write me as follows:

"The Most Excellent Secretary of War and Navy, in an official letter dated the 11th of the past month, has been pleased to write me as follows:='The Most Excellent Secretary of Foreign Relations,'" etc.

I am forwarding it to you for your information and compliance.

God and Liberty. Béxar, October 22, 1830.

[Antonio Elosúa]

To the Military Commandants of Nacogdoches,

Lavaca, Tenoxtitlan, and La Bahía.

---

[1]BA Roll 135, Frame 0632.

ANTONIO ELOSÚA TO THE COMMANDANTS OF THE COMPANIES OF

COAHUILA AND TEXAS, AND TO THE MILITARY

COMMANDANTS OF NACOGDOCHES, LAVACA,

TENOXTITLAN, AND LA BAHÍA[1]

[Translated from Spanish]

[October 22, 1830]

Office of the Principal Commandant of Coahuila and Texas.

The Most Excellent Commandant General Inspector of
these States, in an official letter dated the 27th of September last, has been pleased to write me as follows:

"The Citizen Principal Commandant of San Luis Potosí, in a note dated the 8th of the current month, writes me
as follows:='Most Excellent Sir.=Having terminated the
case drawn up against Lieutenant Colonel Don Juan Malagón,'
etc."

I am forwarding it to you for your information and
guidance.

God and Liberty. Béxar, October 22, 1830.

[Antonio Elosúa]

To the Commandants of the Companies of Coahuila and Texas,
and to the Military Commandants of Nacogdoches, Lavaca,
Tenoxtitlan, and La Bahía.

---

[1]BA Roll 135, Frame 0633.

ANTONIO ELOSÚA TO IGNACIO RODRÍGUEZ[1]

[Translated from Spanish]

[October 22, 1830]

Office of the Principal Commandant of Coahuila and Texas.

Since the Most Excellent Commandant General Inspector of these States, by his superior order dated the 11th of the current month, has issued instructions that Private Damacio Galván, of the Béxar Presidial Company, and Settler Manuel de Luna shall be given a reward of 25 pesos each, you will please go to the Commissariat of this city to inform the Commissar that I have commissioned you to receive the said amounts and sign the corresponding entry in the books in his office, which said sums you will deliver into the hands of the interested parties, and you will report back to me when you have done so.

God and Liberty. Béxar, October 22, 1830.

[Antonio Elosúa]

To Lieutenant Citizen Ignacio Rodrigues.

---

[1]BA Roll 135, Frame 0636.

PETER ELLIS BEAN TO ANTONIO ELOSÚA[1]

[Translated from Spanish]

[October 22, 1830]

Some time ago I heard, from bad reports, that you all have been wanting to file some kind of a charge against my honor and my conduct, saying that I had married two different women.[2] I have waited with much patience, and now I am asking that, if I am delinquent, I be declared as such, and therefore I beg that said charges be presented to me so that, in view thereof, I can vindicate my honor, as I very well can.

God and Liberty. Béxar, October 22, 1830.

Pedro Ellis [*sic*] Bean

[rubric]

To the Principal Commandant,   )
)
Colonel Don Antonio de Elosúa.)

---

[1]BA Roll 135, Frames 0612-0613.

[2]See Sterling C. Robertson's statement concerning Peter Ellis Bean, August 24, 1826, in McLean, *Papers*, II, 629-630.

ANTONIO ELOSÚA TO JOSÉ ORTEGA[1]

[Translated from Spanish]

[October 23, 1830]

Office of the Principal Commandant of Coahuila and Texas.

Colonel Peter Ellis Bean, in an official letter dated yesterday, writes me as follows:

"Some time ago I heard," etc.

And I am copying it for you for your information, urging you to expedite the speedy and most perfect conclusion, according to the instructions sent to you by the Supreme Government, of the case of the said Colonel, which I forwarded to you with an official letter dated the 28th of May of the year just past, and which he, with so much justice, is demanding.

God, etc. Béxar, October 23, 1830.

[Antonio Elosúa]

To Captain Don José Ortega.

---

[1]BA Roll 135, Frame 0654.

ANTONIO ELOSÚA TO PETER ELLIS BEAN[1]

[Translated from Spanish]

[October 23, 1830]

Office of the Principal Commandant of Coahuila and Texas.

Having been informed by Your Lordship's official letter dated yesterday concerning the case which you have seen fit to protest, I wish to report that it is in the possession of Captain Don José Ortega, to whom it was forwarded by me with an official letter dated the 28th of May of the past year in order that it might be documented in the form stipulated by the Supreme Federal Government, and on this very day I am instructing him to expedite it to a speedy conclusion, and by that means I have no doubt that the reputation of Your Lordship will be vindicated in the manner which it justly deserves.

God, etc. Béxar, October 23, 1830.

[Antonio Elosúa]

To Colonel Don Peter Ellis Bean.

---

[1]BA Roll 135, Frame 0656.

ANTONIO ELOSÚA TO JOSÉ DE LAS PIEDRAS[1]

[Translated from Spanish]

[October 23, 1830]

Office of the Principal Commandant of Coahuila and Texas.

.   As soon as I received Your Lordship's official letter dated the 28th of the past month, in which you were
pleased to propose to me a combined expedition against the
Hueco and Tahuacano Indians, I got in touch with the Political Chief of this Department in order to solicit, in advance, the cooperation of the settlers in Austin's Colony,
for which purpose he wrote them, and as yet I do not know
the result.

Subsequently Colonel Peter Ellis Bean arrived, sent
by Your Lordship in this connection, and the two of us have
conferred about the said expedition. We have consulted the
experts who have lived among the Indians and are informed
about their customs and their territories, and we have
examined all the other reports and circumstances that might
be appropriate to the case.

The result has been that the said Indians are not
at present at the points which they have occupied because
in the winter they withdraw to spend that time in the shelter of the forests and creeks, and to occupy themselves in
hunting. Consequently we do not know where they are, or
where they may be found. For a long time it had been sus-

pected that they had gone toward the Comanches, which rumor had been confirmed by the Comanches themselves, and now, after the blow that they suffered from the last expedition, it is to be feared that they have mingled with them, which can be determined whenever they come here next time.

Consequently it appears that the reason or the opportune moment for an expedition to go out has not arrived yet, and that it is necessary to wait for it. I shall be watching for it in order to take advantage of it. Meanwhile it will be possible for almost all of the horses belonging to this garrison, which are in poor condition, to recover. It will be possible to acquire better information and also to get resources with which to supply the troops better, a point which is no less important.

I am reporting all of this to Your Lordship for your information, assuring you that I still have the intention, and will take care to see that the projected expedition is carried out, and that I will keep Your Lordship posted concerning everything that occurs in this connection, by means of reports at the proper time, for your guidance.

God and Liberty. Béxar, October 23, 1830.

[Antonio Elosúa]

To Lieutenant Colonel José de las Piedras,
Commandant of the Frontier at Nacogdoches.
P. S. No matter how much I want to do so, I cannot furnish

Your Lordship any horses from here.

---

[1]BA Roll 135, Frames 0652-0653.

ANTONIO ELOSÚA TO PETER ELLIS BEAN[1]

[Translated from Spanish]

[October 23, 1830]

Office of the Principal Commandant of Coahuila and Texas.

I have forwarded, to the Most Excellent Commandant General of these States, the original official letter from Your Lordship dated yesterday relative to the news that you have to the effect that in the United States of the North they are trying to buy lands from the Indians and make them move over to the west side of the Mississippi, thus coming closer to our frontiers, and, it is to be feared, they may even come beyond them, all of which I am reporting to Your Lordship by way of reply.

God and Liberty. Béxar, October 23, 1830.

[Antonio Elosúa]

To Colonel Peter Ellis Bean.

---

[1]BA Roll 135, Frame 0657.

MINUTES OF THE AYUNTAMIENTO OF SAN FELIPE DE AUSTIN[1]

[October 23, 1830]

[p. 50]   In the Town of San Felipe de Austin on the
23rd day of October 1830. The Ayuntamto. in session this
day pursuant to the adjournment of the extraordinary session of the 18th of this month. The proceedings of the
last meeting as recorded were read over and approved. A
petition was presented by William H. Jack in behalf of Seth
Ingram and Hosea H. League[2] which was read and ordered to
be filed for the purpose of giving the subject matter of
the prayer a full and mature deliberation, in order that
the members may be enabled at the next regular meeting [to]
decide upon its merits.[3] The prest. then represented to
the body that the expense of guarding and securing the persons of the two prisoners now in confinement has become so
considerable as to render it necessary that a different
mode of guarding them should be adopted. The body then
discussed the subject and it was agreed upon that inasmuch
as the 25th Article of the Militia Law of the State pro-
vides that the Militia men shall perform the service and
duty of guards etc. upon occasions like the present, and
of different natures, An official letter shall be addressed
to the Colonel Commandant of the Batallion requiring him to
furnish the necessary and competent number of Militia to
perform the duties of guard for the security of the prisoners now in confinement, either by classing the whole

Militia or by classing the companies in turn or in such
manner as the Col Commandant may deem the least burthen-
some, to secure and effect the objects desired and the body
adjourned

[p. 51] Thos. Barnett

Samuel M Williams

Secy pro tem

---

[1]Eugene C. Barker (ed.), "Minutes of the Ayuntamiento of San Felipe de Austin, 1828-1832," VI, *The Southwestern Historical Quarterly*, Austin, Texas, Volume XXII,
No. 4 (April, 1919), pp. 353-359. This excerpt appears on
pp. 354-355.

[2][Dr. Barker's note:] " ... A letter from Austin
to Ramon Musquiz ... November 30, 1830, ... [reproduced
below] gives some facts concerning this case which became a
cause celebre. John G. Holtham while drunk wandered into
Ira Ingram's yard and was ejected by him. Later he challenged Ingram to a duel and Ingram refused to fight him,
whereupon Holtham posted notices on the court house door
(the alcalde's office) and elsewhere denouncing Ingram as a
coward, a rascal, and a man without honor. He encountered
Seth Ingram, Ira's brother, just after posting one of
these documents, and the latter ordered him to remove it.
He refused, and Ingram killed him. League was in some way,
which Austin does not explain, an accomplice. Ingram was a
man of excellent character, and League was, as we have
seen, a member of the ayuntamiento, while Holtham was,
Austin says, a vagabond. League, however, was extremely
unpopular, and this, conbined with the complexity of criminal judicial procedure, delayed the trial of the defendants for several years, during most of which time they
were kept under guard without bail. For judicial procedure, see *The Quarterly*, XXI, 250."

ANTONIO ELOSÚA TO FRANCISCO RUIZ[1]

[Translated from Spanish]

[October 24, 1830]

Office of the Principal Commandant of Coahuila and Texas.

Colonel Peter Ellis Bean is carrying, for delivery
when he passes through that post, the sum of money that the
Commissar of this city has made available for the relief of
the Álamo Company. I am reporting this fact to you for
your information.

God, etc. Béxar, October 24, 1830.

[Antonio Elosúa]

To Lieutenant Colonel Don Francisco Ruiz,
Commandant of the Tenoxtitlan Detachment.

---

[1]BA Roll 135, Frame 0675.

ANTONIO ELOSÚA TO FRANCISCO RUIZ[1]

[Translated from Spanish]

[October 26, 1830]

Office of the Principal Commandant of Coahuila and Texas.

Having been informed by your official letter dated
the 16th of the present month, and by the original letter
that you enclosed from *Alférez* Don Santiago Navayra concerning the need for the plan which is to be used for
building the fort at that point, and for the advancement of
some funds in order to start building, I wish to report to
you that I will send you the plan just as soon as it comes
to hand, and, with regard to the money that for the present
might be needed in order to start collecting the materials
and begin the work, it is indispensable that *Alférez*
Navayra, as the commissioner, should draw up, on a prudent
basis, the respective budget of the funds that will be
needed right now, and bring it, approved by you, in order
to collect the money from the Commissariat of this city,
all of which I am reporting to you by way of reply.

God and Liberty. Béxar, October 26, 1830.

[Antonio Elosúa]

To the Military Commandant of Tenoxtitlan,

Citizen Lieutenant Colonel Francisco Ruiz.

---

[1]BA Roll 135, Frame 0720.

ANTONIO ELOSÚA TO THE MILITARY COMMANDANTS

OF NACOGDOCHES, LAVACA, TENOXTITLAN,

AND LA BAHÍA[1]

[Translated from Spanish]

[October 26, 1830]

Office of the Principal Commandant of Coahuila and Texas.

The Most Excellent Commandant General Inspector of these States, in an official letter dated the 6th of the present month, has been pleased to write me as follows:

"On this date I am writing the Citizen Vice Consul of the Mexican Republic in New Orleans," etc.

And I am copying it for you for your information and compliance in the part which pertains to you.

God and Liberty. Béxar, October 26, 1830.

[Antonio Elosúa]

To the Military Commandants of Nacogdoches,

Lavaca, Tenoxtitlan, and La Bahía.

---

[1]BA Roll 135, Frame 0722.

ANTONIO ELOSÚA TO THE COMPANIES OF RÍOGRANDE

AGUAVERDE, AND BAVIA, AND TO THE MILITARY

COMMANDANTS OF NACOGDOCHES, LAVACA,

TENOXTITLAN AND LA BAHÍA, AND THE

MAJOR OF THE PLAZA AT BÉXAR

AND THE MILITARY COMPANY

AT MONCLOVA[1]

[Translated from Spanish]

[October 26, 1830]

The Most Excellent Commandant General Inspector of these States, in an official letter dated the 30th of September last, has been pleased to write me as follows:

"The Most Excellent Secretary of War and Navy, in a supreme circular dated the 7th of the present month, writes me as follows:='Most Excellent Sir:=Under date of May 18 last,' etc."

I am forwarding it to you for your information and guidance.

[Antonio Elosúa]

To the Companies of Ríogrande, Aguaverde, and Bavia, and to the Military Commandants of Nacogdoches, Lavaca, Tenoxtitlan, and La Bahía, and the Major of the Plaza at Béxar, and the Military Company at Monclova.

---

[1]BA Roll 135, Frame 0724.

FRANCISCO RUIZ TO ANTONIO ELOSÚA[1]

[Translated from Spanish]

[October 26, 1830]

Office of the Military Commandant)   No. 22
)
of Tenoxtitlan———————————)

By virtue of the fact that the Captain of the Álamo Company has informed me that he has permission from Your Lordship for the individuals of same who have a family at Béxar to go and get them, I have seen fit to permit a first-class corporal, two second-class corporals, and ten privates, of the aforementioned company, to go to that city for the purpose indicated, and I have the honor of reporting this fact to Your Lordship for your information and superior approval.

God and Liberty. Tenoxtitlan, October 26, 1830.

Francisco Ruiz

[rubric]

To the Principal Commandant of Coahuila and)
)
Texas, Colonel Don   )
)
Antonio Elosúa.   )

---

[1]BA Roll 135, Frame 0727.

SEVERO RUIZ TO ANTONIO ELOSÚA[1]

[Translated from Spanish]

[October 26, 1830]

Álamo Presidial Company

On this date the individuals in the Company under my command who have families there [in Béxar] are leaving for that city. The mules of the community are going in order to bring back the supplies from the paymaster's office and to help said families with a part of same. I am reporting this to Your Lordship for your information and to see if you would be so kind as to arrange for that commissariat to help the substitute paymaster in any way that you may deem appropriate.

God and Liberty. Tenoxtitlan, October 26, 1830.

Severo Ruiz

[rubric]

To the Principal Commandant, Colonel)
)
Don Antonio Elosúa.—————————)

---

[1]BA Roll 135, Frames 0728-0729.

MURDER OF JOHN G. HOLTHAM AND FIELDING PORTER[1]

[October 27, 1830]

The Texas Gazette of the 6th ult. [*i.e.*, September 6] states, that a rencountre took place at San Phillippe de Austin, between *Seth Ingram*, H. H. League and J. G. Holtham, in which the latter was killed by a pistol ball passing through his body; that Ingram and League are in close confinement.

The same paper of the 11th, advertised a reward of $100, for the apprehension of *Hiram Friley*,[2] who stands accused of the murder of *Fielding Porter*.--Friley, is described as about 30 years of age, six feet high, stout made, fair complexion, and light hair.

---

[1]*The Nashville Republican and State Gazette*, October 27, 1830, page 3, column 4.

[2]Hiram Friley had located League 14 in Leftwich's Grant on February 25, 1826. See Malcolm D. McLean (compiler and editor), *Papers Concerning Robertson's Colony in Texas, Volume II, 1823 through September, 1826: Leftwich's Grant* (Fort Worth: Texas Christian University Press, 1975), p. 497, and McLean, *Papers*, IV, 467-468.

DISSOLUTION.[1]

[October 27, 1830]

The Copartnership heretofore existing between H. H. LEAGUE
and IRA INGRAM, under the firm of *IRA INGRAM & Co*. is this
day dissolved by mutual and friendly consent.

The said Ingram assumes the payment of all the
debts due by the firm, and is authorized to receive payment
of all debts due it.

H. H. LEAGUE

IRA INGRAM

October 27h, 1830.-46-3t.

---

[1]*The Texas Gazette*, [San Felipe de] Austin, November 6, 1830. See above, Ira Ingram to Hosea H. League, October 16, 1830.

DIEGO CENOVIO DE LACHICA TO ERASMO SEGUÍN[1]

[Translated from Spanish]

Subcommissariat of the State   [October 28, 1830]
of Nuevo León————————

Under the date of August 30 last you were pleased
to inform me that, due to the pressure of duties in that
office, you were not sending me the certificate for seventy
-seven pesos for the charges that I have forwarded to you
on the 23rd of July against the Béxar Company and the First
Permanent Company of Tamaulipas, promising me that you
would do so as soon as you had time, but, since I badly
need the aforementioned document in order to make the
respective entry, I beg you to be so good as not to put off
this reply because I really need it, for in the next mail I
have to send you new charges against Captain Don Severo
Ruiz and Sergeant Juan del Moral, as a result of investigations that are still being carried on in this commissariat.[2]

God and Liberty. Monterrey, October 28, 1830.

Diego Cenovio de Lachica

[rubric]

To Don Erasmo Seguín,   )
)
Commissar of War in Béxar.)

---

[1]BA Roll 135, Frames 0752-0753.

[2]For the background of the charges against Severo
Ruiz, see McLean, *Papers*, IV, 287-288.

FRANCISCO RUIZ TO ANTONIO ELOSÚA[1]

[Translated from Spanish]

Office of the Military Commandant)   [October 28, 1830]
)
of Tenoxtitlan.   )   No. 23.

By the superior official letter from Your Lordship dated the 5th of the present month I have been informed that I should help Colonel Don José de las Piedras with troops, according to the orders issued by the Most Excellent Commandant General Inspector of these States, which said superior order will be duly obeyed, as soon as the said aid is requested. With this I am answering your aforementioned superior official letter which speaks of the matter.

God and Liberty. Tenoxtitlan, October 28, 1830.

Francisco Ruiz

[rubric]

To the Principal Commandant   )
)
of Coahuila and Texas, Colonel   )
)
Don Antonio Elosúa.   )

---

[1]BA Roll 135, Frames 0768-0769.

FRANCISCO RUIZ TO ANTONIO ELOSÚA[1]

[Translated from Spanish]

Office of the Military Commandant)   [October 28, 1830]
)
of Tenoxtitlan.   )   No. 24.

I received the official letter from Your Lordship dated the 5th of the present month, in which you were pleased to insert for me the official letter from the Most Excellent Commandant General Inspector of these States, dated the 19th of September last, relative to the assistance designated for the convict prisoners, the manner in which it is to be administered, and the other matters contained in your aforementioned superior official letter, which I am attentively answering.

        God and Liberty. Tenoxtitlan, October 28, 1830.

                                        Francisco Ruiz

                                        [rubric]

To the Principal Commandant   )
)
of Coahuila and Texas, Colonel)
)
Don Antonio Elosúa.   )

---

[1]BA Roll 135, Frame 0771.

FRANCISCO RUIZ TO ANTONIO ELOSÚA[1]

[Translated from Spanish]

Office of the Military Commandant)   [October 29, 1830]
)
of Tenoxtitlan.   )   No. 25.

We have in this military headquarters the superior official letter from Your Lordship dated the 5th of the month now ending, in which you were pleased to insert for me the official letter from the Most Excellent Commandant General Inspector of these States which speaks about complying with the circular dated June 30 last, which said superior order has been communicated in the order of the day at this point, for observance of same, with which I am answering your aforementioned official letter.

God and Liberty. Tenoxtitlan, October 29, 1830.

Francisco Ruiz

[rubric]

To the Principal Commandant of)
)
Coahuila and Texas, Colonel)
)
Don Antonio Elosúa.)

---

[1]BA Roll 135, Frame 0790.

FRANCISCO RUIZ TO ANTONIO ELOSÚA[1]

[Translated from Spanish]

[October 29, 1830]

Office of the Military Commandant)   No. 26
)
of Tenoxtitlan   )

On the 17th of the month which is now ending this Detachment was transferred to the newly chosen terrain. The change was not effected earlier because the river was on a rise.

The troops are camping out now as best they can until we receive the plan from His Excellency so that we can know more definitely how to locate it in its permanent position. I am reporting these facts to Your Lordship for your information.

God and Liberty. Tenoxtitlan, October 29, 1830.

Francisco Ruiz

[rubric]

To Mr. Principal Commandant of
Coahuila and Texas, Colonel
Don Antonio Elosúa

---

[1]Volume 53, pages 136 and 136 verso, Spanish Archives, General Land Office, Austin, Texas.

FRANCISCO RUIZ TO ANTONIO ELOSÚA[1]

[Translated from Spanish]

Office of the Military Commandant)   [October 29, 1830]
)
of Tenoxtitlan.   )   No. 27.

        On the 23rd of the present month I learned, from

two Americans from Austin's Colony, that from a theft com-

mitted on the 24th of September last, against some Ameri-

cans around the headwaters of Nuncio Creek, there have been

found, in a party of Cado and Hasinae Indians, one of the

horses that was stolen, a carbine, a hat, and other small

items. Consequently they are convinced that these Indians

are the ones who committed the theft. And, since this

incident makes us think that they can do the same thing

around Béxar, La Bahía, and the other establishments in

this Department, it has seemed appropriate to me to call it

to the superior attention of Your Lordship, adding that

there have been several bands of Indians from different

tribes, in small bunches, that have passed along this part

of the Brazos River, among whom there is a band of Quichas

that are very closely related to the Tahuacanos, and they

mix with them, since most of them speak the language of the

Tahuacanos and they are identified with them in every way.

In the aforementioned bands of Indians there are not

included any of the tribes that have just immigrated into

this Department.

God and Liberty.   Tenoxtitlan, October 29, 1830.

Francisco Ruiz

[rubric]

To the Principal Commandant of Coahuila)
)
and Texas, Colonel Don Antonio Elosúa.)

---

[1]BA Roll 135, Frames 0791-0792.

FROST THORN TO STEPHEN F. AUSTIN[1]

Nacogs 29 Oct *1830*

Dear Sir

Coln Piedras it appears has of late received orders, not to suffer any persons to pass here, unless they have actually made a Contract, either with yourself or Dewitt; or have a passport, from the Mexican Consul--in case of a previous Contract being made he requires Documents to that effect-- He has a *strong disposition, to strictly adhere to his order*

The bearer brot with him such voucher as the Colonization Law required--and presented himself to the Alcalde but it appears the Ayuntamiento have not the power of judging of the qualifications requisite, as the Coln took them from the Alcaldies office, and acted on them himself--you will readily see the embarresments, it will place THOSE Innocent persons under, that Emigrate and as a good wisher of the Country, I have always used my feeble exertions to encourage its settlement

You are I presume acquainted with the late regulations on the subject of Terans reserves etc--or I would say more-- If you have any friends Emigrating on the Road, that will pass thró this place, would it not be well to give Coln Piedras a List of the Names, which would supersede the necessity of there riding to Sn Phillepe, and perhaps much difficulty,

I am induced to write to you, as I am told many families are expected--and the advance season will not admit of there delaying much time on the Road--

Coln S. F. Austin   F. Thorn[2]

P. S.   I start for N. Orleans Tomorrow, and expect to be absent 2 Months

F. T

as I deem it expedient that you should receive this as soon as possible, I send it on by mail, under the direction of Colo Ruis, for it is out of my power to see you myself for a few days

[Addressed:] Coln S. F. Austin. St. Phillipe de Austin favd by Mr. [Alexander] *Thomson*

---

[1]*Annual Report of the American Historical Association for the Year 1922. In Two Volumes and a Supplemental Volume. Vol. II. The Austin Papers. Edited by Eugene C. Barker* (Washington: United States Government Printing, 1928), pp. 524-525. Cited hereafter as Barker, *Austin Papers*, II.

[2]Frost Thorn had obtained an empresario contract from the State Government of Coahuila and Texas on April 15, 1825, the same day that Robert Leftwich received his. --*Handbook of Texas*, II, 776.

MANUEL DE MIER Y TERÁN TO ANTONIO ELOSÚA[1]

[Translated from Spanish]

Office of the Commandant General and   [October 30, 1830]

Inspector of the Eastern Interior States.

Your Lordship will please tell me approximately how much
would be needed to provide the capes, *jorongos*, shoes, and
the other things needed by the presidial companies in that
Department and the Béxar garrison. I am saying this to
Your Lordship in reply to your official letter on that subject, dated the 29th of the past month, in which you
inserted the official letter from the Commandant of the
Álamo de Parras Company.

God and Liberty. Matamoros, October 30, 1830.

M. Mier y Terán

[rubric]

To the Principal Commandant)
)
of Coahuiltejas———————)

---

[1]BA Roll 135, Frames 0804-0805.

MANUEL DE MIER Y TERÁN TO ANTONIO ELOSÚA[1]

[Translated from Spanish]

Office of the Commandant General and   [October 30, 1830]

Inspector of the Eastern Interior States.

Your Lordship will order Presbyter Citizen Juan Nepomuceno
Allaya [Ayala?] to pass on to Tenoxtitlan, since there is
already a minister at Nacogdoches, the place to which he
had been assigned. I am saying this to Your Lordship by
way of reply to your official letter dated July 30 last,
No. 304.

     God and Liberty. Matamoros, October 30, 1830.

            M. Mier y Terán

              [rubric]

To the Principal Commandant)
)
of Coahuiltejas———————)

---

[1]BA Roll 135, Frame 0806.

FRANCISCO RUIZ TO ANTONIO ELOSÚA[1]

[Translated from Spanish]

Office of the Military Commandant)   [October 30, 1830]
)
of Tenoxtitlan.   )   No. 28.

The forty men from the Béxar Company who were detached to reinforce this Detachment presented themselves without incident on the 23rd of the present month, and they are now located in this camp. I am reporting this information to Your Lordship for your satisfaction.

God and Liberty. Tenoxtitlan, October 10, 1830.

Francisco Ruiz

[rubric]

To the Principal Commandant of)
)
Coahuila and Texas, Colonel   )
)
Don Antonio Elosúa.   )

---

[1]BA Roll 135, Frames 0865-0866.

FRANCISCO RUIZ TO ANTONIO ELOSÚA[1]

[Translated from Spanish]

Office of the Military Commandant   [October 30, 1830]

of Tenoxtitlan   No. 29

     On the 25th of the month now ending, the foreigner Sterling C. Robertson presented himself to me with six other American individuals proceeding from Tennessee and belonging to the Nashville Company. He showed me the contract made by the said company with the Government of the State of Coahuila and Texas in the early part of 1825 for the introduction of foreign families to settle on these lands, for which purpose he has come to examine the place where they are to form or place their principal settlement, either on the San Andrés [Little River] or the Brazos, according to what he has told me. And, although I gave him to understand that this military point has been occupied for the purpose of forming a new establishment, he showed the greatest pleasure and even said that he would appreciate it if it were even closer to the one to be formed by that Company. Since, when the foreign families come in, they may occupy some of the lands which would be suitable for the inhabitants of the new Tenoxtitlan, I have thought it my duty to notify Your Lordship at the proper time for your information and guidance, adding that both the said Robertson and those in his party have conducted themselves very harmoniously with the Mexicans, and a doctor who came with them even cured some of our sick soldiers without charging them anything.

God and Liberty. Tenoxtitlan, October 30, 1830.

Francisco Ruiz

[Rubric]

To the Principal Commandant of)
)
Coahuila and Texas, Colonel   )
)
Don Antonio Elosúa.   )

---

[1]Volume 54, pages 279 and 279 verso, Spanish Archives, General Land Office, Austin, Texas.

FRANCISCO RUIZ TO SAMUEL M. WILLIAMS[1]

[Translated from Spanish]

Tenoxtitlan, October 30, 1830

Mr. Samuel M. Wil[l]iams:

My fine friend and most esteemed sir: I want to express my most sincere thanks to you for the trouble you took in buying me the *guardapié*[2] which you sent me and which I have received. I like it very much.

I regret extremely the incidents which you indicate to me from the Capital. Ah, my friend, if you could but examine my heart, what sad ideas you would find in it! I no longer desire any power at all; I no longer aspire to anything except to devote my last days to silence. If only I could recover the tranquillity which my spirit has lost. Patience, and let us leave it to time, for perhaps nature will bring things back into order.

I beg you, my friend, not to try to observe with me the etiquette of writing me a reply for then that would deprive me of the pleasure that I get from being able to write you whenever the attentions to my new Tenoxtitlan will allow me to. Please show your confidence in me by not observing any kind of ceremony in our epistolary corre-spondence. I repeat that there should be no etiquette, for we shall unburden ourselves frankly whenever time will give us an opportunity. I hope it will be the same way with our good friend Don Stephen [F. Austin], whom I beg you to ask to do as I have requested, for otherwise I shall find myself isolated without being able to write to the two of you as I desire to do, in order not to obligate you to reply.

Please give my respectful and affectionate regards to your wife and family. I remain your sincere friend who professes invariable friendship to you and kisses your hand.

Francisco Ruiz

[rubric]

P. S. Tell our friend Stephen that it would be better to make a trip up this way than to go off and eat apples and rice.[3] Valid.

---

[1]Samuel May Williams Papers, Rosenberg Library, Galveston, Texas.

[2]The word "guardapié" literally means "guard-foot" or "foot-guard," but it usually occurs in Spanish in the plural, in which case it has two meanings: (1) "a dress of silk or rich cloth which women wore, and which was tied to the waist and descended to the feet," or (2) "a saddle flap of silk or other cloth which men of arms used to wear around their waist, and it extended down over the knees." --Academia Española, *Diccionario de la lengua española* (Madrid: Talleres ESPASA CALPE, S. A., 1936), p. 196. Since Ruiz had left his wife and family in San Antonio and since the age of chivalry was long since dead, we leave it to the reader's imagination to decide just what it was that Williams bought for Ruiz. It probably was a leather cape worn over the saddle horn and descending on either side to protect the rider's legs as he rode through the thick brush of the Brazos River bottoms.

[3]The reader should remember that Austin was a bachelor, that the apple was the Biblical symbol of discord, and that rice denoted matrimony.

THE AYUNTAMIENTO OF SAN FELIPE TO RAMÓN MÚSQUIZ[1]

[Translated from Spanish]

JURISDICTION
   OF
 AUSTIN.
                                              [October 30, 1830]

With the purpose of cooperating with the desires of Your Lordship and those of the Principal Commandant of Arms of the Department in the new expedition which they want to form and send out against the Tahuacano Indians, as Your Lordship was pleased to indicate to this Ayuntamiento in an official letter dated the 14th of the present month, we have published a translation of the aforesaid official letter from Your Lordship, in the gazette of this *Villa*, with an exhortation on behalf of the Ayuntamiento in support of the invitation from Your Lordship so that some of the inhabitants may voluntarily lend their services for their own welfare and that of the country.[2]

This Ayuntamiento will take the greatest pleasure in cooperating with Your Lordship and the Commandant of Arms, in order to obtain the punishment of the said Indians, and, at the opportune time, it will communicate to Your Lordship the result of the measures already taken, for your information and guidance, all of which this Ayuntamiento is reporting to Your Lordship in reply to your aforementioned official letter.

God and Liberty.

Villa of [San Felipe de] Austin on October 30, 1830.

Thos. Barnett

[rubric]

Samuel M. Williams

Temporary Secretary

[rubric]

---

[1]BA Roll 135, Frames 0858-0859. There is another copy in Frame 0999, followed by this note:

"These are copies. Béxar, December 29, 1830.
José Antonio Saucedo, Secretary [rubric]."

[2]See copy under October 14, 1830.

Department of Texas.

Álamo Presidial Company.[1]

November 1, 1830.

	Captains	Lieutenants	Alféreces	Chaplain	Armorer	Sergeants	Bugler	Corporals	Privates	Total	Horses	Mules
Strength from the preceding month	1	1	2	0	1	2	1	7	49	64	115	15
Provided for in vacant positions	0	0	0	0	0	0	0	0	0	0	0	0
Recruits	0	0	0	0	0	0	0	0	0	0	0	0
Deserters presented and apprehended	0	0	0	0	0	0	0	0	1	1	0	0
Horses bought and caught	0	0	0	0	0	0	0	0	0	0	0	0
Strength	1	1	2	0	1	2	1	7	50	65	115	15

	Captains	Lieutenants	Alféreces	Chaplain	Armorer	Sergeants	Bugler	Corporals	Privates	Total	Horses	Mules
Retired, invalids, and promoted	0	0	0	0	0	0	0	0	0	0	0	0
Died	0	0	0	0	0	0	0	0	0	0	0	0
Deserted	0	0	0	0	0	0	0	0	0	0	0	0
Horses dead or strayed	0	0	0	0	0	0	0	0	0	0	0	0
Strength during the present month	1	1	2	0	1	2	1	7	50	65	115	15

Assignments.

	Captains	Lieutenants	Alféreces	Chaplain	Armorer	Sergeants	Bugler	Corporals	Privates	Total	Horses	Mules
On guard duty+	0	0	0	0	0	0	0	1	6	7	7	0
Herding the horses+	0	0	0	0	0	0	0	1	5	6	6	0
In Tamaulipas+	0	0	0	0	0	0	0	0	1	1	1	0
In Nacogdoches+	0	0	0	0	0	0	0	1	0	1	1	0
In Béxar+	0	0	0	0	0	1	0	0	12	12	15	15
Carrying the mail to San Felipe de Austin+	0	1	0	0	0	0	0	0	1	1	1	1
Prisoners in Matamoros+	0	0	0	0	0	0	0	0	1	1	0	0
Ditto in Ríogrande+	0	0	0	0	0	0	0	0	1	1	0	0
Sick+	0	0	0	0	0	0	0	0	3	3	0	0
Prisoners+	0	0	0	0	0	0	0	0	3	3	0	0
Net active strength	1	0	2	0	1	1	1	1	18	25	71	14

[1]BA Roll 135, Frame 0896.

	Captains	Lieutenants	Alféreces	Chaplain	Armorer	Sergeants	Bugler	Corporals	Privates	Total	Horses	Mules
Lacking to complete quota	0	0	0	0	0	0	0	0	1	1	0	0
Detached here from other companies	0	0	0	0	0	0	0	0	0	0	0	0
Invalids added	0	0	0	1	0	1	0	0	57	59	724	113

	Pesos	Rs.	Gs.
Brought forward from previous month	640	6	3
Received during said month	0	0	0
In goods in Paymaster's Office	1.152	5	0
Total	1.793	3	3
Expenses	638	3	0
On hand in present month	1.155	0	3

Supplies prepared to take out against the enemy-------++

Corn in the Paymaster's Barn-------------++

Frijoles in ditto--------------------++

Hardtack-----------------------------++

The horses, although there are not very many of them, are in fairly good condition.

*Note.*1

Severo Ruiz

[rubric]

Indian villages established and at peace.

None-------

	Men	Women	Children	Total
	0	0	0	0

ÁLAMO PRESIDIAL COMPANY[1]

[Translated from Spanish]

[November 1, 1830]

Budget of assests corresponding to the individuals of the said Company in the present month, after deducting for invalids and gratuities for widows and orphans.

Officers.	Pesos,	Reales,	Granos		P.	R.	G.
1 Captain------------	117.	6.	0.	}			
1 Lieutenant---------	62.	6.	6.				
1 First *Alférez*------	47.	0.	10.	}	--288.	6.	3.
1 Second *Alférez*-----	39.	2.	2.				
1 Armorer------------	21.	6.	9.	}			

Enlisted Men.							
2 Sergeants at 29 ps. 1 rl. each---------	58.	2.	0.	}			
1 Bugler-------------	11.	5.	6.				
7 Corporals at 24 ps. 2 rs. 2 gs. each----	169.	7.	2.	}	1.209.	5.	11.
50 Privates at 19 ps. 3 rs. 3 gs. each----	969.	7.	3.*				
[*or	970.	2.	6.?]				

Invalids added.							
1 Private-------------	8.	0.	0.	}			
Gratification.				}	---48.	3.	7.
For the men------------	40.	3.	7.	}			

Rewards for Constancy.							
2 Individuals get 260 rs. pr. mo.------	65.	0.	0.	}			
1 " " 90-	11.	2.	0.				
1 " " 9-	1.	1.	0.	}	---79.	5.	0.
3 " " 6-	2.	2.	0.	}			

Total assets----------1.626. 4. 9.

<u>Bonus for additions.</u>   P.   R.   G.

Add 30 pesos due the apprehended
deserter, José María Vidales, from   }--------   30.   0.
September 16 up to the end of October
last-----------------------------------

                                   Total assets:---1.656.   4.   9.

<u>Deduct for losses.</u>

Deduct from assets 30 pesos drawn in
Monterrey by the family of the Captain }--------30.   0.   0.
of said Company pertaining to the
present month--------------------------

                                   Net assets------1.626.   4.   9.

Tenoxtitlan, November 1, 1830.

                        Santiago Navayra

                            [rubric]

O. K.

   [Severo] Ruiz

          [rubric]

---

[1]BA Roll 135, Frame 0898. There is a duplicate
copy of this report in Frame 0899.

AYUNTAMIENTO.[1]

[November 1, 1830]

Regular session of the Ayuntamiento,

[of San Felipe de Austin] on the

first Monday of November, 1830.

The report of James Kerr, and John H. Scott, commissioners for surveying and examining the route for a road from the La Baca [Lavaca] to the Colorado at Jennings crossing, on H. H. League's tract of land,[2] was read, approved and ordered to be filed.

Henry K. Lewis, Amos Edwards, and George M. Patrick, were appointed commissioners to survey and report the best and most direct route for a road from Harrisburg to Rightor's point; which report must be made at the next regular session, on the 6th of December next.

George Tennell, Josiah H. Bell, George Huff, Jesse Thompson, and Joseph Kuykendall, were appointed commissioners to examine and report the best and most direct route for a road from this town [San Felipe] to Marion, a majority of the five commissioners will be competent to act, and the report must be made at the session of the 6th December next.

Samuel Chance, Thomas F. Tone, Joseph Mims, Caleb R. Bostic, and Moses Morrisson, were appointed commissioners to review and report the best road and most practicable route, for a road from the Colorado at Jenning's crossing to Brazoria, a majority of the five commissioners will be commissioned to act, the report to be made at the session of 6th December next.

The Ayuntamiento ordered the following division of the present precinct of Bastrop, and formed two precincts under the following limits and boundaries: beginning at the crossing of the Cushattee road on the left or east bank of the River Brazos, from thence in a direct line to a point on the Atascosito road which shall be four leagues from the Brazos River, thence along said road to the divide between the San Jacinto and Trinity Rivers, up said divide to the San Antonio road, along said road westwardly to the Brazos River, thence down the river, following its meanders to the place of beginning--The territory comprehended within said limits shall be called the precinct of VIESCA.[3]

The precinct of Bastrop shall be comprised within the following limits, to wit: commencing on the right or west bank of the Brazos river at the point where the Cushatte road crosses, thence in a direct line to the divide between Caney creek and Mill creek, up said divide to the La Bahia road, along said road to the Colorado and across the Colorado to a point two leagues distant from the river, thence along said road to the Brazos river, thence down the river following its meanders to the place of beginning.

The upper line of the precinct of Victoria was

altered as follows: from Newman's Camp on the Bernard, the line shall run to the head of Big creek, in a direct line from said camp, thence down Big Creek with its meanders to its mouth in the Brazos, up the Brazos River to the lower line of Wm. Morton's league, along said lower line north to the north east corner of said Morton's league, thence in a line eastwardly to the old eastern boundary of said precinct.

---

[1]*The Texas Gazette*, San Felipe de Austin, November 6, 1830, page 2, columns 2-3. Microfilm in U. T. Arlington Library. This is only a part of the total minutes for that meeting. For other matters discussed see Eugene C. Barker (ed.), "Minutes of the Ayuntamiento of San Felipe de Austin, 1828-1832," VI, *The Southwestern Historical Quarterly*, Vol. XXII, No. 4 (April, 1919), pp. 353-359.

[2]This phrase is omitted from the Barker version, and there are many other variations throughout the document.

[3]This document has been included to clear up the confusion which has resulted when several amateur historians confused the *Precinct* of Viesca, which lay below the San Antonio-Nacogdoches Road, and the *Municipality* of Viesca, which was located above the road. It is also of interest because it mentions H. H. League and Amos Edwards, two individuals connected with the Texas Association in earlier volumes of these *Papers*.

GASPAR FLORES TO RAMÓN MÚSQUIZ[1]

[Translated from Spanish]

[November 2, 1830]

The haste with which the individuals of the Civic Militia and some residents of this city departed on the expedition that went out against the Tahuacano Indians, under the orders of Citizen Captain Nicasio Sanches did not permit them to supply themselves with the necessary provisions for the time that they were to be gone, and for this reason they arrived in great need at the new military establishment named Tenoxtitlan, where, since these individuals lacked the resources with which to supply themselves, on their own account, with provisions in order to continue on the march, I found myself forced to purchase a beef on credit, and, in fact, one was supplied to me by the foreigner named John Williams for the price of fifteen pesos, and I distributed it to the individuals shown on the list which I am duly enclosing[2] so that, if it should please Your Lordship, you might, as I beg you to do, order that, from the Military Fund, or from whatever fund seems most appropriate, the aforementioned fifteen pesos be handed over to me so that I can place them in the possession of Williams, as I have promised to do.

God and Liberty. Béxar, November 2, 1830.

Gaspar Flores   [rubric]

To the Political Chief of this   )
)
Department, Citizen Ramón Músquiz)

---

[1]BA Roll 135, Frames 0920-0921.

[2]This list was not found with the letter.

RAMÓN MÚSQUIZ TO THE COMMANDANT OF THE SECOND SQUADRON

OF CIVIC MILITIA OF BÉXAR[1]

[Translated from Spanish]

Office of the Political)   [November 2, 1830]
)
Chief of Béxar   )

In an official letter dated today I have been informed by
Citizen Gaspar Flores, Captain of the Second Company of
Civic Militia of the Squadron for this City, as follows:

About the fact that, when he arrived in Tenoxtitlan
he contracted a debt for fifteen pesos, the value of a beef
which was made available to him to take care of the needs
for food on the part of the citizens in the Civic Militia
and the settlers who, under his command, went out with the
expedition of Captain Don Nicasio Sanches, requesting payment of the said fifteen pesos, etc.

And I am forwarding it to you for your information
and so that you will be so good as to order that payment be
made from the fund of the Civic Militia of this City for
the fifteen pesos that are owed to the foreigner John
Williams, for a beef that he made available to Citizen
Captain Gaspar Flores for the citizens of the Militia and
the settlers who, under your immediate orders, went out on
the expedition against the Tahuacanos under the command of
Don Nicasio Sanches, according to the enclosed list of
those among whom said beef was distributed.=God and Liberty.

Béxar, November 2, 1830.=To the Commandant of the Squadron of Civic Militia of this City.

---

[1]BA Roll 135, Frames 0934-0935.

RAMÓN MÚSQUIZ TO GASPAR FLORES[1]

[Translated from Spanish]

Office of the Political)   [November 2, 1830]
)
Chief of Béxar   )

I have forwarded your official letter dated today, with the
list which you enclosed for me, to the Citizen Commandant
of the expedition of Civic Militia from this city, so that
he can order payment from the funds of said militia for the
15 pesos, the value of the beef that the foreigner John
Williams furnished for the party of individuals of the
militia and the settlers who, under your orders, joined the
expedition of Captain Don Nicasio Sanches which went out
against the Tahuacano and assembled at the military post of
Tenoxtitlan, where said beef was distributed to them. I am
reporting this to you in reply to your said official letter.

God, etc. Béxar, November 2, 1830.

[Ramón Músquiz]

To Gaspar Flores, Captain   )
)
of the Second Company of the   )
)
Squadron of Civic Militia   )
)
of this City.   )

---

[1]BA Roll 135, Frame 0933.

EXCERPT FROM THE MINUTES OF THE AYUNTAMIENTO

OF SAN FELIPE DE AUSTIN[1]

[November 2, 1830]

The Ayuntamiento in open session made the following resolution that whereas this municipality from its peculiar situation is much exposed to the inroads of fugitives from justice from the U.S. and other places, vagabonds and men of notorious bad character and it being the duty of the Ayuntamto. to watch over the security and tranquility of the inhabitants of the municipality and also to maintain and support good order and the public tranquility, and prevent the residence of men of bad character, and of idle and vicious habits within the jurisdiction, and taking into consideration that by the 5th article of the Contract made by the Empresario Stephen F. Austin he is bound not to permit, criminals, vagabonds or men of bad character to remain within the limits of his colony but to cause all such to leave it, and if necessary to drive them out by force of arms, it was resolved by the Ayuntamto. that the said Empresario be officially addressed by the Ayunto. and informed that the hereinafter described individuals are men of notorious bad character and ought not to be permitted to remain within the limits of [p.58] the municipality but immediately removed and are Peter Whitstine, Trammel, Pryor, John or Jack House and Brooks Williams.

And further the ayunto. resolved that John Williams[2]

residing near the San Antonio Road is a man of bad character, and in the habit of harboring men notoriously infamous
to the stigma and injury to the peaceable inhabitants of
the Municipality, but inasmuch as he is settled and has
some property and improvements about him, and much pecuni-
ary injury might arrise by his immediate removal the
Ayuntamto. recommended that a further trial be given the
said Williams, but that he shall not be permitted to receive
land until it shall be satisfactorily proven to the Ayunto.
that an entire reformation of character and conduct has
taken place in sd Williams, and further the Ayunto recommended that he be notified that whenever it comes to the
knowledge of the Ayunto. that he has about him or harbors
any men of bad character that he will be instantaneously
removed beyond the limits of the jurisdiction.

The Ayunto. further resolved that John Little has
been guilty of harboring Hiram Friley[3] who fled from this
town being confined in an accusation of a capital crime--
that he shall not be permitted to receive land as a settler
until it shall be satisfactorily proven that he has reformed
his conduct. And also that this Ayuntamto. conceive it
their duty to recommend the said Empresario not to admit
Washington Griffin, Henry P. Welsh, and George Welsh as
settlers as in the opinion of the ayuntamto. they are not
worthy of being admitted.

The subject of the petition presented by H. H.

League and Seth Ingram being introduced the Ayuntamto. considered that as the subject on which it treats is solely of
a judicial nature the ayuntamto. recommended it to the particular attention of the Alcalde[4] and that he adopt such
measures relative to it as in his judgment justice and
equity may require and [p. 59] there being nothing further
before the body it adjourned to Monday the 15th inst. ...

---

[1]Eugene C. Barker (ed.), "Minutes of the Ayuntamiento of San Felipe de Austin, 1828-1832," VII, *The Southwestern Historical Quarterly*, Vol. XXIII, No. 1 (July,
1919), pp. 69-77. The excerpt reproduced here appears on
pp. 69-71.

[2]For previous activities of John Williams, see
McLean, *Papers*, III, 395-396 and 428. This was "Cherokee
John" Williams, who had come into Austin's Colony from the
Pecan Point area.--*Handbook of Texas*, II, 913. The nearest
place for these individuals to go, when they were expelled
from Austin's Colony, was north across the San Antonio-
Nacogdoches Road, into the area that later became known as
Robertson's Colony. The reader should not be surprised,
therefore, when "Cherokee John" Williams comes back into
the story in the summer of 1832, when he rides into Tenoxtitlan and starts shooting up the town.

[3]See McLean, *Papers*, IV, 451-452 and 467-468.

[4]This left the fate of League and Ingram in the
hands of Thomas Barnett, who had been elected Alcalde of
San Felipe de Austin in 1829, and in that capacity he pre-
sided over the meetings of the Ayuntamiento. Born in Logan
County, Kentucky, on January 18, 1798, Thomas Barnett had
moved to Livingston County, Kentucky, before 1821, and he
served as sheriff there for two years. In 1823 he came to
Texas as one of Stephen F. Austin's Old Three Hundred.
About 1825 he married Mrs. Nancy Spencer; they became parents of six children. On February 10, 1828, he had been
elected *comisario* of the district of Victoria in the
Ayuntamiento of San Felipe de Austin, and in 1829 he was
elected Alcalde, as we have mentioned above.--*Handbook of
Texas*, II, 112.

THE GOLIAD AYUNTAMIENTO TO RAMÓN MÚSQUIZ[1]

[Translated from Spanish]

Goliad Civil Court.   [November 4, 1830]

Although this Corporation was most anxious to cooperate in the interesting and very important object of repeating a new expedition against the Tahuacanos, our irreconcilable enemies, we have been unable to do so, in spite of all our efforts and influence, because, first of all, most of our settlers are out of town tending to their own affairs, and, secondly, the few citizens who heard the invitation state, not without justice, that it is impossible for them to abandon their few possessions which they have saved for their own support, but they are willing to donate eleven horses, one mare, one yearling, and seven pesos which were contributed by the citizens of Guadalupe [Victoria], all for the assistance of the expedition which is being planned, all of which I am reporting to Your Lordship in the name of this Ayuntamiento for your superior guidance, in reply to your official letter dated the 14th of the past month which concerns this matter.=God and Liberty. Goliad, November 4, 1830.=José Miguel Aldrete.= Manuel Beserra, Secretary.=To the Chief of this Department, Citizen Ramón Músquiz.————————————————————

—————————————————————————————————————

[1]BA Roll 135, Frames 0998-0999.

SETTLEMENTS IN TEXAS.[1]

[November 5, 1830]

The Mexican Minister to the U. S. has published in a Baltimore paper, the subjoined notification, under date of the 5th ult. It is highly important to emigrants to Texas.

"Having received information that several offers have been made to citizens of the United States to colonize the lands in the States of Coahuila and Texas, I consider it my duty to caution them by publishing the 11th Art. of the law of the 6th of April of 1830, which is as follows:--

"'Art. 11. In virtue of the authority which has been reserved by the General Congress to itself, by Art. 7th of the law of the 16th of August of 1824, all foreigners, whose country is bounding on said State and Territory of the Federation, shall be prohibited from settling within the said State of Territory, in consequence of which all the contracts that have not taken effect, and are opposed to this law, shall be suspended.'

"Wherefore I declare, in the name of the Mexican Government, that whatever contract shall have been made in violation of the said law will be null and void, it being understood that colonization in the States of Coahuila and Texas, and the territory of New-Mexico, by citizens of the United States, has been prohibited.   Jose M. Tornel."

[1]*Arkansas Gazette*, Little Rock, December 22, 1830, page 3, column 2. By comparing the date of this publication with the article above entitled "Robertson Passes Through Little Rock," September 7, 1830, the reader will see that Major Robertson was already enroute to Texas with his first party of emigrants more than *three months* before the Mexican Minister's notice was published in Arkansas, and James W. Breedlove, the Mexican Vice-Consul in New Orleans, did not forward a copy to Stephen F. Austin until December 4, 1830, a month after the original notice was published in Baltimore.--*Austin Papers*, II, 549-550.

ANTONIO ELOSÚA TO FRANCISCO RUIZ[1]

[Translated from Spanish]

[November 5, 1830]

Office of the Principal Commandant of Coahuila and Texas.

The thirteen men of the Álamo de Parras Company who came to this city with the object of transporting their families, as you report to me in your official letter No. 22 dated the 26th of October last, are returning with them to that point. I am reporting this to you by way of reply.

God and Liberty. Béxar, November 5, 1830.

[Antonio Elosúa]

To the Military Commandant of Tenoxtitlan,)
)
Citizen Lieutenant Colonel Francisco Ruiz.)

[1]BA Roll 135, Frame 0727.

ANTONIO ELOSÚA TO SEVERO RUIZ[1]

[Translated from Spanish]

Office of the Principal Commandant)   [November 5, 1830]
)
of Coahuila and Texas   )

The individuals of that company who came to this
city for the purpose of transporting their families and the
supplies from the paymaster's office, as you reported to me
in your official letter dated October 26 just past, are
returning to that point with both items, and supplied as
best we could, the details of which will be reported to you
in due time by Sergeant Francisco Mesa, who has left here
with that assignment. I am reporting this to you in reply.

God and Liberty. November 5, 1830.

[Antonio Elosúa]

To the Captain of the Álamo Company.

---

[1]BA Roll 136, Frames 0045-0046.

MARIANO COSÍO TO ANTONIO ELOSÚA[1]

[Translated from Spanish]

Office of the Military Commandant   [November 5, 1830]
        of Goliad

I have already forwarded [your letter] to the Citizen
Alcalde of this *villa*, in order to reclaim the sword of
Antonio Rodríguez, the Private who deserted from the Álamo
Company, in conformity with what Your Lordship ordered me
to do in your official letter dated the 16th of the past
month, and in reply he tells me that the matter is para-
lyzed until the return of Settler Onorato Moya, who is now
absent, all of which I am reporting to Your Lordship for
your superior information and in reply to the said official
letter.

        God and Liberty. Goliad, November 5, 1830.

                                Mariano Cosío

                                [rubric]

To the Principal Commandant)
)
of This Department———————)

---

[1]BA Roll 136, Frames 0012-0013.

MANUEL DE MIER Y TERÁN TO ANTONIO ELOSÚA[1]

[Translated from Spanish]

Office of the Commandant General)   [November 7, 1830]
and Inspector of the   )
Eastern Interior States   )

Today I am writing Citizen Colonel José de las Piedras as
follows:

"I have received Your Lordship's official letter
dated September 28 last in which is seen the one which on
the same date you wrote Colonel Don Antonio Elosúa relative
to a combination for attacking the Tahuacano and Quichai
Indians. I approve everything that Your Lordship proposes,
and you may proceed forthwith to get in touch with the said
Colonel so that said measures can be put into effect just
as soon as there is a regular remittance of money in order
to give priority to taking care of the expenses that may be
incurred in that useful undertaking, with the understanding
also that I am transmitting this communication to Citizen
Colonel Elosúa so that, with him and Your Lordship working
together, the proposed objective can be achieved."

And I am transcribing it for Your Lordship for your
information as a result of the official letter which was
sent to you on September 28 by the said Colonel Piedras,
with whom Your Lordship will come to an agreement in order
to achieve the proposed object as soon as some money is
received at that point which shall be used preferably in

carrying out the expedition.

God and Liberty. Matamoros, November 7, 1830.

M. Mier y Terán

[rubric]

To the Citizen Principal Commandant

of Coahuiltejas.

---

[1]BA Roll 136, Frames 0076-0077.

JOSÉ DE LAS PIEDRAS TO ANTONIO ELOSÚA[1]

[Translated from Spanish]

Office of the Military Commandant   [November 7, 1830]
of the Frontier

Lieutenant Don Tivurcio de la Garza made a mistake when he said that Corporal José María Sambrano should have been sent to you one day after his departure from this place, for I have not given any order whatsoever for him to leave. On the contrary, I have ordered him to stay here.

The purpose of his coming here was so that we would not slow down the case that is being drawn up against Private Antonio Coy, due to the fact that he is one of the principal witnesses in same. It is possible any day now that that case may be returned for consideration before a Council of War, in which event the witnesses will have to be present, and since one of them, and a very interesting one, is Corporal Sambrano, it would be a very grave mistake for him not to be present. This is the cause of my delay, and with this I am answering Your Lordship's official letter on that subject, dated the 22nd of the past month.

God and Liberty. Nacogdoches, November 7, 1830.

To Colonel Don Antonio   )   José de las Piedras
)
Elosúa, Principal Commandant)   [rubric]
)
of Coahuila and Texas   )

---

[1]BA Roll 136, Frames 0081-0082. Piedras forwarded this letter to the Captain of the Béxar Company on November 23, 1830.--Frame 0083.

JOSÉ DE LAS PIEDRAS TO RAMÓN MÚSQUIZ[1]

[Translated from Spanish]

Office of the Military Commandant   [November 7, 1830]

of the Frontier

I have the honor of enclosing for Your Lordship an investigation which I ordered made concerning the points mentioned
in your official letter dated October 14 with reference to
the conduct of the Alcalde of this place, in order that
Your Lordship may make such use of same as is appropriate.

God and Liberty. Nacogdoches, November 7, 1830.

José de las Piedras

[rubric]

To the Political Chief of the)
)
Department of Texas,   )
)
Don Ramón Músquiz.   )

---

[1]BA Roll 136, Frames 0084-0085.

MANUEL RUDECINDO BARRAGÁN TO ANTONIO ELOSÚA[1]

[Translated from Spanish]

Ríogrande Presidial   [November 8, 1830]
   Company   Number 52.

The Commandant of the Aguaverde Company in reply writes me, in a letter dated the 23rd of the month just past, as follows:

"With your official letter dated the 15th of the current month, in which you inserted for me the official letter from the Principal Commandant, I have received the physical description which you enclosed for me concerning Eduardo Trebiño, the Private who deserted from the Álamo de Parras Company, which said individual I have inquired about, both in this *villa* and in the *Villa* of Morelos, of which he is a native, but it has not been possible to apprehend him."

And I am transcribing this for Your Lordship, for your superior information, as I promised to do in my official letter of reply dated the 25th of last month.

God and Liberty. *Villa* of Guerrero, November 8, 1830.

                    Manuel Ruddo. [Rudecindo?] Barragán [rubric]

To the Principal Commandant,   )
Citizen Colonel Antonio Elosúa)

----

[1]BA Roll 136, Frames 0111-0112.

RAFAEL CHOWELL TO ANTONIO ELOSÚA[1]

[Translated from Spanish]

<u>Lavaca Commissariat</u>   [November 8, 1830]

    With this official letter I am sending a little box
containing the model of the fort that is to be constructed
at Tenoxtitlan, thus complying with the order of His
Excellency the Commandant General.

        God and Liberty. Guade. [Guadalupe?], November 8,
1830.

                                Rafael Chowell
                                    [rubric]

To the Principal Commandant)
)
of Coahuiltejas.   )

---

[1]BA Roll 136, Frame 0123.

ANTONIO ELOSÚA TO MANUEL DE MIER Y TERÁN[1]

[Translated from Spanish]

[November 9, 1830]

Office of the Principal Commandant   No. 394

of Coahuila and Texas

Most Excellent Sir:

The Military Commandant of Tenoxtitlan, Citizen

Lieutenant Colonel Francisco Ruiz, in an official letter

dated October 30 last, writes me as follows:

"On the 25th of the month which is now ending the

foreigner Sterling C. Robertson presented himself to me,"

etc.

And I have considered it my duty to forward it to

Your Excellency for your information and decision.

God and Liberty. Béxar, November 9, 1830.

[Antonio Elosúa]

To the Most Excellent Commandant General

Enclosure for superior decision.

[Endorsed:] Official letter in which the Military

Commandant of Tenoxtitlan reports that the foreigner

Sterling C. Robertson has presented himself at that point

with other Americans to examine lands for colonization.

---

[1]Volume 54, pp. 280 and 280 verso, Spanish Archives,
General Land Office, Austin.

ANTONIO ELOSÚA TO FRANCISCO RUIZ[1]

[Translated from Spanish]

[November 9, 1830]

Office of the Principal Commandant

of Coahuila and Texas

With the official letter from you dated October 30 last, in which you informed me that the foreigner Hesterling [Sterling] Robertson had presented himself at that point with six other Americans from Tennessee who belong to the Nashville Company, who came with the object of examining those lands in order to introduce families and colonize according to the contract made by the said Company with the Government of this State in the early part of the year 1825,[2] I have reported to the Superior Office of the Most Excellent Commandant General Inspector of these States, and I shall inform you of the result for your information and guidance. This is my reply.

God and Liberty. Béxar, November 9, 1830.

[Antonio Elosúa]

To the Military Commandant of Tenoxtitlan

[Francisco Ruiz]

---

[1]BA Roll 136, Frames 0172-0173.

[2]See the "Contract between Robert Leftwich and the State of Coahuila and Texas," April 15, 1825, in McLean, *Papers*, II, 296-301.

ANTONIO ELOSÚA TO FRANCISCO RUIZ[1]

[Translated from Spanish]

Office of the Principal Commandant   [November 9, 1830]

of Coahuila and Texas.

By your official letter dated the 29th of October last I

have been informed of everything you reported to me with

respect to there having been found, among some Indians of

the Cado and Hasinay tribes, a horse, a carbine, and other

small items pertaining to the robbery committed by the

savages in September last against some Americans from

Austin's Colony, and also of the other things that you indi-

cate to the effect that various bands of Indians from dif-

ferent tribes have passed along that part of the Brazos

River, among them being a band of Quichas so closely rela-

ted to the Tahuacanos that they are confused with them,

both in their language and dress.

       I want to thank you for your efficiency in communi-

cating this information, and I urge you to continue to do

so, with due frequency and vigilance, from that post under

your command.

       God and Liberty. Béxar, November 9, 1830.

                              [Antonio Elosúa]

To the Military Commandant of Tenoxtitlan.

---

[1]BA Roll 135, Frames 0793-0794.

ANTONIO ELOSÚA TO FRANCISCO RUIZ[1]

[Translated from Spanish]

Office of the Principal Commandant   [November 10, 1830]

of Coahuila and Texas

As soon as you receive this order you will make arrange-

ments to send an escort of ten men to meet the convoy of

families belonging to the Álamo Company who are now on

their way to that post, accompanied only by the scouting

parties, who are to return as soon as said escort relieves

them, and you will endeavor to speed up both the departure

and the march of the said escort so as to meet the families

a little on the other side of San Marcos.

God and Liberty. Béxar, November 10, 1830.

[Antonio Elosúa]

To the Military Commandant of Tenoxtitlan.

---

[1]BA Roll 136, Frame 0184.

RAMÓN MÚSQUIZ TO THE GOLIAD AYUNTAMIENTO[1]

[Translated from Spanish]

Office of the Political)   [November 10, 1830]
)
Chief of Béxar   )

By your Lordship's official letter No. 128 of the
current month I have been informed of the reasons why the
inhabitants of that municipality cannot persent themselves
as volunteers to go out on the expedition which they are
trying to organize again against the Tahuacano Indians
which are causing so much harm to the lives and property
of the inhabitants along this frontier, and of the offer of
eleven horses, one mare, one yearling, and seven pesos in
cash made by the citizens of the new *Villa* of Guadalupe
Victoria, to whom you will express your deepest appreciation in the name of this office, for the patriotism and
true interest that they have shown in such a just cause,
instructing them to keep the aforementioned items in
reserve until it becomes necessary for us to make use of
them.=God, etc. Béxar, November 10, 1830.=To the Ayuntamiento of Goliad.

---

[1]BA Roll 135, Frame 0994.

SEVERO RUIZ TO ANTONIO ELOSÚA[1]

[Translated from Spanish]

<u>Álamo Presidial Company</u>   [November 10, 1830]

Inserted in the official letter from Your Lordship dated the 22nd of the month just past I have received the superior circular in which Lieutenant Colonel Don Juan Malagón is vindicated of the charge of being involved in a robbery.

God and Liberty. Tenoxtitlan, November 10, 1830.

Severo Ruiz

[rubric]

To the Principal Commandant,)
)
Colonel Don Antonio Elosúa   )

---

[1]BA Roll 136, Frame 0174.

SEVERO RUIZ TO ANTONIO ELOSÚA[1]

[Translated from Spanish]

<u>Álamo Presidial Company</u>   [November 10, 1830]

Inserted in the official letter from Your Lordship dated
the 9th of the month just past, I have received the supreme
resolution of August 7 urging compliance with the circular
dated June 30 preceding, concerning the manner in which
corporals and officers of the army should present themselves in the places designated therein, and the penalties
that are to be imposed upon them if they fail to do so.

God and Liberty. Tenoxtitlan, November 10, 1830.

Severo Ruiz

[rubric]

To the Principal Commandant, Colonel)
)
Don Antonio Elosúa.   )

---

[1]BA Roll 136, Frame 0175.

ANTONIO ELOSÚA TO RAFAEL CHOWELL[1]

[Translated from Spanish]

Office of the Principal Commandant)   [November 11, 1830]
)
of Coahuila and Texas—————————)

The Most Excellent Commandant General Inspector of these States, in an official letter dated October 12 last, was pleased to write me as follows:

"Under this same date I am writing Citizen Rafael Chowell as follows:

"'In a [wooden] box,'" etc.

I am forwarding it [the official letter] to you, hoping that, at the first opportunity, you will be so good as to send me the aforementioned plan so that I can direct it to Citizen Lieutenant Colonel Francisco Ruiz, who is badly in need of it so that he can start building the fort at Tenoxtitlan.

God and Liberty. Béxar, November 11, 1830.

[Antonio Elosúa]

To the Commissar at Lavaca, Citizen R. Chowell.

---

[1]BA Roll 136, Frame 0204.

HOSEA H. LEAGUE TO WILLIAM H. JACK[1]

[San Felipe de] Austin   Nov. 11, 1830--

William H. Jack Esqr

Dear Sir Experience is now about to convince you and every other person who are disposed to take an impartial view of the case of Mr. Seth Ingram and myself that my first impressions about it are substantially correct, that the legal consequences resulting to us on account of the tra[n]saction with which we are Charged is the least evil we have to expect from the arrest and confinement which it has produced. I have known from the beginning that anything like a temporizing course would certainly fail. There are four men (to wit), William Pettus,[2] Oliver Jones,[3] Robert M. Williamson[4] and Luke Lesassier,[5] neither of which will ever relax their exertions in the least possible degree while I have life, or while they are able to make an effort. Their own turpitude has made such a course necessary for them, which they are now compelled to pursue as the last and only means of self preservation. The whole flush of calumny, deffamation and ruin that has overwhelmed me for the last two years has eminated intirely from them and it so hap[p]ens that I am right and they are wrong in the whole matter, or rather that all they have said or done against me is Base false calumny, without the least foundation in truth, but the greatest misfortune for me is that they know the truth of every assertion here made and know that I am able just when I will to establish their infamy beyond the power of contradiction, and they now feel certain that the cruelty injustice and indignity with which they have treated me will bring me out, and well they know that if the world was in possession of the facts that must come out in my justification, that every honest heart in the community would spurn them with just contempt and indignation, to their unalterable ruin, and although their malis has chained me to a wall in heavy Irons until every faculty both bodily and mental are paralized, which together with my being cut off from all intercourse with all persons renders it impossible for me to do myself Justice in any instance, yet under all theas disadvantages, I dare them to an investigation on the assertions I have made, and if I don't succeed, I will take upon myself the charges I have made against them.

Yours &c

H. H. League

[Addressed:] William H. Jack Esqr:

---

[1]Benjamin C. Franklin Papers, The University of Texas Archives, Austin.

[2]"William Pettus was born in Mecklenburg County, Virginia, in 1787. In 1815 he settled near Huntsville, Alabama. Sometime before coming to Texas he married Elizabeth Patrick. With his brother, Freeman Pettus, the James B. Bailey family, and others, he came to Texas on the *Revenge* in 1822. As one of Stephen F. Austin's Old Three Hundred colonists, William Pettus received title to two leagues and a labor of land in present Wharton, Fort

Bend, and Waller counties on July 10, 1824. In August,
1824, he accompanied Austin on a campaign against the
Karankawa Indians. While the expedition was camped near
the site of present Victoria, Pettus, known as Uncle Buck,
and Gustavus E. Edwards entertained the company by running
foot races. The census of 1826 listed Pettus as a farmer
and stock raiser, with a wife, two sons, one servant, and
eight slaves.

"For about a year Pettus lived on Oyster Creek;
from 1824 to 1832 he lived at San Felipe, where he was sindico procurador from 1828 to 1830. ... "--*Handbook of
Texas*, II, 368-369.

"The sindico procurador, combining the duties of a
notary and a city attorney in the Spanish municipality,
handled the legal affairs of the ayuntamiento and sometimes
acted as treasurer of that body. Each municipality was
required to have one sindico ..."--*Handbook of Texas*, II,
614.

[3]"Oliver Jones was born in Connecticut in 1794. He
took part in the War of 1812 and was captured by the
British. Angered at the indifference of the United States
in securing his release, he left the country after the war,
went to Mexico, and there met Stephen F. Austin, with whom
he returned to Texas in 1822. As one of Austin's Old Three
Hundred colonists, Jones received title to one league and
one labor of land in present Brazoria and Austin counties
on August 10, 1824. The census of March, 1826, classified
him as a farmer and stock raiser with six servants. Jones
commanded an expedition against the Karankawa Indians in
1824; in 1829-1830 he was sheriff of Austin's colony.
..."--*Handbook of Texas*, I, 925-926.

[4]"Robert McAlpin Williamson, son of Peter B. and
Ann (McAlpin) Williamson, was born in Georgia in 1804 or
1806. When he was fifteen years old, his school career was
terminated by an illness which confined him to his home for
two years and left him a cripple for life. His right leg
was drawn back at the knee; the wooden leg which he wore
from the knee to the ground resulted in his widely-known
title of 'Three Legged Willie.' Williamson read much during his illness, was admitted to the bar before he was
nineteen, and practiced law in Georgia for over a year. In
1826 he migrated to Texas, locating at San Felipe de Austin.
In 1829, in association with Godwin B. Cotten, he established a newspaper called the *Cotton Plant*, which he edited
from 1829 to 1831. For a short time Williamson edited the
Texas Gazette and the *Mexican Citizen*."

...

--*Handbook of Texas*, II, 917.

[5]The *Louisiana Gazette*, New Orleans, May 7, 1822, page 2, column 1, mentions a "L. Le Sassier" who was elected as a director of the Louisiana State Insurance Company on May 6, 1822. *The Handbook of Texas* gives no details about his life before he came to Texas, picking him up in 1830, when he was a member of the first board of health at San Felipe and a law partner of S. M. Williams.

FRANCISCO RUIZ TO ANTONIO ELOSÚA[1]

[Translated from Spanish]

Office of the Military Commandant   [November 12, 1830]

of Tenoxtitlan————————————   No. 30.

By the superior official letter from Your Lordship
dated October 22 last, in which you were pleased to insert
for me the one from the Most Excellent Commandant General
and Inspector of these States dated the 8th of same, I have
been informed of what the Supreme Government has seen fit
to order with respect to the Spaniards who may present
themselves without a passport, and the requirements that
are to be met for same, which said superior resolution will
receive my punctual compliance and due fulfillment in the
part that pertains to me.

God and Liberty. Tenoxtitlan, November 12, 1830.

Francisco Ruiz

[rubric]

To the Principal Commandant of Coahuila   )
)
and Texas, Citizen Colonel Antonio Elosúa   )

---

[1]BA Roll 136, Frames 0216-0217.

FRANCISCO RUIZ TO ANTONIO ELOSÚA[1]

[Translated from Spanish]

Office of the Military Commandant)   [November 12, 1830]
)
of Tenoxtitlan————————————)   No. 31.

      Colonel Peter Ellis Bean, when he passed through
this post, delivered the funds that he brought for the
Álamo Company, and about which you were pleased to notify
me in your official letter dated October 24 last, which I
am attentively answering.

      God and Liberty. Tenoxtitlan, November 12, 1830.

                               Francisco Ruiz

                                [rubric]

To the Principal Commandant of)
)
Coahuila and Texas, Citizen   )
)
Colonel Antonio Elosúa—————)

---

[1]BA Roll 136, Frame 0218.

FRANCISCO RUIZ TO ANTONIO ELOSÚA[1]

[Translated from Spanish]

Office of the Military Commandant)   [November 12, 1830]
)
of Tenoxtitlan————————————)   No. 32.

    We now have, in this military headquarters, the
official letter from Your Lordship dated October 26 last in
which you were pleased to forward to me the one from the
Most Excellent Commandant General and Inspector of these
States dated September 30 last relative to the deserters
who by law may be assigned to Veracruz, which said superior
order will be observed in all its parts, and with this letter I am attentively answering your aforementioned superior
official letter which speaks of the matter.

        God and Liberty. Tenoxtitlan, November 12, 1830.

                              Francisco Ruiz

                              [rubric]

To the Principal Commandant   )
)
of Coahuila and Texas, Citizen)
)
Colonel Antonio Elosúa————————)

---

[1]BA Roll 136, Frames 0219-0220.

FRANCISCO RUIZ TO ANTONIO ELOSÚA[1]

[Translated from Spanish]

Office of the Military Commandant)   [November 12, 1830]
)
of Tenoxtitlan———————————)   No. 34.

As soon as I received the superior official letter from

Your Lordship dated the 22nd of October last, in which you

were pleased to insert for me the one from the Most Excel-

lent Commandant General and Inspector of These States dated

the 27th of September last, which speaks about the indemni-

zation of Lieutenant Colonel Don Juan Malagón, accused of

being an accomplice in a robbery, the said letter was com-

municated in the order of the day for the information of

this garrison, and I am notifying Your Lordship of this

fact by way of giving you an attentive reply.

    God and Liberty. Tenoxtitlan, November 12, 1830.

                                    Francisco Ruiz

                                      [rubric]

To the Principal Commandant   )
)
of Coahuila and Texas,   )
)
Citizen Colonel Antonio Elosúa)

---

[1]BA Roll 136, Frames 0221-0222.

JOSÉ DE LAS PIEDRAS TO ANTONIO ELOSÚA[1]

[Translated from Spanish]

Office of the Military Commandant   [November 12, 1830]
of the Frontier

    In compliance with the superior orders which I have
to the effect that I shall not permit the entry of any
American without a valid passport from the Mexican Consul
in [New] Orleans, or unless they belong to the Colony of
Stephen F. Austin, I detained Alexander Thomson, James
Ledbetter, Thomas Sherman, and Everton Kennerly, who, with
nine families, were coming in to settle wherever they could
find the best land, and, in view of the fact that they have
indicated to me that they have some matters to clear up in
the *Villa* of [San Felipe de] Austin, I permitted them to go
on alone, leaving the families at the ranch which they call
"El Carrizo" ["The Ditch Reeds"] five miles from this town
on the road to Natchitoches, on the condition that they
will return within twenty days to go back to their country.
Two days after they had been detained, aided by the darkness of the night, they took roundabout roads in order to
hide themselves from this post, and they continued their
journey toward [San Felipe de] Austin, according to the
news I have, thus mocking the authorities of the country
and the laws which prohibit their entry.

    This deed shows what kind of people they must be,
and the advantages which the country will derive from them,

for, if a person who, on asking for permission to enter the country, mocks the laws thereof, what hope can we have that they will obey them later? Add to this the precedent which they have established, which will be followed by others in the same situation, if they are not forced to leave in compliance with the laws, and for the satisfaction of the authority which they have mocked, by giving them to understand that we know how to enforce them, at the same time that they are boasting that they have scorned our laws.

Please report this matter to the Most Excellent Commandant General and to the Political Chief of the Department so that they may order the posts wherever the said individuals may be not to admit them and to force them to leave the territory, in compliance with the Law of April 6, [1830].

God and Liberty. Nacogdoches, November 12, 1830.

José de las Piedras

[rubric]

To Colonel Don Antonio)
)
Elosúa, Principal Commandant of Texas)

---

[1]Nacogdoches Archives, Texas State Library, Austin. There is another English translation in the typed "Nacogdoches Archives," Vol. 41, pp. 251-252, in The University of Texas Archives, Austin.

JOSÉ DE LAS PIEDRAS TO STEPHEN F. AUSTIN[1]

Office of the Military Commandant   [November 12, 1830]

of the Frontier.

The Americans Alexander Thompson [Thomson], James Ledbetter, Thomas J. Wooten, John Sherman, and Everton Kennedy [Kennerly], were found passing through this town with their families, and in conformity with the law of the 6th April and my orders from the government to prevent the entrance of Americans, I required of them the necessary passports, but as they had none, and as they belong neither to your Colony nor to any other I notified them to return; But as they had some business to transact in your Town, I permitted them to proceed on condition that they would return to this place in twenty days, then to leave the Republic, their families meanwhile remaining at the "Rancho del Carrizo," but in contempt of the laws of the country and of its authorities and a total disregard to my orders which they promised to obey availing themselves of the obscurity of the night and unfrequented roads they took off their families, and are now on their way to your Town as I am informed by Col Bean who met them on that side of the Trinity.

Aware of your disposition to preserve good order and sustain the laws, I request you will please order Alexander Thompson to be notified to leave the country immediately, together with the nine families of which he was the head, obligating him to return through this place in order that the authorities whom he has thus contemptuously treated may be satisfied of his departure, the bad conduct of this man and his companions have rendered them unworthy to be admitted into a country, into which they had no sooner entered, than they make a mockery of its laws and authorities. You will I have no doubt take the necessary means to see that the laws are obeyed, and cause the aforesaid individuals to depart without fail. This I have under this date communicated to the Political Chief of the Department and to the Commander in Chief of the State in order that they may issue such orders as they may deem expedient in the case, should those individuals have deseminated and established themselves in some other colony not within your jurisdiction.

God and Liberty Nacogdoches November 12th 1830. (Signed) José de las Piedras. To Stephen F. Austin. Esqr.

They will endeavor I suppose to obtain admission as Settlers in your Colony, but as they have come into this Country contrary to law, and have disrespected the Authorities of this Town, and treated them with contempt, I think they ought not to be admitted.

The foregoing including the paragraph inserted above is a correct Translation of the Copy in Spanish on file in this Office. General Land Office of the Republic of Texas, City of Austin May 26th 1840. The words "I suppose" interlined before signing.

Thomas G. Western

Translator pr. Contract

---

[1]"Translations of Empresario Contracts," pp. 224-225, Spanish Archives, General Land Office, Austin.

ANTONIO ELOSÚA TO FRANCISCO RUIZ[1]

[Translated from Spanish]

Office of the Principal Commandant)   [November 13, 1830]
)
of Coahuila and Texas———————)

The most Excellent Commandant General Inspector of These States, in a superior official letter dated October 12 last, has been pleased to write me as follows:

"Under this same date I am writing Citizen Rafael Chovvell as follows:

"'In a wooden box,'" etc.

I am forwarding it to you, remitting to you the aforementioned model and plan so that immediately you can begin to construct the fort at that post, as His Excellency orders.

God and Liberty. Béxar, November 13, 1830.

[Antonio Elosúa]

To the Military Commandant of Tenoxtitlan.

---

[1]BA Roll 136, Frame 0236. Antonio Elosúa, in his official letter No. 425, reported to Manuel de Mier y Terán that he had received and forwarded to Tenoxtitlan the plan that was to be used in building the fort.--Entry dated 12-3-1830, Frame 0853, BA Roll 136.

ANTONIO ELOSÚA TO JUAN NEPOMUCENO DE AYALA[1]

[Translated from Spanish]

Office of the Principal Commandant)   [November 13, 1830]
)
of Coahuila and Texas_____)

        The Most Excellent Commandant General Inspector of

These States, in an official letter dated the 30th of

October last, has been pleased to write me as follows:

        "Your Lordship will arrange for Presbyter Citizen

Juan Nepomuceno Ayala to transfer to Tenoxtitlan," etc.

        I am forwarding this to you for your information

and so that you can arrange to make your departure for that

post at the first opportunity.

        God and Liberty. Béxar, November 13, 1830.

                                        [Antonio Elosúa]

To Citizen Presbyter Juan Nepomuceno de Ayala.

---

[1]BA Roll 136, Frame 0237.

FRANCISCO RUIZ TO ANTONIO ELOSÚA[1]

[Translated from Spanish]

Office of the Military Commandant)   [November 13, 1830]
)
of Tenoxtitlan—————————————)   No. 35.

The consumption of paper which, up to the present, has come out of my personal supply, in this military command, has motivated me to trouble you and beg you to be so good as to tell me to whom I should apply in the future for reimbursement for the amount that may be used in correspondence, as well as for the paper that is indispensable for recording the proceedings in legal cases that may come up.

God and Liberty. Tenoxtitlan, November 13, 1830.

Francisco Ruiz

[rubric]

To the Principal)
)
Commandant of Coahuila & Texas,)
)
Citizen Colonel Antonio Elosúa)

---

[1]BA Roll 136, Frames 0228-0229.

FRANCISCO RUIZ TO ANTONIO ELOSÚA[1]

[Translated from Spanish]

Office of the Military Commandant of)   [November 13, 1830]
)
Tenoxtitlan—————————————————————)   No. 36

      The foreigner Sterling C. Robertson, about whom I wrote to Your Lordship in my official letter of October 30 last, presented himself to me again yesterday with two other individuals and informed me that some foreign families, of those who are coming by virtue of the contract celebrated with the Government of this State to colonize on the San Andrés [Little River] or the Brazos, are about to arrive. Of these families, nine have stopped on the land first occupied by this detachment, and it is in Mr. Austin's colony. Many more are due to arrive at the same place within a very few days, but, since I have before me Your Lordship's superior official letter dated October 26 last, which instructs me not to permit the introduction of North Americans, I have prevented them from going on without obtaining the corresponding permission. Consequently the journey of the aforesaid families has been suspended, but, since the aforesaid Robertson presents in his favor the contract made with the Government of the State, and likewise the damages which will result to him if he is delayed for a long time, after such a long journey, and the expenditures which it will be necessary for him to make in order to support the families at that place, I am reporting the

situation to Your Lordship for your information and decision.

        God and Liberty. Tenoxtitlan, November 13, 1830.

                    Francisco Ruiz

                        [rubric]

To the Principal Commandant of)
)
Coahuila and Texas, Colonel   )
)
Antonio Elosúa———————)

---

[1]Volume 54, pp. 281-281 verso, Spanish Archives,
General Land Office, Austin.

FRANCISCO RUIZ TO SAMUEL M. WILLIAMS[1]

[Translated from Spanish]

Tenoxtitlan, November 13, 1830

Mr. Samuel M. Wil[l]iams:

My very esteemed friend: I want to express my most sincere thanks for the wafer [of sealing wax?] which you sent me, and which I received in due time.

The bearer of this letter is going only for the purpose of bringing the mail from that post. He is not carrying any correspondence because tomorrow, without fail, an officer is leaving here for Béxar, and he will carry what I have to send.

Just yesterday Mr. Sterling C. Robertson arrived here with other individuals who have left some families in the home, or on the land, of Yony [Johnny] Wil[l]iams, and who are coming to colonize. They have encountered a difficulty: in the last mail an order came not to permit the introduction of North Americans without the corresponding passport. Consequently I should appreciate it if our friend Don Stephen [F. Austin] would write, immediately, something in favor of the aforesaid families, for to me the ones I have seen look like very good people, and this very day I am writing a letter, to be sent tomorrow to [Ramón] Músquiz and the Principal Commandant [Antonio Elosúa], in favor of these individuals, for I think they deserve it.

I hope that you are happy, and please feel free to

call on your intimate friend who loves you and kisses your
hand.

                              Francisco Ruiz

                                   [rubric]

P. S.

        The enclosure is for our friend Don Stephen, with
my regards. Valid.

                         [rubric]

        [Endorsed:] Francisco Ruiz, November 13, 1830.

_____

        [1]Samuel May Williams Papers, Rosenberg Library,
Galveston, Texas.

STERLING C. ROBERTSON TO RAMÓN MÚSQUIZ[1]

[Translated from Spanish]

Tenoxtitlan, November 13, 1830

Dear Sir:

Some of the families whom I have engaged have
arrived ... on the San Antonio Road, brought by Alexander
Thomson from Giles County, Tennessee, one of the United
States of the North, to settle in the colony granted to the
Nashville Company, of which I am a member and one of the
first petitioners when the colony was granted to Leftwich,
and I was also one of the petitioners when the colony was
confirmed to the Nashville Company, at which time Hosea H.
League was [appointed as agent by the said] company ...,
and he appointed Colonel Stephen F. Austin as his agent,
who [obtained a confirmation of the contract] to the said
company, and its management was placed in the hands of [a
board of directors]: namely, James Overton, N. Patterson,
John Davis, Richard Hyde, [Samuel B. Marshall], Andrew
Hynes, James Roan, and John Shel[b]y, to whom the Government gave the management of the colony, passing a law that
nobody could settle in it without the knowledge of the
aforesaid company. For three years I had been trying to
get [an interview with the directors in order to obtain] an
order from them authorizing me to come to establish a colony, offering to establish two hundred families, and I
could not get [their approval until] June [of the present

year], at which time they did grant me permission to do so.
Since that time I have done everything in my power to
collect families, and finally I succeeded in engaging two
hundred which I had contracted to assemble, ten of whom
have arrived on the Brazos on the San Antonio Road. Part
of the balance are on their way, and the rest will arrive
here during this winter and next spring and ... in order to
establish themselves in the Nashville Colony. As soon as I
arrived here I considered it my duty to go with those who
came with me to the colonel who was in command of this
place, and I did so, carrying the number of souls (which
totaled fifty), and the colonel informed me that a few days
earlier he had received an order from General [Mier y]
Terán not to permit the establishment of families in the
Nashville Colony until he received new orders from the same
Gentleman. I came to this Country with the firm intention
of obeying and being submissive to the laws because I have
adopted it as my Country, and I will reside in silence
until I can proceed according to the laws. The families
whom I caused to emigrate are in the same situation, and,
furthermore, they are extremely poor, for they [brought]
nothing [with them except] those things which are necessary
... for the order and for their transportation to ... and
furnishing them the expenses which they incurred in 900
miles ... [during the sixty-three] days. I have to return
to Tennessee ... by January 1 to bring out the rest of the

families, for they have sacrificed everything they had, all
for the laudable desire to emigrate and establish themselves in the Nashville Colony, and, with these developments, there can be no doubt that both those families as
well as those who are here with me, will all be enveloped
in ruin. In view of the foregoing circumstances, I have
taken the liberty of addressing this communication to you
without ... for your consideration, with the just purpose
of begging you to intercede with General [Mier y] Terán so
that he will permit me to establish the families in the
manner in which I am obligated to the Nashville Company to
do, for which favor I shall be extremely grateful.

I remain your most attentive and humble servant,

Sterling C. Robertson

---

[1]Nacogdoches Archives, Texas State Library, Austin.
There is also a typed copy in Volume 53, pp. 7-9, of the
"Nacogdoches Archives," The University of Texas Archives,
Austin.

ALEXANDER THOMSON TO STEPHEN F. AUSTIN[1]

Tenoxtitlan--Novr 13th 1830

Respected Sir,

I am unacquainted with you personally, yet situated as I am, I think it necessary, to address you, and apprise you of a considerable difficulty, that now exist[s] in the settlement of your colony, and the others also; namely, the order from General Teran, to the Colo at Nacogdoches to suffer no person to pass, unless, they have a passport, I was not apprised of that order, and came here [there], I think on the 28 ultmo--, the Alcalde inform'd me when the families came into town I must collect them all together, and present them, I done so, then the Coll, sent for me, and inform'd me that he had the saturday before recd- the above mentioned order and could not consistent with his order, let me pass, but as we were ignorant of the late Law, having our certificates Legally arra[n]ged, by the proper authorities, he would venture to give five of us a permit to you, who he said was authorised to give us pass- ports; but the families must remain until our return, we had traveled better than 8 weeks, had spent a great deal of money, and was much fatigued, we could not feel willing to remain in that part of the country on expences so Long, we therefore came round, which caus'd us to loose 2 1/2 days travel, we are now at the barracks, at Mr [Johnny] Williams that is the families, We arrived there Last night,

Today I came up to the new garrison to see the commander
here he says that he has recd the same order, and advises
us to remain where we are, until he receives further orders
in answer to his letter that he had written after Majr
Robertson had inform'd him that I was on the road,[2] which
answer he expected would arrive in four days, mean-while
he gave us permission to explore the country, which we
intend to do immediately-- Col, Thorn has sent you a letter
by me on the subject,[3] We, him and myself think it advis-
able for you to have an agent appointed in Nacogdoches, he
says he is willing to act for you if you wish him, but he
expected to start in a day or two for New Orleans and be
absent two months, There ought to be some person there
authorised immediately, for since I left there I have been
informed of two more families that have been stopped, and
detain'd,-- I have been particular in giving the particu-
lars of my detention, to you, in order that, you may have a
clear view of the impediment, emigrants will meet with in
comeing to the colonies-- So soon as I can, I expect to
see you, but can not for a few days,-- Majr Robertson has
inform'd you that I am interested in the settlement of this
colony--

                                        Alexander Thomson

        [Addressed:] Colo S. F. Austin San Phillipi De
Austin

[1]*Austin Papers*, II, 534-535. A printed copy also appeared in the *Quarterly of the Texas State Historical Association*, II (January, 1899), 237-238, and a facsimile was reproduced in Ernest William Winkler, *Manuscript Letters and Documents of Early Texians, 1821-1845. In Facsimile. Folio Collection of Original Documents. Selected and Annotated by E. W. Winkler, Bibliographer, The University of Texas Library* (Austin: Published by The Steck Company, 1937), pp. 101-103.

[2]See Francisco Ruiz to Antonio Elosúa, November 13, 1830.

[3]See Frost Thorn to Stephen F. Austin, October 29, 1830.

THOMSON'S CLANDESTINE PASSAGE AROUND

NACOGDOCHES[1]

W. P. ZUBER

[Entered under November 13, 1830]

[*Note by McLean*: Now that we have seen the two
eyewitness accounts, written by Sterling C.
Robertson and Alexander Thomson, at the time
these events occurred, it is interesting to
compare them with the following version published
by William Physic Zuber more than sixty years
later, in the first issue of the first volume of
what was later to become known as the *Southwestern
Historical Quarterly*. Then it was called *The
Quarterly of the Texas State Historical Association*.
This item appeared on pp. 68-70. The text reproduced here was taken from a reprint by the Johnson
Reprint Corporation, 111 Fifth Avenue, New York,
N. Y. 10003, "with the permission of the Texas
State Historical Society [*sic*]." The notes are
those that accompanied the original article. At
first we thought that the route used might have
been the Old Smuggler's Road, but that ran south
of Nacogdoches, whereas the road used by Thomson's
party passed north of town. See Edward Blount's
article entitled: "Location of the Old Contraband
Trace in Nacogdoches County," *The Junior Historian
of the Texas State Historical Association, Austin,*
Vol. VI, No. 3 (December, 1945), pp. 7-11, which
is accompanied by an excellent map of the Contraband
Trace.]

In 1830, after the passage of the exclusion act, a
large body of families sent by Sterling C. Robertson from
Tennessee were conducted into Texas by Alexander Thomson.[2]
Before reaching Nacogdoches, they learned that they could
not pass the garrison at that place without passports, and
they encamped about three miles east of that town.

Mr. Thomson and two other men went into Nacogdoches

to confer with Colonel Piedras. They stated their condition to the colonel and requested him to permit the families to pass. Piedras had no authority to comply with their request, and so informed them. They then said that, if the immigrants would consent to do so, they would change their destination to Austin's colony, and asked Colonel Piedras whether they could pass thither. He replied that they could do so only after procuring permits from Austin, and advised them, if they should so decide, to let the families stay in their present encampment while a messenger should proceed to San Felipe and procure the needed permits from Austin. They told him that they would return to the camp and try to persuade the immigrants to do as he advised, but they thought that two or three days might elapse before they could determine what to do. But they promised to come again and inform Colonel Piedras of whatever decision the immigrants should make.

They returned to their encampment, and reported to their friends their interview with Colonel Piedras. They soon determined what to do. On the next day, they cut a road around Nacogdoches. This required comparatively little work: the opening of two connecting roads, through open woods, between that on which they were encamped and another, nearly parallel with it, which lay about a mile north of Nacogdoches. Thus their route led from their encampment, or from a point a little west of it, nearly

north to another road; thence with said road nearly west to
a point several miles northwest of Nacogdoches; and thence
nearly south to a point on the San Antonio road a few miles
west of Nacogdoches.

On the following morning, very early, the families
decamped and proceeded for their destination in Robertson's
colony, the beginning of their journey being on their
improvised road. But Mr. Thomson and the two men who had
previously accompanied him went through Nacogdoches to see
Colonel Piedras. They told him that, after thoroughly considering their situation, the immigrants had unanimously
determined to settle in Austin's colony, and would stay
in their present encampment till receipt of their permits,
and that they--Mr. Thomson and the two men with him--were
en route for San Felipe to procure the permits, and hoped
soon to return and conduct the families into Austin's
colony. Piedras wished them God-speed, and they proceeded
on their journey. But a few miles west of Nacogdoches, Mr.
Thomson and the two others rejoined the families, and they
all proceeded together for Robertson's colony.

My father was then in Texas, about twenty-five
miles east of Nacogdoches, and soon learned the facts of
this passing around that place by Mr. Thomson's immigrants.
The same account was confirmed to my father by Mr. Thomson
himself at Harrisburgh, Texas, in 1831. His statement to
my father was substantially as I have here repeated it.

The road which those immigrants made around Nacogdoches was known as the "Tennesseans' road," and was used
by many subsequent immigrants, who were not provided with
passports or permits.

After Thomson's immigrants had passed around Nacogdoches, some gentlemen reported their action to Colonel
Piedras. He replied: "I can not recall them. I can not
prevent people from passing *around* Nacogdoches, whether
their route be half a league or a hundred leagues distant.
All that I can do is to prevent intruders from passing
through this town."

However, Colonel Piedras, of course, must have
reported the affair, both to the State authorities and to
the general commanding the troops of the department. This
conduct of the immigrants was regarded by the authorities
as treacherous and defiant to the laws, and to the Federal
and State governments. Of course, it greatly aggravated--
if it did not cause--all the troubles that afterward beset
the settlement of Robertson's colony.

Yet justice to Mr. Thomson demands full consideration of the circumstances which impelled his action, which,
if they do not justify his conduct, at least greatly dimin-
ish the blame due thereto. I can not see that he could
have done better. He was under obligation to the Nashville
Company, to Robertson, and to the immigrants themselves, to
conduct them to Robertson's colony, in which only they were

willing to settle. He had conducted them thus far in good faith, anticipating no opposition, but there they were halted; no arrangement could be made to procure passports to their desired destination without a trip to the State capital west of the Rio Grande, either by Robertson, who was in Tennessee,[3] or by a messenger to be sent by him; the delay for such a trip would quite exhaust their funds for travel, which were limited. Yet, they could not otherwise obtain the needed passports. Deluded by the hope that if they could, *by any means*, pass Nacogdoches, they would encounter no further trouble, they adopted the plan, which they executed, of passing clandestinely around that place. Mr. Thomson keenly felt his obligations to his company, to his empresario, and to his immigrants. His condition was extremely distressing. He and his companions adopted this clandestine passage as the best proceeding in their power. I am safe in saying that he would not have done as he did if he had not believed that the circumstances morally justified his action. Both my father and myself knew him as an honorable and conscientious gentleman. His necessity resulted from the seemingly unavoidable neglect of Empresario Robertson to provide for the needed passports.

In January, 1831, my father, with his family, en route from Ayish to Austin's colony, passed around Nacogdoches on the "Tennesseeans' road," which had been improvised by Thomson's immigrants for Robertson's colony,

though he had a permit from Austin. My father did so on
the entreaty of a Tennesseean, who, with his family, had
overtaken us, and who had no permit, though he, too, was
going to Austin's colony. I have always regretted this
incident, for it deprived me of an opportunity to pass
through the old historical town of Nacogdoches, which I
have never yet seen.

---

[1] I narrate these facts from my own knowledge, as I
do not know that they have ever yet been published.

[2] He spelled his name Thomson, not Thompson.

[3] [Note added by McLean:] This statement is incorrect: Robertson was in Texas. See the letter he wrote
Ramón Músquiz from Tenoxtitlan on November 13, 1830.

For the first printing of Zuber's article, see
The Quarterly of the Texas State Historical Association,
Volume I, Number 1 (July, 1897), pp. 68-70.

STEPHEN F. AUSTIN TO M. B. MENARD[1]

San Felipe de Austin Novr 13. 1830

Mr M. B. Menard[2]

Dr Sir, The enclosed letter from T. F. McKinny
Esqr. will explain to you the reasons why I have taken the
liberty of troubling you with this letter and the enc[l]osed
instructions. I applied to Mr. McKinney to recommend to me
a suitable person in Nacogdoches as agent to give certificates of reception to emigrants bound to this Colony, who
pass through that place. On his recommendation I have sent
to you the enclosed appointment and instructions made out
in Spanish. He has aprised me that you would attend to it,
and that full confidence might be placed in you. I hope
this will be sufficient to explain to you why I have
troubled you with this matter. Should you feel any unwill-
ingness to attend to it, you can return the papers to me,
or to Mr. S. M. Williams at this place by some safe con-
veyance.

The object of the certificates which you are to
issue to the emigrants, is to place Evidence in their hands
that they are a part of the Settlers who enter into my contracts, which they can present to Col. Piedras, so as to
avoid any detention or difficulty in pursuing their journey
to this place.

I send you a pamphlet containing translations of
the colonization laws, and of my contracts with Government.

You will see that the 5 article of my contract (page 49) prohibits me from admitting criminals etc etc (see the said article) This article is cited in the 2d. article of your instructions. I wish to do my duty strickly. The object of the government I understand to be, to keep out bad and useless men, and to admit all who are honest, industrious and moral, and I wish you to keep that rule in view in giving the certificates. Men of families who bring their wives and children are less objectionable in general than single men, and I wish you to be more cautious and partic- ular with the latter class, than with the former.

I do not require that all should be rejected who bring no recommendations with them, for I know that many good men emigrate without providing themselves with recommendations, because they are not apprised of the necessity of doing so. A vagabond or an indolent drunken, or disorderly person is very apt to shew what he is by his appearance, conversation or deportment and a nice observer may generally form a pritty correct idea of him on a short acquaintance

I must request that you take pains to impress upon the emigrants the necessity of presenting themselves, imme- diately to Col. Piedras, and that they treat him with respect and attention which is due to the commanding offi- cer of this nation on that frontier, and also that they treat all the officers and authorities of this government

with proper respect, and I hope you will refuse certificates to all who fail to do so.

Shew your instructions to Col. Piedras, as you are
required to do in the 7 article and have a friendly understanding with him. try to remove all difficulties to the
emigration of good men, and get all through you can who are
worthy of being admitted: Trouble Piedras as little as
possible; but call on him often enough to shew that you
respect his authority and wish to act in concert with him.

You will of course expect a compensation for your
trouble. This business is for the benefit of the emigrant,
and I think that each certificate ought to entitle you to
receive half a dollar from the person who gets it, and you
can charge that sum-- Should you think this insufficient
write me frankly your views on the subject

S. F. Austin [rubric]

N. B. I hope you will keep me informed of whatever
may occur of interest. In my absence your letters will be
answered by Mr S. M. Williams--

Austin [rubric]

---

[1]*Austin Papers*, II, 535-536.

[2]"Michel Branamour Menard was born of French paren-
tage near Montreal, Canada, on December 5, 1805. After 1819
he roamed the Northwest, living with trappers and trading
with the Indians until he joined the service of the Northwest Fur Company with headquarters at Detroit. About 1823
he went to Kaskaskia, Illinois, to make his home with his
uncle, Pierre Menard, an Indian agent. He entered the

employ of his uncle as an Indian trader and moved with
Indians to the Arkansas area. He traded with the Shawnee
on White River making friends with the tribe and eventually
becoming a chief. After 1825 the Indians migrated into the
Louisiana region, and Menard moved to Shreveport in 1826.
He arrived in Texas on November 28, 1829, and traded some
time at Nacogdoches before returning to Illinois. ..."
--*Handbook of Texas*, II, 170.

APPOINTMENT OF M. B. MENARD AS MY

AGENT IN NACOGDOCHES[1]

[Translated from Spanish]

[November 13, 1830]

Some immigrants, who are honorable and worthy of being received into the colonization contracts which I have made with the Mexican Government, are entering Mexican territory without the necessary passports, some of them because they did not know that it was necessary to have passports, and others because they were unable to secure them because there was no agent authorized to issue them at the port from which they came. In order to remedy these obstacles which are impeding the settlement and progress of the country, and in order to comply more exactly with the colonization law, and with the contracts I have made with the Government, relative to the introduction of families, I have appointed M. B. Menard, a resident of Nacogdoches, as my agent to issue certificates for this colony to the immigrants who are passing through Nacogdoches. My said agent shall observe the following instructions in the matter:

1st. He shall issue to the immigrants a certificate in this form: "I certify that _____ is entering the colonization contracts of Empresario Don Stephen F. Austin, and this certificate may be taken away from him if it should ever be proved that the said _____ is a bad man, a fugitive, or vagabond." Date and sign as Agent of the said Empresario.

2nd.   In issuing the said certificates my said agent shall keep before him Article 5 of my contract made with the Government on July 4, 1825.

3rd.   He shall take special care not to issue certificates to any bad man, or even one of suspicious customs which might lead one to believe that he is a drunkard, idler, rebel, fugitive, or vagabond.

4th.   He shall examine bachelors more carefully than the men with families, because having a family offers a kind of guarantee for the conduct and industry of the individual.

5th.   He shall not give certificates to anyone who has failed to respect any Mexican Authority.

6th.   He shall, from time to time, make a report to me on the certificates he has issued, specifying the name of each head of a family, the number in same, and their class, origin, and occupation.

7th.   He shall show these instructions to the Commandant of the frontier, Colonel Don José de las Piedras, and he shall reach an agreement with the said gentleman whenever necessary, in order to work more efficiently and not give certificates to bad people, and to remove obstacles for good and useful people to come to this colony.

San Felipe de Austin, November 13, 1830.

Stephen F. Austin [rubric]

[Enclosure: Blank certificate.[2]]

---

[1]*Austin Papers*, II, 536-537.

[2][Dr. Barker's note:] See Austin to Williams, Dec. 28, 1830.

HOSEA H. LEAGUE TO STEPHEN F. AUSTIN[1]

[November 13, 1830]

Col. Stephen F. Austin

Dear Sir my wife will start tomorrow morning to remove to Jennings Camp it is unnecessary for me to attempt a description of her deplorable situation and feelings, or my own I have not sufficient use of my faculties to address you as I would wish, but I call upon your humanity and merciful feelings to come down and see and have an interview with Mrs. League before she starts and also with myself

H H League

Nov--13th--1830

---

[1]*Austin Papers*, II, 537.

SEVERO RUIZ TO ANTONIO ELOSÚA[1]

[Translated from Spanish]

Álamo de Parras   [November 14, 1830]
Presidial Company.

Corporal José Chacón has grown worse from that shortness of breath which keeps him from taking any kind of exercise, and, since at this post we have absolutely no resources with which to effect his cure, he is going to that city [Béxar], accompanied by a Private from the Company, in order to see whether, with the assistance of his family, he can succeed in regaining his health.

The individual who is accompanying him has no other assignment except to assist him on the road, and, consequently, he must return as soon as Your Lordship orders him to do so, in case you should not consider it appropriate for him to wait for the return of the paymaster.

God and Liberty. Tenoxtitlan, November 14, 1830.

Severo Ruiz

[rubric]

To the Principal Commandant,)
)
Don Antonio Elosúa_____)

_____

[1]BA Roll 136, Frames 0240-0241.

FRANCISCO RUIZ TO ANTONIO ELOSÚA[1]

[Translated from Spanish]

Office of the Military Commandant)   [November 14, 1830]
)
of Tenoxtitlan._____)   No. 37.

Alférez Don Santiago Navayra is going to that city
[Béxar] for the sole purpose of obtaining, from the office
of the commissar of same, some kind of an advance, in cash,
so that he can start collecting timber for the fortified
house, for which purpose he is carrying the budget approved
in duplicate.

He is being accompanied by four men from the Álamo
Company and the picket from Béxar, who are going along as
an escort.

God and Liberty. Tenoxtitlan, November 14, 1830.

Francisco Ruiz

[rubric]

To the Principal Commandant   )
)
of Coahuila and Texas,   )
)
Citizen Colonel Antonio Elosúa   )

---

[1]BA Roll 136, Frames 0242-0243.

FRANCISCO RUIZ TO ANTONIO ELOSÚA[1]

[Translated from Spanish]

Office of the Military Commandant   [November 14, 1830]

of Tenoxtitlan_____.   No. 38.

At the moment when I received the superior official letter

from Your Lordship dated the 10th of the current month, in

which you ordered me to send out an escort of 10 men to

meet the convoy of families of the Álamo Company who are

coming to this post, I ordered the said escort to go out,

as it is now doing, at seven o'clock in the morning on this

date, with orders to make forced marches until they meet up

with the said families, and I am reporting this fact to you

by way of reply.

God and Liberty. Tenoxtitlan, November 14, 1830.

Francisco Ruiz

[rubric]

To the Principal Commandant of Coahuila)
)
and Texas, Colonel Don   )
)
Antonio Elosúa_____)

_____

[1]BA Roll 136, Frames 0244-0245.

ANTONIO ELOSÚA TO RAFAEL CHOWELL[1]

[Translated from Spanish]

Office of the Principal Commandant)   [November 16, 1830]
)
of Coahuila and Texas_____   )

        I received the box with the model that is to serve

for the construction of the fort at Tenoxtitlan, which you

announced to me in your official letter dated the 8th of

the present month, which I am now answering.

        God and Liberty. Béxar, November 16, 1830.

                                    [Antonio Elosúa]

To Commissar Citizen Rafael Chowell.

_____

        [1]BA Roll 136, Frame 0304.

EXCERPT FROM THE RECOLLECTIONS OF

BARZILLAI KUYKENDALL[1]

[Entered under November 16, 1830][2]

In the month of November 1830, a Chickasaw Indian
brought intelligence from the frontier that a party of
eleven Wacoes were on their way to the neighborhood in
which I resided (22 miles northwest from San Felipe) for
the purpose of stealing horses. The approach of the
Indians was very soon confirmed by one of my neighbors who
had seen them on his return from the up country. He stated
that they were provided with ropes and bridles. He also
learned that at one or two houses where they had called
their deportment had been menacing and insulting. The day
this news was received a few of the neighbors armed and
assembled for the purpose of seeking and attacking the
Indians, who, we learned late in the evening, were camped
near the residence of James Stephenson, on Caney creek. As
the Indians outnumbered our little party, William Cooper
and I rode nearly all night to raise more men. At the dawn
of next day, with a force of eleven men, precisely that of
the Indians--we stole upon their camp which was a little
grove on the bank of a spring branch within less than a
hundred yards of Stephenson's house. Favored by a gully
and a dense fog we approached within thirty feet of the
Indians, (part of whom had not yet risen) before they

perceived us, at which moment we delivered our fire. One of the Indians also fired and William Cooper fell, exclaiming that he was shot. The Indians ran and were pursued a short distance by our leader, Adam Lawrence, who reloaded his rifle and fired at them again--but further pursuit was prevented by the fall of young Cooper, who was shot through the heart and expired in a few minutes.

Late in the morning the trail of the Indians was followed as far as the bottom of Caney creek, some five or six hundred yards. Seven red stripes marked their course across the prairie and two or three conically shaped pieces of spongy, rotten wood, with which these Indians are generally provided to plug their wounds, were picked up on their trail, saturated with blood. The carcass of one of the Indians was afterwards found in Caney bottom. Seven of the eleven never reached home as will appear in the sequel. One shot gun, several bows, and arrows, and ropes, and bridles fell into our hands. It was my painful duty to take the news of young Cooper's death to his parents who resided about five miles from the spot where he was killed. Of the eleven men engaged in this affair only the following names are recollected, viz: Adam Lawrence, Thomas Stevens, Adam Kuykendall, Charles Gates, George Robinson, William Cooper, B. Kuykendall.

About a fortnight after the above events, Col. Austin sent father, with six or seven men, of whom I was one, to Tenoxtitlan, then a recently established military post on the Brazos, garrisoned by one or two companies of Mexican regulars under the command of Capt Ruis. The precise object of our mission I have forgotten, but it had reference to the relations of the colonists with the Wacoes and Tawacanies. When we arrived at Tenoxtitlan several northern Indians and two or three Wacoes were there. One of the latter was a chief. These Wacoes informed the Mexicans that in the late affair on Caney they sustained a loss of seven men--which corresponded well with my own opinion. Father having dispatched his business with Capt. Ruis, we were about to start home, when James Cooper of our party and brother of the young man killed in the recent attack on the Indians, to avenge the death of his brother, shot at one of the Wacoes and would probably have killed him had not his gun hung fire. The Indian escaped with the loss of a thumb. Cooper immediately secreted himself to avoid being arrested by the Mexicans. The rest of us, after a short delay, left the place, but Cooper did not rejoin us until the succeeding day. He skulked for several hours in the thickets about the post, seeking an opportunity to shoot at the Wacoes again; nor did he depart until he ascertained that they had been escorted away from the post by a file of soldiers.

---

[1]J. H. Kuykendall, "Reminiscences of Early Texans.

A Collection from the Austin Papers .... 4. Recollections of Barzillai Kuykendall," *The Quarterly of the Texas State Historical Association*, Volume VI (July, 1902, to April, 1903), pp. 317-319.

[2]The approximate of this incident has been determined from information contained in the letter that Francisco Ruiz wrote Stephen F. Austin on November 22, 1830. See copy below.

RAFAEL CHOWELL TO ANTONIO ELOSÚA[1]

[Translated from Spanish]

Lavaca Commissariat.   November 17, 1830

Under date of the 8th of the present month I sent Your

Lordship the model [and] plan that are to serve for the

construction of the fort at Tenoxtitlan. I had not done so

before because my duties prevented me from making a copy

of them with all due promptness.

All of which I have the honor of reporting to Your

Lordship by way of reply to your note dated the 11th of

the present month.

God and Liberty. Guadalupe, November 17, 1830.

Rafael Chowell

[rubric]

To the Principal Commandant)
)
of Coahuila and Texas.   )

---

[1]BA Roll 136, Frame 0312.

MANUEL DE MIER Y TERÁN TO ANTONIO ELOSÚA[1]

[Translated from Spanish]

Office of the Commandant General and   [November 18, 1830]

Inspector of the Eastern Interior States

By the official letter from Your Lordship dated the 22nd of
last month, and the original which you enclosed from the
Commandant of the Frontier at Nacogdoches, Citizen Colonel
José de las Piedras, I have been informed of the combination which this Chief proposes in order to make an expedition against the Tahuacano and Hueco Indians who are being
so hostile toward that city [Béxar]; as well as about the
coming of Colonel [Peter Ellis] Bean, and about what you
have discussed with him concerning this manner, and in
reply I wish to state to Your Lordship that I repeat to
you what I have said about the combination undertaken by
the said Colonel Piedras, taking advantage, as that Chief
proposes, of the most opportune time, with Your Lordship
limiting yourself, for the present, to whatever is appropriate for the safety of the new establishment at Tenoxtitlan.

God and Liberty. Matamoros, November 18, 1830.

M. Mier y Terán

To the Citizen Principal   )
Commandant of Coahuiltejas   )   [rubric]

---

[1]BA Roll 136, Frames 0324-0325.

ANTONIO ELOSÚA TO MANUEL DE MIER Y TERÁN[1]

[Translated from Spanish]

[November 19, 1830]

Office of the Principal Commandant

of Coahuila and Texas   No. 408

Most Excellent Sir:

The Military Commandant of Tenoxtitlan, Citizen Lieutenant Colonel Francisco Ruiz, in an official letter dated the 13th of the present month, writes me as follows:

"The foreigner Sterling C. Robertson, about whom I wrote you in my official letter of October 30," etc.

And I am forwarding it to Your Excellency for your information and superior decision.

God and Liberty. Béxar, November 19, 1830.

[Antonio Elosúa]

He inserts, for a superior decision, the official letter in which the Military Commandant of Tenoxtitlan reports that the foreigner Sterling C. Robertson has presented himself to him again to report that some foreign families, of those who are coming to settle on those lands by virtue of the contract celebrated with the Government of the State, are about to arrive.

---

[1]Volume 54, pp. 282-282 verso, Spanish Archives, General Land Office, Austin, Texas. This document is summarized on the incomplete list of correspondence filed in the Béxar Archives under November 23, 1830.--BA Roll 136, Frames 0501-0502.

THE COMMISSAR GENERAL OF BÉXAR TO

MANUEL DE MIER Y TERÁN[1]

[Translated from Spanish]

[November 19, 1830]

Most Excellent Sir:

To the Commissar of the Villa of San Felipe de
Austin I am communicating the superior order of Your Excellency dated the 3rd of the present month, and with it I am
enclosing the Law of April 6 of the present year for his
compliance, which Your Excellency had the kindness to
enclose for me with the aforecited order. I got in touch
precisely with that commissar because he is the only
employee of the Treasury Department whom I recognize and
because I do not know whether there is another one in
Brazoria, which I have the honor to report to Your Excellency in reply to your said order.

God and Liberty. Béxar, November 19, 1830.

To the Commandant General,)
)
Manuel de Mier y Terán   )

---

[1]BA Roll 135, Frame 0227.

THE COMMISSAR GENERAL OF BÉXAR TO

MANUEL DE MIER Y TERÁN[1]

[Translated from Spanish]

[November 19, 1830]

Most Excellent Sir:

By the official letter from Your Excellency dated
October 11, in which you copied for me the one you were
sending under that date to the Principal Commandant of this
Department, and in which you state, among other things,
that the spies in the expedition against the Tahuacanos,
Damasio [sic] Galván and Manuel Luna, should be rewarded
with 25 pesos each, I appreciate the good will of Your
Excellency, and I have the honor to inform you that every-
thing has been complied with, except the said rewards to
Galván and Luna.

God and Liberty. Béxar, November 19, 1830.

To the Most Excellent Commandant General)
)
Don Manuel de Mier y Terán.   )

---

[1]BA Roll 135, Frame 0229.

JUAN NEPOMUCENO DE AYALA TO ANTONIO ELOSÚA[1]

[Translated from Spanish]

[November 19, 1830]

In submissive and respectful reply to the superior official
letter from Your Lordship dated the 13th of the present
month, in which Your Lordship was pleased to forward to me
the superior order from the Most Excellent Commandant General Inspector of these States, for me to go to Tenoxtitlan,
I must tell Your Lordship that I find myself in the best
disposition to go to that post, but certainly two very
powerful motives prevent me from doing so. The first one
is that for a very long time I have been suffering from
venereal disease and I find it impossible to ride on hors-
back, as is shown in the certificate which I am attentively
enclosing for Your Lordship.[2] In the second place, the
great poverty in which I find myself prevents me from
undertaking the said journey, due to a lack of pay from
which I have been suffering for a long time, as is well
known, and now I find myself deprived of all help, and if,
despite my infirmities, I must go, I ask and beg Your Lordship to order that I be protected as is necessary, both
with regard to food on my journey as well as to cover my
honor, which does not amount to much, in this city, and to
make a place in which to live at that post, and that I be
assured of my pay in the Álamo Company, which is garrison-
ing it, for it is quite clear and sad to see the constancy

with which I have suffered my labors, and scarcities, which,
if it were not for the charity of the Parish Priest of this
City, I would have already perished or become a beggar, and
I beg Your Lordship earnestly to call this to the attention
of the Most Excellent Commandant General so that he can
provide a remedy for these ills.

God and Liberty. Béxar, November 19, 1830.

Juan Nepomuceno de Ayala

[rubric]

To the Principal Commandant,)
)
Colonel Don Antonio Elosúa   )

---

[1]BA Roll 136, Frames 0385-0387.

[2]No certificate was found with this letter.

ÁLAMO DE PARRAS PRESIDIAL COMPANY[1]

[Translated from Spanish]

[November 20, 1830]

Report showing the amount that is needed, more or less, in order to provide capes, *jorongos*, shoes, and other very necessary things, for the individuals of the said Company.

	Pesos	R.	G.
For 119 positions from Sergeant on down, we need an equal number of capes which, at 6 1/2 varas of cloth each, amount to 773 [1/2] varas, which, at the price of 22 reales per vara, bought in Querétaro and delivered to this City, amounts to---	2.109.	2.	"
	[*sic*]		
For the same number of positions we need an equal number of sarapes which, at the price of 3 pesos each, delivered here, amounts to-------------------------------	.357.	0.	0
For the said force we need 39 dozen pairs of shoes which, at the price of 10 reales each, delivered here, is----------	.590.	0.	0
For the said force we need 119 complete saddles, except for the trees and bows, and, bought in the *Villa* of León and delivered here, that amounts to 23 pesos each-------------------------------	2.737.	0.	0
For ditto we need 119 hats which, delivered here at 12 reales each------------------	.178.	4.	0
TOTAL:	5.971.	6.	0

Béxar, November 20, 1830.

---

[1]BA Roll 136, Frame 0415.

MANUEL DE MIER Y TERÁN TO ANTONIO ELOSÚA[1]

[Translated from Spanish]

Office of the Commandant General and   [November 22, 1830]
<u>Inspector of the Eastern Interior States</u>.

<u>Circular</u>.

The Most Excellent Secretary of War and Navy, in a note
dated the 30th of last month, was pleased to write me as
follows:

"Most Excellent Sir:=Since one of the greatest services that can be rendered to the Nation is to avoid its
being defrauded of its income and taxes, never more than at
the present time, when smuggling has risen to imponderable
proportions, and when the Treasury finds itself as over-
loaded with demands, as it is short on resources to cover
them, the Most Excellent Vice President, considering that
none of the classes in the State is as interested as the
military in seeing that the said acts of fraud are avoided,
since the products of said income are invested, for the
most part, in paying them, and, since the said class has
the best attitude and disposition for apprehending the
smugglers, since they are armed and have other useful
means, due to the fact that the citizens have for them the
esteem which they deserve, and adding to this the fact that,
when the seizure is made by the troops, it will achieve the
advantage of increasing the income from which they derive
their subsistence, and the amount of the seizure which,

according to law, belongs to the one who makes the arrest, with the result that the apprehension of contraband by parties of troops must be considered as a means for the relief and better support of the corps, His Excellency has ordered that, despite what has been ordered previously to the effect that Commandant Generals and Principal Commandants should make available, to the administrators and guards of the income from tobacco, such assistance as may be requested of them, you are to be ordered to exercise the greatest diligence to see that the parties under your command pursue the smugglers tenaciously, and from the fruit thereof, that they send the items apprehended to the head office in this capital, where they will be liquidated instantly, and the value of same will be handed over to them, without any deduction except twenty-five percent for excise taxes, as prescribed by law, all of which I am communicating to you from said superior order for your punctual compliance."

And I am inserting it for Your Lordship for your information, recommending that, on your part, you exercise the most exact compliance with said superior order.

God and Liberty. Matamoros, November 22, 1830.

M. Mier y Terán

[rubric]

To the Principal Commandant of Coahuila and Texas.

---

[1]BA Roll 136, Frames 0431-0433. On December 9,

1830, Elosúa forwarded this order from Béxar to the Companies of Coahuila and Texas and to the Military Commandants of Nacogdoches, Galveston, Lavaca, La Bahía, and Tenoxtitlan.--BA Roll 136, Frame 0982.

JOSÉ DE LAS PIEDRAS TO ANTONIO ELOSÚA[1]

[Translated from Spanish]

Office of the Military Commandant   [November 22, 1830]
of the Frontier

Colonel Peter Ellis Bean has returned to this post, and, from the official letter from Your Lordship which he has delivered to me, dated October 23, I see the just motive which exists for the suspension of the expedition against the Tahuacanos, and I shall wait, as you suggest, for a more opportune occasion to undertake it.

God and Liberty. Nacogdoches, November 22, 1830.

José de las Piedras

[rubric]

To the Colonel Don Antonio   )
)
Elosúa, Principal Commandant   )
)
of Coahuila and Texas_____)

---

[1]BA Roll 136, Frames 0441-0442.

JOSÉ ORTEGA TO ANTONIO ELOSÚA[1]

[Translated from Spanish]

12th Permanent Battalion   [November 22, 1830]

Having received Your Lordship's official letter dated the
23rd of the past month, in which you recommend that I proceed as quickly as possible to conclude the case which I
am prosecuting against Colonel Don Peter Ellis Bean, I must
tell you that said case has been suspended while we are
waiting for the reply from the judge in the district where
they say he was married, to whom I wrote asking him to send
either a certificate that said marriage did take place, or
a statement that no record of same could be found, without
which document it is impossible to prove in court the
charge of bigamy which has been filed against him.

        I repeated my request yesterday, through the great
judge at Natchitoches, and if, within a reasonable period
of time, I do not receive a reply, I will report to Your
Lordship on the status of the case.

        God and Liberty. Nacogdoches, November 22, 1830.

                                        José Ortega

To the Principal Commandant)   [rubric]
)
of the Department, Colonel)
)
Don Antonio Elosúa   )

_____

[1]BA Roll 136, Frames 0445-0446.

FRANCISCO RUIZ TO STEPHEN F. AUSTIN[1]

[Translated from Spanish]

[November 22, 1830]

Office of the Military Commandant of Tenoxtitlan

With singular appreciation I received your official letter of the 6th of the current month in which you were pleased to communicate to me the measure dictated by the illustrious Ayuntamiento of that municipality, and likewise the objective of Captain Abner Cuikendoll [Kuykendall], commandant of the first company of the battalion of civilians under your command, and consequently I offered to the said captain such assistance as I found at my disposal in order to comply fully with such a just and beneficent measure, and to let him proceed to comply with same without any fear that the individuals against whom the writ had been issued should be able to elude it by having heard about it from that jurisdiction so that they could flee from the just punishment to which his harmful conduct made him subject, for under no condition would the office of this military commandant permit him to come into this new establishment; on the contrary, it would expel all those therein who find themselves in a similar situation, in order to comply in every respect with the superior orders which I now have.[2]

I want to thank you most profusely for the assistance which you promise me in the persecution of people wandering through this part of the country, and also for the good attitude of the illustrious Ayuntamiento and the inhabitants of that Colony for the same purpose, as you indicate to me in your aforesaid official letter which I have the pleasure of answering. At the same time I beg you to thank for me the esteemed corporation and the community, and accept for yourself the manifestations of my most sincere and respectful consideration and appreciation.

God and Liberty. Tenoxtitlan, November 22, 1830.
To Lieutenant Colonel Stephen F. Austin

Francisco Ruiz

[rubric]

---

[1]*Austin Papers*, II, 538-539.

[2]See above, "Excerpt from the Minutes of the Ayuntamiento of San Felipe de Austin," November 2, 1830.

FRANCISCO RUIZ TO STEPHEN F. AUSTIN[1]

[Translated from Spanish]

[November 22, 1830]

Office of the Military Commandant of Tenoxtitlan

With regret I saw, on the morning of the 16th of the current month, a Kichas [Keechi] Indian, one of three who were here in this camp on a peaceful mission, who showed me the thumb of his right hand, broken by a shot from a carbine which he said an American had fired at him without any cause whatsoever,[2] and, although at the moment I could not find out who had been the aggressor, I have learned later, from various witnesses, that it was an individual named *Cúpar* [James Cooper] who was in the party of civil militia led by Captain Cuikendoll [Abner Kuykendall], and such a procedure is unworthy of men who respect the lawfully constituted authorities and subject themselves to the law. It caused me the greatest displeasure, for, in case the Indian had infuriated Mr. Cúpar, he first should have filed his complaint and not trampled upon reason and justice, since he was in a place where he could have done so without giving cause for the just sentiment with which I have the honor of reporting it to you, while at the same time reassuring you of my highest esteem and appreciation.

God and Liberty. Tenoxtitlan, November 22, 1830.

Francisco Ruiz

[rubric]

To the Lieutenant Colonel of Civic Militia,

Citizen Stephen F. Austin.

---

[1]Barker, *Austin Papers*, II, 538.

[2]This Indian had been in the party which killed James Cooper's brother, William Cooper, Jr., on Caney Creek.--*Handbook of Texas*, I, 408-409. Also see above, "Excerpt from the Recollections of Barzillai Kuykendall," November 16, 1830.

ARTICLES OF AGREEMENT BETWEEN ROBERTSON & THOMSON

AND JAMES G. HOOKER[1]

[Entered under November 22, 1830]

[Arti]cles of agreement made this 2... 1830 [bet]ween
Sterling C. Robertson of Da[vidson County] and [Sta]te of
Tennessee and Alexr Tho[mson of Giles] County [an]d State
aforesaid and Jas. G. [Hooker of the C]ity of [Na]shville,
Witnesseth, that the [said Roberts]on and [Th]omson agrees
and binds themselves [to convey] unto the said Hooker his
heirs or assigns one [hundred] and sixty acres of good land
in Leftwichs grant [in the] province of Texas also eight
hundred and forty acres [of land in an]other and separate
place the whole being one thous[and ac]res of land in said
Grant in said province all of [good qu]ality. for and in
consideration of said one thousand [acres of] land the said
Hooker agrees and binds himself to settle and remain on
said land so as to enable the said Robertson & Thomson [to]
obtain & perfect a title to a league of land by virtue of
said settlement un[d]er the Mexican Re[publi]c, and said
Hooker also binds [hi]mself to erect h[ouses necessary] for
a permanent reside[nce] and to open and [fence] a sufficient
portion of the said land which may be [set] apart for him
the said Hooker and the said Robertson and Thomson agrees
to lay off and survey the said one [hun]dred and sixty
acres and also with the assistance of said Hooker in chain
carrying and chopping to lay off and s[urvey] the ballance

of the one thousand acres, viz. eight h[undre]d and forty acres of land.

In testimony whereof we have [hereunto] set our hands and affixed our seals this day and year [first abov]e written

S. C. [Robertso]n (Seal)

Alex[r Thom]son (Seal)

Jam[es G. Hooke]r (Seal)

[Endorsed:] Agreement & Robertson & Thomson & James G. Hooker.

---

[1]Papers of Mrs. Thomas Shelton Sutherland, Sr., in the Robertson Colony Collection, The University of Texas at Arlington Library. The closest that we have been able to date this document is November 22, 1830, the last date for which we have a printed form issued by Robertson & Thomson. After that date the agreements were written entirely in longhand, as is the case in this instance.

VICENTE CÓRDOVA TO RAMÓN MÚSQUIZ[1]

[Translated from Spanish]

Nacogdoches)   [November 23, 1830]
)
Court   )   Confidential.

It has come to my attention that, by order of Your Lordship, the Commandant of Arms of this Frontier has been instructed to draw up a report on my judicial procedure in the case which is being prosecuted, by order of Your Lordship, against Don Juan Antonio Padilla and his employees, Don Justo Liendo and Don Joaquín Rumayor. If this is true, I beg Your Lordship to make me a transcript of said report so that I can answer any charges against me that may be made therein, and so that Your Lordship, or the judge who may be assigned to handle the case, may pass judgment with a complete knowledge of the facts; otherwise please tell me what the outcome of the case has been, for my information and guidance.

God and Liberty. Nacogdoches, November 23, 1830.

Vicente Córdova

[rubric]

To the Political Chief)
)
of This Department   )

---

[1]BA Roll 136, Frames 0484-0485.

MANUEL DE MIER Y TERÁN TO ANTONIO ELOSÚA[1]

[Translated from Spanish]

Office of the Commandant General and   [November 24, 1830]
Inspector of the Eastern Interior States.

Please order the commandants of the posts in the Principal

Commandancy under your supervision, whenever they report

deserters they have apprehended, to give the name of the

offices that have paid the reward to the person who made

the arrest, which said payment I recommend that they make

with all due promptness.

     God and Liberty. Matamoros, November 24, 1830.

           M. Mier y Terán

              [rubric]

To the Citizen Principal Commandant)
)
of Coahuila and Texas_____)

---

[1]BA Roll 136, Frames 0503-0504. On December 9,
1830, Elosúa forwarded this order from Béxar to the Companies of Ríogrande, Aguaverde, and La Bavia, to the Major of
the Plaza at Béxar, and to the Military Commandants of
Nacogdoches, Galveston, Lavaca, La Bahía, and Tenoxtitlan.
--BA Roll 136, Frame 0981.

MANUEL DE MIER Y TERÁN TO ANTONIO ELOSÚA[1]

[Translated from Spanish]

Office of the Commandant General and   [November 24, 1830]
Inspector of the Eastern Interior States

Confidential.

I have seen the documented reports on what has been furnished to the Presidial Companies in that Department, and,
pursuant to what Your Lordship reported to me in your official letter No. 317 of the 21st of last month, I am satisfied that the individuals of same have received what is
shown therein. At the time that they were totaled up I was
informed, through various channels, that those well deserving troops were not receiving even half a *real* in cash, and
that the soldiers were being forced to receive, for their
allowance, ornamental shell combs, carding combs, and other
articles which they sacrificed with a loss of three-fourths
of their value in order to get actual cash that they could
use freely for themselves and their families. It would not
be strange if this had happened, for Your Lordship well
knows how far the monopolists can go with their arbitrary
actions, and I am not unaware of the fact that the helpless
and innocent soldier down in the ranks is threatened and
frightened so that he says nothing about these excesses and
has to be satisfied with whatever charges they take a
notion to make against him, just as though it had been cash
in hand that he received. Therefore, desiring to uproot

these abuses, I once again admonish Your Lordship to use every means at your disposal to investigate, every time that the companies receive money, to find out whether the individuals in same actually receive in their hands the amount which justly belongs to them according to their rank and according to the other ways by which their monthly allotment is supposed to be paid, satisfying yourself that they are actually getting what belongs to them in proportion to what each paymaster draws from the Commissariat. I am reporting this to Your Lordship by way of reply so that you can carry out these instructions and, if you notice any irregularities in the matter, you can report them to me so that I can file charges against the offender.

God and Liberty. Matamoros, November 24, 1830.

M. Mier y Terán

[rubric]

To Citizen Colonel Antonio Elosúa.

---

[1]BA Roll 136, Frames 0505-0506.

MANUEL DE MIER Y TERÁN TO THE COMMISSAR AT BÉXAR[1]

[Translated from Spanish]

Office of the Commandant General and   [November 24, 1830]
Inspector of the Eastern Interior States

To Citizen Subcommissar Lieutenant Colonel Francisco Lojero

I am writing today as follows:

"Out of the first remittance of money that is sent
to Texas you will designate two thousand pesos to be used
exclusively for the expenses of the fort which is to be
built at the new establishment of Tenoxtitlan, at the same
time making the corresponding report to the Citizen Commissar in Béxar."

Which I am inserting for you, for your information
and by way of reply to your official letter dated the 15th
of the past month which deals with the matter.

God and Liberty. Matamoros, November 14, 1830.

M. Mier y Terán

[rubric]

To the Citizen Commissar of Béxar.

---

[1]BA Roll 136, Frames 0509-0510.

ANTONIO ELOSÚA TO FRANCISCO RUIZ[1]

[Translated from Spanish]

Office of the Principal Commandant   [November 24, 1830]

of Coahuila and Texas

Alférez Citizen Santiago Navayra, about whom you

wrote me in your official letter dated the 14th of the pre-

sent month, has presented himself in this city, and he will

return to that post just as soon as we receive here a ship-

ment of funds which is about to arrive. I am reporting

this to you by way of reply.

God and Liberty. November 24, 1830.

[Antonio Elosúa]

To the Military Commandant of Tenoxtitlan,

[Francisco Ruiz]

---

[1] BA Roll 136, Frame 0514.

ANTONIO ELOSÚA TO FRANCISCO RUIZ[1]

[Translated from Spanish]

Office of the Principal Commandant)   [November 24, 1830]
)
of Coahuila and Texas_____)

    By your official letter dated the 13th of the pre-
sent month I have been informed of everything that you
report therein with respect to the fact that the foreigner
Sterling Robertson has presented himself again at that
post, saying that some of the foreign families who are coming to colonize those lands by virtue of the contract made
with the Government of the State are about to arrive, and
about everything else you indicate in said letter. I am
reporting this to you by way of reply, and with the understanding that I have already reported all this to the Most
Excellent Commandant General Inspector of These States, for
his information and superior decision.

    God and Liberty. Béxar, November 24, 1830.

                      [Antonio Elosúa]

To the Military Commandant of Tenoxtitlan.

---

[1]BA Roll 136, Frames 0515-0516.

ANTONIO ELOSÚA TO FRANCISCO RUIZ[1]

[Translated from Spanish]

Office of the Principal Commandant)   [November 24, 1830]
)
of Coahuila and Texas_____)

You will forward the charges, for paper for that Military Headquarters under your command, to the Álamo Company so that there they may be repaid to you and charged to the Gratification Fund, which said measure is in conformity with instructions issued for that same purpose during the last few years by the Most Excellent Commandant General Inspector of these States, for the Military Headquarters at La Bahía. I am reporting this to you in reply to your official letter dated the 13th of the present month relative to the matter, adding that in the Office of the Principal Commandant under my command we at present do not have any stamped paper to furnish you.

God and Liberty. Béxar, November 24, 1830.

[Antonio Elosúa]

To Lieutenant Colonel Citizen Francisco Ruiz.

---

[1]BA Roll 136, Frames 0518-0519.

ANTONIO ELOSÚA TO SEVERO RUIZ[1]

[Translated from Spanish]

Office of the Principal Commandant)   [November 24, 1830]
)
of Coahuila and Texas_____)

By your official letter dated the 14th of the present month I have been informed of the illnesses from which
Corporal José Chacón is suffering, in that Company under
your command, and in reply I must tell you that, if he con-
tinues to be sick and there is no hope of his recovering at
that Post, you may make arrangements for him to come to
this City.

God and Liberty. Béxar, November 24, 1830.

[Antonio Elosúa]

To Captain Don Severo Ruiz.

_____

[1]BA Roll 136, Frame 0517.

ANTONIO ELOSÚA TO JUAN NEPOMUCENO AYALA[1]

[Translated from Spanish]

Office of the Principal Commandant)   [November 24, 1830]
)
of Coahuila and Texas_____)

I have been informed of everything that you reported to me in your official letter dated the 19th of the present month with respect to the illnesses from which you are suffering, but, since it is not within my power to permit you to remain in this city, I urge you, on the first occasion that presents itself, to plan to begin your journey to Tenoxtitlan in compliance with the order of the Most Excellent Commandant General Inspector of these States, which I have communicated to you, with the understanding that, as far as your wants are concerned, I am issuing appropriate orders so that your pay can be made available to you by the Álamo Company, and it being understood that from the first remittance that arrives in this city there will be made available to you funds for your journey. I am reporting this to you by way of reply, and I am returning to you the certificate which you enclosed with your aforementioned official letter.

God and Liberty. Béxar, November 24, 1830.

[Antonio Elosúa]

To Chaplain Citizen Juan Nepomuceno Ayala.

---

[1]BA Roll 136, Frames 0520-0521.

RAMÓN MÚSQUIZ TO JOSÉ DE LAS PIEDRAS[1]

[Translated from Spanish]

Office of the Political Chief, etc.   [November 24, 1830]

        With Your Lordship's official letter dated the 7th

of the present month, I have received the documentation

which, at the request of this office, you were kind enough

to have drawn up concerning the conduct of the Alcalde of

that place in the case which was filed against Don Juan

Antonio Padilla. I have the honor to report this to Your

Lordship by way of reply, repeating to you the expressions

of my particular respect and esteem.

        God, etc. Béxar, November 24, 1830. R. M. [Ramón

Músquiz].

To Colonel Don José de las Piedras,   )
)
Military Commandant of the Frontier.   )

---

[1]BA Roll 136, Frame 0085.

RAMÓN MÚSQUIZ TO THE ALCALDE OF NACOGDOCHES[1]

[Translated from Spanish]

Office of the Political Chief)   [November 24, 1830]
)
[of the Department of Béxar])

I have noticed that by means of the printing press[2] in that town they are validating paper bearing the fourth seal[3] for use by the public in the years of 1830 and 1831, and, since they usually do the same thing whenever they run out of the other kinds of paper, thus exceeding the power which the law grants to employees in the tax collector's office for that purpose, it is indispensable to warn you to be careful to see that the laws and orders in force governing the matter are obeyed. Consequently the fourth seals now on hand validated in this form should be voided by the tax collector in that office, and you should take charge of those that have already been issued, so that, the tax collector can request in advance, from his head office, the paper bearing the seals that he considers necessary for use, and he should limit himself to validating in longhand, with your intervention, the paper bearing the seals that the public urgently needs for private transactions that cannot be delayed. God, etc. Béxar, November 14, 1830.= To the Citizen Alcalde of Nacogdoches.

---

[1]BA Roll 136, Frames 0522-0523.

[2]This must have been the printing press operated by Milton Slocum, who was listed as a printer in Nacogdoches from 1829 to 1832. Mr. Streeter does not report any Nacogdoches imprints for 1830, but this letter gives us a clue as to what the press was being used for.--Streeter, *Bibliography of Texas, 1795-1845*, Part I, Volume I, pp. 27-28.

[3]For the law governing the use of stamped paper, see Decree of October 6, 1823, in McLean, *Papers*, II, 128-138. In a future volume we shall see how this official paper became more precious than gold.

FRANCISCO RUIZ TO STEPHEN F. AUSTIN[1]

[Translated from Spanish]

Tenoxtitlan, November 26, 1830

Mr. Stephen Austin:

My very esteemed friend: By your fine letter of the 17th of the current month I have learned, with the greatest satisfaction, that you will do everything within your power to remove obstacles in the way of colonization in this part of the country. As for me, I have written so much in favor of the subject, both officially and privately, that I am afraid they will come to believe that I have something personal at stake, which is not far from the truth, since I think only of the welfare of my country and my fellow man. I shall regret it very much if my record is spoiled by some manifestation of distrust, but I will not for that reason cease to talk about the advantages which, in my opinion, would result if we would admit hardworking, honest people, regardless of the country they come from, as you say, or from hell itself, as long as they are useful, for otherwise the country, or, to put it more accurately, the greater part of this Department, will be inhabited only by Indians and wild beasts that will devour us. This is the truth. The truth.

I do not want to talk about the condition in which the political affairs of our Republic find themselves at the moment, for it grieves me, and I despair, but it would be better if I talked about something else. Please do not hesitate to tell me frankly your opinion on any subject you like, with the understanding that I hope you will do me the justice to believe that I am your true friend, and that my breast will be an archive for your secrets or confidential matters, regardless of what they may be, for, even though I may not agree with you, that will not be any reason for me to go back on my promise, which I solemnly vow to keep.

My friend, I am already tired of my post after such a short time. It seems to me that I won't last very long here. I realize that it would be better for me to get out of the military service because I am not of the right temperament to command in such calamitous times, and much less at a post which is so advanced and without resources, for we are already beginning to run short of troops, and pretty soon the bare necessities will begin to play out. It is impossible for me to describe to you the condition in which I find myself with my garrison. Suffice it to say that I am performing or acting a very sad part, and I don't know what is going to become of this establishment. Time will tell, and meanwhile I shall turn to another subject.

I am enclosing for you two official letters: one in reply to yours dated the 6th of the present month, and the other one is about a Kichas Indian who got the thumb of his right hand shot off by an individual in the party of civil militia which was brought by Captain Cuikendoll

[Kuykendall]. I don't expect you to do anything more than give the aggressor to understand (if you think it would be a good idea) that he committed an error in trampling upon the authority which I represent, and that it was not right to try to avenge his wrong in the way that he tried to do it, in cold blood, within sight of a post occupied by troops with competent authority, and perhaps with an Indian who was not to blame. You are not unaware of the fact that I detest Indians, because I know what they are, and I tolerate them only because circumstances demand prudence. In short, I am sending you my official letter, and you may receive it with the confidence of a friend, for, as far as I am concerned, whatever you do and say will be all right.

I am sending you, by the bearer, six *reales*, the value of two letters for which you paid the postage and forwarded them to me: one for Captain Severo [Ruiz] and the other one was mine.

Please give my regards to my friend Don Samuel [M. Williams] and family, and for yourself please receive the singular affection of one who professes to be, and repeats in all truth, that he is your friend who kisses your hand.

Francisco Ruiz   [rubric]

P. S.

I am planning to build a house where I can raise cattle, and, if possible to bring out my family from Béxar. Consequently I want to find a piece of unclaimed land that is safe from the Indians.[2] I want your advice about the land, for you may know if there is any in your Colony, so that I could be near you as a new settler, because that is all I want. Valid.

---

[1]Barker, *Austin Papers*, II, 541-542.

[2]On August 31, 1833, Francisco Ruiz received 9 leagues of land from Commissioner Luke Lessassier, distributed as follows: 4 in present Robertson County, 2 in Brazos County, 2 in Milam, and 1 in Burleson. Then on March 16, 1834, he completed his total of 11 leagues by receiving 2 leagues from Commissioner Vicente Aldrete in present Karnes County.--Virginia H. Taylor, *The Spanish Archives of the General Land Office of Texas* (Austin: The Lone Star Press, 1955), p. 235.

MICHEL B. MENARD TO STEPHEN F. AUSTIN[1]

Nacogdoches. Nov. 27th. 1830.

Col Stephen F Austin

San phillippe

Dear sir I receved this morning by Mr. Novara your
Letter and document[2] appointing me your agent to give certificat to such deserving persons as should wish to Emigrate to your Colony I felt disposed to Accept of the
apointment for three Reason 1er to oblige a man who had
done the most for the Interest and promotion of this province 2er to satisfy the desire that I have if I had the
power to promogate the growth and importance of this province 3er to the Request of Mr. McKinney a man that I have
the highest Estime and Consideration for.

But not wishing to Expose myself being a Stranger
in the Contry I thought proper (allso in accordance with
your Instruction) to call on Col Piedras to give his appro-
bation on the Subject after due Consideration he said that
he did not think he Could give his assent being Contrary to
his Superior order that he had order to stop any one who
Should not have a passport from a Mexican Agent that you
had a wright youself to give pasport or Certificat to such
Number or persons as by your Contract with Government you
were to settle in your Colony and no more. that having the
wright youself (to give Certificat) it was surpassing your
faculty to Extend that wright to other and in short that

the power and Instruction you give me were (if Complyed
with) in direct violation of his order and to the 9th:
article of the Law of the Sixth of aprill Last for he said
by those Instruction you are impowered to give Certificat
to any men (if good men) who Should say that he is Emigrating to Austin Colony not specifying the Number while your
Contract with Government Specify a Limited Number and that
no one ells ought to be admitted in the province besides:
it is an affair of too much Responsability for him to permit it he said if you would furnish him with a List of the
names of those persons you have Contracted with which are
to settle in your Colony or them to have a Certificat of
your own Signature he has no objection to Let him pass. but
upon no other term--Saying it would be transgressing his
order to do the Contrary.--he Requested me to Let him take
a Copi of your Instruction to me and that he would Write to
the Govment to know whether they would allow you to appoint
an agent for this business not finding it objectionable I
Let him have the paper and he took a Copie of it I am no
Lawyer therfore I do not know whether Col. Piedras is
wright or wrong in this affair nor do I wish to have any
Contantion with him on the Subject therfore I wrote you the
Subtance of what he said it is for you to Juge or to do as
you plaese about it

Notwithstanding my Willingness to be of Service to
you--you see it is imposible for the present But in this or

other Case here after if I Can be of any help or service to you I prey you to Request it of me and I will if in my power do it with greatest pleasure

With Respect and Consideration I am your Obed. Sert.

Michel B. Menard   [rubric]

To. Col. Stephen F Austin

Ville de Austin

Addressed: Col. Stephen F. Austin. Villa de Austin Texas

Per Mr. Foster

PS. the Comisionner Novara Receved order to day from the Governor of the State not to proceed any farther in his business unless he is sure that Col. Milam Colonist are not North American Emigrant that Col. Milams Contract with Govt. his to settle European Emigrant the Gentlemen is very much dissapointed I am sorry for it.

M. B. Menard

---

[1]Barker, *Austin Papers*, II, 543-544.

[2]See "Stephen F. Austin to M. B. Menard" and "Appointment of M. B. Menard as My Agent in Nacogdoches," both under November 13, 1830.

CERTIFICATE OF CHARACTER FOR FRANCIS SLAUGHTER[1]

[November 27, 1830]

We the undersigners, Citizens of Maury County, Tennessee, *do certify*, that we have been acquainted with Francis Slaughter Esqr of Maury County, for about Ten years, we *do believe* him, to be an honest, good citizen, harmless and peaceable towards every body, we never knew him to be ingagued in quarrels, strifes, or contentious lawsuits, and in all his business, officially, & privately, we, believe he has conducted himself, as a gentleman.

Given under our hands 27th November 1830.

Lawyers Names	*Names*
Thomas B Craighead	George M. Martin C.M.C.C.
Will. E. Erwin.	W. E. Gillespie clk ch. cort
R. L. Cobbs	Wm. Voorhies
Saml. D. Frierson	John Porter
A. O. P. Nicholson	Nimrod Porter
Jo. Herndon	H. Grove
P. R. Booker	Hugh Bradshaw
Robt Mack	W. B. Porter
Gideon J. Pillow	Thos. Jefferson Porter
Allen Brown	Americus Bradshaw
J. A. Mack	
Edmund Dillahunty	B. F. Herndon
Wm. McNeill	William Kerr
Elias Pullin Frierson	William McCandless

	Gideon B. McCandless
H. Ward	Lorenzo Hitchcock
Wm. R. Miller	Jas. B. Jopling
R. M. Booker	W. E. Hodge
Joel B. Sanders, M.D.	James Hodge
Levi Ketchum	R. C. K. Martin
Sml. B. Reavis	A. C. Hays
Abraham Looney	Simon Johnson
Saml McBride	Wm. S. Moore
David Looney	Edwd M Sheegog
J. Pittillo	Charles Colhoun
John Hill	T. M. Terrell
Taswell S. Aldissan	Jeremiah Cherry
John Kisney	
Nathon Coffey	P. Nelson
Leml. Phillips	John Lomax
Saml. McDowell	Caleb Thomas
Thos. C. McDowell	Pleasant D Cocke
L. H. Duncan	
Evan Young	Edwd. H. Chaffin
Butler Noles	H. Langtry
John R. Groves	Thos Bradshaw
G. W. Campbell	Barton W Jenkins
Nathan Vaught	Parry W. Porter
Isaac S. Goff	James R Plummer
Wm K Hill	T Maddin

State of Tennessee Maury County

I Thomas J Porter clerk of the court of pleas and quarter sessions for said county [do] certify that I am well acquainted with Francis Slauter [Slaughter] who has obtained the foregoing certificate and believe him justly entitled to the reputation therein certified. I am also well acquainted with all the persons who have signed and certified his character and know them to be men of fair and honorable standing and of strict veracity In testimony of

[Seal:]   all which I have hereunto set my hand

STATE OF TENNESSEE and seal this 2nd day of December A.D.
   MAURY COUNTY
   COURT OF PLEAS   1830 and 54th year of American indepen-
      AND
QUARTER SESSIONS dence.

                                        Thos J Porter

State of Tennessee)   I James Walker, Presiding Justice of
)
Maury County   )   the Court of Pleas & Quarter Sessions

for said county, do hereby certify that Thomas J. Porter, whose name is officially signed to the foregoing certifi- cate is at this time, and was at the time of signing the same clerk of our said court and that full faith & credit is due and given to all his official acts as such. Given under my hand & seal this 16th day Dec. 1830

                              James Walker P.J.M.C.C.

                              State of Tennessee

                              Executive Department.

I, William Carroll, Governor in and over the said State do, hereby, certify that James Walker whose name is subscribed to the foregoing certificate was on the 16th day of December 1830 Presiding Justice of the Court of Pleas and Quarter Sessions of said County of Maury and that his official acts are entitled to full faith and credit.

[Seal:]
SEAL OF THE STATE
OF TENNESSEE
1796

In testimony whereof I have hereunto set my hand and caused the Great Seal of the State to be affixed at Nashville this

24th December 1830

Wm. Carroll

By the Governor

Thos H Fletcher

Secretary of State

[Endorsed:] Francis Slaughter recommendation

---

[1]Harllee Collection. This character certificate with 79 signatures, extending from the county level all the way up through the governor, is the most elaborate document we have ever seen of this nature. It was executed to comply with Article 5 of the State Colonization Law of Coahuila and Texas, March 24, 1825, which stipulated that "the new settlers who present themselves to be admitted, will have to establish, by means of certificates from the authorities in the place from which they come, their christianity, morality, and good customs." (See McLean, *Papers*, II, 271.) Many such documents eventually came to rest in the "Character Certificates" file in the Spanish Archives of the General Land Office in Austin, Texas, but this one did not, apparently because Francis Slaughter was delayed in coming to Texas. Sterling C. Robertson paid his fare when they embarked from Nashville on board the Steamboat *Criterion* on March 29, 1831, but Francis Slauter [*sic*] and his family were not sworn in as Robertson colonists until January 9, 1836, which was after the outbreak of the Texas Revolution

and the land offices in the various colonies had been
closed. This probably accounts for the fact that the document remained in Robertson's personal papers instead of
being filed with the records of his land office, which were
delivered to the General Land Office after the Revolution.

GENERAL AGREEMENT BETWEEN ROBERTSON & THOMSON

AND THEIR COLONISTS[1]

[November 28, 1830]

Know all men by these presents that whereas Sterling C Robertson and Alexander Thompson [Thomson] citizens of the State of Tennessee one of the United States of North America have contracted with us the subscribers to emigrate with them to the Province of Texas for the purpose of making settlements under the colonization laws of the Federal government of the Republic of Mexico in the grant formerly made to Robert Leftwich, but since ceded to a company of enterprisers in the City of Nashville in said State of Tennessee, and whereas they have executed their bonds to us severally for certain quantities of land as soon as they obtain their titles, now as the grant, titles, or patents, may be issued in our names, for the quantity to which we may as settlers be entitled, in that event, we bind ourselves, our heirs, executors, & administrators, severally, to convey to sd Robertson & Thompson, their heirs, or assigns, that they may designate all the lands that may be thus granted to us as settlers; except that portion for which we severally hold their bonds, to make us a title, said Robertson and Thompson affording to us the right, aids and facilities in making our settlements as stipulated in their bonds to us.

T Joins

Jeremiah Tinnin

James Ledbetter

John Ledbetter

       his
Stephen X Ledbetter
    mark

     his
Isaah X Curd
   mark

Daniel Koonce

      his
Elijah X Koonce
    mark

       his
William X Joines
     mark

John Massey

James Parker

    his
John X Wilson
   mark

Henry J. Pair

Quintin Dines

      his
Nathan X Weaver
    mark

William B. Wilks

James Farmer

Everton Kennerly

Thos. Wootton

The above contract was Renewed in the province of

Texas on the 28th day of Novr. 1830 Nashvilles company
colony by the persons assignd below this

Thos. Wootton

Everton Kennerly

Quintin Dines

his
Isaah X Curd
mark

Henry J. Pair

George A Kerr

J Tinnin

James Farmer

his
John X Wilson
mark

[Endorsed:] A general Agreement between Robertson,
Thomson & others.

A general agreement between Alex Thompson [Thomson]
Sterling C. Robertson & others upon emigrating to Texas.

---

[1]Sutherland Collection.

ANTONIO ELOSÚA TO FRANCISCO RUIZ[1]

[Translated from Spanish]

Office of the Principal Commandant)   [November 29, 1830]
)
of Coahuila and Texas_____)

In an official letter dated the 24th of the present month I wrote Citizen Severo Ruiz, Captain of the Álamo Company, as follows:

"The Most Excellent Commandant General Inspector of these States, in an official letter dated the 30th of October last," etc.

And I am copying it for you for your information and guidance.

God and Liberty. Béxar, November 29, 1830.

[Antonio Elosúa]

To the Military Commandant of Tenoxtitlan.

---

[1]BA Roll 136, Frame 0607.

STEPHEN F. AUSTIN TO JOSÉ DE LAS PIEDRAS[1]

[Translated from Spanish]

[November 29, 1830]

[From Austin's Blotter, in file of June 5, 1830]

Official letter to Colonel José de las Piedras,

Commandant of the Frontier:

I have received from Your Lordship your official letter dated the 12th of the present month relative to the conduct of the immigrants from the North--Alexander T[h]omson, James Ledbetter, Thomas J. Wooton, John Sherman, and Everton Kennerly--which individuals, with others, passed that post with their families without the necessary passports and in defiance of the orders which Your Lordship had given them, and, supposing that they had entered this colony, Your Lordship begs me to warn them to return immediately so that they can leave the country.

None of the said individuals has come to this *villa* nor have they presented themselves to me as colonists of this establishment, or in any other manner whatsoever. I understand that they emigrated from the State of Tennessee as part of the families contracted by the Nashville Company to settle above the Béxar Road--that they left the country from which they came without knowing that their entrance was forbidden, that they have come in good faith with the intention of settling permanently in this country as adopted citizens under the Law of March 24, 1825, and that

they never intended to violate any law, nor to defy any
authority.

I believe it is true that the families are innocent
of any intention of violating the law. They thought that
the Nashville Company had the authority to introduce colonists into its enterprise. They have come under this
impression and under the direction of the agent of the said
company.

It seems, therefore, that the families are not to
be blamed, nor can one rightly say that the company is at
fault, or its agent, because the Government granted it full
and ample authority to introduce families, and the fact
that it has introduced them indicates that the company
thought its contract was still in force. In view of these
circumstances it seems that the conduct of the said families does not provide sufficient grounds for charging them
with having violated the law, for that would require that
one prove their intent to violate it, with the previous
knowledge that such a law existed. But this can be said
only up to the time of their arrival at that post, when
they learned from Your Lordship that they could not pass
on, and there is no doubt that they did a very bad thing in
passing that town during the night over roundabout roads,
after receiving orders from Your Lordship to halt. Without
desiring to take it upon myself to defend their case, I
beg Your Lordship to permit me to point out the unfortunate

and desperate situation in which they found themselves, according to what I have heard. They had traveled some 500 leagues overland with their families; their resources were almost exhausted; they had sold their possessions in the country from which they came and made all the preparations and calculations for establishing themselves in this one. Their only hope was to reach their destination before the rigorous winter set in, so they could build houses, cut down the brush, and clear off fields with which to support their families during the coming year, in a country unpopulated and lacking in resources, as is the case above the Béxar Road. Under such circumstances to return to the north, or to remain in the vicinity of Nacogdoches, meant ruin to them, and it is quite probable that they continued their journey because they were convinced that there was no other remedy or any other recourse, trusting to the humanity and justice of Your Lordship and the Government to support their case.

As soon as I can get in touch with Mr. Alexander Thomson I shall point out to him the bad step which he has taken, and I have no doubt that he will do everything possible to remedy it--and meanwhile I beg that Your Lordship will permit me to ask that, out of deference to the circumstances in the case, all possible leniency be extended to the said unfortunate immigrants by reporting the matter in their favor to your superior officers, and for that purpose Your Lordship may make such use of this official

letter as you consider appropriate.   God and Liberty.

Villa [of San Felipe] de Austin, November 29, 1830.

Stephen F. Austin   [rubric]

---

[1]Barker, *Austin Papers*, II, 545-546.

STEPHEN F. AUSTIN TO RAMÓN MÚSQUIZ[1]

[Translated from Spanish]

[November 30, 1830]

For the purpose of providing myself with what I need for travel expenses, etc., from this *villa* to the Capital [Saltillo] in order to go to take possession of my position as Deputy in the Honorable Congress of the State, I beg Your Lordship to be so good as to issue me a draft, on the administrator of taxes on stamped paper in this *Villa*, for 250 or 260 pesos which he tells me he owes to the State, and, for the rest that I have coming to me for travel expenses, Your Lordship will make it available to me in any way that you deem best.

According to the calculation that I have made, it is 270 leagues from this *Villa* to the Capital, which, at the rate of 10 *reales* for each league, amounts to a sum of three hundred and thirty-seven pesos and 4 *reales*. I shall leave the arrangement of this matter to you, in case my ideas are mistaken.

On the 15th day of next month I shall begin my journey to the Capital, for which reason I must beg Your Lordship to be so good as to take care of the aforementioned matter by return mail.

God and Liberty.

Villa of [San Felipe de] Austin, November 30, 1830.

Estevan F. Austin

[rubric]

To the Chief of the Department,)
)
Citizen Ramón Músquiz   )

---

[1]BA Roll 136, Frames 0616-0617. The entire letter, except for the signature, is in the handwriting of Samuel M. Williams. A draft copy of this letter, in Spanish, was published in Barker, *Austin Papers*, II, 548. Incidentally, the "administrator of taxes on stamped paper" was none other than Samuel M. Williams.

STEPHEN F. AUSTIN TO RAMÓN MÚSQUIZ[1]

[Translated from Spanish]

[November 30, 1830]

[From Austin's Blotter, in file of June 5, 1830]

Official letter to the Chief of the Department, Citizen

Ramón Músquiz, concerning the prisoners Ingram and

League.

On the 2nd day of the month of September last a
difficulty occurred in the street of this town between Seth
Ingram and H. H. League against John G. Holtham in which
the latter was killed with a pistol bullet by Ingram.
Holtham was also armed with pistols. League was accused as
an accomplice in the death of Holtham because he was with
Ingram. The cause of the difficulty was that the deceased
had posted lampoons on the door of the Alcalde's office,
announcing to the public that Ira Ingram, Seth's brother,
was a coward, a rogue, and a man without honor, etc. It
seems that the motive which stimulated Holtham to this measure was that some time earlier he had gone into Ira
Ingram's yard gate drunk, and Ingram kicked him out.
Holtham wrote to Ira Ingram demanding satisfaction, and I
believe that it was well understood that the object was to
challenge Ira Ingram to a duel in case he should refuse to
give satisfaction of any kind. Then Holtham posted lampoons against Ira Ingram, and his brother, Seth Ingram, met
Holtham in front of the house where he had posted one of

the said lampoons, and he ordered him to take it down, which Holtham refused to do. The fight followed, and Seth Ingram killed Holtham. As a consequence Seth Ingram and League have been imprisoned in irons from that time until now. The Alcalde refuses to release them on bond because he has his doubts as to whether that would be legal or not. The case has not been concluded, due to the lack of a translator,[2] according to what the Alcalde told me day before yesterday, and it appears that for the same reason it will take many months, perhaps years, to finish it, if they continue the same system of administering justice which now prevails. There is no jail nor any other way of guarding them except by using the civil militia, and they had been using this method until the militia refused to serve, and there is no other remedy except to impose excessive fines against a very large number of militiamen, and collect them by force, or to send the prisoners to Béxar to that jail, or to release them on bond. They could make bond with the best men there are in the colony, both from the point of view of property as well as their other qualities, and I am convinced that nobody has any suspicion that either of the prisoners will try to escape. These prisoners are not vagabonds. Holtham was, but that is no excuse for having killed him. I do not think there is a better man than Seth Ingram anywhere in the colony. The other fellow, League, has few friends, almost none, and the reason is that he is very hot-headed by nature, and it has been his custom to curse almost everybody. I do not approve of his conduct in any way. The question is: Are these men to be kept in chains forever, or could the Alcalde put them at liberty under bond. I have told the Alcalde that I thought he ought to designate a definite place where they are to stay and take a strong bond stipulating that they shall not leave there without an order from the Alcalde. I desire the opinion of Your Lordship so that I can give information to the Alcalde so that he can dispose of this matter in the best way for the general welfare, and in order to comply with the law and justice. God and Liberty. Villa [of San Felipe] de Austin, November 30, 1830.

Stephen F. Austin   [rubric]

---

[1] Barker, *Austin Papers*, II, 547-548. There is another copy of this document in Austin's own handwriting, in Spanish, in BA Roll 136, Frames 0618-0619. For the background of this case, see McLean, *Papers*, IV, 453-456.

[2] Any serious student of Texas history, if he has seen the hundreds and hundreds of pages written in very fluent Spanish by both Stephen F. Austin and Samuel M. Williams, may wonder why one of them did not offer to serve as translator in this case. A possible explanation is found in Noah Smithwick's *The Evolution of a State*, page 82, where he says: "... at the period at which we have arrived, Austin had been divested of every semblance of authority; his colony being under the domination of a ring, the leader of which had skipped his bonds in Alabama to avoid prosecution on a criminal charge, bringing with him all his personal property and leaving his friends to mourn his departure to the tune of several thousand dollars."

This same source gives more details concerning the relationship between League and the Ingrams, explaining that "the Ingram brothers, Seth and Ira, had a store, with them being associated Hosea H. League, a lawyer by profession, who with his wife lived near by. League later formed a law partnership with David G. Burnet, their office being in the immediate vincinity."--*Ibid.*, p. 56.

Smithwick also makes it easy to visualize the place where Ingram and League were chained to the wall:

"The alcalde's office was in a large double log house standing back some distance from the main thoroughfare almost immediately in the rear of the Whiteside Hotel, which building it much resembled. By whom it was built, or for what purpose, I do not now remember, but my impression is that it was designed for a hotel. The walls of hewn logs were roofed in and abandoned at that stage. It was here the ayuntamiento held its sittings, and this windowless, floorless pen, through the unchinked cracks of which the wild winds wandered and whistled at will, was presumably the Faneuil Hall of Texas."--*Ibid.*, p. 57.

As for the shooting scrape itself, Smithwick disposes of it in a very few words as follows:

"There was a lawyer who had a penchant for dueling, to which men paid no attention. He sent a challenge to a merchant with whom he had trouble. The challenged party made no reply and the challenger proceeded to post him as a coward. A brother of the man who was being thus maligned, ordered him to take down the poster, and upon his refusal he was shot dead."--*Ibid.*, p. 80.

J. U. EVANS TO STERLING C. ROBERTSON[1]

Camp Contentian   [Entered under] Nov [30] 1830
Majr. Roberson

        To avoid further deficualties I take this method to
Let you know that I have understood whilst I was on the
other side of the river you abused me in a manner not even
becoming a master to his servant. This is not the first
offence of the kind but I hope it will be the Last I wish
you to understand that I am not used to Such language &
that I am as free & as respectable a man as your honor and
have recd as much of your abuse as I can bare & for the
future I wish you to have nothing more to do with me pass
me as you did the first time you saw me I depend on you
for nothing[2] nor neither do I wish you to depend or ask any
thing of me unless you are possessed [of] honor enough to
make gentlemanly acknowledgements before the company you
gave me the last abuse
I am at A Thomsons Esqr Service I beleive him to be a
gentleman & will go any length for him to do anything to
forward or advance his buisness.

                              J. U. Evans

        [Addressed:] Sterling C Roberson   Present

---

[1]Harllee Collection.

[2]See "Agreement of Jesse M. [or U.?] Evans with
Sterling C. Robertson and Alexander Thomson," June 28,
1830, in McLean, *Papers*, IV, 225-226.

ÁLAMO DE PARRAS PRESIDIAL COMPANY[1]

[Translated from Spanish]

[December 1, 1830]

Budget showing the amounts due the individuals of said company in the present month, after deducting for invalids and pensions.

Officers	Pesos	R.	G.	Pesos	R.	G.
1 Captain-----------------------------------	117.	6.	0.			
1 Lieutenant---------------------------------	62.	6.	6.			
1 First *Alférez*----------------------------	47.	0.	10.	.266.	7.	6.
1 Second Ditto-------------------------------	39.	2.	2.			

Enlisted Men						
2 Sergeants-------at 29ps. 1r.-----------	58.	2.	0.			
1 Bugler-------------------------------------	11.	5.	6.			
6 Corporals---------------------------------	145.	5.	0.	1.185.	7.	0.
50 Privates---------------------------------	970.	2.	6.			

Invalids Added						
1 Private------------------------------------	8.	0.	0.			

Gratification						
				. 48.	3.	7.
For the men---------------------------------	40.	3.	7.			

Rewards for Constancy						
1 at 260 reales----------------------------	32.	4.	0.			
1 at 90 reales----------------------------	11.	2.	0.			
1 at 9 reales----------------------------	1.	1.	0.	. 47.	1.	0.
3 at 6 reales----------------------------	2.	2.	0.			

Credit for Additions   # 1.548. 3. 1.

None.

Deduct for Losses

Deduct from this amount 30 pesos that
are being received by the family of the
Captain of said Company in Monterrey
for the present month--------------------. 30. 0. 0.

From José Chacón, who died on the 13th
of November, for 18 days that he did not

serve in the said month, deduct----------. 15. 0. 0. ⎫ . 63. 7. 6.

From the same, deduct the reward of 260
reales for the 18 days that he did not
serve----------------------------------. 18. 7. 6. ⎭

1.484. 3. 7.

Add to this amount the pay of Chaplain
Don Juan Nepomuceno Ayala, who is
serving as attaché in this Company--------------------   . 40. 0. 0.

NET ASSETS---# 1.524. 3. 7.

Tenoxtitlan, December 1, 1830.

O. K.   Santiago Navayra

[Severo] Ruiz   [rubric]

[rubric]

---

[1]BA Roll 136, Frames 0671-0672. There is a duplicate copy in
Frames 0672-0673.

ANTONIO ELOSÚA TO MANUEL DE MIER Y TERÁN[1]

[Translated from Spanish]

Office of the Principal Commandant)   [December 2, 1830]
)
of Coahuila and Texas_____)

Most Excellent Sir:

In the terms which Your Excellency was pleased to instruct

me, in your superior official letter dated the 9th of

November last, and as soon as we know the day which the

Government of this State has designated, the Chiefs and

Officers who are under my orders will wear the mourning

which, by supreme order, is to be worn because of the death

of His Majesty George IV, King of the United Kingdom of

Great Britain. I am reporting this to Your Excellency by

way of making an attentive reply.

God and Liberty. Béxar, December 2, 1830.

[Antonio Elosúa]

To the Most Excellent Commandant General

Replies that, as he has been ordered to do, the Chiefs and

Officers under his command will wear the mourning that is

supposed to be worn according to the supreme order occa-

sioned by the death of His Majesty George IV.

---

[1]BA Roll 136, Frames 0747-0748. Elosúa forwarded
this order to the Companies of Ríogrande, Aguaverde, and
Bavia, to the Military Commandants of Nacogdoches, Lavaca,
La Bahía, and Tenoxtitlan, and to the Major of the Plaza at
Béxar, on December 2, 1830.--Ibid., Frame 0751. Since
George IV had died on June 26, 1830, we can see that it
took more than five months for the news to reach Texas.

ANTONIO ELOSÚA TO THE MILITARY COMMANDANTS OF NACOGDOCHES,

LAVACA, LA BAHÍA, AND TENOXTITLAN[1]

[Translated from Spanish]

[December 2, 1830]

Office of the Principal Commandant)
)
of Coahuila and Texas_____)

The Most Excellent Commandant General Inspector of
these States, in a superior official letter dated October 1
last, has been pleased to write me as follows:

"Confidential.=The Most Excellent Secretary of War
and Navy, in an official letter dated August 31 last has
been pleased to write me as follows: 'Most Excellent Sir:
=Under this date I am writing the Commandant General of
Veracruz,' etc."

And I am copying it for your information and compliance.

God and Liberty. Béxar, December 2, 1830.

[Antonio Elosúa]

To the Military Commandants of Nacogdoches, Lavaca, La
Bahía, and Tenoxtitlan.

---

[1]BA Roll 136, Frame 0752.

ARTICLES OF AGREEMENT BETWEEN ROBERTSON & THOMSON

AND WILLIAM W. FORD[1]

[December 2, 1830]

[Articles of agreement made and entered into] this

2nd day of December one [thousa]nd eight hundred and thirty

between St[erling] C Robertson of the county of Davidson,

state of Tennessee, and [Alex]ander Thomson of the county

of Giles and both of [th]e State of Tennessee of the one

part and William W Ford of the County of Marengo and State

of Alabama of the other part   (Witnesseth)

The Said Robertson & Thomson agrees & binds themselves to

[con]vey unto the said Ford one hundred acres of Land for

each and every Famaly that the said Ford may Influence to

Imigrate Settle and remain in the Nashville Grant in the

state of Co[a]h[u]ila & Texas and c[o]mply with these pre-

sent terms of colo[niz]ing said grant so as to enable the

said Rober[tson and] Thomson to obtain & p[erf]ect a title

to [a league of land in virtue of said se]ttlem[ent under

the Mexican R]epublic and [said Robertson and Thomson] binds

themselves to convey unto the said [Ford] One thousand

acres of land provided he the s[ai]d Ford settles a Famaly

by the 15th of April next or so as to inable them the said

Rober[t]son & Thompson to obtain & perfect a title to a

League [of] Land in virtue of said Settlement and the said

Ford binds himself to convey unto the said Rober[t]son &

Thomso[n] the remainder of said Leag[u]e of Land after

reserv[in]g to himself the said one thousand acres of

La[nd.]   ...tle Should ... in his ... the said ... name or

his settlers In testi[mon]y whereof we have her[e] unto set

our hands and af[f]ixed our Seals this day and date above

mentioned.

Signed sealed &c   S. C. Robertson (Seal)

In the presents of   Alexr. Thomson (Seal)

J. U. Evans   Wm. W. Ford (Seal)

        [Endorsed:] Articles Between Rober[t]son & Thomson

& Wm. W. Ford

---

[1]Original in the Sterling C. Robertson Papers, The
University of Texas Archives, Austin. These papers passed
down through Sterling Clack Robertson's son, Elijah Sterling
Clack Robertson, to E. S. C.'s daughter, Mrs. Cone Johnson
(nee Eliza Sophia "Birdie" Robertson), and from her to her
niece, Mrs. William Curry Harllee, who deposited them for
safekeeping at UT-Austin.

ARTICLES OF AGREEMENT BETWEEN ROBERTSON & THOMSON

AND TANDY WALKER[1]

[December 2, 1830]

Articles of Agreement made and entered into this

2nd day of December in the year of our Lord one Thousand

eight hundred and thirty between Sterling C Robertson of

the county of Davidson and State of Tennessee and Alexander

Thomson of the county of Giles and State aforesaid of the

one part and Tandy Walker formaly from the county of Perry

and State of Alabama and now an Inhabitant of the State of

Co[a]h[u]ila and Texas and the grant of the Nashville Com-

pany of the other part.   (Witnesseth)

That the said Rober[t]son and Thomson binds themselves to

convey unto the said Walker his heirs or assigns one Thou-

sand acres of Land whereon the said Walker now resides to

be layd off as the said Walker may request and to pay all

expences pretaining to obtaining said title Which Said

Walker for and in consideration of the said one thousand

acres of Land agrees and binds himself to continue on said

primacies or tract [of] land so as to inable Said Rober[t]-

son & Thomson to obtain and perfect a title to a league of

land in virtue of Said settlement under the Mexican Republic

and Should the Said title come out in the name of the said

T[an]dy Walker he the said (Tandy Walker) for and in con-

sideration of the said one thousand acres of Land and the

expences of obtaining a title to the same Binds himself

heirs and assigns to convey to the Said Rober[t]son and

Thomson the remainder of said League after resurve[y]ing

the above named one thousand acres And the Said Robertson

and Thomson further agrees and binds themselves to convey

to the said Tandy Walker his heirs &c. one hundred acres

of Land for each and every Famaly that he the said Walker

may Introduce in said colony through his influence and

cause to remain so as to Enable the said Rober[t]son &

Thomson to obtain and perfect a title to a Leag[u]e of

Land in virtue of each famaly Settlement In Testimony

whereof we have hereunto Set our hands and af[f]ixed our

seals this day & date above written

Signed in the presents of   S. C. Robertson (Seal)

J. U. Evans   Alexr. Thomson (Seal)

                                   Tandy Walker (Seal)

        [Endorsed:] Agreement between Robertson & Thomson

& Tandy Walker

---

[1]Original in the Sterling C. Robertson Papers, The
University of Texas Archives, Austin. Published in Harllee,
Kinfolks, III, 2823, 2825.

        Although Tandy Walker was already residing on land
in the Robertson Colony area in 1830 when this contract was
made, the only land that he received title to in Texas
before the Texas Revolution was 1 league in Stephen F.
Austin's Second Colony, in present Grimes County, which he
received on April 27, 1831.

        For genealogical information concerning Tandy
Walker, see Worth S. Ray, *Austin Colony Pioneers. Includ-
ing history of Bastrop, Fayette, Grimes, Montgomery and
Washington Counties, Texas* (Austin: The Pemberton Press,

Jenkins Publishing Company, 1970), p. 232.

There is an article in *A Memorial and Biographical History of McLennan, Falls, Bell and Coryell Counties, Texas* ... (Chicago: The Lewis Publishing Company, 1893), pp. 850-851, which mentions Jessie Walker, a daughter of Tandy Walker.

L. W. Horton, in his article entitled: "General Sam Bell Maxey: His Defense of North Texas and the Indian Territory," *Southwestern Historical Quarterly*, Vol. LXXIV, No. 4 (April, 1971), pp. [507]-524, mentions a "Tandy Walker's Choctaw Brigade."

In view of the span of years involved between these various dates, it is possible that there may have been more than one person named Tandy Walker.

FRANCISCO RUIZ TO ANTONIO ELOSÚA[1]

[Translated from Spanish]

Office of the Military Commandant)   [December 3, 1830]
)
of Tenoxtitlan_____)   No. 39.

With the greatest regret I see myself in the difficult situation of having to report to Your Lordship the pitiful
condition of the party of 40 men who came from the Béxar
Company to reinforce this Detachment. From the 15th of
November last up to the present they have been maintained
with only two pesos for each individual, which it was possible to obtain under my responsibility, while at the same
time it finds itself at an advanced post where there is no
capitalist whatsoever or any inhabitant capable of being
able to help with anything for them to live on. For this
reason on this very day they do not have a thing to eat,
and they are incapable of rendering any service whatsoever,
being exposed to commit grave offenses, and even abandoning
the camp. For these reasons from this day forward I remain
free of any responsibility which I may be charged with in
the future with respect to the security of this new establishment, the subordination and discipline appropriate for
the military, for it is not within my power to achieve all
the interesting objectives which have been entrusted to me,
with subordinates who breathe nothing but the necessity
which surrounds them on all sides, with me having to suffer

as an eyewitness to the sad state which they present in the midst of their misery, for, although it might be said that hunting could, in part, cover their insufferable need, the poor condition of what few horses they have, and the rough terrain, does not afford them this consolation. Finally, Your Lordship will please permit me to tell you, with the greatest respect, that if, within ten or twelve days, at the least, the said party does not receive some supplies, I shall have no other alternative than to have them march to that city [Béxar], rather than give them an opportunity to do inevitable harm, for I have the well founded fear that, if they do not receive help in the very near future, the Álamo Company may, in part, do likewise. All of which I regret to report to Your Lordship for your information and superior decision.

God and Liberty. Tenoxtitlan, December 3, 1830.

Francisco Ruiz

[rubric]

To the Principal Commandant of)
)
Coahuila and Texas, Colonel   )
)
Don Antonio Elosúa._____)

---

[1]BA Roll 136, Frames 0770-0772.

ALEXANDRO TREVIÑO TO ANTONIO ELOSÚA[1]

[Translated from Spanish]

Béxar Presidial Company   [December 3, 1830]

In the allotment made by the Commissariat of this City on
this date, there has fallen to the lot of this Company
under my command, the sum of one thousand and one hundred
pesos. With this sum I need to take care of the Detachment
at Tenoxtitlan, to complete their pay for the past month,
of which they have received only one half, and the pay that
they have coming for the present month, according to the
order given by Headquarters, to the effect that we should
take care of them first because they are located at a post
where they have no other assistance. These two sums amount
to five hundred and nineteen pesos.

In addition to this, I have to pay, without fail,
three hundred pesos, which is the cost of the seeds that
they have let me have on credit in order to support the
company during the past month, when it did not receive anything, and all that I have left is just two hundred and
eighty-one pesos with which to help the rest of the company
that is located here, and the families of those who are on
detached service.

All of which I am reporting to Your Lordship for
your superior information.

God and Liberty. Béxar, December 3, 1830.

                                        Alexandro Treviño

                                          [rubric]

To the Principal Commandant,)
)
Colonel Don Antonio Elosúa__)

_____

        [1]BA Roll 136, Frames 0835-0836.

REFUGIO DE LA GARZA TO ANTONIO ELOSÚA[1]

[Translated from Spanish]

[December 3, 1830]

The paymaster of the Tenoxtitlan Company is resisting, unjustly, the payment of the amount owed by the soldiers of same, as appears in the documents issued by the paymaster himself.

I hope, I beg you to be so good as to order that on this very day payment be made of the total amount stated in the promissory note, for my obligations are such that they are carrying me to the extreme of feeling that my honor has been offended, and consequently I am unable to avoid causing you this trouble.

God and Liberty. Béxar, December 3, 1830.

Refugio de la Garza

[rubric]

To Lieutenant Colonel   )
)
Citizen Antonio Elosúa.)

---

[1]BA Roll 136, Frames 0837-0838.

JUAN NEPOMUCENO DE AYALA TO ANTONIO ELOSÚA[1]

[Translated from Spanish]

[December 3, 1830]

I am attentively enclosing for Your Lordship a list of what
is needed, both for the Holy Sacrifice of Mass and for the
administering of the Sacraments, at the new military establishment of Tenoxtitlan, so that, if Your Lordship should
consider it appropriate, you may get in touch with the
Priest of this City and get him to provide said articles
free of charge.

  God and Liberty. Béxar, December 3, 1830.

          Juan Nepomuceno de Ayala

           [rubric]

To the Principal Commandant, Citizen)
)
Colonel Antonio Elosúa_____)

List of Ornaments and Sacred Vessels that are needed for
the Sacrosanct Sacrifice of Mass and the administering of
the Sacraments in the new Parish of Tenoxtitlan.

  1 white chasuble, one flesh-colored, and one mulberry-colored.
  1 black cape
  1 alb [priest's white linen robe]
  1 altar cloth
  1 missal [Mass book]
  1 altar
  1 hand bell
  1 very small vial for the holy oil for the sick
  2 ditto for the oil of the catechumens and holy
   chrism

Béxar, December 3, 1830.

Juan Nepomuceno de Ayala

[rubric]

---

[1]BA Roll 136, Frames 0839-0840. We are indebted to Sister M. Dolores Kasner, Catholic Archives of Texas, North Congress & 16th Street, Austin, Texas, for checking our translation of the Catholic terminology used in this document.

ANTONIO ELOSÚA TO REFUGIO DE LA GARZA[1]

[Translated from Spanish]

Office of the Principal Commandant)   [December 3, 1830]
)
of Coahuila and Texas_____)

    The Chaplain from the La Bavia Company, Citizen
Presbyter Juan Nepomuceno Ayala, assigned by Superior
Authority to the military post at Tenoxtitlan, in an offi-
cial letter dated today writes me as follows:

    "I am attentively enclosing for Your Lordship a
list of what is needed, both for the Holy Sacrifice of
Mass," etc.

    And I am forwarding it to you, inserting a copy of
the note, so that, if you think it appropriate for the welfare of the troops and the other individuals located at
that post, you will be so good as to make available the
ornaments and sacred vessels requested by the said Chaplain,
either as a loan or in any other way that seems most appropriate to you.

    God and Liberty. Béxar, December 3, 1830.

                                   [Antonio Elosúa]

To the Parish Priest of this City,)
)
Citizen Refugio de la Garza.   )

---

[1]BA Roll 136, Frames 0841-0842.

RAMÓN MÚSQUIZ TO JOSÉ MARÍA VIESCA[1]

[Translated from Spanish]

Office of the Political Chief)   [December 5, 1830]
)
[of the Béxar Department]   )

No. 279.

Most Excellent Sir:

I happened to find out that abuses were committed by the Alcalde of Nacogdoches, Citizen Vicente Córdova, and the First *Regidor* of that Ayuntamiento, Citizen Luis Procela, in drawing up the case that is being prosecuted against Don Juan Antonio Padilla, accused of complicity in the assassination executed upon the person of Preciliano Fuentes. Therefore I requested information from Colonel Citizen José de las Piedras, Military Commandant of that frontier.=This Chief, who has given evidence of the best sentiments which incline him in favor of the law and good administration of justice at that post, complying with my request, ordered a report drawn up, the original of which I am respectfully enclosing for Your Excellency so that you can be so good as to inform yourself as to whether, in fact, the legal formulas have been followed in drawing up the case against Don Juan Antonio Padilla; whether, either through ignorance or malice, the Alcalde allowed the accused to question himself in the preliminary examination; whether, by a special commission conferred upon the First *Regidor*, in violation of Article 170 of the State Constitution, the latter has made

himself the judge in the case, and has released on bond the
said Don Juan Antonio Padilla, against whom charges have
been made that he was the author of the death of Fuentes.
Consequently there must be grounds for bringing to bear the
second part of Article 184 of the said Constitution, which
was explained in Article 107 of Reglamentary Law No. 39,
and, finally, Your Excellency will see from said infraction
that both the Alcalde and the *Regidor* turn out to be
accused of prevarications which they have committed against
the strict administration of justice by protecting the
crime committed against the public welfare, which is interested in correcting or punishing the real criminals, and
therefore, complying with the duty imposed upon me by
Article 76 of Law No. 97 [?], dated June 13, 1827, I am
hereby reporting the matter to Your Excellency by means of
said report which contains facts which have been sufficiently documented concerning the injustices which I have
mentioned above.=God, etc. Béxar, December 5, 1830. R. M.
[Ramón Músquiz]=To the Most Excellent Governor [of Coahuila
and Texas].

Extract

Encloses a report drawn up against the Alcalde of Nacogdoches, in which it is evident that the First *Regidor* of
that Ayuntamiento has committed a prevarication in drawing
up the case against Don Juan Antonio Padilla, with a violation of Articles 170 and 184 of the State Constitution [of

Coahuila and Texas].[2]

---

[1]BA Roll 136, Frames 0887-0888.

[2]Our translation of Articles 170 and 184 appears below:

"Article 170. Every inhabitant of the state must be judged by competent tribunals and judges, established prior to the act which is being judged, and under no circumstances by a special commission nor under a retroactive law."

"Article 184. He who gives bond, in cases where the law does not expressly prohibit it, shall not be taken to jail, and, in any case where it may appear that corporal punishment cannot be imposed upon the prisoner, the latter shall be placed at liberty under bond."

--*Colección de constituciones de los Estados Unidos Mexicanos. Tomo I.* (México: Imprenta de Galvan á cargo de Mariano Arévalo calle de Cadena núm. 2, 1828), pp. 258, 261-262.

JOSÉ DE LAS PIEDRAS TO ANTONIO ELOSÚA[1]

[Translated from Spanish]

Office of the Military Commandant   [December 5, 1830]

of the Frontier

By virtue of the order of the Most Excellent Commandant

General, Chaplain Don Ignacio Galindo[2] is beginning his

journey today to incorporate himself into his Company.   I

am reporting this to you for your information.

            God and Liberty. Nacogdoches, December 5, 1830.

                                José de las Piedras

                                        [rubric]

To Colonel Don Antonio   )
)
Elosúa, Principal Commandant   )
)
of Coahuila and Texas   )

---

[1]BA Roll 136, Frames 0876-0877. Elosúa acknowledged receipt of the Piedras letter on December 29, 1830.
--BA Roll 136, Frame 0881.

[2]Ygnacio Galindo, born about 1792, had been listed
as a priest in Nacogdoches in the census records of 1828
and 1829.--Carolyn Reeves Ericson, *Nacogdoches--Gateway to
Texas, A Biographical Directory, 1773-1849* (Fort Worth:
Arrow/Curtis Printing Company, Publishing Division, 1974),
p. 56.

On November 9, 1830, José Ignacio Galindo had filed
an application in Nacogdoches, Texas, for eleven leagues of
land, but he did not receive the grant until April 13, 1833,
so the main documents concerning that transaction will be
entered under the latter date. These eleven leagues,
located in the Robertson Colony area, were distributed as
follows: 9/10 in present McLennan County and 1/10 in present Falls County.--Taylor, *The Spanish Archives of the
General Land Office of Texas*, p. 187.

RAMÓN MÚSQUIZ TO THE GOVERNOR

OF COAHUILA AND TEXAS[1]

[Translated from Spanish]

Office of the Political Chief)   [December 6, 1830]
[of the Béxar Department]   )
No. 284   )

Most Excellent Sir:

In an official letter dated August 30 of this year, which I inserted for Your Excellency in my official letter No. 211 of September 25 last, Citizen Hosea H. League, agent of the Nashville Company for establishing a colony in this Department, reported that, in the coming year and during this winter the aforesaid company was going to send, from the State of Tennessee, three hundred honorable families to settle the land transferred to it by Empresario Leftwich. Some of them have arrived at the said point and have encountered a difficulty in that the military commandant of the new establishment of Tenoxtitlan on the bank of the Brazos River has informed them that he has an order from the Most Excellent Commandant General of said states not to permit the introduction of families belonging to the aforementioned enterprise, as indicated by the author of the letter written in the English language and in the translation,[2] the originals of which I am forwarding to the superior hands of Your Excellency, hoping that in reply you will tell me what to do so that I can transmit your decision to these families or to their agents, in case they should file a claim for the damages which of necessity must result for them if they are prevented from emigrating to the points of colonization contracted for with the Government, upon whose good faith they have undertaken long and difficult journeys with the expectation of improving their own interests. ...

God, etc. Béxar, December 6, 1830.

To the Most Excellent Governor, etc.

Extract

Relative to a communication from the agent of the Nashville Company inserted in official letter No. 211 of September 25. Encloses a letter written in English with a translation of same indicating the arrival of some 8 families of those contracted for the said enterprise, and their difficulty in not being admitted arises from an order which the military commandant of the new establishment of Tenoxtitlan has concerning said subject. Asks how he can satisfy the agent of said families in case they should file a suit for damages.

---

[1]Translated from a typescript in the Nacogdoches Archives, Texas State Library, Austin. Original not seen.

[2]Sterling C. Robertson to Ramón Músquiz, November 13, 1830.

ANTONIO ELOSÚA TO FRANCISCO RUIZ[1]

[Translated from Spanish]

Office of the Principal Commandant)   [December 6, 1830]

)

of Coahuila and Texas_____)

By your official letter dated the 3rd of the present month
I have been informed of everything you report therein concerning the shortages being suffered by the forty men of
the Béxar Company who are now stationed at that post, and
the Álamo de Parras Company, as well as of the measures
which you suggest that you will take if I do not send them
help within ten or twelve days, and in reply I must tell
you that tomorrow, without fail, *Alférez* Citizen Santiago
Navayra is departing for that post, carrying the funds for
the Álamo Company and the supplies for the picket from
Béxar. You should not doubt that in the future we will
continue to forward the necessary supplies to that post in
order to decrease all the sufferings. Meanwhile I urge you
to use all your zeal and efficiency to preserve that important post, at all costs, by exhorting the troops who garrison it to remain loyal, with the understanding that the
merit which you are earning for your Country with your honorable sufferings will be duly appreciated. And I conclude
by assuring you that, as far as I am concerned, I shall
continue sending in reports at the appropriate time to
headquarters so as to provide the rest of the assistance

needed in order to take care of their needs.

     God and Liberty. Béxar, December 6, 1830.

                          [Antonio Elosúa]

To the Military Commandant of Tenoxtitlan.

---

[1]BA Roll 136, Frames 0772-0773.

ANTONIO ELOSÚA TO RAMÓN MÚSQUIZ[1]

[Translated from Spanish]

[December 7, 1830]

Office of the Principal Commandant

of Coahuila and Texas

Colonel Citizen José de las Piedras, Commandant of the Frontier at Nacogdoches, in an official letter dated November 12 last, has been pleased to write me as follows:

[Here he quotes the letter. See text under November 12, 1830.]

I am forwarding it to Your Lordship for your information and so that you may take such measures as you deem appropriate with reference to the aforementioned individuals.

God and Liberty. Béxar, December 7, 1830.

Antonio Elosúa

To the political Chief,

Citizen Ramón Músquiz

---

[1]Translated from a typescript in the "Nacogdoches Archives," Vol. 53, pp. 76-78, The University of Texas Archives, Austin. Original in the Nacogdoches Archives, Texas State Library, Austin.

ANTONIO ELOSÚA TO JOSÉ DE LAS PIEDRAS[1]

[Translated from Spanish]

Office of the Principal Commandant)   [December 7, 1830]
)
of Coahuila and Texas_____)

I have reported to the Most Excellent Commandant General
Inspector of these States, for his information and superior
decision, everything that Your Lordship reported to me in
your official letter dated November 12 last concerning the
illegal manner in which the foreigners Alexander Thomson,
Santiago [James] Ledbetter, Thomas Sherman, and Everton
Kennerly have introduced themselves, according to reports,
headed for the Villa of [San Felipe de] Austin with their
families, and I have sent an official letter to the Citizen
Political Chief of this Department so that he will be so
good as to take the proper measures concerning said individuals. I am reporting this to Your Lordship in reply.

God and Liberty. Béxar, December 7, 1830.

[Antonio Elosúa]

To the Commandant of the Frontier at Nacogdoches.

---

[1]BA Roll 136, Frame 0943.

EXCERPT FROM THE MINUTES OF THE AYUNTAMIENTO

OF SAN FELIPE DE AUSTIN[1]

[December 7, 1830]

...

The Ayuntamto. then ... further ordered ... that Samuel M. Williams be and is hereby invested with the office of Secretary of the Ayuntamto with the salary of Eight hundred dollars per annum, and that the said Williams be allowed for the services which he has rendered as Secretary pro tem. from the time he commenced up to the present at the same rate, to wit at the rate of 800$ per year which salary and services are to be paid him out of the funds of the Municipality.[2]

...

---

[1]Eugene C. Barker (ed.), "Minutes of the Ayuntamiento of San Felipe de Austin, 1828-1832," VII, in *The Southwestern Historical Quarterly*, Volume XXIII, Number 1 (July, 1919), pp. 69-77. The passage quoted appears on p. 76.

[2]On April 6, 1830, Samuel M. Williams had applied to the State Government of Coahuila and Texas for a grant of an additional seven leagues of land on the grounds that, among other things, he had performed the duties of Secretary of the Ayuntamiento of San Felipe for two years, without salary. He received title to the seven leagues on December 28, 1831, as we shall see later. The question which naturally arises, therefore, is whether he was paid twice for the same servies: once "out of the funds of the Municipality," as stipulated in these minutes, and once with land from the public domain, as evidenced by the grant of the seven leagues on December 28, 1831. For the answer see the excerpt from the minutes of December 31, 1830.

VICENTE CÓRDOVA TO RAMÓN MÚSQUIZ[1]

[Translated from Spanish]

[December 7, 1830]

NACOGDOCHES COURT

No. 196

On the 1st day of the current month I was notified
by José María Hernández, a resident of Béxar, that he had
learned, from a resident of this town [Nacogdoches], whom I
did not summons because he happened to be at a great distance from here, that some wagons with foreign families,
individuals who have not presented themselves in this Court,
had passed by, and they are entering the country by a
roundabout road. Consequently, in order to avoid this
abuse, I sent an official letter to the Military Commandant
of this Frontier asking for help, and he sent back word by
an officer under his command, to the effect that he was
ready to furnish such assistance as I might need, provided
that I needed infantry, but that, if I needed cavalry, I
should furnish him animals on which to mount them, since
they were all afoot. In view of the difficulties which
arose, I sent out an order which was to be carried from one
house to the next until we could learn whether we could
succeed in getting these individuals to return and present
themselves in this Court. We know nothing of the results
up to this date. I am reporting this information to Your
Lordship so that, if you consider it appropriate, you may

send it by messenger to Mr. Stephen F. Austin so that, in case these individuals should present themselves in that colony, they may be made aware of the error which they have committed, and so that they may be examined as required by the law governing the matter.

God and Liberty. Nacogdoches, December 7, 1830.

Vicente Córdova

[Rubric]

To the Political Chief of the

Béxar Department

---

[1]Nacogdoches Archives, Texas State Library, Austin. For the reply of Músquiz, see below, January 25, 1831.

RAMÓN MÚSQUIZ TO VICENTE CÓRDOVA[1]

[Translated from Spanish]

Office of the Political Chief)   [December 8, 1830]
[of the Department of Béxar])

By the last mail I made a report to the Most Excellent

Governor of the State, enclosing the documents in the case

drawn up by the Military Court of that Town by order of the

Citizen Commandant of the Frontier, as a result of my ask-

ing him for a report concerning the abuses or violations of

the law that might have been noticed as having been commit-

ted by you in documenting the case drawn up against Don

Juan Antonio Padilla, and, since the customary procedure is

to handle the case as provided by law, you must wait until

the proper authority makes the charges against you for the

faults indicated therein, since all that this Office is

supposed to do in such cases is to make a report, with the

respective documents, concerning the abuses and violations

of the Law which the judicial authorities may have commit-

ted in the exercise of their functions. All of which I am

reporting to you in reply to your confidential official

letter dated November 23 last, in which you ask me for a

transcript of the aforementioned information.

        God, etc. Béxar, December 8, 1830.

                                        [Ramón Músquiz]

To the Citizen Alcalde of Nacogdoches.

---

[1] BA Roll 136, Frame 0485.

RAMÓN MÚSQUIZ TO STERLING C. ROBERTSON[1]

[Translated from Spanish]

[December 9, 1830]

... *[From the xerox copy that we have before us, it appears that the top three inches of the original document must have been so badly stained that they would not copy clearly. The remaining fragment, as best as we have been able to decipher it, reads as follows:]*

1st. Bearing date of September 25 relative to whether the admission of families contracted by the Nashville Company is opposed to the spirit of the Law of April 6. [See text in McLean, *Papers*, IV, 546-547.]

2nd. Dated November 13 last enclosing for him the original of the explanation by Sterling C. Robertson wherein he states that the Military Commandant of the new establishment at Tenoxtitlan has orders not to admit the families contracted by the said Company.

All of which I am transcribing for you for your information and in reply to the letter from you dated the [13th] of November last ... with which this Headquarters earned the scorn shown by you and the other families who accompanied you, by order of the Military Commandant of the Frontier at Nacogdoches, and that all the persons who immigrated with you must remain subject to whatever is decided in the matter by the Most Excellent Commandant General ... .

God and Liberty. Béxar, December 9, 1830.

[Ramón Músquiz]

To Sterling C. Robertson.

---

[1]Original in drawer marked: "1830 Dec. 9-31,"
Nacogdoches Archives, Texas State Library, Austin, Texas.

ANTONIO ELOSÚA TO MANUEL DE MIER Y TERÁN[1]

[Translated from Spanish]

Office of the Principal Commandant)   [December 9, 1830]
)
of Coahuila and Texas _____)

Most Excellent Sir:

I have already received, from Citizen Assistant
Commissar of Lavaca, Rafael Chovell, the plan which is to
be used in building the fort at Tenoxtitlan, to which place
I have forwarded it. I am reporting this fact to Your
Excellency in reply to your official letter dated November
18 last.

God and Liberty. Béxar, December 9, 1830.
To the Most Excellent Commandant General

He replies that he has received, and forwarded to
Tenoxtitlan, the plan which is to be used in building the
fort.

---

[1]Volume 53, p. 119, Spanish Archives, General Land
Office, Austin, Texas.

FRANCISCO RUIZ TO ANTONIO ELOSÚA[1]

[Translated from Spanish]

Office of the Military Commandant)   No. 40.
)
at Tenoxtitlan_____)   [December 9, 1830]

With the sole object of escorting Citizen Anastacio Mansolo,
who brought an oxcart loaded with freight for the Álamo
Company, twelve men from the said Company and the Picket
from Béxar, including one corporal, are going to that city
[Béxar], all of which I am reporting to Your Lordship for
your satisfaction and superior information.

        God and Liberty. Tenoxtitlan, December 9, 1830.

                                        Francisco Ruiz

                                           [rubric]

To the Principal Commandant)
)
of Coahuila and Texas,   )
)
Colonel Don Antonio Elosúa_)

_____

    [1]BA Roll 136, Frame 0966.

SEVERO RUIZ TO ANTONIO ELOSÚA[1]

[Translated from Spanish]

Álamo de Parras   )   [December 9, 1830]
)
Presidial Company.)

Last night three privates belonging to the Béxar Company deserted, taking with them three horses belonging to individuals in the Company under my command. I beg Your Lordship to be so good as to order that they [the horses] be gathered up and deposited in the herd of horses at Béxar, if perchance they should arrive at that City

God and Liberty. Tenoxtitlan, December 9, 1830.

Severo Ruiz

[rubric]

To the Principal Commandant)
)
of Coahuila and Texas,   )
)
Colonel Don Antonio Elosúa.)

---

[1]BA Roll 136, Frame 0970. Notice that Severo Ruiz respects the delicate line of authority by giving orders concerning only the *horses*; the *men* who deserted belonged to the Béxar Company, not the one commanded by Ruiz. However, from a practical point of view, this document leaves several things to be desired. For instance, what were the names of the men, and what were the colors, marks, brands, and numbers of the horses?

SEVERO RUIZ TO ANTONIO ELOSÚA[1]

[Translated from Spanish]

Álamo de Parras)   [December 9, 1830]
)
Company_____)

The former Armorer of this Company, Antonio Salazar, is now departing for that City [Béxar], taking advantage of the opportunity afforded by the escort for the oxcarts that are returning. He is not carrying his permit because I have to wait for the arrival of the paymaster, who is expected soon, in order to record it properly. I am reporting this to Your Lordship for your guidance, and so that the interested party will not suffer any harm for lack of that credential, which will be forwarded to him in due time.

God and Liberty. Tenoxtitlan, December 9, 1830.

Severo Ruiz

[rubric]

To the Principal Commandant)
)
of Coahuila and Texas,   )
)
Colonel Don Antonio Elosúa.)

---

[1]BA Roll 136, Frames 0971-0972.

LEANDRO AGUILAR TO THE SUBALTERN COMMISSAR AT BÉXAR[1]

[Translated from Spanish]

Subaltern Commissariat)   [December 9, 1830]
)
at Monterrey_____)

We have, in this office under my supervision, the three
certificates crediting the documents made for Captain Don
Severo Ruiz in the months from July up to the end of September, at the rate of thirty pesos per month, which his
wife, Doña María del Refugio, received from this commissariat, and I hope, in view of your efficiency, you will continue to handle the matter the same way for the subsequent
months. I have the honor of answering your official letter
concerning this matter, dated November 22 last.

        God and Liberty. Monterrey, December 9, 1830.

                                        Leandro Aguilar

                                        [rubric]

To the Subcommissar)
)
at Béxar_____)

_____

    [1]BA Roll 136, Frames 0962-0963.

STERLING C. ROBERTSON TO JOHN LUKER: DEED TO 101 1/2 ACRES

OF LAND IN GILES COUNTY, TENNESSEE

[December 9, 1830]

CERTIFIED COPY

Sterling C Robertson   for 101 1/2 acres of land in
Deed to   Giles County
John Luker   Registered the 24th March, 1831

This Indenture made and entered into this ninth day of

December 1830 by and between Sterling C Robertson one of

the heirs of Elijah Robertson deceased of the State of

Tennessee Davidson County of one part and John Tucker

[Luker] of Giles County of said State of the other part

Witnesseth that for and in consideration of the sum of

Fifty dollars to me in hand paid by the said John Luker the

receipt whereof is hereby acknowledged has this day bar-

gained sold aliened conveyed and confirmed to him the said

John Luker his heirs and assigns forever, a certain tract

or parcel of land lying and being in the County of Giles in

the said state and granted by the state of North Carolina

to Thomas Polk by grant number _____ and conveyed by

said Polk to the heirs of Elijah Robertson and bounded as

follows to wit:

Beginning at a sugar tree Joseph Lukers south west corner

running from thence North with said Lukers west boundary

line one hundred and sixteen poles[1] to a chestnut said

Lukers North West corner, thence West one hundred and forty

poles to a dogwood on the top of a ridge thence south one

hundred and sixteen poles to two hickories near a spring on the road leading from Robert Gordons to Huntsville, thence East to the Beginning containing by estimation one hundred and one acres and a half. It being a part only of the of the aforementioned grant _____. To have to hold the aforesaid land and bargained premises with all and singular the rights uses benefits emoluments and appurtenances to the only proper use behoof and benefit of him the said John Luker his heirs and assigns forever. And I the said Sterling C Robertson one of the heirs of Elijah Robertson deceased for my myself my heirs executors administrators and assigns do and forever will warrant and defend the right of said land against all and every person or persons whatsoever in any wise lawfully claiming the same. In testimony whereof I have set my hand and seal on the day and date above written.

                                        S C Robertson   (Seal)

In presence of

Alexander Thompson [Thomson]

James Ledbetter

State of Tennessee

Giles County S ct. Circuit Court February Tern 1831

        Then was the within deed of conveyance from Sterling C Robertson to John Luker produced in Court and the execution thereof proven by the oaths of Alexander Thompson

[Thomson] and James Ledbetter the Witnesses thereto and ordered to be certified for registration. In testimony whereof I have hereunto set my hand and affixed my private seal there being no seal of office at office in Pulaski the 9th day of March, 1831.

(SEAL)   S. H. Lester Clk

STATE OF TENNESSEE

COUNTY OF GILES

        I, Thurman P. Bass, Register in and for the State and County aforesaid, do hereby certify that the foregoing instrument is a true, perfect and complete copy of the Deed from Sterling C Robertson to John Luker, as the same appears of record in Deed Book "H" page 451, in my said office.

        Given under my hand and official seal this the 7th day of November, 1969.

                        [Signed:]   _____
                                        Thurman P. Bass

                                    Thurman P. Bass,

                                    County Register

My commission expires September 1, 1970.

[Impressed seal:] SEAL
                   REGISTER OF DEEDS.
                   GILES COUNTY, TENN.

---

        [1]"POLE: 5 1/2 yards or 16 1/2 feet; also called *perch* or *rod*."--*The Researcher's Guide to American Genealogy, By Val D. Greenwood. With an Introduction by Milton Rubicam* (Baltimore: Genealogical Publishing Co., Inc., 1973; Fourth Printing, 1977), p. 291.

RAMÓN MÚSQUIZ TO ANTONIO ELOSÚA[1]

[Translated from Spanish]

Office of the Chief of the   [December 10, 1830]

Béxar Department

In the next to the last mail from the frontier I received notice from Sterling C. Robertson, communicated from Tenoxtitlan under date of November 13 last, advising me of his arrival at that post with the nine families referred to by Colonel José de las Piedras in his official letter of the 12th of said month, which Your Lordship was pleased to forward to me under date of the 7th of the present month.

The said Sterling says nothing in his communication about the furtive way in which they passed Nacogdoches, contrary to the instructions of Mr. Piedras, because they had not come with the things required by law, and because the Law of April 6 has impeded the immigration of Anglo Americans, for he only refers to the fact that said families belong to the colony contracted for by Empresario Leftwich and transferred by him to the Nashville Company, and to the fact that Lieutenant Colonel Francisco Ruiz, the commander of that post, has prevented them from settling, according to orders which he has from the Most Excellent Commandant General, for which reason, and because I was unaware of the circumstances under which they had entered, I made a report to the Most Excellent Governor of this

State, for his information, asking him to clear up for me
certain doubts which I had as to the true meaning of the
aforesaid Law of April 6, in the part which speaks of
established colonies, and those which, by virtue of the
contracts made by Empresarios like Leftwich's and others,
are to be established.[2] For these reasons, and because the
said nine families happen to be in a place which is not
under the jurisdiction of this office, I find myself
deprived of the authority to do anything about the just
excitement of Colonel José de las Piedras, but Your Lordship in this matter will do whatever you may consider proper, since it happened at a post under your jurisdiction.

I have the honor of reporting this information to
Your Lordship by way of a reply, and to repeat to you my
expressions of attention and esteem.

God and Liberty. Béxar, December 10, 1830.

Ramón Músquiz

To the Principal Commandant of this

Department, Colonel Antonio Elosúa.   A copy.

---

[1]Volume 54, pp. 284-284 verso, Spanish Archives,
General Land Office, Austin, Texas. There is also a typed
copy in the "Nacogdoches Archives," The University of Texas
Library, Austin. A copy of this document, made by J. M.
Guerra, Matamoros, December 31, 1831, is in the Nacogdoches
Archives of the Texas State Library, Austin.

[2]See above, Ramón Músquiz to José María Viesca,
December 6, 1830.

STERLING C. ROBERTSON TO PEYTON ROBERTSON: DEED TO

2 1/2 ACRES OF LAND NEAR THE NASHVILLE GRAVEYARD

[December 10, 1830]

[Marginal note:]   Peyton Robertson of Sterling C.

Robertson: a Deed for 2 1/2 acres of land on Browns Creek

near the Nashville Grave Yard

Registered January 21=1831

This Indenture made this tenth day of December in the year

of our Lord one thousand eight hundred and thirty between

Sterling C. Robertson of Davidson County and State of

Tennessee of the one part and Peyton Robertson of County of

Davidson & State of Tennessee on the other part: Witnesseth

that Sterling C. Robertson for and in consideration of the

sum of six hundred & twenty-five dollars to him in hand

paid by the said Peyton Robertson the receipt whereof is

hereby acknowledged hath given, granted, bargained sold

aliened conveyed and confirmed and by these presents doth

give grant bargain sell alien convey and confirm unto the

said Peyton Robertson his heirs and assigns forever a cer-

tain tract piece or parcel of land situate lying and being

in the County of Davidson and State of Tennessee on the

south side of Cumberland river on the waters of Browns

Creek Beginning at a post on the west side of the Hunts-

ville road and Thomas Spences line and runs south 88 1/2

west twenty and two tenth poles to a very small elm on the

line of the Nashville Graveyard tract thence south fifteen

poles and eight tenths to a stake thence north 88 1/2
degrees east thirty and a half poles to a stake on the margin of the Huntsville road, thence with the Huntsville road
to the beginning containing two acres and a half be the
same more or less To Have & To Hold the aforesaid land with
all and singular the rights profits emoluments heredita-
ments and appurtenances of in and to the same belonging and
in any way appertaining to the only proper use benefit and
behoof of the said Peyton Robertson heirs and assigns forever and the said Sterling C. Robertson for himself, heirs
executors and administrators do covenant and agree to &
with the said Peyton Robertson, heirs or assigns that the
before recited land bargained premises he will warrant and
forever defend against the right, title interest or claim
of all & every person or persons whomsoever. In witness
whereof the said Sterling C. Robertson has hereunto set his
hand & affixed his seal the day & year first above written.

Sterling C. Robertson (Seal)

By his attorney in fact E. B. Robertson

Signed sealed & delivered in purview of State of
Tennessee Davidson Circuit Court November Term 1830

Probate

This Indenture of bargain and sale between Sterling C.
Robertson by his attorney in fact Eldridge B. Robertson of
the one part & Peyton Robertson of the other part was

acknowledged in open court by the said E. B. Robertson as attorney as aforesaid to be his act & deed and ordered to be registered ....

[Endorsed:] I, Felix Z. Wilson II, Register for Davidson County, hereby certify that the foregoing is a true and correct copy of the *Warranty Deed* from *Sterling C. Robertson* to *Peyton Robertson* as same appears of record in my office in book No. *S*, page *756*, witness my official signature at office this *15th* day of *July*, *1968*

Felix Z. Wilson, II

Register of Davidson County

By *Allen Lantz*

Deputy Register

[*The following entry, although taken from a different source, probably concerns the document reproduced above:*]

[December 15, 1830]

An Indenture of bargain & sale between Eldredge B. Robertson attorney in fact for Sterling C. Robertson of the one part and Peyton Robertson of the other part was acknowledged in open Court by Said Eldredge B. attorney as aforesaid to be his act and deed and ordered to be Registered.[1]

---

[1]Davidson County, Tennessee, Circuit Court Minutes, Microfilm Roll 524, Books F-G, 1826-1831, Book G, Page 360, Wednesday morning, December 15, 1830.

ANTONIO ELOSÚA TO MANUEL DE MIER Y TERÁN[1]

[Translated from Spanish]

[December 11, 1830]

Office of the Commandant General
Inspector of the Interior States of the East.

Office of the Principal Commandant)
)
of Coahuila and Texas._____)   No. 430

Most Excellent Sir:

        Colonel Citizen José de las Piedras, Commandant of

the Frontier at Nacogdoches, in an official letter dated

November 12 last, writes me as follows:

        [Here he quotes the letter from Piedras. See copy

under November 12, 1830.]

        Which I am forwarding to Your Excellency for your

superior information and decision. I am enclosing the

original of the reply which I have received from the Poli-

tical Chief of this Department as a consequence of having

sent him a copy of this same official letter, adding that I

understand that those individuals are the same ones whose

arrival at Tenoxtitlan was reported to Your Excellency by

official letter on the 9th and 19th of November last.

        God and Liberty. Béxar, December 11, 1830.

                                    Antonio Elosúa

To the Most Excellent Commandant)
)
General of these States._____)

[1]Volume 54, pp. 139-141, "Nacogdoches Archives,"
The University of Texas Library, Austin. A copy of this
document, made by J. M. Guerra, Matamoros, December 31,
1830, is in the Nacogdoches Archives, Texas State Library,
Austin. Elosúa's rough draft for forwarding this letter is
in BA Roll 136, Frames 1022-1023.

FRANCISCO RUIZ TO ANTONIO ELOSÚA[1]

[Translated from Spanish]

[December 13, 1830]

Office of the Military Commandant

of Tenoxtitlan   No. 41

With the greatest satisfaction I have received the official letter from Your Lordship dated November 13 last in which you were pleased to insert for me the one from the Most Excellent Commandant General Inspector of these States, dated October 12 last, and, having taken note of its contents, I wish to inform you that I did not receive the Plan and model which you mention for the construction of the fort which is to be built at this post,[2] and consequently I am waiting for it to be sent to me so that I can carry out what was ordered by Your Excellency in your aforementioned superior order. Please consider this as my reply to the official letter from Your Lordship cited above.

God and Liberty. Tenoxtitlan, December 13, 1830.

Francisco Ruiz

[Rubric]

To the Principal Commandant of Coahuila and)
)
Texas, Colonel Antonio Elosúa.   )

---

[1]Volume 53, pp. 138-138 verso, Spanish Archives, General Land Office, Austin, Texas.

[2]However, the plan and model did arrive later. See Ruiz to Williams, December 26, 1830.

ALEXANDRO TREVIÑO TO ANTONIO ELOSÚA[1]

[Translated from Spanish]

Béxar Presidial Company   [December 13, 1830]

Francisco Uriegas, the Private from this Company who
deserted from the detachment at Tenoxtitlan, presented himself night before last in the barracks [here], but, from his
enclosed declaration it will be noted that he did not have
any basis for the reasons he gives for having committed
this offense, and since this is the first time that he has
deserted, he deserves a punishment of four months cleaning
up the barracks. Therefore it has seemed best to me, if
Your Lordship is in agreement, for this individual to set
out immediately for that post [Tenoxtitlan], where he has
duties to perform with the picket from this Company which
is stationed there.

God and Liberty. Béxar, December 13, 1830.

Alexandro Treviño

[rubric]

To the Principal Commandant,

Colonel Don Antonio Elosúa.

---

[1]BA Roll 137, Frames 0006-0007. No enclosure was
found with this letter.

STEPHEN F. AUSTIN TO GOVERNOR ECA Y MÚSQUIZ[1]

[Translated from Spanish]

[December 14, 1830]

[From Austin's Blotter, in file of June 5, 1830]

(official letter)

I have had the honor to receive the official communication which Your Excellency was pleased to send me under date of the 12th of the past month of November, transcribing for me the petition of Messrs. Villaveque and Company of Paris, and Messrs. Villaveque and Brothers, with the map on which have been outlined the lands which they are requesting in order to settle them with European families.

Tomorrow I shall set out on the road to that capital, and, since it is my intention to speed up my journey so as to arrive on January 1, I do not have enough time to answer the aforesaid communication from Your Excellency with the necessary precise examination of the map, in the presence of the contracts already made by the Government with various Empresarios for parts of the same territory designated by Messrs. Villaveque. For this reason, and also because I need some data concerning the contracts already made with other Empresarios which I can obtain only in the archive of that Government or from the copies brought by Commissioner General Juan Antonio Padilla, which are all in Nacogdoches (according to what I have heard), I find myself forced to carry the said communication from

Your Excellency with me to that capital, in order to draw up my report more accurately.

Up until now I have not received any copies of the map of Texas which I compiled, and which was published in Philadelphia, but I have received news of the arrival of a little schooner which they say has the maps on board, and I have dispatched a courier to bring them. He is due to return tomorrow, and, in case he gets them, I shall bring with me the number of copies which you indicate. One of my principal objects in ordering these copies (which is all the remuneration I am to receive for the manuscript copy which I compiled) was to have some to present to the State and National Governments, as a manifestation, although far short of my desires, to reward, as far as I can, the public service with an increase in the geographical knowledge of this part of the republic.

God and Liberty.

Villa [of San Felipe] de Austin, December 14, 1830.

Stephen F. Austin

To the Most Excellent Governor of
the State of Coahuila and Texas.

---

[1]Barker, *Austin Papers*, II, 554-555.

MANUEL DE MIER Y TERÁN TO ANTONIO ELOSÚA[1]

[Translated from Spanish]

Office of the Commandant General   [December 15, 1830]
Inspector of the Eastern Interior States.

The Most Excellent Secretary of War and Navy, in a superior note dated the 18th of the month just past, has been pleased to write me as follows: "Most Excellent Sir:=The Most Excellent Vice President has been informed of Your Excellency's official letter No. 460, dated October 11 last, in which you were pleased to give a report on the results of an expedition sent from Béxar against the Tahuacano and Hueco Indians, and he has instructed me to tell Your Excellency that he approves all the measures taken in this matter, and he wants you to convey the most expressive thanks of the Supreme Government to the officers who have had a part in these events, assuring them that they will be kept in mind in the future because of their good conduct and military honor, which His Excellency values so highly. This is a reply to your aforementioned note, which he has forwarded to the Most Excellent Secretary of Foreign Relations so that he can dictate such measures as lie within his jurisdiction." I am transcribing the foregoing for Your Lordship for your information and for the information of the citizen officers and enlisted men who composed the said section.

God and Liberty.   Matamoros, December 15, 1830.

M. Mier y Terán

[rubric]

To the Citizen Principal Commandant)
)
of Coahuila and Texas, Colonel   )
)
Antonio Elosúa._____)

[Marginal note:] This was copied into the general order of
the day for the satisfaction of the garrision, and particularly for those individuals who took part in the expedition.

Elosúa

[rubric]

---

[1]BA Roll 137, Frames 0085-0086.

ANTONIO ELOSÚA TO RAMÓN MÚSQUIZ[1]

[Translated from Spanish]

Office of the Principal Commandant) [December 15, 1830]
)
of Coahuila and Texas._____)

In view of the reasons which Your Lordship was pleased to report to me in your official letter dated the 2nd of the present month, I ordered that Private Jesús Rocha, of the Béxar Company, should be punished for the act of insubordination which he has committed, and he has gone on to Tenoxtitlan to suffer the punishment which he deserves. I am reporting this to Your Lordship by way of making an attentive reply.

   God and Liberty. Béxar, December 15, 1830.

          Antonio Elosúa

           [rubric]

To the Political Chief,)
)
Citizen Ramón Músquiz.)

---

  [1]BA Roll 137, Frame 0091. Elosúa's rough draft of this letter is in Frame 0092.

ANTONIO ELOSÚA TO FRANCISCO RUIZ[1]

[Translated from Spanish]

Office of the Principal Commandant)   [December 17, 1830]
)
of Coahuila and Texas_____)

    The twelve men from the troops of that garrison who have come to this City [Béxar] escorting Citizen Anastacio Mansolo, as you informed me in your official letter dated the 9th of the present month, are returning to that post, all of which I am reporting to you by way of reply.

    God and Liberty. Béxar, December 17, 1830.

                                     [Antonio Elosúa]

To the Military Commandant of Tenoxtitlan.

---

[1]BA Roll 136, Frame 0967.

ANTONIO ELOSÚA TO SEVERO RUIZ[1]

[Translated from Spanish]

Office of the Principal Commandant)   [December 17, 1830]
)
of Coahuila and Texas._____   )

      I have been informed of everything that you reported to me in your official letter dated the 9th of the present month concerning the coming to this City of Citizen Antonio Salazar, former Armorer of that Company under your command, whose permit you promise to forward to him at the first opportunity.

      God and Liberty. Béxar, December 17, 1830.

                    [Antonio Elosúa]

To the Captain of the Álamo Company.

---

[1]BA Roll 136, Frame 0972.

ANTONIO ELOSÚA TO ALEXANDRO TREVIÑO[1]

[Translated from Spanish]

Office of the Principal Commandant)   [December 17, 1830]
)
of Coahuila and Texas._____)

It is all right with me for Francisco Uriegas, the Private who deserted from that Company under your command, to return to the detachment at Tenoxtitlan to suffer there the punishment stipulated by law for deserting the first time, and for this reason I am returning to you, with my decree, the deposition of this individual, which you sent me with the official letter dated the 13th of the present month, which I am now answering.

God and Liberty. Béxar, December 17, 1830.

[Antonio Elosúa]

To the Captain of the Béxar Company.

Béxar, December 17, 1830

Decree.=Send Private Francisco Uriegas back to the detachment at Tenoxtitlan, from which he deserted, so that there he may suffer the four months of cleaning up the barracks which is stipulated for him by law for deserting for the first time, and file this deposition.

---

[1]BA Roll 137, Frames 0153-0154.

ANTONIO ELOSÚA TO SEVERO RUIZ[1]

[Translated from Spanish]

Office of the Principal Commandant)   [December 17, 1830]
)
of Coahuila and Texas._____)

I have been informed of the fact that, on the night of
the 8th day of the present month, three Privates from the
Béxar Company deserted, according to what you reported to
me in your official letter dated the 9th of the same month,
and, despite the fact that you did not tell me who they
were, I must tell you, in reply, that Francisco Uriegas,
who, according to the way I understand it, was one of them,
presented himself in this City and has already been sent
back to that post, and the same will be done with the
others, if they present themselves here or are apprehended.

God and Liberty. Béxar, December 17, 1830.

[Antonio Elosúa]

To Captain Citizen Severo Ruiz.

---

[1]BA Roll 137, Frame 0159.

ON THE NEXT TWO PAGES WE ARE REPRODUCING A

FACSIMILE COPY OF WHAT PURPORTS TO BE A

POWER OF ATTORNEY ISSUED BY SAMUEL M.

WILLIAMS TO STEPHEN F. AUSTIN IN SAN FELIPE

ON DECEMBER 17, 1830, BUT LATER AUSTIN HAD

TO WRITE WILLIAMS AND TELL HIM HOW THE

DOCUMENT WAS MADE OUT. THE ORIGINAL HAS

BEEN STOLEN FROM THE STATE ARCHIVES IN

SALTILLO, SO WE ARE REPRODUCING THIS FAC-

SIMILE TO FACILITATE IDENTIFICATION AND

DENUNCIATION OF THE DOCUMENT WHENEVER IT

SURFACES FOR SALE IN THE UNITED STATES.

> --Photos by BRUCE AUSTIN, *from a
> photostatic copy on file in
> the Archives of the University
> of Texas at Austin.*

POWER OF ATTORNEY FROM SAMUEL M. WILLIAMS

TO STEPHEN F. AUSTIN[1]

[Translated from Spanish]

[December 17, 1830]

971   175

SELLO SEGUNDO: DOCE REALES.

HABILITADO POR EL ESTADO DE COAHUILA Y TEXAS PARA EL BIENIO
DE 1828 Y 29.   [Added in manuscript:]   30 y 31[2]
                                    Williams
                                    [rubric]

In the *Villa* of San Felipe de Austin on the seventeenth day

of the month of December of 1830, before me, the Citizen

Thomas Barnett, Constitutional Alcalde of this Jurisdiction,

appeared the Citizen Samuel M. Williams, resident and

Administrator of Mails for this *Villa*, and he said that he

gives and grants a power of attorney, as ample and general

as is legally required, to the Citizen Esteven [Stephen] F.

Austin, Deputy in the Honorable Legislature of this State,

so that in his name he may present himself before the

Supreme Government of the State, and may propose and cele-

brate, for his constituent [*i.e.*, the one who gave him the

power of attorney] a contract, or contracts, for the colo-

nization of foreign families, or others, with the said

Supreme Government, in conformity with the Colonization Law

of this State dated March 24, 1825, or in conformity with

any other law which in the future may be promulgated by the

Honorable Congress and Supreme Government, to which end,

and in order that the powers of his agent may extend as far

as necessary in order to smooth out the circumstances which

may arise, the grantor confers upon his agent free, unre-

stricted, general, and ample power to do, by virtue thereof,

everything that he could and would do for himself if he

were present.[3]=Therefore, in order to hold securely what-

ever his agent may do, and in order that it may be used for

legal purposes whenever and wherever he sees fit, he is

signing it with me, and before my attendant witnesses,

> [*At this point in the original, although there was
> room for at least two more lines of text, the writer
> went on to the next page, where he started about an
> inch and a quarter from the top. Then he filled in
> the unused space, at the bottom of the first page
> and at the top of the second, with wavey lines and
> curlicues.*]

972   176

with whom I am acting in the absence of a notary public,

for there is none in this *Villa*, all of which I certify.=

Samuel M. Williams.=Witness: Manuel Vidal.=Witness: Robert

Taylor jr._____

This agrees with its original which remains on file in this

Archive under my supervision, from which it was

ordered taken at the verbal request of the interested

party. It has been faithfully corrected, and the Citizens Thomas Westall and C. C. Givens, in addition to myself, were present to see it copied, corrected, and proofread, all of which I certify.

Villa of [San Felipe de] Austin,

December 17, 1830.

Thos. Barnett

[rubric]

Witness: Witness:

Manuel Vidal   Robert Taylor jr.

[rubric]

---

[1]This certified copy was originally on file on pp. 971-972 of *Expediente* 1061, *Legajo* 25, Archivo de la Secretaría de Gobierno del Estado, Saltillo, Coahuila, from which I copied it in 1940, but, when I went back to check it on July 11, 1967, it had disappeared. However, there is a photostatic copy on file in the "Saltillo Archives," Vol. XXX, pp. 175-176, The University of Texas Archives, Austin.

[2]Since the original of this document has been stolen from the State Archives in Saltillo, we have left these lines in the original Spanish in order to facilitate the identification and recovery of this item whenever it surfaces and is offered for sale. In English they would read as follows: "SECOND SEAL: TWELVE REALES. VALIDATED BY THE STATE OF COAHUILA AND TEXAS FOR THE BIENNIUM OF 1828 AND 29. 30 and 31."

[3]Opposite this point, in the righthand margin of the original, there was a penciled note written vertically which said: "Original bad." There are heavy black spots over about 20 lines, making them very difficult to read. This note was probably added by the photostat operator to explain why the copy was so poor.

RAMÓN MÚSQUIZ TO THE GOVERNOR

OF COAHUILA AND TEXAS[1]

[Translated from Spanish]

Office of the Political Chief,   [December 19, 1830]
etc.
No. 291.

                    Most Excellent Sir:

I am forwarding, to the superior hands of Your Lordship,

five applications from the [following] inhabitants of the

town of Nacogdoches: Citizen Atanacio de la Cerda, Pres-

byter [?] Carlos Ocampo,[2] Ignacio Carrillo, and H. Rueg,

asking that there be adjudicated to them the lands which

they are asking for, some as settlers and others as pur-

chasers.=God, etc. Béxar, December 19, 1830.=To the Most

Excellent Governor.

                    Extract:

Encloses five applications from the [four] individuals whom

he names, asking that the lands which they are requesting

be adjudicated to them.

---

[1]BA Roll 137, Frame 0192.

[2]Carlos Ocampo received a grant for 5 leagues of
land in the Robertson Colony area, in present McLennan
County, from Commissioner Luke Lessassier on October 19,
1833. The other three applicants (Atanacio de la Cerda,
Ignacio Carrillo, and H. Rueg) did not receive any land in
Texas under the Mexican Government. The fifth application
may have been for the 6 leagues granted to Carlos Ocampo by
Commissioner Radford Berry, Alcalde of Nacogdoches, on
December 16, 1835, but the titles that Berry issued were
lated voided by the Texas constitution of 1836.--Taylor,
Spanish Archives, pp. 57, 222.

MANUEL DE MIER Y TERÁN TO ANTONIO ELOSÚA[1]

[Translated from Spanish]

Office of the Commandant General   [December 20, 1830]
and Inspector of the Eastern Interior States.

      The official letters from Your Lordship numbered 394 and 408, and dated the 9th and 19th of November last, inform me of what the Citizen Commandant of the Tenoxtitlan Detachment told you about what was reported to him by the foreigner Sterling Robertson (who in the report of colonies granted by the Government of the State appears with the name of Robert Leftwich) to the effect that the families were about to arrive who were going to settle on the land where said detachment is located. Your Lordship may reply to the Commandant thereof that he should inform Robertson that colonization has been suspended by the Law of April 6 of this year, which excepts only the existing colonies, and Your Lordship will please report the same to the Citizen Political Chief of that Department, so that he can take such measures as may be necessary in order to comply with the said Law, by suspending the operations of said empresarios. I am reporting this information to Your Lordship by way of reply and for your information so that you may help to carry out said measures insofar as they may pertain to you.

      God and Liberty. Matamoros, December 20, 1830.

      M. Mier y Terán

[Rubric]

To the Citizen Principal Commandant of

Coahuila and Texas

[Endorsed in English:] Order of the Comdt. Genl.

of the Eastn. Internl. States, and Commissr. of the Genl.

Govt. of Mexico, to the Principl. Comdr. in Texas, at Bexar,

requiring him to issue his orders to the Military Comdt of

Tenoxtitlan on the Brazos, to prevent Sterling C. Robertson

from carrying the Colonization Contract of the Nashville

Colony into effect. The said Colonizn. Contract being

suspended by the provisions of the law of 6th April 1830.--

Rec'd from the Sec'y of State Austin 13th Octr.

1846.

Geo: Fisher,

Sp. Clk. G. L. Of.

[Spanish Clerk, General Land Office]

---

[1]Volume 54, pp. 283-283 verso, Spanish Archives,
General Land Office, Austin, Texas.

FRANCISCO RUIZ TO ANTONIO ELOSÚA[1]

[Translated from Spanish]

Office of the Military Commandant)   [December 22, 1830]
)
of Tenoxtitlan_____)   No. 42.

I have been informed, by Your Lordship's official letter dated November 29 last, concerning the coming of Presbyter Don Juan Nepomuceno Ayala to his assignment at this post, according to the orders of the Most Excellent Commandant General and Inspector of these States, as well as of what Your Lordship wrote to the Captain of the Álamo Company relative to the said Chaplain, in the official letter which you were pleased to insert for me in the one which I am attentively answering.

    God and Liberty. Tenoxtitlan, December 22, 1830.

    Francisco Ruiz

    [rubric]

To the Principal Commandant)
)
of Coahuila and Texas, Citizen)
)
Colonel Antonio Elosúa._____)

----

[1] BA Roll 137, Frames 0247-0248.

FRANCISCO RUIZ TO ANTONIO ELOSÚA[1]

[Translated from Spanish]

Office of the Military Commandant)   [December 22, 1830]
)
of Tenoxtitlan_____)   No. 43.

The superior official letter from Your Lordship dated the
2nd of the current month leaves me informed about the
mourning that the Citizens, Chiefs, and Officers must wear
because of the death of the King of Great Britain, George
IV, whenever the Government of this State issues the order,
and it will be duly obeyed. With the foregoing I am making
a respectful reply to your said official letter.

                God and Liberty. Tenoxtitlan, December 22, 1830.

                                        Francisco Ruiz

                                        [rubric]

To the Principal Commandant)
)
of Coahuila and Texas,   )
)
Colonel Don Antonio Elosúa.)

_____

        [1]BA Roll 137, Frame 0249-0250.

FRANCISCO RUIZ TO ANTONIO ELOSÚA[1]

[Translated from Spanish]

Office of the Military Commandant)   [December 22, 1830]
)
of Tenoxtitlan._____)   No. 44

The superior note from Your Lordship dated the 2nd of the
present month, in which you were pleased to insert for me
the note from the Most Excellent Commandant General of
these States, leaves me informed of the fact that Commandant
General Don Manuel Gómez Pedraza[2] had been forbidden to
enter the Republic, no matter where he tries to come in,
all of which, as far as I am concerned, will be punctually
obeyed, in case the said Chief should arrive at this post,
and I am reporting this fact to Your Lordship by way of
making an attentive reply.

        God and Liberty. Tenoxtitlan, December 22, 1830.

                                    Francisco Ruiz

                                        [rubric]

To the Principal Commandant   )
)
of Coahuila and Texas,   )
)
Citizen Colonel Antonio Elosúa.)

---

[1]BA Roll 137, Frames 0251-0252.

[2]Manuel Gómez Pedraza (1789-1851) had served as
Mexican Minister of War and Navy from January 8 to June 7,
1825, under President Guadalupe Victoria, and from that
Ministry he had prepared his campaign for the presidency,
as chief of the moderates. He opposed the candidacy of

General Vicente Guerrero, and even had the support of the majority of the state legislatures, but the revolution in Veracruz and the riot in the Acordada forced him to abandon Mexico City on December 3, 1829, and go abroad to live in France. He had returned to Mexico in October of 1830 but had been forced to re-embark for New Orleans, and from there the Mexican authorities were apparently expecting him to try to return through Texas.--*Diccionario Porrúa de historia, biografía y geografía de México*, 3d ed. (2 vols.; México, D. F.: 1970-71), I, 888.

FRANCISCO RUIZ TO ANTONIO ELOSÚA[1]

[Translated from Spanish]

Office of the Military Commandant)   [December 24, 1830]
)
 of Tenoxtitlan_____)   No. 45.

I received the superior communication which Your Lordship

was pleased to send to me with your note dated the 3rd of

the present month relative to the rules which are to be

observed in collecting the taxes on foreign goods, and the

excise tax on domestic items, and I am reporting this fact

to Your Lordship by way of making an attentive reply.

God and Liberty. Tenoxtitlan, December 24, 1830.

Francisco Ruiz

[rubric]

To the Principal Commandant   )
)
of Coahuila and Texas,   )
)
Citizen Colonel Antonio Elosúa.)

---

[1]BA Roll 137, Frame 0283.

FRANCISCO RUIZ TO ANTONIO ELOSÚA[1]

[Translated from Spanish]

Office of the Military Commandant)   [December 24, 1830]
)
of Tenoxtitlan_____)   No. 46.

I received the Sovereign Decree which Your Lordship was

pleased to send me with your note dated the 3rd of the cur-

rent month, relative to the establishment of a loan bank

for the development of national industry, and I am notify-

ing Your Lordship of this fact by way making an attentive

reply.

                God and Liberty. Tenoxtitlan, December 24, 1830.

                                        Francisco Ruiz

                                           [rubric]

To the Principal Commandant   )
)
of Coahuila and Texas,   )
)
Citizen Colonel Antonio Elosúa.)

---

[1]BA Roll 137, Frame 0284.

FRANCISCO RUIZ TO ANTONIO ELOSÚA[1]

[Translated from Spanish]

Office of the Military Commandant)   [December 24, 1830]
)
of Tenoxtitlan_____)   No. 47.

I received the Sovereign Decree approving the division of the State of Sonora and Sinaloa[2] which Your Lordship was pleased to send me with your note dated the 3rd of the present month, which I am attentively answering.

       God and Liberty. Tenoxtitlan, December 24, 1830.

                     Francisco Ruiz

                       [rubric]

To the Principal Commandant)
)
of Coahuila and Texas,)
)
Citizen Colonel Antonio Elosúa.)

---

[1]BA Roll 137, Frame 0285.

[2]In 1824 Sonora had been joined with Sinaloa, forming an entity which was called the "Estado de Occidente" ("Western State"), but, by a decree dated October 13, 1830, Sonora and Sinaloa were divided.--*Diccionario Porrúa*, 3rd ed., II, 2011.

FRANCISCO RUIZ TO ANTONIO ELOSÚA[1]

[Translated from Spanish]

Office of the Military Commandant)   [December 24, 1830]
)
of Tenoxtitlan_____)   No. 48.

I received the Sovereign Decree which speaks of the "Estado
de Occidente" ["Western State"] having been constitution-
ally divided, and of the Departments composing the State of
Sinaloa, and I am reporting this fact to Your Lordship by
way of making an attentive reply to your note dated the 3rd
of the present month, with which you were pleased to send
it to me.

        God and Liberty. Tenoxtitlan, December 24, 1830.

                                        Francisco Ruiz

                                        [rubric]

To the Principal Commandant   )
)
of Coahuila and Texas,   )
)
Citizen Colonel Antonio Elosúa.)

---

[1]BA Roll 137, Frame 0286.

FRANCISCO RUIZ TO ANTONIO ELOSÚA[1]

[Translated from Spanish]

Office of the Military Commandant)   [December 24, 1830]
)
of Tenoxtitlan_____)   No. 49.

We have on file in this military command the Sovereign

Decree relative to the charge that must be made to those

who ask for passports to enter or leave the Republic, also

for letters of safeconduct and certification of signature,

and I am notifying Your Lordship of this fact by way of

making an attentive reply to your note dated the 3rd of the

current month, with which you were pleased to send it to

me.

      God and Liberty. Tenoxtitlan, December 24, 1830.

                         Francisco Ruiz

                           [rubric]

To the Principal Commandant   )
)
of Coahuila and Texas,   )
)
Citizen Colonel Antonio Elosúa.)

----

[1]BA Roll 137, Frame 0287.

FRANCISCO RUIZ TO SAMUEL M. WILLIAMS[1]

[Translated from Spanish]

Tenoxtitlan, December 26, 1830

Mr. Samuel Wil[l]iams:

My most esteemed and fine friend:

By order of the Most Excellent Mr. Commandant General, Don Manuel de Mier y Terán, there is to be constructed at this post a fortified house, for which purpose he sent me the plan and model for same, but, since the plan is in Spanish and there is no interpreter here capable of translating it into English, nor do the Americans understand Spanish, I find myself in a difficult position to begin the work. For these reasons the bearer of this letter, whose name is *Alférez* Don Santiago Navayra, who has been commissioned to supervise the work, is going to that *villa* [San Felipe de Austin] for the purpose of troubling you, and I on my part beg you, to be so kind as to copy the plan or draft it in English, for which purpose he is carrying with him both the plan and the model. Also he is to look for a man capable of building the said house. I hope that you will tell him about some individual who can do it, and that you will use your influence to get him to take the job. In conclusion I repeat my request to you, and I hope you will give the aforesaid official the benefit of your knowledge, for by so doing you will render a service to your country as well as to me, for I have an interest in the project, and I find myself without the necessary knowledge for building fortifications. I shall be forever grateful to you for this service.

Please remember me to your wife and give her my most affectionate greetings, and for yourself receive the invariable affection which is professed for you by your true friend who loves you and kisses your hand.

Francisco Ruiz

[Rubric]

P. S. Please give my regards to our good friend Don Stephen [F. Austin], if he is still there. Valid.

---

[1]Samuel May Williams Papers, Rosenberg Library, Galveston, Texas. It is interesting to note that apparently Ruiz was going to employ Anglo Americans to build this fort whose purpose was to keep Anglo Americans out of Texas.

STEPHEN F. AUSTIN TO SAMUEL M. WILLIAMS[1]

Bexar 28 December 1830

Dr Sam,

I arrived here last evening, and shall leave the day after tomorrow by the upper road. I get an escort from here as far as Río Grande, and another from there to Saltillo--Madero[2] will leave in a few days for that place. I wish you to pay him all the attention you can. Shew him some of the deeds that are finished & explain the mode of translating the Surveyors returns &c--also the general plots--he is (I have no doubt) as true and warm a friend as the North Americans have--he is a devoted friend of Guerrero[3] and opposed to [Manuel de Mier y] Teran and the present administration--on subjects of this kind it is best to be silent unless directly questioned, in the latter case you will of course give prudent answers. The people of this place are, in heart, unanimously hostile to the present administration, and they are more friendly to the North American emigration than they ever were-- The state of affairs in Mexico is, if any thing, more unsettled than ever-- Teran I believe will not go to Mexico [City], & I think it not improbable that he may turn his course this way-- from what I can learn both Piedras and the General [Terán] are desirous to have a good standing with the settlers-- we ought to encourage this idea for we may derive much benefit from it, at least so far as to keep off harsh orders &c--

        I send you two hundred signatures, have certificates
printed over them verbatim like the others and fill them
up, all except the name[4]-- give as many to R. Williamson[5]
as he wants and send some to McGuffin[6] and some to Piedrass,
and some to Col Thorn[7]-- Try and have them printed at
night when no one is present, & take care that none of the
blanks get into other hands. let none know any thing of
this but Lesassier,[8] & Williamson--

        Settlers can get in with certificates from De Witt[9]
and he ought to have about 200 struck off & sent to Arkansa,
and Nachitoches &c--

        I presume you have heard all the news from Pettus &
Johnson, in this place there is Novidad de indios [reports
of Indians] every hour-- a large party were discoverd yesterday on Medina near the road.

        Arciniega[10] will be on by the 15 of next month try
and get the coast colony[11] out of the way by that time-- I
will write another letter by him & one by Madero both of a
public character, that is you can shew them if you think
proper, but this one, no person must see except Lesassier--

        There can scarcely be a more difficult thing than
to play a double game, it is dangerous, and it is at times,
a nice point to draw the distinction between such a game,
and dishonor-- we are so situated that we must keep a good
understanding with Teran and Alaman--[12] but at the same

time all our best friends at Saltillo & in Mexico [City]
are very hostile to both those men-- Silence, prudence,
and vigilince, must all be called in requisition-- I shall
have a dreadfull task at Saltillo= if I am compelled to
come out and take sides openly, I must go with the Viescas[13]
of course, in this event the whole pack with Licenciado
Aguirre at the head will open against me-- Tho, it is best
not to anticipate trouble, in two weeks after I get there
you shall hear what the prospect is--Viesca[14] has returned
to the Govt.-- this is a good sign-- I say nothing for,
nor against Zavala, very rigid orders have been issued by
Teran prohibiting the admission of Zavalas families[15]

        Keep peace & union at home. I shall not be idle
abroad. I have written to DeWitt to get 200 certificates
of the same kind of mine printed and signed by by [*sic*] him
and sent in blank to different places aid the poor fellow
along with it-- Chambers[16] has not yet arrived-- I cannot
concieve what detains him-- Pettus and myself partd on
such terms as I wish to be with all the settlers. I have
confidence in him now, & I think he has in me-- The Chiefs[17]
answer to Williamson will inform you what has been done in
his business-- a consulta with the Superioridad [higher
authority] & nothing can be done untill an answer is
obtaind

        attend to the printing of the certificates a[nd]
take care of my signature, dont put m[e] in the power of

the printer or his boys. I have written to Sastre[18] on

this subject.

remember me to Mrs Sweet[19]

--and Sarah[20]

Yours

S. F. Austin

Politnes [?] by Madero--

---

[1]Samuel M. Williams Papers, The Rosenberg Library, Galveston, Texas.

[2]Francisco Madero had been appointed General Land Commissioner of Texas on September 27, 1830, by Governor José María Letona to succeed Juan Antonio Padilla.--*Handbook of Texas*, II, 127. Padilla had been removed from office on April 6, 1830, on a charge of having a man murdered so that Padilla could enjoy the favors of the victim's widow.-- McLean, *Papers*, III, 60.

[3]Vicente Ramón Guerrero, President of Mexico, April 1, 1829--December 31, 1830.--*Handbook of Texas*, I, 744-745.

[4]A version of this letter, not quite as complete as the one reproduced here, was published in Barker, *Austin Papers*, II, 567-569, and at this point Dr. Barker inserted the following note: "For a copy of these certificates, which were intended to relieve immigrants from the embarrassments imposed by the law of Apr. 6, 1830, see Austin to Menard, Nov. 13, 1830." That was published in 1928. However, Mr. Streeter, in his *Bibliography of Texas*, expressed the opinion that "The form of certificate described in Austin's letter of November 13, 1830, to M. B. Menard ... was almost certainly not printed." For the complete text of Mr. Streeter's entry for the printed form of the certificate, see January 15, 1831. Meanwhile, on December 29, 1830, Austin wrote Williams as follows: "I sent you 200 signatures by Williamson, attend to that without delay."--Barker, *Austin Papers*, II, 569-570.

[5]Robert McAlpin Williamson, editor of a newspaper called the *Cotton Plant*, 1829-1831, in San Felipe de Austin. --*Handbook of Texas*, II, 917.

[6]Probably Hugh McGuffin, who was living midway between Natchitoches, Louisiana, and the Sabine River when Moses Austin made his trip to Texas in 1820.--*Handbook of Texas*, II, 113-114.

[7]Frost Thorn, a resident of Nacogdoches.--*Handbook of Texas*, II, 776.

[8]Luke Lesassier, a law partner of Samuel M. Williams in San Felipe.--*Handbook of Texas*, II, 50.

[9]Green C. DeWitt, Empresario of DeWitt's Colony.--*Handbook of Texas*, I, 496.

[10]Miguel Arciniega, who had been appointed on November 13, 1830, as Commissioner for the distribution of land in Stephen F. Austin's colonies.--*Handbook of Texas*, I, 67.

[11]"Austin's 'Coast Colony,' by contract of July 9, 1828, was established with a view of extending settlement to the coast and developing harbors and ports of entry. The territory comprised the littoral leagues between the Lavaca and San Jacinto rivers. The contract called for the settlement of 300 families. ..."--Taylor, *Spanish Archives*, p. 45. This contract was also known as Austin's Fourth Colony.

[12]Lucas Alamán y Escalada (1792-1853), Mexican Minister of Foreign Relations, January 12, 1830--May 20, 1832. --*Diccionario Porrúa*, 3rd ed., I, 47-48.

[13]Two brothers: José María Viesca and Agustín Viesca y Montes, both of whom played an important part in the history of Coahuila and Texas.

[14]On December 4, 1830, José María Viesca had written Antonio Elosúa, Principal Commandant of Coahuila and Texas, that on that same date he had recovered his health and resumed his duties as Governor of Coahuila and Texas.--BA Roll 137, Frames 0295-0296.

[15]Lorenzo de Zavala, on March 12, 1829, had received an empresario contract to introduce 500 families into Texas. Then, on October 16, 1830, he, with David G. Burnet and Joseph Vehlein, transferred his contract to the Galveston Bay and Texas Land Company.--*Handbook of Texas*, I, 498.

[16]Thomas Jefferson Chambers (1802-1865), on February 12, 1830, together with Juan Antonio Padilla, had received an empresario contract to introduce 800 families into Texas, but the land granted them lay in the present bounds

of Oklahoma and Kansas; so the contract was never fulfilled.
--*Handbook of Texas*, I, 326.

[17]This was probably a reference to Ramón Músquiz,
Political Chief of the Department of Béxar.

[18]Dr. Barker marked this word as "name illegible" in
his version. There is a possibility that it was "Sastre,"
a Spanish word meaning "tailor," which in turn could have
been a code word for somebody named Taylor: for instance,
the "Robert Taylor jr." who witnessed the power of attorney
from Samuel M. Williams dated December 17, 1830, or it
could have been a reference to Charles Stanfield Taylor,
who had taken his citizenship oath before the ayuntamiento
at Nacogdoches on April 1, 1830. He boarded in the home of
Adolphus Sterne until May 28, 1831, at which time he
married Mrs. Sterne's sister, Anna Marie Ruoff.--*Handbook
of Texas*, II, 714-715.

[19]Mrs. Eliza Williams Sweet was the widowed sister
of Samuel M. Williams.--Margaret Swett Henson, *Samuel M.
Williams, Early Texas Entrepreneur* (College Station:
Texas A&M University Press, 1976), p. 24.

[20]Mrs. Sarah Patterson (Scott) Williams was the wife
of Samuel M. Williams.--Henson, *Samuel May Williams ...*,
p. [19].

MANUEL DE MIER Y TERÁN TO JOSÉ MARÍA VIESCA[1]

[Translated from Spanish]

[December 30, 1830]

Most Excellent Sir:

As a consequence of what was ordered by the Law of April 6 last, and being interested in the security of the Department of Texas, whose military part is under my orders, I have selected some points which have appeared to me the most appropriate for locating detachments of troops: at the mouth of the Lavaca River, at the crossing of the Brazos River on the Upper Road from Béxar to Nacogdoches (a place which has been given the name of Tenoxtitlan), and at the point at the head of Galveston Bay, on the left bank at the mouth of the Trinity River. These establishments are already approved by the Supreme Government, and there is no doubt that upon their progress depends the union of said Department. The Federation, by stationing troops there, is going to give a beginning to the formation of towns, and it is appropriate that they should be formed with Mexicans, and for that purpose we need for that Government [*i.e.*, the State Government of Coahuila and Texas] which Your Excellency is directing so skillfully, with all its power, and for the Honorable Legislature, with all its wisdom, to promote the transfer of national families by granting them privileges which will put them on an equal footing with the North Americans who, in addition to the advantages which

they have for moving naturally into Texas, have been
encouraged by concessions and exemptions which will make
them, if it has not already done so, exclusive masters of
a country which it is so important for our Republic to
retain, both because in it alone can a barrier be erected
against the Republic to the North [*i.e.*, the United States],
as well as because, due to the fact that it is the nearest
frontier, and because it has the qualities of being fertile
and communicable with the coast and with the roads to the
interior, it will be the first place which the Mexicans are
bound to occupy when they extend their excess population
from the states in the center of the country. Since the
said detachments are to be permanent and, since the objective is to establish towns with them, Your Excellency will
please declare that the land where they have been located
shall be set aside for that purpose, and designate the
limits thereof, either as a concession from the State, or
under the terms prescribed in Article 4 of the said law.
For this purpose I consider that it would be appropriate to
designate how much is to be set aside for each of the families who may be transferred there, with special attention
to the military families. It seems to me that the amount
assigned by the Colonization Law is sufficient, in which
case Your Excellency will please authorize the Chief of the
Department to grant the pieces of land and proceed to lay
out the town, with authority to delegate said commission to

another, in order to save on expenses. Among others, I believe this work could be done by those who have been commissioned as paymasters for the troops, or by those whom Your Excellency may consider worthy of this confidence.

Please be kind enough to carry out the foregoing with the speed which the circumstances require, and to admit the sincerity with which I profess for you my distinguished consideration and particular esteem.

Manuel de Mier y Terán

To the Governor of Coahuila and Texas,

José María Viesca

---

[1]Quoted in José María Viesca to the Political Chief of the Department of Texas, January 22, 1831, Volume 53, pp. 97-98 verso, Spanish Archives, General Land Office, Austin, Texas.

JOSÉ MARÍA VIESCA TO RAMÓN MÚSQUIZ[1]

[Translated from Spanish]

[December 31, 1830]

[Seal:]   SUPREME GOVERNMENT OF THE
          FREE STATE OF COAHUILA AND TEXAS.

On this date I am writing to the Most Excellent
Commandant General of these States as follows:

"Most Excellent Sir.=In view of what Your Excellency
was pleased to write me in your official letter dated the
13th of the present month and the news contained in the copy
which you enclosed for me of the confidential note which,
through the First Secretariat of State, was passed on to
Your Excellency on the 25th of last October, which said
communication was also sent to this Government, all relative to the sales that are being made in the United States
of the North, of the lands which have been granted in the
Department of Béxar[2] in conformity with the colonization
laws, which certainly in no way give any right to the
grantees of said lands to sell them to foreigners, nor
could they grant any such right when it is considered that
there are still in force the ancient legal orders to the
effect that foreigners cannot acquire territorial properties
in the Republic, until after they become naturalized therein
by means of fulfilling the necessary prerequisites, it has

appeared to me that the measure which Your Excellency saw
fit to propose to me should effectively cut off the aforesaid abuses, and therefore I say to Your Excellency, since
you are the one commissioned by the Supreme Government of
the Federation to intervene in matters concerning the colonization of Texas, by virtue of the Law of April 6 of the
current year, and in compliance also with the decree which
has been issued to us concerning all the points respecting
the manner and terms under which we are to carry out, in
the said Department, the settlement of colonists who come
from abroad, it being stipulated by the laws of the State
that there shall not be granted to *empresarios*, for colonization in the public domain of said State, more land in full
ownership than the amount designated for them as premium
lands under the Law of March 24, 1825, and this only after
they have introduced a certain number of families of those
called for in the respective contracts, and without the
right of being able to sell yet, the said land thus granted
in full ownership, except to Mexicans, and by no means to
subjects of foreign Governments. Nor do they have the
right to transfer their contracts, either to Mexicans or to
foreigners, without the knowledge and consent of the Government of this State. Therefore we should consider as null
and void, according to the laws, everything that has been
done that is not in conformity with the aforementioned
regulations. I am making this clarification solely for the

purpose of avoiding, for the interested parties, the making of deceptive contracts that might be declared null and void, warning them of the damages that may result therefrom if the case should arise in which they are declared to be of no legal value, by means of the judgment and action of the corresponding authorities, according to the nature and terms under which the aforesaid contracts may have been made.=On this date I am transcribing this communication for the Chief of the Department of Béxar and the other authorities of the State under my supervision, so that they can make it known to all the inhabitants of said State, and particularly to the inhabitants of that country, admonishing them to use to that end every possible means, no matter how superfluous such efforts might appear under other circumstances, for such is required by the magnitude of the disorder that we are trying to avoid.=I repeat to Your Excellency, with the greatest consideration, the expressions of my most decided affection and high esteem."

And I am transcribing it for Your Lordship for your information and so that, within the district under your command, you can give the decision all the publicity possible, for the information of those who might be considered to be interested in the matter.

God and Liberty. Leona Vicario [Saltillo], December 31, 1830.

[José María] Viesca

[rubric]

Santiago del Valle

[rubric]

To the Political Chief of the)
)
Department of Béxar_____)

    [Marginal note:] Circulated to the Alcaldes
      of this Department on January 28, 1831.

---

[1]BA Roll 137, Frames 0355-0356. An extract of this circular was published in the newspaper called the *REGISTRO OFICIAL DEL GOBIERNO DE LOS ESTADOS-UNIDOS MEXICANOS*, [Mexico City], February 9, 1831, p. [157], column 1. Francisco Pizarro Martínez, the Mexican Consul in New Orleans, made an English translation from the *Registro Oficial* and sent it to the editor of the *Louisiana Courier* on March 29, 1831. See his English version below, under that date.

[2]Instead of *Béxar*, Governor Viesca was actually referring to the Department of *Texas*, which had been set up on February 1, 1825, by Decree No. 13 of the Congress of the State of Coahuila and Texas, which provided that the ordinary residence of the Chief of the Department should be at the city of *Béxar* (present San Antonio), and it also stipulated that this newly created "Department of *Texas*" would cover the same area formerly known as the "Province of Texas."--Kimball, *Laws and Decrees of the State of Coahuila and Texas* ..., pp. 11-14. However, on January 31, 1831, when this Department was divided into two districts by Decree No. 164, it was referred to as the "Department of *Béxar*." See text below under that date.

The ruling set forth in the letter from Governor Viesca to General Mier y Terán would make it difficult, if not impossible, to carry out the provisions of the contracts made by Robertson & Thomson with their prospective settlers, as reported in McLean, *Papers*, III, 519-528, and the provisions of the general agreement between Robertson & Thomson and their colonists, included under November 28, 1830, in this present volume. At best, they would have had to wait until they themselves had become naturalized citizens and had complied with all the provisions of their own land grant before they could have deeded any portion of it to Robertson.

MANUEL DE MIER Y TERÁN TO ANTONIO ELOSÚA[1]

[Translated from Spanish]

[December 31, 1830]

Office of the Commandant General
Inspector of the Eastern Interior States.

Your Lordship will give orders to the effect that
neither Sterling Robertson nor any other North American
family shall be permitted to settle in Tenoxtitlan, and
issue instructions to find out the names of those who
entered that part of the country, as reported in Your Lordship's official letter No. 430 dated the 11th of the month
now ending, and, with respect to what the Political Chief
says in his official letter, the original of which Your
Lordship enclosed for me, I am reporting same to the Governor of the State and asking him to enforce the Law of April
6 last.

God and Liberty. Matamoros, December 31, 1830.

M. Mier y Terán

[Rubric]

To the Principal Commandant
of Coahuila and Texas

[Endorsed in English:] C. Order The Comdt. Gl. of
the Eastn. Intl. States to the Principl. Comdt. of Texas at
Bejar, requiring him, to issue his orders to the Mility.

Comdrs. at various points in Texas, to oppose the Settlement of Sterling C. Robertson, or any other N. American families, at Tenoxtitlan, as being contrary to the provisions of the Law of 6th April 1830. dated Matams. 31 Decr. 1831 [1830]

Rec'd. from the Sec'y of State Austin 13th Octr. 1846.

Geo: Fisher,

Sp: Clk. G. L. Of.

---

[1]Volume 54, pp. 286-286 verso, Spanish Archives, General Land Office, Austin, Texas.

DIARY OF EVENTS AT BÉXAR FOR DECEMBER, 1830[1]

[Translated from Spanish]

[December 31, 1830]

Department of Texas.   Plaza of Béxar.

     Diary of events that have occurred in the said plaza during the month of December, 1830.

Days	Events
1st....	The First Permanent Company of Tamaulipas reported that a soldier had been found dead at dawn, and that the evildoers had been taken prisoners.
2......	Without incident.
3......	One sergeant and 2 privates reported from the Río-grande Company.
4......	*Alférez* Don Eugenio Navarro left with 7 privates for the *Villa* of Goliad with the money for their company.
5......	One sergeant, one corporal, and 5 privates from the Third Active Company of Tamaulipas left for Goliad.
6......	2 privates carrying the mail from Tenoxtitlan reported, and another two left for the same post. 2 privates left carrying the mail to Ríogrande, and the scouting parties were relieved without incident.
7......	A corporal reported with 3 privates who went to Laredo last month. They brought in a private who had deserted from the Béxar Company. An *Alférez* left with 8 men for Tenoxtitlan with the money for the Álamo Company.
8......	Without incident.
9......	The sergeant and soldiers from the Ríogrande Company who came in on the 3rd returned [*i.e.*, started back to Ríogrande]. And the two privates who left on the 6th with the mail for Ríogrande came back.
10.....	Without incident.
11.....	A private who had deserted from the Garrison at Tenoxtitlan came in.

12..... Without incident.

13..... Private Eucevio Farías, of the Béxar Company, reported that he had noticed, in the suburb of Laredo [a part of Béxar?] that some Tahuacano Indians were carrying off his horse, so he attacked them and took a musket and a buffalo hide away from them.

14..... The scouting parties were relieved without incident. And 3 privates departed, taking with them the private who had deserted from the Garrison at Tenoxtitlan who came in on the 11th.

15 and 16. Without incident.

17..... 1 corporal and 11 privates from the Tenoxtitlan Garrison came in escorting the oxcarts.

18..... 2 privates left carrying the mail to La Bahía.

19..... Without incident.

20..... The scouting parties were relieved without incident.

21 and 22. Without incident.

23..... One sergeant left with 30 men in pursuit of wild Indians.

24..... Without incident.

25..... One sergeant left with 12 men in pursuit of Indians; 2 privates came in with the mail from La Bahía.

26..... The scouting parties were relieved without incident.

27..... The 3 privates who left on the 14th for Tenoxtitlan came in, and 2 couriers came in from La Bahía.

28..... 5 privates came in from the Nacogdoches Garrison.

29..... The sergeant and 12 privates who left on the 25th came in.

30..... 2 privates left for Ríogrande. The sergeant and 29 men who left on the 23rd came in.

31..... Without incident.

Béxar, December 31, 1830.

Alexandro Treviño
[rubric]

---

[1]BA Roll 138, Frames 0222-0223.

EXCERPTS FROM THE MINUTES OF THE AYUNTAMIENTO

OF SAN FELIPE DE AUSTIN[1]

[December 31, 1830]

...

An account was presented to the body containing a charge of 20 50/100 for ironing [Hosea H.] League and [Seth] Ingram and taking off their irons and fifty dollars for a horse, which had been lost by Mr. Thos Gray on the expedition to Gonzales--The Ayuntamto. refused to admit the first charge inasmuch as the expense was incurred for the special convenience of sd Ingram and League and therefore considered it right they should pay it themselves ....

...

Third That Citizens Abner Lee, John P. Coles, Nestor Clay John Cole and George Erving be and are hereby appointed Commissioners to lay out a road from the present residence of Joel Laky to the garrison [Tenoxtitlan] on the river Brasos.

...

On motion of William Pettus Sindico procurador, it was ordered that the amt due to Samuel M Williams for his services as Secretary protem and Secretary of the body since the removal of George Fisher, up to the end of the present year, the same being two months and a half at the rate of 800$ per annum amtg to 166 dollars 66/100 be and is hereby allowed and awarded to said Williams to be paid out of the first funds of the municipality. The body then

adjourned until tomorrow at 10 oclock

Thos Barnett

Samuel M. Williams

Secy

---

[1]Eugene C. Barker (ed.), "Minutes of the Ayuntamiento of San Felipe de Austin, 1828-1832," IX, in *The Southwestern Historical Quarterly*, Volume XXIII, pp. 214-223. The excerpts reproduced here appear on pp. 216-218.

DEED OF TRUST BY NATHANIEL B. ATWOOD

TO WALTER D. DABNEY[1]

[Entered under December 31, 1830]

THIS INDENTURE made and entered into this _____

day of _____ in the year of our Lord one thousand eight

hundred and thirty between Nathaniel B. Atwood of the County

of Fayette and State of Tennessee of the first part and

James Robb of the county of Shelby and State aforesaid

WITNESSETH, That whereas the said Nathaniel Atwood and

James Robb together with one John T. Foster on the _____

day of _____ in the year of ____ by certain Articles of

Copartnership made an[d] executed by the said Atwood Robb &

Foster bearing date the said last mentioned day entered

into trade in the town of Memphis and county of Shelby

aforesaid, and whereas the said Nathaniel Atwood then by

said articles agreed to pay and advance to the firm of Robb

Atwood & Foster the sum of Five thousand Dollars, as his

part of the capital invested in trade of the house of Robb

Atwood & Foster, and whereas the said house of Robb Atwood

& Foster is greatly indebted to wit in the sum of _____

Dollars and whereas the said Atwood hath not as yet advanced

or paid to the firm of Robb Atwood & Foster the said sum of

Five thousand Dollars, and whereas the property of each and

every of the firm of Robb Atwood & Foster is bound for the

payment of the debts of said firm, and whereas also the

said James Robb hath advanced to said firm of Robb Atwood &

Foster the sum of ____ dollars NOW THEREFORE to make the said James Robb secure and safe and to ensure on the part of the said Atwood the payment in full of the Five thousand dollars aforesaid to meet the engagement and debts of the said firm, the said Nathaniel B. Atwood hath this [day] made and appointed Walter D. Dabney of the county of Shelby and State aforesaid his Trustee to carry into full & perfect effect the foregoing purposes. Therefore in consideration of the [p]remises and of the sum of five Dollars lawful money of the United States to the said Nathaniel B Atwood in hand paid the receipt of which is hereby acknowledged the said Nathaniel B Atwood hath this day bargained and sold aliened, enfeoffed and conveyed and by these presents doth bargain & sell aliene enfeoff and convey to the said Walter D. Dabney his heirs and assigns forever those certain tracts or parcels of land lying being and situate in the town of Memphis county of Shelby and State aforesaid known and designated on the Master Platt of said town as Lots Nos (128) one hundred & twenty eight (130) one hundred & thirty (131) one hundred & thirty one (132) one hundred and thirty two (211) two hundred and eleven and (212) two hundred and twelve.

TO HAVE and TO HOLD the above described lots or parcels of ground together with all and singular the appurtenances thereto belonging to the only proper use benefit and behoof of him the said Walter D Dabney his heirs and assigns forever

IN TRUST NEVERTHELESS and for the following and no other use, towit in the event that the said Nathaniel B Atwood should fail refuse or neglect to pay the said sum of Five thousand dollars above specified or so much thereof as may be due to the said Firm of Robb Atwood & Foster on or before the ____ day of _____ in the year of our Lord one thousand eight hundred and thirty three then and in that event the said Walter D Dabney his Executors Administrators or Attorney shall and may after giving ten days notice thereof by advertising in any of the newspapers published in the Town Memphis aforesaid of the time and place of sale immediately offer and expose to sale at public auction the several lots or parcels of land above described and to him conveyed and the proceeds of said sale apply to the payment of the debts of the said firm of Robb Atwood & Foster after deducting therefrom enough to pay all the necessary expences of said sale. And the said Nathaniel B Atwood doth hereby covenant and agree with the said Walter D Dabney his heirs executors administrators that after a sale made in pursuance of the foregoing provisions and the above named uses and purposes, and after the payment of the purchase money that he or they may convey the said lots or parcels of land to the purchaser or purchasers in fee simple by deed of general warranty. And the said Nathanel B Atwood doth hereby solemnly and fully and without reservation of

any kind relinquish all right or equity of redemption in &
to the above described lots or parcels of land in favor of
the purchaser at the sale made as above directed. But
until the happening of the contingency on which by the
terms of this Indenture the sale of said Lots or parcels
land is to be made the said Nathaniel B. Atwood reserves to
himself the free and undisturbed use and possession thereof

IN TESTIMONY WHEREOF the said Nathaniel B. Atwood
hath set his hand & seal the day and year first above
written.

(Seal)

Interlined before signing

[Endorsed:] Nathl B Atwood to Walter D. Dabney
Deed of Trust.

5 00

2.54

2.66

---

[1]This document probably came into Empresario Robert-
son's papers after the death of his brother-in-law, Wash-
ington L. Hannum, who had apparently practiced law in
Memphis before coming to Texas.--James D. Davis, *History of
Memphis* ... (Memphis: Hite, Crumpton & Kelly, Printers,
1873), pp. 80-81. There was an N. B. Attwood who served
Memphis as an alderman during its first corporate year
(March, 1827, to March, 1828).--*Ibid.*, p. [33].

RAMÓN MÚSQUIZ TO THE GOVERNOR

OF COAHUILA AND TEXAS[1]

[Translated from Spanish]

Office of the Political Chief, etc.   [January 1, 1831]

No. 2

Most Excellent Sir:

On the thirty-first day of December last the person elected as Deputy for this Department, Citizen Stephen F. Austin, began his journey from this City to that Capital, assisted with the amount of three hundred and thirty-seven pesos, four reales, which he has coming to him for travel expenses, due to the fact that he is traveling two hundred and seventy leagues, from the place of his residence to that Capital, all of which I am reporting to Your Excellency for your proper superior information.=God, etc. Béxar, January 1, 1831. To the Most Excellent Governor, etc.

Extract

Reports the day that Deputy Stephen F. Austin departed for the state capital, assisted by the travel money he had coming to him.

---

[1]BA Roll 137, Frame 0511. This document was not included in the published *Austin Papers*.

FUNDS FOR THE ÁLAMO COMPANY AT TENOXTITLAN[1]

[Translated from Spanish]

[January 1, 1831]

*[When Erasmo Seguín, the Subaltern Paymaster at
Béxar, balanced his books on January 1, 1831, he
included the following entries concerning funds
for the Álamo Company at Tenoxtitlan:]*

...

Disbursements.

...

To the Paymaster of the Álamo de Parras
    Presidial Company, *Alférez* Don Santiago
    Navayra, on account for funds due same-2.321.   3.   3.

To the same as the one in charge of build-
    ing the barracks now being constructed
    at Tenoxtitlan, and to take care of
    the expenses required by same----------""358.   0.   0.

...

To the unattached Lieutenant Colonel Cap-
    tain of Cavalry Don Francisco Ruiz,
    on account for the payments that are
    owing to him---------------------------""150.   0.   0.

...

---

[1]BA Roll 137, Frames 0512-0513.

ÁLAMO DE PARRAS PRESIDIAL COMPANY[1]

[Translated from Spanish]

[January 1, 1831]

Budget showing the amounts due the individuals of said Company in the present month, after deducting for invalids and pensions.

Officers.	Pesos	R.	G.	Pesos	R.	G.
1 Captain--------------------#.	117.	6.	0.			
1 Lieutenant----------------#.	62.	6.	6.			
1 1st *Alférez*-------------#.	47.	0.	10.	.266.	7.	6.
1 2nd ditto-----------------#.	39.	2.	2.			

Enlisted Men.

	Pesos	R.	G.	Pesos	R.	G.
1 Sergeant------------------#.	29.	1.	0.			
1 Bugler--------------------#.	11.	5.	6.			
6 Corporals at 24ps.2rrs.2gs.#.	145.	5.	0.	1.156.	6.	0.
50 Privates at 19ps.3rrs.3gs.#.	970.	2.	6.			

Invalids Added.

	Pesos	R.	G.	Pesos	R.	G.
1 Private------------------#.	8.	0.	0.			

Gratification.

	Pesos	R.	G.	Pesos	R.	G.
For the men------------------#.	40.	3.	7.	. 48.	3.	7.

Rewards for Constancy.

	Pesos	R.	G.	Pesos	R.	G.
1 at 90 rrs.----------------#.	11.	2.	0.			
1 at 9 rrs.----------------#.	1.	1.	0.	. 14.	5.	0.
3 at 6 rrs.----------------#.	2.	2.	0.			
				"1.486.	6.	1.

Credit for Additions.

None.

Deduct for Losses.

	Pesos	R.	G.	Pesos	R.	G.
Deduct from this total 30 pesos that are being enjoyed in Monterrey by the family of the Captain of said Company pertaining to the present month-----------------------#.	30.	0.	0.	. 30.	0.	0.
				"1.456.	6.	1.

Add to this total the pay of Chaplain Don
    Juan Nepomuceno Ayala, who is serving
    as an attaché in this Company------------# . 40. 0. 0.
                        Net assets-----#1.496. 6. 1.

        Tenoxtitlan, January 1, 1831.

                    Santiago Navayra

                        [rubric]

O. K.

[Severo] Ruiz

    [rubric]

_____

    [1]BA Roll 137, Frames 0496-0497.

MINUTES OF THE AYUNTAMIENTO OF SAN FELIPE DE AUSTIN[1]

[January 1, 1831]

[p. 87]   In the Town of San Felipe de Austin first
January 1831 conformably with the municipal ordinances The
Ayuntamto. met this day the following members being present
Thomas Barnett prest. Jesse H. Cartwright 2d Regidor, Walter C. White 3d Regidor Churchill Fulchear 4th Regidor and
William Pettus Sindico procurador, and the session being
declared by the president as open, and on account of a previous notification to that effect, Mr. Francis W. Johnson,
the Alcalde elect presented himself before the body and
took the oath prescribed by the 22d article of the Constitution which was administered by the prest. of last year--
After which act the Sindico procurador notified the body
that there were no others of the new members present, and
this act was closed.   The prest. of the old body then presented a written report of the general affairs of the
Municipality during last year and of the reforms necessary
after its having been read the new president ordered a
session to be held on the 17th for the purpose of appointing committees and the Ayunto. adjourned.

Thos. Barnett
Samuel M. Williams
Secy ...

[1]Eugene C. Barker (ed.), "Minutes of the Ayuntamiento
of San Felipe de Austin, 1828-1832," IX, *The Southwestern
Historical Quarterly*, January, 1920 (Vol. XXIII, No. 3),
pp. 214-223. The portion reproduced here appears on p. 218.

RAMÓN MÚSQUIZ TO THE GOVERNOR

OF COAHUILA AND TEXAS[1]

[Translated from Spanish]

Office of the Political Chief   [January 3, 1831]
[of the Béxar Department]
No. 3

Most Excellent Sir:

The Tahuacano Indians, who at all times have made war on these settlements, without paying any attention to the fact that they have had their periods of peace which they have broken many times, violating the good faith of their treaties, without any other motive than their desire to assassinate and steal, toward which they are naturally inclined, at this time, when it was believed that, on account of the attack which they suffered on September 15 last, from the expedition under the command of Captain Don Nicacio Sanches, which I have reported to Your Excellency,[2] would suspend hostilities, everything has turned out to the contrary, for toward the end of the said month of September they stole twenty-some-odd animals, most of them belonging to me. In October they murdered a soldier and a settler in the vicinity of the Medina River. On the 16th of November they stole the herd of horses belonging to the La Bahía Company and settlers in Goliad. On the 22nd of December they stole, from the outskirts of this City and vicinity, fifteen animals, for which reason a party of thirty men from the permanent militia went out in pursuit of them and suffered the

misfortune of having one man killed at the hands of these
savages on the night of December 24, in an encounter that
they had with another band that was coming in on Cíbolo
Creek. On that same night they killed three Americans from
Austin's Colony on the road to Gonzales, out of five that
were driving a herd of hogs. On the 28th they killed an
inhabitant of DeWitt's Colony, and that *Empresario* [DeWitt]
is complaining about the thefts of horses and cattle from
which they are suffering very frequently, and about the
imminent risk which that settlement is running of being
sacrificed, and recently, on the morning of the 1st of the
present month, those who were guarding the herd of horses
belonging to the Béxar Company noticed that during the preceding night they had been robbed of forty-six animals belonging to the troops and to individuals of this community,
and for that reason an officer with fifty-some-odd troops
went out to overtake them, and I hope that the result will
be favorable. I will report to Your Excellency at the
earliest opportunity. For the present I regret to report
to that supreme government these unfortunate events, at the
same time that the troops of this garrison, who are few in
number and poorly equipped, have not been paid what they
have coming to them, and therefore they should be given
such consideration as Your Excellency can grant them, due
to the condition in which they find themselves, unable to
accomplish the objects for which they were intended. All

this has placed this community in the most melancholy situation that can be imagined, because they fear, and I
believe with good foundation, that the assassinations and
thefts which have taken place, and which it has not been
possible to correct, may provoke the numerous Comanche
Nation to declare a devastating war such as has been experienced on other occasions, and which has caused great harm.
This supposition is not lacking in foundation, if one takes
into consideration the mysterious and not at all frank conduct which they are observing, having reduced the visits by
families, which used to come frequently, and in large numbers, to do their trading, which they commonly refer to as
"*el cambalache*," and to receive the present which it has
been the custom to give them, and, finally, because on
December 30 last some Comanche Indians approached the ranch
of Citizen Ignacio Pérez and, in the presence of the people
who were there, carried off three horses.

What has been set forth above, Most Excellent Sir,
gives an idea of the disadvantageous status of the public
tranquillity during the last three months of this year,
around this city, Goliad, Gonzales, and Guadalupe Victoria,
where the Carancahuases [Karankawa Indians] have done harm
to those settlers, as I have reported to Your Excellency,
and I would like for you to be so good as to demand of the
Supreme Executive Power that an end be put to the aforesaid
evils, for only by bringing to bear all of the resources

under its administration will it be possible to do so.

God, etc. Béxar, January 3, 1831.=To the Most
Excellent Governor of the State.

Extract

Makes a summary of all the assassinations and thefts
committed by the Tahuacano Indians, from the latter part of
September up through December last; indicates his suspicion
that the Comanches will go on the war path; promises to
report the result of the last party that went out in pursuit of the former [the Tahuacanos], stating that the
public tranquillity of the settlements he mentions has been
upset by these events.

---

[1]BA Roll 137, Frames 0615-0617.
[2]See McLean, *Papers*, IV, 584-585.

MANUEL DE MIER Y TERÁN TO STEPHEN F. AUSTIN[1]

[Translated from Spanish]

Matamoros, January 5, 1831

Mr. Stephen Austin:

Dear Sir and most esteemed friend: The same variations as the ones which you indicate to me in your fine
letters have occurred to me because of my election as
Deputy to the General Congress, and consequently I have
gotten behind with my things, but, now that the Government
has decided to continue me in my post in these countries, I
am busy pushing everything that has fallen behind, and
especially my trip, for which nothing stands in the way now
except the uncomfortable weather.

During the time that we stopped writing to each
other, the Fisher incidents occurred, but I have not given
you my opinion about that. There is no doubt that he went
out to take charge of two things that had no connection
with each other and which should have been considered from
different points of view: as Administrator of the Maritime
Customs House, the Ayuntamiento of [San Felipe de] Austin
had nothing to do with him, but, as Secretary of that corporation he was subordinate to it, and, in that case, I
have nothing to do with the matter. I have told him so in
an official letter so that he can take his complaints to
the Chief of the Department.

I have no knowledge that Colonel Piedras or anybody

else has detained families belonging to your enterprise,
nor, much less, because they were bringing in servants.
Furthermore, no instructions have been sent out on this
point, since we always assumed that your colonists were
being introduced in compliance with the laws.

The incident about which I have received an official
report is the one involving the introduction of some families who, because they did not have any documents with them,
were detained in the vicinity of Nacogdoches and they,
scorning the authority of Colonel Piedras, have come in at
night like fugitives and malefactors. At first they mentioned your name, and they were not detained when they
affirmed that they belonged to your Colony. It appears that
these families were following the envoys of the Nashville
enterprise, whose conduct corresponds to your indication
that it is not very well organized. The enterprise also
has against it the Law of April 6, and its origin is not
very pure, for, as you know, it is a transfer made by
another empresario to said group, and in the transaction it
must result naturally that the Colonization Laws have been
broken, for otherwise no benefit could result for the said
company. Concerning the intentions of these families I
have made a report to the Government of the State, urging
that they not be admitted, an action which seems just to
me, in view of the fact that they scorned the authorities.

The Governor has promised me that in the next

Legislature they will discuss the establishing of a Political Chief in Nacogdoches, and, as for the administration of
justice, the thing that I think would work, and I have even
said so to the Supreme Government, is trial by jury, and a
review by a judge of letters who would visit the settlements
periodically, as is done in Louisiana. I wish that, once
and for all, they would decree the freedom of religion in
Texas, for it seems to me that it is worse for them to have
none at all, which is the case now.

I no longer have any hope of our seeing each other,
since you will be in congress by the time that I arrive in
Texas, but our correspondence will be more frequent.

Your most devoted friend who attentively kisses
your hand and wishes you the best of health and happiness,

Manuel de Mier y Terán   [Rubric]

---

[1]Barker, *Austin Papers*, II, 576-577.

ANTONIO ELOSÚA TO SEVERO RUIZ[1]

[Translated from Spanish]

Office of the Principal Commandant)   [January 5, 1831]
)
of Coahuila and Texas_____)

    The 600 cartridges which that company under your command made available to the expedition of Captain Nicacio Sanches, and about which you wrote me in your official letter dated December 24 last, remained already packed in the Paymaster's office at Béxar, due to the lack of an animal on which to load them, so I understand, but you can rest assured that they will be sent to you at the first opportunity. All of which I am writing you by way of reply.

    God and Liberty. Béxar, January 5, 1831.

                      [Antonio Elosúa]

To Captain Citizen Severo Ruiz.

---

[1]BA Roll 137, Frame 0659.

SEVERO RUIZ TO ANTONIO ELOSÚA[1]

[Translated from Spanish]

Álamo de Parras   [January 6, 1831]

Presidial Company

I have in my possession the circular from the Supreme Government which Your Lordship transcribed for me in your
official letter dated the 9th of the month just past,
recommending the pursuit and apprehension of smugglers.

God and Liberty. Tenoxtitlan, January 6, 1831.

Severo Ruiz

[rubric]

To the Principal Commandant,)
)
Colonel Don Antonio Elosúa.   )

---

[1]BA Roll 137, Frame 0697. Notice that Ruiz does
not add the customary phrase: "and it will be duly obeyed
as far as I am concerned."

FRANCISCO RUIZ TO ANTONIO ELOSÚA[1]

[Translated from Spanish]

Office of the Military Commandant)   [January 7, 1831]
)
of Tenoxtitlan._____)   No. 50.

By the superior official letter from Your Lordship dated

December 9 last, I have been informed of the provisions

contained in the one which you were pleased to insert for

me from the Most Excellent Commandant General and Inspector

of these States, dated November 22 last, relative to the

pursuit of contraband, which said superior resolution will

be punctually and properly obeyed, and I am informing Your

Lordship of this fact by way of reply.

        God and Liberty. Tenoxtitlan, January 7, 1831.

                                        Francisco Ruiz

                                           [rubric]

To the Principal Commandant,)
)
Colonel Don Antonio Elosúa.)

_____

[1]BA Roll 137, Frames 0706-0707.

FRANCISCO RUIZ TO ANTONIO ELOSÚA[1]

[Translated from Spanish]

Office of the Military Commandant)   [January 7, 1831]
)
of Tenoxtitlan._____)   No. 51.

We have in this Military Headquarters the superior official

letter from Your Lordship dated December 9 last, in which

you were pleased to insert for me the one from the Most

Excellent Commandant General and Inspector of these States,

dated November 24 last, which speaks of deserters that may

be apprehended, and of the reward paid to the one who makes

the arrest, which said superior order will be most exactly

complied with in the part that concerns me. With the fore-

going I am attentively answering your said superior offi-

cial letter on that subject.

          God and Liberty. Tenoxtitlan, January 7, 1831.

                                        Francisco Ruiz

                                        [rubric]

To the Principal Commandant   )
)
of Coahuila and Texas,   )
)
Citizen Colonel Antonio Elosúa.)

---

[1]BA Roll 137, Frames 0708-0709.

FRANCISCO RUIZ TO SAMUEL M. WILLIAMS[1]

Tenoxtitlan, 7th January, 1831

Senor Don Samuel M. Williams

My Most esteemed and fine friend:

The same confidence which you have deigned to lavish upon me on so many occasions frequently prompts me to bother you, and accordingly I take advantage of it again in this instance, asking that you please assist me in favor of the bearer of this letter, who is my son, and who is going to·Brazoria carrying some money to buy some things for Captain Severo [Ruiz] and me. He has no acquaintances there, and therefore I hope you will receive him with the thought that if you have a correspondent there, to assure him that if the *amount of* money which my son carries *is not sufficient* to cover goods up to three or four hundred pesos, they will be paid for by sight draft mailed in San Felipe; the reason that he is not carrying this amount now is because I do not know what the conditions are in Brazoria, or what kind of stock they may have on hand. In conclusion, I repeat my request to you, without demanding that you compromise yourself one way or the other, that you will instruct him in the manner in which he should deal with the customs men, in case they have any in Brazoria, as I suppose they do. I hope you will forgive my troubling you so much. I shall never forget my gratitude, and promise to reciprocate in any way possible, perpetuating your memory. My attentive and affectionate greetings to your excellency,

and I beg you to call with frankness on your constant

friend, assuring you of my debt and attentively kissing

your hand

Fran[cis]co Ruiz

---

[1]See a xerox copy of the Spanish original and a
typed English translation, Item 23-0533, Samuel May
Williams Papers, The Rosenberg Library, Galveston, Texas.
Cited hereafter as Williams Papers.

ANTONIO ELOSÚA TO MANUEL DE MIER Y TERÁN[1]

[Translated from Spanish]

Office of the Principal Commandant)   [January 8, 1831]
)
of Coahuila and Texas_____)

Most Excellent Sir:

Barbaquista, the principal chief of the Comanches, came in yesterday with several of his men and some families to visit us in peace, and I have the satisfaction of announcing to Your Excellency that, having encountered, on his march, the Tahuacano Indians with the 42 animals [horses] which they were carrying off stolen from the herd belonging to the Béxar Company, about which I informed Your Excellency in my official letter No. 442 dated the 7th of the current month, he took 30 away from them, not being able to get the others because they fled mounted on them, and he has delivered them here, an action which I have praised him for taking, as is just, and which shows the good sense he has manifested in order to preserve the peace.

God, etc. Béxar, January 8, 1831.

Reports that Barbaquista, the principal chief of the Comanches, has delivered in Béxar 30 animals that he took away from the Tahuacanos, of the 42 that were stolen from the herd on the night of the 30th of December.

---

[1]BA Roll 137, Frame 0732. For previous activities of a Comanche chief named Barbaquista, see McLean, *Papers*, IV, 34-35.

STEPHEN F. AUSTIN TO SAMUEL M. WILLIAMS[1]

[From Williams Papers, Rosenberg Library, Galveston, Tex.]

Monclova Jany 9 1831

Dr Sir.

I arrived here yesterday sin novedad [without inci-
dent], and shall leave in the morning. Dn Victor Blanco[2]
recd me in him home with great friendship and attention--he
has truly an amiable and interesting family. I wrote you
by Madero that Dn Victor would appoint you his agent to
select his land--by this mail he will send you a power of
attorney[3] to act as his agent, and also as the agent of
many others. I most particularly request that you will try
and make good selections for Dn Victor, he wants the most
of his land on the Trinity low down or on San Jacinto.
This gentleman is a very warm and sincere friend and I hope
you will spare no pains to get good selections for him.

The accounts given to me here by Dn Victor, Tijerina
and others, as to the general aspect of political affairs,
amount in substance to this--that the present administration
have all the effective portion of the Army and all the
Legislatures and Governors of all the States in their favor,
and most of the Talents and wealth of the nation. They are
of opinion that the present Govt. will sustain itself and
that Guerrero must soon be put down entirely. Dn Victor
and others here, think that this administration is not hostile to North American emigration to Texas, and that the

present restrictions will be removed before this year concludes.   They all say that my Colony stands very high with
the Govt. both in Mexico and in Saltillo.   The answer of
our Ayto [Ayuntamiento] to that of Leona Vicario has given
general satisfaction to all intelligent and reflecting men
and has raised our character more than you have any idea of.
The Senate has approved of Carrillo's credentials as Senator, *unanimously*, not one vote in favor of the Jalapising
System proposed by the Saltilleros.[4]

In Rio Grande and in this place (the only towns I
have passed through) I have been treated with more attention
and respect that I had any reason to expect.   The opinion
here is that Teran will not go to Mexico, but that he will
proceed to Texas in a short time.   The enemies to North
American emigration are beginning to suspect that he is
more friendly to them [*i.e.*, the North Americans] than they
wish etc. etc.   I give these ideas as I have recd. them.
You see that they differ very much from those intertained
in Bexar.   When I get to headquarters I shall be able to
form some certain opinion on these subjects, in the mean-
time it is best to pursue a prudent and *silent* course as to
all matters of politics.

The town at the crossing of the upper road on the
Colorado is yet to name.[5]   I wish you would request
Arciniega not to name it until he hears from me on the sub-
ject.

My colleague Padre Murquis [Músquiz] passed here on the 3d of this month. I am told he intends to ask leave to resign, but Dn Victor thinks that it was under a belief that I would not come on.

Try and get the coast colony out of the way, before Arciniega gets there so that you may have nothing to interfere with the other business.

The mountains round this place are white with snow and ice and the weather very cold and wet--my health is good. The horses stand the journey very well--corn in this place is only 75 cents to a dollar the fanega I again recommend Dn Victor's land matter to you particularly--that is, his *own claims*, the others are for his friends and are of secondary consideration in comparison with his, for they want the land for speculation--he wants it for his family, he has ten children, and a more promising family I have never seen.

       remember me to Mrs. Sweet and Sarah

                       S F Austin   [Rubric]

---

[1]Barker, *Austin Papers*, II, 581-583.

[2]"Victor Blanco, brother-in-law of Ramón Músquiz, was a citizen of Monclova, and represented his state as alternate deputy of the provincial deputation on September 8, 1823. Considering the establishment of a colony in Texas on the Trinity River, he appointed Samuel May Williams as his agent to select a site, but his plans never materialized. Blanco was governor of the state of Coahuila and Texas from May 30, 1826, to January 27, 1827, during which time he suppressed Haden Edwards and B. W. Edwards in the

Fredonian Rebellion of 1826. On July 4, 1827, Blanco was elected the first vice-governor under the Constitution of Coahuila and Texas. He represented the state as a senator in the national legislature from 1833 to 1835 and was re-elected to the same office in 1835; while in the legislature, he opposed Stephen F. Austin's request that Texas be separated from Coahuila."--*Handbook of Texas*, I, 171.

[3]See below, J. Francisco Madero to Samuel M. Williams, March 15, 1831, for an indication of the contents of that power of attorney. That document will also show that the statement in *The Handbook of Texas*, to the effect that Blanco's plans never materialized, is slightly misleading. He did not establish a colony, it is true, but he did get the land.

[4]See "Ayuntamiento of San Felipe to Ayuntamiento of Saltillo," September 27, 1830, in Barker, *Austin Papers*, II, 500-502.

[5]Bastrop, Texas.

ANTONIO ELOSÚA TO THE MAJOR OF THE PLAZA AT BÉXAR[1]

[Translated from Spanish]

[January 10, 1831]

Office of the Principal Commandant of Coahuila and Texas.

The Captain of the Álamo Company, Citizen Severo Ruiz, in an official letter dated the 3rd of the present month, writes me as follows:

"This morning Privates Tomás Lazo and Manuel Tarín deserted from the detail that was guarding the horses," etc.

I am forwarding it to you for your information and so that you can endeavor to apprehend the said deserters.

God and Liberty. Béxar, Januray 10, 1831.

[Antonio Elosúa]

To the Major of the Plaza

[at Béxar]

---

[1]BA Roll 137, Frame 0508. Note: This document is misfiled under January 1 instead of January 10, 1831, on the microfilm.

ANTONIO ELOSÚA TO SEVERO RUIZ[1]

[Translated from Spanish]

Office of the Principal Commandant)   [January 10, 1831]
)
of Coahuila and Texas_____)

     Timoteo Núñez, the retired Sergeant from that Com-
pany under your command, and Private Sesario de la Serda,
about whom you wrote me in your official letter[2] dated the
3rd of the present month (which I am now answering), have
presented themselves in this City.

     God and Liberty. Béxar, January 10, 1831.

                                        [Antonio Elosúa]

To Captain Citizen Severo Ruiz

_____

     [1]BA Roll 137, Frame 0775.

     [2]This letter was not found on Roll 137.

JOSÉ MARÍA ROMÁN TO RAMÓN MÚSQUIZ[1]

[Translated from Spanish]

[January 10, 1831]

José María Román, a Private in the Álamo de Parras Company, presented a petition on January 10, [1831], asking that he be placed in possession of a lot that was granted to him during the time of the Spanish Government, located to the east of the wall of the secularized Balero [Valero] Mission [San Antonio de Valero, now known as the Alamo], and his petition was sent to the Ayuntamiento of this City [Béxar] for a report, with the following decree.=Béxar, January 13, 1831.=The Illustrious Ayuntamiento of this City, in view of what has been stated by the interested party in this petition, and after having made the necessary investigations, will make a recommendation as to what should be done concerning the contents of same.=R. Músquiz.

---

[1]BA Roll 137, Frame 0665.

ARTICLES OF AGREEMENT BETWEEN ROBERTSON & THOMSON
AND HANNAH ALLEN[1]

[January 11, 1831]

District of Attuskasito [Atascosito][2]

Articles of agreement made and entered into this 11th day
of January in the year of our lord one thousand eight hundred & thirty one between Sterling C Robertson and Alexander
Thomson both of the State of Tennessee one of the United
States of the North of the one part and Hannah Allen[3] formerly of the State of Louisana also one of the United States
of the North but now a resident of the District aforesaid
of the other part (Witnesseth) That the said Robertson and
Thomson agrees and binds themselves to give to the said
Hannah Allen one thousand acres of good land in the Nash-
v[ill]e Colony in the State of Cohuila and Texas in the
Mexic[an] Republic, viz. one labour which she the said
Hann[ah] Allen agrees and binds herself to settle and
rem[ain on] so as to enable the said Robertson & Thomson to
obta[in and pe]rfect a title to a league of lan[d] by virtue
of [said settlemen]t under the Mexican Re[public] and the
[balance of the land to make] one th[ous]and acres she is
to [take in another] and seperate place so as n[ot to]
interfear wi[th the settlem]ent on the St. Andress or
Little River and she [the said] Hannah Allen agrees and
binds herself that in [case] the title for the league
should come out in [her] name she will convey to the said

Robertson and Thomson all but the one thousand acres above mentioned [as] soon as they the said Robertson and Thomson shall have her title made by the commissioner appointed by the government to make titles to land in said colony.

In testimony whereof we have hereunto set our hands and seals this day and year above written

test	S. C. Robertson	(Seal)
C. West	Alexr Thomson	(Seal)
	By S. C. Robertson	
	Hannah Allen	(Seal)
	By George Allen	

[Endorsed: Agree]ment [Ro]bertson & Thomson & Hannah Allen, District of Attuskasito.

---

[1]Collection of Mrs. T. S. Sutherland, Sr.

[2]Apparently Robertson was returning to the United States over the Atascosito Road, which is described by *The Handbook of Texas* (I, 75) as follows: "The Atascosito Road, established by the Spanish prior to 1757 as a military highway to East Texas, took its name from Atascosito, a Spanish settlement and military outpost on the Trinity River near present Liberty, Texas. The road extended from Refugio and Goliad to Atascosito Crossing on the Colorado River, on to the Brazos near San Felipe de Austin, and across present northern Harris County to the Trinity. The eastward extension of the trail was known as the Opelousas or La Bahía Road. After the development of the cattle industry in Texas, the old Atascosito road was followed by cattle drivers from South Texas to New Orleans."

[3]For a biography of Hannah (Pride) Allen, see *A Memorial and Biographical History of McLennan, Falls, Bell and Coryell Counties, Texas. Illustrated. Containing a History of this Important Section of the Great State of Texas, from the Earliest Period of its Occupancy to the Present Time, together with Glimpses of its Future Prospects;*

also Biographical Mention of Many of the Pioneers and Pro-
minent Citizens of the Present Time, and Full-page Portraits
of Some of the most Eminent Men of this Section (Chicago:
The Lewis Publishing Company, 1893), pp. 379-381. Her
daughter, Sarah, married George A. Pattillo.

ARTICLES OF AGREEMENT BETWEEN ROBERTSON & THOMSON

AND GEORGE A. PATILLO[1]

[January 11, 1831]

Attaskasito [Atascosito] D[is]trict   State of Co[a]huila &
Texas

Articles of agreement made & entered into this 11th day of
January in the year of our lord one thousand eight hundred
and thirty one between Sterling C Robertson and Alexander
Thomson both of the State of Tennessee one of the United
States of the North of the one part and George A Patillo[2]
formerly of the State of Louisiana also one of the United
States of the North but now a resident of the District
aforesaid of the other part (witnesseth) that the said
Robertson & Thomson agrees and binds themselves to give the
said Patillo one thousand acres of good land in the Nashville Colony in the State of Coahuila & Texas clear of all
cost and charges and for the consideration of said one
thousand acres of land he the said Patillo agrees and binds
himself to settle and remain on one labour of said land so
as to enable the said Robertson and Thomson to obtain and
perfect a title to a league [of] land by virtue of said

settlement under the Mexican Republic and the ballance of the land to make the one thousand acres he is to take in another and separate place so as not to interfear with the settlement on the St. Andress or Little river and in case the title for the league should come out in his said Patillo['s] name he will convey to the said Robertson and Thomson all but the one thousand acres above mentioned as soon as they the said Robertson and Thomson shall have his title made to him by the commissioner appointed by the government to make titles to la[nd] in said Colony. In testimony whereof we have hereunto set our hands and seals this day and year above written.

test	S. C. Robertson (Seal)
C. West	Alexander Thomson (Seal)
	by
	S C Robertson
	George A. Patillo (Seal)

[Endorsed:] Agreement Robertson & Thomson & George A. Patillo District of Atuskasito.

---

[1]Sterling C. Robertson Papers in the E.S.C. Robertson Home, Salado, Texas.

[2]For biography of George A. Patillo, see [E.R. Lindley (compiler),], *Biographical Directory of the Texas Conventions and Congresses, 1832-1845* (no place, no publisher, 1941), p. 150. Also see Lewis Publishing Company, *A Memorial and Biographical History of McLennan, Falls, Bell and Coryell Counties*, pp. 379-381.

ANTONIO ELOSÚA TO SEVERO RUIZ[1]

[Translated from Spanish]

Office of the Principal Commandant)   [January 12, 1831]
)
of Coahuila and Texas_____)

    I have already issued orders for the apprehension

of Privates Tomás Laso and Manuel Tarín, deserters from

that company under your command, about whom you wrote me in

your official letter dated the 3rd of the present month,

which I am now answering.

    God and Liberty. Béxar, January 12, 1831.

                                    [Antonio Elosúa]

To Captain Citizen Severo Ruiz

_____

    [1]BA Roll 137, Frame 0804.

ANTONIO ELOSÚA TO THE COMMANDANT OF ARMS AT LAREDO[1]

[Translated from Spanish]

Office of the Principal Commandant)   [January 12, 1831]
)
of Coahuila and Texas _____)

The Tahuacano Indian that Private Estevan León, of the first Permanent Company of Tamaulipas, is taking to deliver to you has as his destination the Commissariat of the City of Monterrey, as the result of an order by the Most Excellent Commandant General Inspector of these States, and consequently I would appreciate it if you would be so good as to have him, and the enclosed document, conducted to said City, via the post at Lampazos, by two or three soldiers, with the understanding that he is leaving here with funds and supplies for his journey, but if, in spite of this, he should need any help, I hope that you will be so good as to make it available to him, which said charge you can forward with the said escort to the aforementioned Commissariat, where I believe that it will be immediately repaid to you.

God and Liberty. Béxar, January 12, 1831.

[Antonio Elosúa]

To the Commandant of Arms at Laredo

---

[1]BA Roll 137, Frames 0802-0803.

ANTONIO ELOSÚA TO THE COMMISSAR AT BÉXAR[1]

[Translated from Spanish]

Office of the Principal Commandant)   [January 12, 1831]
)
of Coahuila and Texas_____)

The Most Excellent Commandant General Inspector of these States, in an official letter dated October 11 last, was pleased to write me, among other things, as follows:

"Your Lordship will make arrangements for the children who were taken prisoners to be forwarded to Monterrey," etc.

I am forwarding it to you for your information, and with the understanding that one of the said children is to leave here tomorrow for the City of Monterrey as a result of the order of His Excellency, so I would appreciate it if you would place at the disposal of Captain Don Alexandro Treviño ten pesos which have been approved for his provisions, and eight more that are due Private Francisco Calvillo for food that he has given him [the Indian boy] since he was taken prisoner and he [Calvillo] has kept him in his home.

God and Liberty. Béxar, January 12, 1831.

[Antonio Elosúa]

To the Commissar of this City

---

[1]BA Roll 137, Frames 0805-0806.

RAMÓN MÚSQUIZ TO ANTONIO ELOSÚA[1]

[Translated from Spanish]

[January 12, 1831]

Office of the Political Chief of the Department of Béxar.=
When Citizens José Antonio Salinas and Juan Casanova learned
that the Most Excellent Commandant General of these States
had ordered that the children who were taken prisoners from
the Tahuacano Indians in the action of September 15 of the
past year[2] should be gathered up and forwarded to the City
of Monterrey, they presented themselves to this Office, and
the first one [Salinas] stated that, of the two that he
brought in, at the cost of many cares because of their ten-
der age, one of them died after having received the water
of baptism, as a result of not having his mother's milk,
and from an illness which he contracted from the food with
which he fed him until his arrival in this City, and that
the other one, without opposing the orders of His Excellency, begged most fervently that he [the Indian boy] be
left with him because it would grieve him deeply to be
separated from him, due to the affection that he had developed for him as a result of the care that both he and his
family had exercised to raise him and feed him, and that,
futhermore, he intended to adopt him as his only son, with
all the formalities required by law, and the second one
[Casanova] said that he has another one [Indian boy] who is
very young, for whom he has not spared any paternal care in

order to guide him and bring him up along with his own
children. He wants him to be left with him, just like
Salinas does.=Your Lordship will do me the justice to
believe that these citizens, solely out of the affection
which is normally felt for children by those who raise
them, are moved to ask, with an interest prompted by their
humane feelings, that the children that were given to them
not be taken away. Therefore I have decided to send you
this communication, on behalf of the interested parties,
and for the purpose of seeing whether you might be able to
prevail upon the Most Excellent Commandant General to coun-
termand his order relative to this matter.=God and Liberty.
Béxar, January 12, 1831.=Ramón Músquiz.=To the Principal
Commandant of this Department, Colonel Don Antonio Elosúa.

---

[1]BA Roll 137, Frames 0807-0808.

[2]See McLean, *Papers*, IV, 495-524.

LEANDRO AGUILAR TO ERASMO SEGUÍN[1]

[Translated from Spanish]

Monterrey Subcommissariat   [January 13, 1831]

I am including for you two original receipts for what was
furnished by this Commissariat to the wife of Captain Don
Severo Ruiz in the present month and for the pay of Juan
del Moral, Sergeant of the First Company of Tamaulipas,
pertaining to the month just past, so that you, after
posting the charge in the proper place, may be so good as
to send me a certificate for fifty-eight pesos and four
reals, the total amount of said documents, in order to
support the entries in my accounts.

God and Liberty. Monterrey, January 13, 1831.

Leandro Aguilar

[rubric]

To Citizen Erasmo Seguín,)
)
Subcommissar at Béxar____)

_____

[1] BA Roll 137, Frames 0813-0814.

ANTONIO ELOSÚA TO THE MILITARY COMMANDANTS

OF THE DEPARTMENT OF TEXAS, AND

TO THOSE OF THE COMPANIES

OF COAHUILA AND TEXAS[1]

[Translated from Spanish]

Office of the Principal Commandant)   [January 13, 1831]
)
of Coahuila and Texas_____)

The Most Excellent Commandant General Inspector of these States, in an official letter dated December 23 last, has been pleased to write me as follows:

"The Most Excellent Secretary of War and Navy, in an official note dated the 1st of the current month, has been pleased to write me what I am copying below:='Most Excellent Sir.=The Most Excellent Secretary of Foreign Relations,' etc. To the effect that the Constitution and Laws should be observed."

I am forwarding it to you for your information and compliance in the part that pertains to you.

God and Liberty. Béxar, January 13, 1831.

[Antonio Elosúa]

To the Military Commandants of the Department of Texas, and to Those of the Companies of Coahuila and Texas.

---

[1]BA Roll 137, Frame 0834.

ANTONIO ELOSÚA TO THE MILITARY COMMANDANTS AND THE
CAPTAINS OF COMPANIES IN COAHUILA AND TEXAS[1]

[Translated from Spanish]

Office of the Principal Commandant)   [January 13, 1831]
)
of Coahuila and Texas_____)

The Most Excellent Commandant General Inspector of
these States, in an order dated December 9 last, has been
pleased to write me as follows:

"Having noticed that in the trials," etc.

I am forwarding it to you for your information and
compliance.

God and Liberty. Béxar, January 13, 1831.

[Antonio Elosúa]

To the Military Commandants and to Those of the Companies
in Coahuila and Texas.

---

[1] BA Roll 137, Frame 0835.

ANTONIO ELOSÚA TO THE MILITARY COMMANDANTS AT LAVACA,

GALVESTON, NACOGDOCHES, GOLIAD, AND TENOXTITLAN[1]

[Translated from Spanish]

Office of the Principal Commandant)   [January 13, 1831]
)
of Coahuila and Texas_____)

The Most Excellent Commandant General Inspector of
these States, in a superior official letter dated December
18 last, has been pleased to write me as follows:

"I am enclosing for Your Lordship a copy of what
has been sent to me by the Citizen Chief of that Department," etc.

And I am forwarding it to you and enclosing the
copy cited therein, for your information and guidance.

God and Liberty. Béxar, January 13, 1831.

[Antonio Elosúa]

To the Military Commandants at Lavaca, Galveston, Nacogdoches, Goliad, and Tenoxtitlan.

---

[1]BA Roll 137, Frame 0842.

ANTONIO ELOSÚA TO THE COMMISSAR AT MONTERREY[1]

[Translated from Spanish]

Office of the Principal Commandant)   [January 13, 1831]
)
of Coahuila and Texas_____)

The Most Excellent Commandant General Inspector of these States, in an official letter dated October 11 last, was pleased to write me, among other things, what I am copying below:

"Your Lordship will make arrangements to send to Monterrey the children who were taken prisoners," etc.

I am forwarding it to you for your information, with the understanding that I am sending you one of the four children prisoners. He is suffering from epilepsy which, so I understand, and as I have learned from the Comanches, he acquired after he grew up. The others are not going because one died and the other two have not been weaned yet.

God and Liberty. Béxar, January 13, 1831.

[Antonio Elosúa]

To the Commissar in the City of Monterrey

---

[1]BA Roll 137, Frame 0844.

JOSÉ MARÍA VIESCA TO MANUEL DE MIER Y TERÁN[1]

[Translated from Spanish]

[January 14, 1831]

Supreme Government of the Free

State of Coahuila and Texas

Most Excellent Sir:

Citizen Francisco Madero, who has been commissioned by this Government to place some people in possession of tracts of land from the public domain, under date of the 6th of December last, writes me as follows:

"Most Excellent Sir:

"Having been informed that in this Department there are almost no other unclaimed lands outside the colonization enterprises, except those that are occupied by the belligerent tribes, I cannot find any place to locate the Mexican citizens whom that Supreme Government has commissioned me to put in possession of the lands which it has conceded to them by sale. In view of this fact, and knowing that the Most Excellent Commandant General [Mier y] Terán has ordered suspended the introduction of the families corresponding to the enterprise contracted for by Mr. Zavala and the one that Mr. Leftwich contracted for, which belongs today to the Company formed in Nashville, it has seemed appropriate for me to consult Your Excellency about whether, upon any of the lands of the two aforesaid enterprises, I may place the citizens to whom I have referred at the beginning of this note."

The Chief of the Béxar Department, under date of November 22 last, also writes me as follows:
"Most Excellent Sir:

"The Most Excellent Commandant General of these States, under date of October 26 last, was pleased to send me the communication which follows:

"On this date I am writing the Citizen Principal Commandant of Coahuila and Texas, Colonel Antonio Elosúa, as follows:

"I am writing Citizen Colonel José de las Piedras today as follows:

"Your Lordship shall not permit the establishment of the colony of Don Lorenzo [de] Zavala on the banks of the Sabine River, nor the establishment of his representative for twenty *sitios* of land: namely, Jorge Fisher, because same is prohibited thus in Article II [*i.e.*, 11] of the Law of April 6 of this year."

"I am transcribing it for Your Lordship for your information and guidance.

"I have the honor of forwarding it to Your Lordship for your information."

And I have the honor of communicating it to Your Excellency for your superior information.

In view of the communications inserted above it has appeared appropriate to me to report to Your Excellency that, in my opinion, the contract which Mr. Zavala has made with this Government to colonize Texas lands may, or it may not, be opposed to the 11th Article of the Decree of April 6 of the past year, depending on the kind of foreigners with which he undertakes to settle the land which has been conceded to him, in view of the fact that, when he speaks of this point in the document concerning the aforesaid contract, he uses the words *he obligates himself to settle, with five hundred Mexican and foreign families*; consequently, if these families are to be from any other countries except the United States of the North, I understand that, according to the aforecited law, he has the right to retain his contract.

I should appreciate it very much if Your Excellency would be so kind, and I beg you, to give me the reasons which caused Your Excellency to declare null, and contrary to the said law, the fulfillment of the aforesaid contract, for, since I know that Mr. Zavala proposes to do his colonizing with German, Dutch, and Mexican families, I really do not see any way to prevent it and dispose, in a legal manner, of the land which belongs to his enterprise by allocating it to other individuals who might want it.

I repeat to Your Excellency the sincere manifestations of my high consideration and decided affection.

God and Liberty. Leona Vicario [Saltillo], January

14, 1831.

J[osé] M[arí]a Viesca

Santiago del Valle,

Secretary

To the Most Excellent Commandant General

of the Eastern Interior States.

_____

[1]México. Fomento. Colonización. Legajo IV,
1823-1835, pp. 177-178. Typed transcripts in The University
of Texas Archives, Austin.

FRANCISCO RUIZ TO SAMUEL M. WILLIAMS[1]

[Translated from Spanish]

Tenoxtitlan, January 15, 1831

Mr. Samuel M. Williams:

My very esteemed and appreciated friend: On the
8th of the current month I had the satisfaction of receiving your fine letter of the 3rd of the same, which was
handed to me by Mr. Thomas McQueen, whom I had the honor of
meeting and offering him my respects. The only thing I
regret is that he presented himself to me on foot, and,
although I offered him my rustic hut, he gave me to understand that he was staying in the home of a trader named
Smith. After he had talked a little while, he told me
goodbye, and I repeated to him the desires which I had of
pleasing him. After a very short time had passed, I went
to look for him at Smith's house, and I did not find him
because he had gone off with John Williams. From the said
Smith I learned that he was due to come back the next day;
consequently I ceased to worry about it and was looking
forward to seeing him again, but, since he has not returned
up to now, I find myself regretting that I was not able to
serve him like I wanted to. Nevertheless, I beg you, on my
behalf, to be so good as to assure him of my positive
desires to serve him in every way possible, as a friend,
with which honorable title I hope he will honor me from now
on.

I give you, my friend, my most expressive thanks for all the trouble you took to help Navayra by smoothing out his difficulties, as well as for the services which by so doing you have rendered to Our Country or Mexican soil.

I have so many Indians on my hands that I do not know what I am writing. Consequently I shall conclude by giving my affectionate regards to your wife and family, and you can always call on your invariable friend who loves you and really kisses your hand.

Francisco Ruiz

[Rubric]

[Endorsed:] Fran[cis]co Ruiz January 15, 1831.

---

[1] Xerox copy of Item 23-0547, Williams Papers.

LATE IN DECEMBER OF 1830, WHEN STEPHEN F.
AUSTIN WAS IN BÉXAR ON HIS WAY TO SALTILLO,
HE SIGNED HIS NAME TO 200 BLANK SHEETS OF
PAPER AND SENT THEM TO SAMUEL M. WILLIAMS
IN SAN FELIPE, WITH INSTRUCTIONS FOR
WILLIAMS TO HAVE CERTIFICATES PRINTED ABOVE
THE SIGNATURE, "AT NIGHT WHEN NO ONE IS
PRESENT," TO "FILL THEM UP, ALL EXCEPT THE
NAME," AND THEN TO FORWARD THEM TO VARIOUS
PEOPLE IN STRATEGIC POSITIONS ALONG THE
EAST TEXAS FRONTIER, WHERE THEY COULD BE
SOLD TO IMMIGRANTS WHO MIGHT OTHERWISE BE
EXCLUDED FROM TEXAS BY THE LAW OF APRIL 6,
1830. THE DOCUMENT WOULD PERMIT THE PUR-
CHASER TO SETTLE IN AUSTIN'S COLONY. A
FACSIMILE COPY OF ONE OF THESE DOCUMENTS
APPEARS ON THE NEXT PAGE. THE ORIGINAL IS
IN THE SAMUEL M. WILLIAMS PAPERS, ROSENBERG
LIBRARY, GALVESTON, TEXAS.

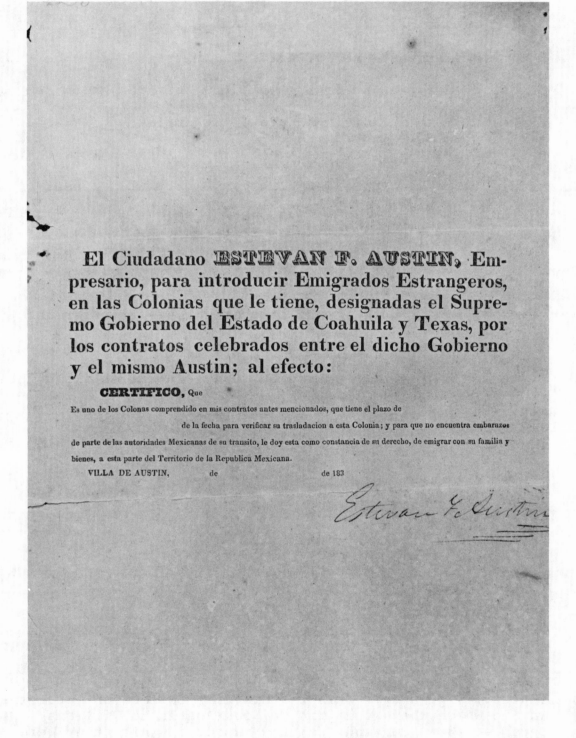

El Ciudadano **ESTEVAN F. AUSTIN**, Empresario, para introducir Emigrados Estrangeros, en las Colonias que le tiene, designadas el Supremo Gobierno del Estado de Coahuila y Texas, por los contratos celebrados entre el dicho Gobierno y el mismo Austin; al efecto:

CERTIFICO, Que

Es uno de los Colonas comprendido en mis contratos antes mencionados, que tiene el plazo de

de la fecha para verificar su trasladacion a esta Colonia; y para que no encuentra embarazos de parte de las autoridades Mexicanas de su transito, le doy esta como constancia de su derecho, de emigrar con su familia y bienes, a esta parte del Territorio de la Republica Mexicana.

VILLA DE AUSTIN,   de   de 183

PRINTED FORM FOR ADMITTING AUSTIN COLONISTS[1]

[Translated from Spanish]

[Entered under January 15, 1831]

Citizen STEPHEN F. AUSTIN, Empresario, in order to introduce Foreign Immigrants into the colonies which the Supreme Government of the State of Coahuila and Texas has designated for him, by the contracts celebrated between the said Government and the said Austin, for that purpose:

I HEREBY CERTIFY, That [blank for name of colonist] if one of the colonists included in my aforementioned contracts, that he has a period of [blank for the amount of time] from this date in which to effect his transfer into this Colony, and, in order that he may not encounter any obstacles on the part of the Mexican authorities along the way, I hereby give him this writ as evidence of his right to immigrate with his family and property, to this part of the Territory of the Mexican Republic.

VILLA [OF SAN FELIPE] DE AUSTIN [blank for the day] of [blank for the month], 183[blank].

[Signed in advance in manuscript:] Estevan F. Austin

[Rubric]

---

[1]Xerox copy of Item 23-4230, Williams Papers. There are two other similar blanks (Items 23-0512 and 23-4229) signed by Austin in this same collection. For the way in which they were printed, see Austin to Williams, December 28, 1830, and, for the manner in which they were to be issued, see Austin to Menard, November 13, 1830. Notice, however, that the wording of this printed certificate

is entirely different from the manuscript version suggested
in Austin's letter of November 13, 1830. Mr. Thomas W.
Streeter, in his *Bibliography of Texas, 1795-1845, Part I.
Texas Imprints, Volume I. 1817-1838* (Cambridge: Harvard
University Press, 1955), p. 27, says: "As it is unlikely
that Austin's letter dated from Bexar on December 28, 1830,
reached San Felipe and was acted on by Cotten by the time,
on or before January 15, 1831, he had sold his *Texas
Gazette* press to the printers of the *Mexican Citizen*, I
have supplied the imprint of the latter to this piece."
Following Mr. Streeter's reasoning, we have assigned this
item the date of January 15, 1831.

ARTICLES OF AGREEMENT BETWEEN ROBERTSON & THOMSON
AND JOSEPH PEVETO[1]

[January 15, 1831]

Riven Mountain [?]   state of Louisiana

Articles of agreement made this 15th day of January in the
year of our lord one thousand eight hundred and thirty one
between Sterling C Robertson and Alexander Thomson both of
the state of Tennessee of the one part and Joseph Peveto of
the state of Louisiana of the other part all of the United
States of the North (witnesseth): that the said Robertson
and Thomson agrees and binds themselves to give to the said
Peveto one thousand acres of land in the [N]ashville colony
in the state of Co[a]huila and Texas in the Mexican Republic. One labour of said land the said Peveto agrees and
binds himself to set[tle] and remain [on] so as to enable
the said Robertson and Thomson to [obtain] and perfect a
title to a league of land in [the] Republic aforesaid and
if the title for the league [s]hould come out in his the
said Peveto['s] name he will convey all to the said
Robertson a[nd] Thomson but the one thousand acres above
mentioned the said thousand acres to be given to the said
Peveto clear of all expences

In testimony whereof we have hereunto set our hands
and seals this day and year above written

S C Robertson (Seal)

Alexander Thomson (Seal)

by S C Robertson

his

Joseph ┼ Peveto (Seal)

mark

[Endorsed:] agreement Robertson & Thoms[on] &

Joseph Peveto Louisiana

---

[1]Sterling C. Robertson Papers, The University of Texas Archives, Austin. Facsimile and printed copies of this document have been published in William Curry Harllee, *Kinfolks* (3 vols.; New Orleans: Searcy & Pfaff, Ltd., 1934-1937), III, 2825-2827. Notice that Robertson signs this contract for both himself and Thomson, and that he refers to both Robertson and Thomson as being from the State of Tennessee, whereas by March 25, 1831, Robertson was signing for himself only, with no mention of Thomson, and he said that he was from the State of Coahuila and Texas.

ARTICLES OF AGREEMENT BETWEEN ROBERTSON & THOMSON
AND WILLIAM G. EVANS[1]

[Entered under January 15, 1831]

[ARTICLES OF A]GREEMENT, Made and entered into th[is] ...th day of ... in the year of our Lord, one tho[usa]nd [eight hundred and] thirty one [between [STERLIN]G. C. ROBERTSON, of the County of Davidso[n and Alexander Thomson] of the County of Giles [and State of Te]nnessee, and [Willi]am G. Evans -- of the County of Giles and State of Tennessee, WITNESSETH: That the said ROBERTSON and Thomson bind themselves to convey unto the said William G. Evans his heirs or assigns, one hundred and sixty acres of good Land, in Leftwich's Grant, in the Province of Texas, and also eight hundred and forty acres of Land, in another and separate place--the whole being one thousand acres of Land, all of good quality, in said Province--which said -- William G. Evans -- for and in consideration of the said one thousand acres of land, agrees and binds himself to settle and remain upon said land, so as to enable the said Robertson and Thomson to obtain and perfect a title to a league of land, in virtue of said settlement, under the Mexican Republic.

_____ and the said William G. Evans -- binds himself to erect houses necessary for a permanent residence, and to open and fence a sufficient portion of the land, which shall be set apart for him, the said William G. Evans. And the said ROBERTSON and Thomson agree to survey and lay off the

said one hundred and sixty acres of land; and also agrees,
with the assistance of the said William G. Evans -- to
survey and lay off the balance of the one thousand acres;t
to wit, eight hundred and forty acres of land.

IN TESTIMONY WHEREOF, we have hereunto set our
hands and affixed our seals, the day and year first above
written.

Test	Sterling C Robertson (Seal)
W. D. Thomson	Alex[and]r Thomson (Seal)
John Kerr	W[illia]m G. Evans (L. S.)

As ... that the wit... Leag[ue] ... may be Granted
... to me; ... should that be the ca[se] ... myself to convey unto the said Robertson [and] Thomson all of s[ai]d
League except that part for which we hold their bond.

W[illia]m G. Evans (L. S.)

[Endorsed:] Robertson & Thomson and William G.
Evans agreement.

---

[1]Collection of Mrs. T. S. Sutherland, Sr.

JOSÉ DE LAS PIEDRAS TO ANTONIO ELOSÚA[1]

[Translated from Spanish]

Office of the Military Commandant   [January 17, 1831]

of the Frontier

On the 12th of the current month Manuel Tarín, a Private

from the Álamo Company, was apprehended. He said that he

had deserted from the detachment at Tenoxtitlan in the com-

pany of Tomás Lazo of the same company, bringing with him

four horses, two of which they left in the possession of

the Quicapú [Kickapoo] Indians because they had played out

on them, and they came on to this town riding the others,

but one of them strayed away on the night that they were

apprehended.

They pursued Lazo so hard that he was forced to

turn himself in on the 16th of the current month, saying

that they had robbed him of the horse and saddle on which

he was riding. I have ordered that the corresponding

investigation be drawn up concerning everything, and I will

make a report to Your Lordship. Meanwhile the two indivi-

duals have been confined to the barracks.

They assert that they left Tenoxtitlan on an

assignment to look for part of a herd of horses that had

strayed off from that troop. They found it in a short time

and left it in the same place. I believe that it is appro-

priate for Your Lordship to have this information so that

you can communicate it to the commandant of that detachment.

God and Liberty. Nacogdoches, January 17, 1831.

José de las Piedras

[rubric]

To Colonel Don Antonio)
)
Elosúa, Principal   )
)
Commandant of Texas   )

---

[1]BA Roll 137, Frames 1011-1013. Notice the strict formality of going through channels that is being observed in this letter. The courier carrying the letter from Nacogdoches to Béxar would have to go via Tenoxtitlan, since General Manuel de Mier y Terán had ordered that the official correspondence be carried that way, so he could have just handed the letter to Francisco Ruiz, the Commandant at Tenoxtitlan. Instead, Piedras, Military Commandant of the Frontier, is sending the information to an officer of equal status, Antonio Elosúa, Principal Commandant of Texas, who is over the area in which Ruiz is serving, and Elosúa has to turn right around and send another letter back over the same road from Béxar to Tenoxtitlan. Meanwhile, since the mail was delivered only once every two weeks, considerable time must have elapsed before this information reached its destination.

ANTONIO ELOSÚA TO THE MILITARY COMMANDANTS

IN THE DEPARTMENT OF TEXAS AND THE

COMPANIES OF COAHUILA AND TEXAS[1]

[Translated from Spanish]

Office of the Principal Commandant)   [January 18, 1831]
)
of Coahuila and Texas _____)

The Most Excellent Commandant General Inspector of these States, in an official letter dated the 29th of December last, has been pleased to write me as follows:

"The Most Excellent Secretary of War and Navy, in an official letter dated the 30th of last month [November], has been pleased to write me as follows:

"'Most Excellent Sir: Today I am writing the Inspector General,' etc."

I am forwarding it to you for your information and guidance.

God and Liberty. Béxar, January 18, 1831.

[Antonio Elosúa]

To the Military Commandants in the

Department of Texas.

To the Companies of Coahuila and Texas.

---

[1]BA Roll 138, Frame 0003.

ANTONIO ELOSÚA TO FRANCISCO RUIZ[1]

[Translated from Spanish]

Office of the Principal Commandant)   [January 18, 1831]
)
of Coahuila and Texas_____)

The Most Excellent Commandant General Inspector of these States, in an official letter dated the 20th of December last, has been pleased to write me as follows:

"The official letters from Your Lordship Nos. 394 and 408, of the 9th and 19th of November," etc.

I am forwarding it to you for your information and guidance.

God and Liberty. Béxar, January 18, 1831.

                                    [Antonio Elosúa]

To the Military Commandant of Tenoxtitlan.

---

[1]BA Roll 138, Frame 0006.

ANTONIO ELOSÚA TO THE MILITARY COMMANDANTS OF NACOGDOCHES,

TENOXTITLAN, LAVACA, AND GOLIAD AND TO THE

LA BAHÍA AND ÁLAMO COMPANIES[1]

[Translated from Spanish]

Office of the Principal Commandant)   [January 18, 1831]
)
of Coahuila and Texas_____)

The Most Excellent Commandant General Inspector of
these States, in an official letter dated the 29th of
December last, has been pleased to write me as follows:

"I am writing Citizen Colonel Juan Davis Bradburn
today as follows:

"'In view of the good situation, etc."

I am forwarding it to you for your information and
guidance.

God and Liberty. Béxar, January 18, 1831.

[Antonio Elosúa]

To the Military Commandants of Nacogdoches,

Tenoxtitlan, Lavaca, and Goliad, and

To the La Bahía and Álamo Companies, and

To the Major of the Plaza [at Béxar].

---

[1]BA Roll 138, Frame 0004.

ANTONIO ELOSÚA TO FRANCISCO RUIZ[1]

[Translated from Spanish]

Office of the Principal Commandant)   [January 18, 1831]
)
of Coahuila and Texas_____)

The Most Excellent Commandant General Inspector of these States, in a superior official letter dated December 31 last, has been pleased to write me as follows:

"Your Lordship will give orders to the effect that there shall not be permitted in Tenoxtitlan the establishment of Sterling," etc.

I am forwarding it to you for your information and fulfillment, and as a result of your official letter of November 13 last relative to the matter.

[Antonio Elosúa]

God and Liberty. Béxar, January 18, 1831.

To the Military Commandant of Tenoxtitlan

---

[1]Volume 54, p. 287, Spanish Archives, General Land Office, Austin, Texas.

JOSÉ DE LAS PIEDRAS TO ANTONIO ELOSÚA[1]

[Translated from Spanish]

Office of the Military Commandant)   [January 18, 1831]
)
of the Frontier_____)

As I am offering to do in a separate official letter, I am
enclosing for you the declarations taken from the deserters
from the Álamo Company, so that in view thereof you may
decide what should be done.

   God and Liberty. Nacogdoches, January 18, 1831.

         José de las Piedras

           [rubric]

To the Principal Commandant)
)
of this Department, Colonel)
)
Don Antonio Elosúa_____)

---

[1] BA Roll 138, Frame 0025.

EXCERPTS FROM THE MINUTES OF THE AYUNTAMIENTO

OF SAN FELIPE DE AUSTIN[1]

...   [January 18, 1831]

[p. 2] In the town of [San Felipe de] Austin 18th
Jany 1831 the Ayuntamto. met pursuant to the adjournment of
yesterday present F. W. Johnson president and Walter C.
White 1st Regidor, Randall Jones 3d Regidor and R. M.
Williamson Sindico procurador.

...

The Ayuntamto. further ordered that the president
be authorised to pay out of the first funds collected and
belonging to the Municipal funds for the translation of the
evidence taken in the case of Ingram and League.[2]

It was further ordered by the Ayuntamto. that the
president of the body adopt such measures not [p. 3] contrary to the existing laws, as [several illegible words
interlined] may secure the persons of the criminals now
under restraint and also all others that may hereafter
require confinement while the municipality is without a
public prison or jail, as in his judgment may fulfil the
objects and intentions of the laws and at the same time be
the least bothersome and expensive to the municipality, and
defray the expenses which may be incurred from any funds of
the municipality not otherwise appropriated.

...

The body adjourned--the 2d and 4th Regidors not

having attended the session.

                                   Samuel M. Williams

        ...

---

[1]Eugene C. Barker (editor), "Minutes of the Ayuntamiento of San Felipe de Austin, 1828-1832," IX, *The Southwestern Historical Quarterly*, Austin, Texas, XXIII, 214-223. The passages quoted appear on pp. 219-220, and 222.

[2]For the background of this case, see McLean, *Papers*, IV, 64-65, 453-454, and 533-534.

LIST OF FOREIGNERS IN NACOGDOCHES[1]

January 18, 1831

List of foreigners resident in this municipality that in compliance with the order of His Excellency Minister of State and of Relations of the 17th of November past communicated by the Senor Political Chief of this Department for the renewal of the Card of Security, and under the solicitation provided in the superior order, have proceeded to make the following:

	Carta de *Security* [sic]
Pierre Robleau	None
Jean Baptiste Cazenave	
Julian Fonteno	
Antonio Grillet	
Remigio Toten	
Francisco Delile	
Michel Sacco	
Adolphus Sterne	
George Pollitt	
Daniel Clark	
Frost Thorn	
John M. Daniels	
Haden Edwards	
Michel B. Menard	
Milton Slocum	

G. S. Thomas

Samuel B. Marshall[2]

Hyman Hertz

Thomas Hastings

William Elliot

David Towns

Joseph L. Hood[3]

Augustus Hotchkiss

Eliel Melton[4]

Chas. H. Sims

Charles S. Taylor

William R. D. Speight

James Olds

Amos Donavan

William Donavan

John S. Morrison

L. Hopkins

Joseph Whitcomb

Radford Berry[4]

Bernard Pantaleon

William Goyens

Henry Stockman

Baptiste Porrier

Louis Rose

Andrew Henry

John S. Roberts

Nacogdoches, January 18, 1831.

Manuel de los Santos Coy

---

[1]"Nacogdoches Archives," Volume 55, pp. 80-82, The University of Texas Archives, Austin. This document is included to illustrate how many settlers from East Texas later moved to the Robertson Colony area.

[2]Samuel B. Marshall was one of the original stock-holders of the Texas Association.

[3]Joseph L. Hood received a grant of 1 league of land in present Bell County on December 23, 1834.

[4]Eliel Melton and Radford Berry were living in the Upper Colony on August 13, 1832.

ANTONIO ELOSÚA TO RAMÓN MÚSQUIZ[1]

[Translated from Spanish]

Office of the Principal Commandant)   [January 19, 1831]
)
of Coahuila and Texas_____)

The Most Excellent Commandant General Inspector of these States, in an official letter dated December 20 last, has been pleased to write me as follows:

"The official letters from Your Lordship Nos. 394 and 408, of the 9th and 19th of November last, inform me of what the Citizen Commandant of the Tenoxtitlan Detachment told Your Lordship," etc.

And I have the honor of forwarding it to Your Lordship for your information and guidance.

God and Liberty. Béxar, January 19, 1831.

[Antonio Elosúa]

To the Political Chief, Citizen Ramón Músquiz.

---

[1]BA Roll 138, Frame 0044.

ANTONIO ELOSÚA TO FRANCISCO RUIZ[1]

[Translated from Spanish]

Office of the Principal Commandant)   [January 19, 1831]
)
of Coahuila and Texas_____)

   I am enclosing for you the indictment that was
drawn up against Francisco Castañeda, a Lieutenant in the
Álamo Company, because of the shortage of funds that was
discovered in the accounts of said Company, so that you can
proceed with the investigation in the manner prescribed by
the Most Excellent Commandant General Inspector of these
States in his superior decree dated October 9 of last year,
bearing in mind that, since Lieutenant Tomás Munguía, who
was serving as secretary, is no longer in the service, I
have appointed in his place Francisco de Porras, an *Alférez*
in the First Permanent Company of Troops, who is going to
that post to present himself to you for that purpose.

   The aforementioned Lieutenant Castañeda, who had
remained here under arrest, is also going to that post
because I believe that you will find his presence necessary
in order to continue the investigation, and you may ask for
the appearance of any witnesses whom you deem necessary,
or, if they cannot come because the distance is too great,
or for any other just reason, you will forward the interro-
gatories and do whatever else is necessary in the case, all
for the purpose of expediting the investigation.

   Since, according to the ruling of the official

appointed to investigate the case, with which His Excellency

has agreed, Severo Ruiz, Captain of the said Company, has

also turned out to be responsible and subject to charges,

I have thought that, for that reason, he should be relieved

of his command of same, at least until he has had a chance

to clear himself, and, since there is no other official

available to replace him, you will, for the time being,

take command of the said Álamo Company, receiving it with

all the formalities prescribed by military regulations. I

am notifying the superior office of the Most Excellent

Commandant General Inspector of this change.

God and Liberty. Béxar, January 19, 1831.

[Antonio Elosúa]

To Lieutenant Colonel Citizen Francisco Ruiz.

---

[1]BA Roll 138, Frame 0052.

CONTINUATION OF THE CASE AGAINST SEVERO RUIZ AND

FRANCISCO DE CASTAÑEDA[1]

[Translated and summarized from Spanish]

[January 19, 1831]

[At this point we find a continuation of the inves-
tigation which we first mentioned in Volume IV of
these Papers, *on pages 176-178. Since the manu-*
script records of this one case alone fill 248
frames, with two pages to each frame, it is materi-
ally impossible to reproduce the full text here.
Consequently we have been forced to be content with
giving the very brief summary which appears below.
Omission of the full text can be justified to a cer-
tain extent because most of the crimes involved were
committed toward the latter part of 1829 and early
in 1830, before the Álamo de Parras Company was
ordered into the Robertson Colony area, and also
because many of the activities took place outside
the area, and a good part of the depositions were
taken elsewhere. However, we do want to include
an outline of the case because it demonstrates very
vividly the legal machinery that was in use in Texas
by the Mexicans at the time when Robertson began
bringing in his colonists. The highlights of the
case are given below.]

This case began on May 30, 1830, when Severo Ruiz, Captain of the Álamo de Parras Company, reported to Antonio Elosúa, the Adjutant Inspector in Béxar, that, when Lieutenant Francisco de Castañeda, Paymaster of the Álamo Company, turned his accounts over to his successor, *Alférez* Santiago Navayra, on December 31, 1829, Castañeda had been short 901 pesos, 7 reales, and 1 1/2 granos. Proceedings in the case were suspended on August 15, 1832.

Lieutenant Colonel Francisco Ruiz, the Military Commandant of Tenoxtitlan, was appointed to gather the evidence in the case, and Tomás Munguía, a lieutenant from the Monclova Company, was appointed to serve as secretary.

Francisco Ruiz made the preliminary investigation in Tenoxtitlan and reported the results to Colonel Elosúa in Béxar, who sent them on to General Manuel de Mier y Terán, the Commandant General, in Matamoros, and he, in turn, requested an opinion from Lic. Ignacio de Cárdenas in Ciudad Victoria. Cárdenas ruled that the documentation

was incomplete and sent the case back with specific
instructions as to how to proceed to establish the guilt
or innocence of Castañeda and Severo Ruiz, and to use
every possible means to find out about the illicit trade
that Severo was carrying on with the Álamo Company. Consequently, because of all of these delays, Elosúa was not
able to send a reply back to Francisco Ruiz until January
19, 1831, which is the point where we resume the story
here.

By this time Tomás Munguía had been mustered out
of the service, so Francisco de Porras, First *Alférez* of
the First Permanent Company of Tamaulipas, was appointed to
replace him as secretary, and Castañeda, who had been held
under arrest in Béxar, was sent to Tenoxtitlan so that he
would be available to testify in the trial.

Then, since charges had been made against Severo
Ruiz, he was relieved of his command, placed under arrest,
and ordered to make bond for 1,200 pesos, which he did by
depositing 600 pesos in cash and submitting titles to land
to cover the other 600. (Unfortunately, the records do
not reveal what land was covered by the titles.) Since
there was no strong box in Tenoxtitlan, and since both the
outgoing and incoming paymasters were under investigation,
Francisco Ruiz had to take the bond money and documents
into his personal custody. Also, since there was no other
officer available to replace Severo as Captain of the
Álamo Company, Francisco Ruiz had to take on that additional responsibility, so now we find Francisco Ruiz func-
tioning simultaneously as Military Commandant of Tenoxtitlan, Captain of the Álamo Company, judge, and paymaster.
Two sergeants (Manuel de León from the Béxar Company, and
Francisco Mesa from the Álamo Company) served as witnesses
to the proceedings.

When they went to the house where Lieutenant Francisco de Castañeda was living, to seize his property in
case he could not make bond, they found that all his
worldly possessions consisted of a single bed, a trunk containing a few articles of used clothing, a saddle, a pair
of pistols, and a sword, whereupon Francisco Ruiz ruled
that, since those items were of no great value, and since
Castañeda had been suffering a discount of two-thirds of
his salary for so long that most of the shortage had
already been made up, his property should not be seized,
and that they should proceed with the case.

At this point, as was customary whenever a member
of the Mexican Army was being tried, the complete service

records of both Severo Ruiz and Francisco de Castañeda were added to the file, but they are of such great importance that we are reproducing them in their entirety elsewhere in these *Papers*, under March 19, 1831. During the course of the next seventeen months depositions were taken from the following witnesses:

     1.   Santiago Navayra, former paymaster of the Álamo Company.

     2.   Corporal Antonio Soto, of the Álamo Company, 36 years old.

     3.   Corporal Antonio de León, of the Álamo Company.

     4.   First Corporal José María de la Garza, of the Álamo Company, 32 years old.

     5.   Corporal José María Román, of the Álamo Company.

     6.   Private Antonio Herrera, of the Álamo Company.

     7.   Private Santos Mansolo, of the Álamo Company.

     8.   Private Anestacio Guerrero, of the Álamo Company.

     At this point Francisco de Castañeda filed a complaint that Francisco Ruiz should not be allowed to serve as judge in the case because Francisco Ruiz and Severo Ruiz both had the same surname and were relatives, so Francisco Ruiz suspended the proceedings and forwarded the testimony to Manuel de Mier y Terán, who appointed Lieutenant Nicolás Flores to replace Francisco Ruiz as judge and sent the case back to Elosúa, who turned it over to Nicolás Flores and ordered him to go to Tenoxtitlan to continue the investigation.

     Meanwhile, on June 6, 1830 [*sic*], Francisco de Castañeda had filed a petition with Miguel Arciniega, Alcalde of Béxar, asking him to question certain witnesses concerning the smuggling activities of Severo Ruiz. Arciniega, assisted by Bruno Huizar and Ignacio Arocha, approved the request and ordered José Flores, the Fourth *Regidor*, to summon the witnesses and take their testimony, acting as *Síndico Procurador* (attorney for the municipality), and to forward the documents to Castañeda. In this manner statements were taken from the following additional witnesses:

9. José María de Cárdenas, a native and resident of Béxar, a farmer, 34 years old, and a Catholic.

10. José Luis Carabajal, a native and resident of Béxar, a farmer, 24 years old, and a Catholic.

11. Felipe Jaime, a native and resident of Béxar, a farmer and rancher, 25 years old, and a Catholic.

12. José María Músquiz, a native of Goliad and resident of Matamoros, a cowboy, 18 years old, and a Catholic.

13. Manuel Vidal, a native of the Valley of Santa Rosa and resident of Monclova, a farmer, 45 years old, and a Catholic.

14. Laureano Granados, a native and resident of Béxar, a silversmith (?), 22 years old, and a Catholic.

Then Alcalde Miguel Arciniega ordered that the depositions which had been taken should be turned over to Francisco de Castañeda, but a little later, on July 30, 1830, Castañeda again appeared before Alcalde Arciniega and asked for additional depositions, as a result of which the following witnesses were questioned:

15. José Antonio Salinas, a native and resident of Béxar, a farmer, over 50 years of age, and a Catholic.

16. José María Herrera, a native and resident of Béxar, a rancher, 50 years old, and a Catholic.

The two depositions mentioned above were also given to Castañeda.

Lieutenant Nicolás Flores, from the Fifth Permanent Batallion, was transferred from Goliad to Tenoxtitlan to replace Francisco Ruiz as *Fiscal* (State's Attorney) in the case being prosecuted against Severo Ruiz and Francisco de Castañeda, and he was sworn in on June 18, 1831. His first step was to take a deposition from:

17. Francisco de Castañeda, who, when asked to mention any persons who might be able to give additional information about the illicit trade carried on by Severo Ruiz, gave the names of Juan Martín de Veramendi, José Antonio de la Parra, Pedro del Toro, Santos Mansolo, Anestacio Guerrero, Fernando Rodríguez, Agapito Hernández, José Antonio Navarro, José María Román, and Manuel Barbe-

rena. Then Nicolás Flores sent a copy of Castañeda's
deposition to Antonio Elosúa so that he could take depositions there from the individuals cited. Judge Flores also
wrote Francisco Ruiz and asked him to furnish copies of
documents involving transactions by Severo Ruiz.

On July 12, 1831, a letter was received from the
Mexican Secretary of War and Navy, ordering Nicolás Flores
to turn over to Captain Mariano Sandoval his duties as
judge in the case, and for Flores to return immediately to
the Fifth Permanent Battalion.

Meanwhile Elosúa had authorized a transfer of the
case from Tenoxtitlan to Béxar, where Mariano Sandoval
arrived on July 30, 1831, with the two defendants (Severo
Ruiz and Francisco de Castañeda). Mariano Sandoval became
ill, and Captain Vicente Arreola was commissioned to conclude the case. Statements were taken from the following
witnesses:

18. Juan Martín De Veramendi, Vice Governor of
Coahuila and Texas.

19. Pedro del Toro, 40 years old.

20. José Antonio de la Garza, 58 (?) years old.

21. Fernando Rodríguez, a retired lieutenant, 41
years old.

22. José María Román, 40 years old.

23. Trinidad Guerra, a private in the Álamo Presidial Company, 32 years old.

24. Nicolás Mendes, a private in the Álamo Company, 25 years old.

25. Tomás Ramón, a private in the Álamo Company,
20 years old.

On September 22, 1831, Severo Ruiz filed a complaint that Francisco de Porras should not be allowed to
serve as secretary in the case because of his connections
with Francisco de Castañeda, so next day Ignacio Rodríguez
was appointed to replace Francisco de Porras as secretary.
Severo also complained that Francisco de Castañeda was a
brother-in-law of Ramón Músquiz, who had also become
implicated in the case. Then additional depositions were
taken as follows:

26. Agapito Hernández, 35 years old.

On September 26, 1831, Severo Ruiz complained that his trial had been prolonged so much that his health was suffering from his imprisonment, so the judge authorized Severo to go out and take exercise "or do anything else he wanted to within the City of Béxar."

27. A second deposition was taken from Fernando Rodríguez because in his first statement (see No. 21 above), he had not told the truth, and his conscience had been hurting him.

28. A second deposition was taken from Agapito Hernández because he said he had not told the truth the first time (in No. 26 above).

29. Deposition of Francisco Esquivel, 49 years old.

30. Deposition of Anastacio Treviño, 29 years old.

On October 6, 1831, the judge ordered Severo Ruiz to appear and make his deposition, but Severo replied that he was sick in bed, so ill that he could not testify.

On October 14, 1831, the judge ruled that all the testimony against Francisco de Castañeda had been heard, Castañeda had made his own statement, and charges had been drawn up against him, so Castañeda was instructed to choose an officer to defend him before a Council of War. Castañeda appointed José María Díez Noriega, who at that time was residing in Matamoros. That same day Castañeda, having heard that an expedition was being organized to go out against the Tahuacano Indians, asked Elosúa to let him go with them, even though charges were pending against him, and Elosúa approved his request.

Finally, on November 16, 1831, Severo Ruiz appeared in court to make his confession, and he appointed Manuel Moutom, Captain of the Eleventh Battalion, then living in Matamoros, to defend him. Severo Ruiz made a 25-page statement, saying that he was 33 years old, a native of the *Villa* of Santa Bárbara, and a Catholic. His memory was very vague about everything that happened.

In November of 1831, orders were sent to Manuel Moutom and José María Díez Noriega to come from Matamoros to defend Severo Ruiz and Francisco Castañeda, but they did not arrive in Béxar until March of 1832.

Finally, in August of 1832, after 117 pesos had been deducted from the bond posted by Severo Ruiz, the case was suspended, insofar as the shortage of funds was concerned, and the balance of the bond posted by Severo was returned to him. However, he was admonished that he would still have to stand trial on all of the other charges which had developed against him in the course of this investigation. These, briefly, were as follows:

1. Taking advantage of his position as Captain of the Álamo de Parras Company to carry on illicit trade with his troops, selling them corn, men and women's shoes, soap, flour, castrated young goats, muttons, chile, ribbons, silk, ornamental combs, and liquor, all at exorbitant prices. Sometimes he used Pedro del Toro, a merchant in Béxar, as a front.

2. Selling mules belonging to the company, and carrying them on the books in such a way that one could not tell whether the mules had died, or strayed, or been stolen by Indians, and then replaced.

3. Sending government soldiers and government mules down into Austin's Colony to receive contraband tobacco at Brazoria and smuggle it to Goliad, San Felipe, Gonzales, Béxar, Laredo, and even beyond the Río Grande, to Revilla, Mier, El Pilón, Cadereita, and Gualeguas. He also carried chamois skins and buffalo robes. On the return trip he smuggled *piloncillo* (brown sugar in cones). He also rented the mules to private parties and pocketed the charges for the freight. The point of rendezvous, where the mules loaded with contraband tobacco joined the army convoy on its way from Béxar to Laredo, was a mesquite thicket near the Espada Mission. Other shipments were unloaded on a lot behind the Álamo Chapel and carried on foot to Pedro del Toro's store.

The net result of all this litigation, so far as the Robertson Colony area was concerned, was to keep the personnel at Tenoxtitlan so tied up with taking depositions that they had little time left for building the permanent fort, patrolling the frontier against Indian attacks, or carrying the mail between Béxar and Nacogdoches.

---

[1]BA Roll 131, Frames 0001-0248.

ANTONIO ELOSÚA TO THE COMMANDANT
OF THE ÁLAMO COMPANY[1]

[Translated from Spanish]

Office of the Principal Commandant)   [January 19, 1831]
)
of Coahuila and Texas_____)

    Alférez Don Francisco de Porras, who is going to that post, will deliver to you the amount of the budget for the company under your command, which he took out of the Paymaster's Office in this city for that purpose, and at the same time he is carrying the corresponding allotments for the picket from the Béxar Company.

    Béxar, January 19, 1831.

[Antonio Elosúa]

To the Commandant of the Álamo Company.

---

[1]BA Roll 138, Frame 0049. Elosúa sent a copy of this letter to Francisco Ruiz on that same date (January 19, 1831), but the draft of that letter is misfiled in the Bexar Archives under January 29, 1831. See BA Roll 138, Frame 0351.

RAMÓN MÚSQUIZ TO THE GOVERNOR OF COAHUILA AND TEXAS[1]

[Translated from Spanish]

Office of the Political Chief)   [January 20, 1831]
)
of Béxar   )

No. 22

Most Excellent Sir:

I am forwarding to the superior hands of Your
Excellency the petitions of José María Román, Corporal of
the Álamo de Parras Company, and Citizen José Manuel de la
Garza, of this community, with the enclosed documents asking for revalidation of the grants which they obtained
under the Spanish Government for the lands described therein; plus those of Lieutenant Juan José Gallardo and Sub-
lieutenant Mariano López, residents in the town of Nacogdoches, who are asking that the lands for which they are
petitioning be adjudicated to them as purchasers.

God and Liberty. Béxar, January 20, 1831.

[Ramón Múquiz]

To the Most Excellent Governor of the State.

Extract:

Encloses four petitions from the citizens named
therein, asking that the lands requested be granted to
them.

---

[1]BA Roll 138, Frame 0065.

ANTONIO ELOSÚA TO FRANCISCO DE PORRAS[1]

[Translated from Spanish]

Office of the Principal Commandant)   [January 20, 1831]
)
of Coahuila and Texas _____)

Since you must go to the Tenoxtitlan Detachment,
please receive, in the Paymaster's office of this City,
the amount of the budget for the Álamo Company and deliver
it at that post to Don Severo Ruiz, Captain of the said
Company.

To Lieutenant Francisco Castañeda you will deliver
the part of the pay that he has coming to him from the
said budget, and, in addition, you will issue an allotment
of four pesos to the invalid Diego Pérez, and you will
turn in, as money, the receipts that both of them will
give you.

Also you will pick up, from the Captain of the
Presidial Company in this City, the allotments for the
picket from the said company that is detached there [at
Tenoxtitlan], and you will deliver them to the person
designated by the said Captain.

God and Liberty. Béxar, January 20, 1831.

[Antonio Elosúa]

To *Alférez* Don Francisco de Porras.

---

[1]BA Roll 138, Frames 0060-0061.

ANTONIO ELOSÚA TO FRANCISCO DE PORRAS[1]

[Translated from Spanish]

Office of the Principal Commandant)   [January 20, 1831]
)
of Coahuila and Texas _____)

You will set out without any loss of time for the Detachment at Tenoxtitlan, and you will present yourself to the Commandant there, Lieutenant Colonel Francisco Ruiz, so that you can exercise the functions of Secretary in the case which, by orders from headquarters, is being drawn up against Lieutenant Francisco Castañeda, of the Álamo Company, for a shortage of funds which has been discovered in the accounts of said company.

God and Liberty. Béxar, January 20, 1831.

[Antonio Elosúa]

To *Alférez* Don Francisco de Porras.

P. S. The enclosed document is to be delivered by you into the hands of Lieutenant Colonel Don Francisco Ruiz.

---

[1]BA Roll 138, Frame 0062.

ANTONIO ELOSÚA TO MANUEL DE MIER Y TERÁN[1]

[Translated from Spanish]

Office of the Principal Commandant)   [January 21, 1831]
)
of Coahuila and Texas _____)   No. 454.

Most Excellent Sir:

By the superior official letter from Your Excellency dated
December 15 last, in which you were pleased to insert for
me the official letter from the Most Excellent Secretary
of War and Navy, I have been informed, with satisfaction,
that the Most Excellent Vice President was pleased to
approve the measures taken with reference to the Tahuacano
and Hueco Indians, and in the name of the Supreme Government I have thanked the citizens, officers, and enlisted
men who took part in the expedition against them. I am
reporting this to Your Excellency by way of reply.

God and Liberty. Béxar, January 21, 1831.

[Antonio Elosúa]

To the Most Excellent Commandant General.

Replies that he has thanked the officers and
enlisted men who took part in the expedition against the
Tahuacanos and Huecos.

---

[1]BA Roll 138, Frames 0101-0102.

ANTONIO ELOSÚA TO MANUEL DE MIER Y TERÁN[1]

[Translated from Spanish]

Office of the Principal Commandant)   [January 21, 1831]
)
of Coahuila and Texas _____)   No. 455.

Most Excellent Sir:

In compliance with the superior order from Your Excellency
dated October 11 of last year, I have forwarded to the
Citizen Commissar of the City of Monterrey one of the four
children who were taken prisoners from the Tahuacano Indians. I did not do the same with the other three because
one of them died, and the other two have not been weaned
yet.

On this occasion I should report to Your Excellency that the individuals who have had the two unweaned
babies in their possession up to the present have made
every effort, and have tried in every way, to raise them
and feed them, and consequently they ask that each one of
them be granted the favor which Your Excellency will find
stated in the original official letter from the Citizen
Political Chief of this Department, which I am respectfully enclosing for your information and guidance.

[Antonio Elosúa]

To the Most Excellent Commandant General.

Reports having forwarded to the City of Monterrey
one of the four children who were taken prisoners from the

Tahuacano Indians, and what happened to the other three.

---

[1]BA Roll 138, Frames 0103-0104.

ANTONIO ELOSÚA TO ERASMO SEGUÍN[1]

[Translated from Spanish]

Office of the Principal Commandant)   [January 21, 1831]
)
of Coahuila and Texas_____)

    Since *Alférez* Don Francisco de Porras has to go to Tenoxtitlan to perform a commission of the service, and since he is taking with him an adequate escort, I should appreciate it if you would take advantage of this opportunity to send the amount of the budget for the Álamo Company, which it is already in need of.

    God and Liberty. Béxar, January 21, 1831.

                            Antonio Elosúa

                                [rubric]

To the Paymaster of this City,)
)
Citizen Erasmo Seguín_____)

---

[1]BA Roll 138, Frame 0095. Both the rough draft and the final copy of this letter are in this same frame.

ANTONIO ELOSÚA TO JORGE DE CEVALLOS[1]

[Translated from Spanish]

Office of the Principal Commandant)   [January 21, 1831]
)
of Coahuila and Texas_____)

Alférez Manuel Menchaca, in an official letter dated today, has written me as follows:

"Private Luciano Flores," etc.

I am copying it for you with reference to the official letter cited therein, so that, accepting the appointment as defender of the aforementioned Luciano Flores, you may set out for this City for the purpose of carrying out your assignment, after giving the proper notices to the Commandant of your Company and to the Commandant of that post.

God, etc. Béxar, January 21, 1831.

[Antonio Elosúa]

To *Alférez* Jorge Cevallos.

---

[1] BA Roll 138, Frame 0861.

JOSÉ MARÍA VIESCA TO RAMÓN MÚSQUIZ[1]

[Translated from Spanish]

[January 22, 1831]

The Most Excellent Commandant General of these
States, under date of December 30 last, writes me as
follows:

[Here he copies the letter from Manuel de Mier y
Terán to José María Viesca, December 30, 1830. See copy
above.]

Consequently, and in view of the fact that the
establishments under consideration deserve all the attention of this Government, I hereby appoint Your Lordship so
that, as commissioner of the said Government, with the
power to delegate the said commission to persons in whom
you have confidence, you may proceed with the formal erec-
tion of said establishments and designate the lands which
they are to occupy, according to the number of families who
are going to settle, as well as those lands which may be
needed for the military posts or detachments which are to
be located, carrying out the respective measures in complete accord with the Colonization Laws, both the general
laws and the individual State laws, and the instructions
which have been given by the Government for the commissioners,
with the understanding that the aforementioned concessions
of land shall be made without injury to the rights which,
according to law, belong to the empresarios within whose

contracts the lands on which the aforesaid establishments are going to be founded happen to lie.

The lands which are to be granted for the aforesaid purpose shall be understood as being granted by the State to the Supreme Government of the Union, according to the terms, prices, and periods of time prescribed by the Colonization Law of March 24, 1825, where it speaks of contracts for colonization by empresarios.

God and Liberty. Leona Vicario [Saltillo], January 22, 1831.

> J[osé] M[arí]a Viesca
>
> Santiago del Valle
>
> Secretary
>
> [Rubric]

To the Political Chief of the)
)
Department of Texas_____)   Béxar

---

[1]Volume 53, pp. 97-98 verso, Spanish Archives, General Land Office, Austin, Texas.

RAMÓN MÚSQUIZ TO VICENTE CÓRDOVA[1]

[Translated from Spanish]

[January 25, 1831]

Office of the Political Chief, etc.

The Law of April 6 of the past year, and the regulations governing passports, dated May 1, 1828. The first one has prohibited the immigration of Anglo-American families, except those who belong to the colonies already established, and the second determines the formalities with which foreigners must comply in order to enter the country. In view of the foregoing, and pursuant to what you tell me in your official letter of December 7 last relative to what you have heard about the furtive manner in which some families entered the country, and the measures which you took to have them appear before you in that court, I am waiting for you to report to me the result they have produced, as you offer to do. Meanwhile you should see to it that the law and the regulations cited above are strictly enforced.

God, etc. Béxar, January 25, 1831.

R[amón] M[úsquiz]

To the Citizen Alcalde of Nacogdoches

---

[1]Nacogdoches Archives, Texas State Library, Austin. The draft of this reply is written on the back of Córdova to Músquiz, December 7, 1830. See text above.

CERTIFICATES OF CHARACTER FOR EPHRAIM RODDY[1]

[January 25, 1831]

State of Tennessee.

I Blackman Coleman, Clerk of the Circuit Court of Law and Equity for the County of Haywood in the State of Tennessee aforesaid do hereby Certify that, I have for some years known & been well acquainted with Ephraim Roddy[2] esquire of said County, and I take much pleasure in stating to all whom it may concern, that he has always been considered here as an upright, correct, honest and Honorable man.

In testimony whereof I have set my hand & affixed the [seal] seal of my office at Brownsville, the 25th of January

A.D. 1831.

Blackman Coleman, Clerk

State of Tennessee)
)
Haywood County   ) Having been well acquainted with Ephraim Roddy Esqr for many years do take pleasure in certifying that he has supported a correct upright & honorouble character during my acquaintance with him.

Brownsville Feb. 21st, 1831.

James Smith

Thos. B. Coleman

M. H. Bradford

J. T. Dobyn

Edmund Richmond
  Atto. at Law

James Tisdale

Mason. F. Johnson   *Physician*

Will H. Loving   Atto: at Law

Will B. Grove

James H. Sims   J. P.

R. B. Harper

L. H. Peters

---

[1]Austin Papers, Unpublished, The University of Texas, Austin. Sterling C. Robertson, in his suit to recover the colony (filed under May 22, 1834) mentioned Ephraim Roddy as one of the colonists he had contracted with before January 2, 1832, to settle in Robertson's Colony.

[2]See Roy Fletcher, "Like Father Like Son," biographical sketch of Ephraim Roddy, in Lee County Historical Survey Committee, *History of Lee County, Texas* (Quanah, Texas: Nortex Press, 1974), pp. 29-30.

SEVERO RUIZ TO ANTONIO ELOSÚA[1]

[Translated from Spanish]

Álamo de Parras   [January 28, 1831]

Presidial Company

Enclosed I am forwarding to Your Lordship the case drawn up against Private José María Vidales, who deserted, so that in view thereof you can decide what should be done. It is written on ordinary paper because here we are completely out of the stamped paper which should have been used.

God and Liberty.   Tenoxtitlan, January 28, 1831.

Severo Ruiz

[rubric]

To the Principal Commandant,)
)
Colonel Don Antonio Elosúa__)

---

[1]BA Roll 138, Frame 0322.

ANTONIO ELOSÚA TO RAMÓN MÚSQUIZ[1]

[Translated from Spanish]

Office of the Principal Commandant)   [January 29, 1831]
)
of Coahuila and Texas _____)

With the official letter from Your Lordship dated the 12th of the present month, in which you were pleased to report to me the petition of Citizens José Antonio Salinas and Juan Casanova, residents of this city, asking that each of them be allowed to keep the boy he has in his possession from those that were taken prisoners from the Tahuacano Indians, I have made a report to the Most Excellent Commandant General Inspector of these States, with my endorsement. I have the honor of reporting this to Your Lordship by way of reply, with the understanding that I will communicate His Excellency's decision to you at the proper time.

God and Liberty. Béxar, January 29, 1831.

                                          Antonio Elosúa

                                          [rubric]

To the Political Chief,)
)
Citizen Ramón Músquiz___)

---

[1]BA Roll 138, Frames 0347-0348. The rough draft of this letter is in Frames 0348-0349.

FRANCISCO RUIZ TO ANTONIO ELOSÚA[1]

[Translated from Spanish]

[January 30, 1831]

Office of the Military Commandant of Tenoxtitlan.
= With the greatest regret I find myself forced to report
to Your Lordship that, in spite of my desires and the
interest I have taken in order to get started on the construction of the fort which both the Most Excellent Commandant General Inspector of these States, and Your Lordship, have repeatedly recommended, up to this date I do
not have the pleasure of telling you that it has been
started. On the contrary, I regret to report that the
official commissioned to build it is incapable of carrying out the assignment, for, despite two trips to San
Felipe de Austin in search of experts for the formation of
the budget, he has only been able to bring back some very
brief notes. I, for my part, lack the necessary knowledge,
and, even if I did have it, since there is no expert to be
found here, and, since I cannot go out personally to hunt
for one elsewhere, I find myself faced with many obstacles
to starting the construction. Consequently I am of the
opinion that, if an expert is not sent, and a commissioner
trained in the matter, it is going to be difficult to
build the said fortification. In view of what has been
stated above, *Alférez* Don Santiago Navayra, the present
commissioner, is going to that city, carrying with him the

notes which I have mentioned above, so that he can show them to Your Lordship, with the results of his commission and the obstacles which are keeping him from carrying out his assignment, as well as the details which he can explain to you, either orally or in writing, for your better information, all of which I regret to report to Your Lordship, so that, if you should see fit, you may forward it to the Most Excellent Commandant General and Inspector of these States, or do whatever you think best.= God and Liberty. Tenoxtitlan, January 30, 1831.=[signed:] Francisco Ruiz.=To the Principal Commandant of Coahuila and Texas, Citizen Colonel Antonio Elosúa.

A copy.

---

[1]BA Roll 138, Frames 0358-0359.

SEVERO RUIZ TO ANTONIO ELOSÚA[1]

[Translated from Spanish]

Álamo de Parras   [January 30, 1831]

Presidial Company

Sergeant Citizen Francisco Mesa has concluded his commission, and he is returning to report to Your Lordship, now
that *Alférez* Don Santiago Navayra is departing [for that
post].

God and Liberty. Tenoxtitlan, January 30, 1831.

Severo Ruiz

[rubric]

To the Principal Commandant,   )
)
Citizen Colonel Don Antonio Elosúa)

---

[1]BA Roll 138, Frame 0353.

SEVERO RUIZ TO ANTONIO ELOSÚA[1]

[Translated from Spanish]

Álamo de Parras   [January 30, 1831]

Presidial Company

Alférez Don Santiago Navayra is departing for that city on
matters pertaining to the fort which he has been commissioned to build. This individual, as former Paymaster of
my Company last year, has not yet closed out his books for
the end of the year so that he can turn them over to his
successor. In order that he may do so, I would appreciate
it if Your Lordship would be so good as to arrange matters
so that his return will not be delayed, at the same time
bringing with him some money for the troops, for which
purpose is taking with him the respective budgets.

God and Liberty. Tenoxtitlan, January 30, 1831.

Severo Ruiz

[rubric]

To the Principal Commandant,   )
)
Citizen Colonel Antonio Elosúa)

---

[1]BA Roll 138, Frames 0355-0356.

DECREE DIVIDING THE DEPARTMENT OF BÉXAR

INTO TWO DISTRICTS[1]

[January 31, 1831]

DECREE No. 164.

The Congress of the State of Coahuila and Texas, consider-

ing the evils experienced in the political and

financial administration of the department of Texas

for the reason that the extensive territory thereof

is comprised in one sole district, and populated

mostly by foreign colonists, thinly settled therein;

exercising the power conferred by article 8 of the

constitution, decrees:

ART. 1. The department of Bexar shall be divided

into two districts, and the following shall be the dividing

line--commencing at Bolivar Point on Galveston Bay; thence

running northwesterly to strike between the San Jacinto and

Trinity rivers, following the dividing ridge between the

said rivers to the head waters of San Jacinto; thence

following the dividing ridge between the Brazos and Trinity

to the head waters of the latter, and terminating north of

the source of the said Trinity upon Red River.

ART. 2. The territory situated east of said line

shall be called the District of Nacogdoches, and the town

of the same name shall be the capital.

ART. 3. A district chief shall reside in said

town, or at such place as the executive shall think most

proper, whose appointment, removal, attributes, salary and office expenses shall be in the manner and form provided by the constitution and laws in force with respect to that class of officers.

ART. 4. The aforementioned department shall continue to be governed agreeably to the provision of this decree, and such as was established for that effect prior thereto.

ART. 5. On receipt of this decree, measures shall be taken for the appointment of the district chief herein mentioned.

For its fulfilment, the Governor of the State shall cause it to be printed, published, and circulated.

Given in the city of Leona Vicario [Saltillo] on the 31st of January, 1831.

JOSÉ CAYETANO RAMOS, President.

PEDRO de la FUENTE FERNÁNDEZ, D. S.

JOSÉ de JESÚS GRANDE, D. S.

---

[1]H. P. N. Gammel (compiler and arranger), *The Laws of Texas, 1822-1897* (10 vols.; Austin: The Gammel Book Store, 1898), I, (281). This document also appears, in both Spanish and English, in J. P. Kimball (translator), *Laws and Decrees of the State of Coahuila and Texas, In Spanish and English. To Which is Added the Constitution of Said State: Also:--The Colonization Law of the State of Tamaulipas, and Naturalization Law of the General Congress. By Order of the Secretary of State. Translated by J. P. Kimball, M. D.* (Houston: Telegraph Power Press, 1839), p. 171. The Béxar Department was divided, by Decree No. 270, of March 18, 1834, into the Béxar Department and the Brazos Department. See text below under that date.

ANTONIO ELOSÚA TO JOSÉ DE LAS PIEDRAS[1]

[Translated from Spanish]

Office of the Principal Commandant)   [February 1, 1831]
)
of Coahuila and Texas_____)

By your official letter dated the 17th of the month
just past, I have been informed of the circumstances under
which Private Manuel Tarín was apprehended at that post and
Tomás Lazo turned himself in, both of them being from the
Álamo Company. I am reporting this to Your Lordship in
reply, with the understanding that, at the first opportunity, I hope you will be so good as to have them conducted
to this City, or to Tenoxtitlan, which I believe would be
easier.

God and Liberty. Béxar, February 1, 1831.

[Antonio Elosúa]

To Colonel Citizen José de las Piedras.

---

[1]BA Roll 137, Frame 1013.

ANTONIO ELOSÚA TO JOSÉ DE LAS PIEDRAS[1]

[Translated from Spanish]

Office of the Principal Commandant)   [February 1, 1831]
)
of Coahuila and Texas_____)

I received, with the official letter from Your Lordship dated the 18th of last month, the declaration taken from the soldiers who deserted from the Álamo de Parras Company, Manuel Tarín and Tomás Lazo. I am writing you this by way of reply.

God and Liberty. Béxar, February 1, 1831.

[Antonio Elosúa]

To Colonel Citizen José de las Piedras.

---

[1]BA Roll 138, Frame 0026.

ÁLAMO DE PARRAS PRESIDIAL COMPANY[1]

[Translated from Spanish]

[February 1, 1831]

Budget showing the amounts due the individuals of said Company in the present month, after deducting for invalids and pensions.

Officers.	Pesos	R.	G.	Pesos	R.	G.
1 Captain--------------------#.	117.	6.	0.			
1 Lieutenant----------------#.	62.	6.	6.			
1 1st *Alférez*---------------#.	47.	0.	10.	.266.	7.	6.
1 2nd ditto-----------------#.	39.	2.	2.			

Enlisted Men.	Pesos	R.	G.	Pesos	R.	G.
1 Sergeant-------------------#.	29.	1.	0.			
1 Bugler--------------------#.	11.	5.	6.			
6 Corporals at 24ps.2rrs.2gs.#.	145.	5.	0.	1.117.	7.	6.
48 Privates at 19ps.3rrs.3gs.#.	931.	4.	0.			

Invalids Added.	Pesos	R.	G.	Pesos	R.	G.
1 Private-------------------#.	8.	0.	0.			
Gratifications.				.48.	3.	7.
For the men------------------#.	40.	3.	7.			

Rewards for Constancy.	Pesos	R.	G.	Pesos	R.	G.
1 at 90 rrs.----------------#.	11.	2.	0.			
1 at 9 rrs.----------------#.	1.	1.	0.	.14.	5.	0.
3 at 6 rrs.----------------#.	2.	2.	0.			
				#1.447.	7.	7.

Credit for Additions.

None.

Deduct for Losses.

	Pesos	R.	G.
Deduct from this total 30 pesos that are being enjoyed in Monterrey by the family of the Captain of said Company pertaining to the present month------------------------#.	30.	0.	0.

Deduct also 36ps.2rrs.6gs.
that failed to be earned in
the month of January last by
Privates Tomás Lazo and
Manuel Tarín because they
deserted beginning with the
3rd day of said month--------#. 36. 2. 6.

. 66. 2. 6.

#1.381. 5. 1.

Add to this total the pay of Chaplain Don
    Juan Nepomuceno Ayala, who is serving
    as an attaché in this Company------------# . 40. 0. 0.
                              Net assets-----#1.421. 5. 1.

    Tenoxtitlan, February 1, 1831.

O. K.   As the one in charge of the Paymaster's Office.

    [Severo] Ruiz   Francisco Mesa

        [rubric]   [rubric]

---

[1]BA Roll 138, Frames 0432-0433. There is a duplicate copy of this report in Frames 0433-0434.

JOSÉ ANDRÉS DE SOBREVILLA TO ANTONIO ELOSÚA[1]

[Translated from Spanish]

Office of the Military Commandant)   [February 2, 1831]
)
of the Garrison at Laredo_____)

With the official letter from Your Lordship dated the 12th of the past month, Private Estevan León, of the First Permanent Company of Tamaulipas, has delivered to me the Tahuacano Indian which Your Lordship tells me is on his way to the Commissariat in Monterrey, as the result of an order from the Most Excellent Commandant General and Inspector of these States, in view whereof you ask me to be so good as to have him conducted, with a document which you enclosed for me, to said city, with two or three soldiers, with the understanding that he has come furnished with sufficient money and supplies for the trip, adding that if, in spite of this, he should need any help, I am to make it available to him. In view of the foregoing I wish to inform Your Lordship that, within two or three days, I will duly comply with those instructions. I have not been able to do so during the past week because I had sent out what few troops I had to pursue some Indians who stole a herd of horses within the limits of this jurisdiction. I am writing you this by way of reply to your aforementioned letter.

God and Liberty. Laredo, February 2, 1831.

José Andrés de Sobrevilla

[rubric]

To the Principal Commandant,   )
)
Citizen Colonel Antonio Elosúa)   Béxar.

---

[1]BA Roll 138, Frames 0490-0491.

STERLING C. ROBERTSON *VS*. THE STATE OF TENNESSEE[1]

[Wednesday, February 2, 1831]

No. 1   Sterling C. Robertson   Plaintiff
              vs   In Error
           The State   Defendant

By Consent said Cause[2] is Set for trial, on the

third Thursday of this month.[3]

Court adjourned until tomorrow morning 10 o'clock.

J[oh]n Catron

Isaac Peck

---

[1]"Minute Book of Tennessee State Supreme Court of Errors and Appeals, 1831-1834," Department of Archives, Fifth Floor, Tennessee State Library and Archives, 403 Seventh Avenue North, Nashville, Tennessee 37203.

[2]For the background of this case, see McLean, *Papers*, III, 440-453: "The State of Tennessee *vs* Sterling C. Robertson: Indictment for murder of Edward Randolph." Those proceedings ended on December 30, 1829, with this statement: "This day came the Attorney General, and said Defendant [Sterling C. Robertson] by his atto[rney] [and] tendered a bill of exceptions to the opinion of the Court which was received signed and sealed by the Court and ordered to be made a part of the record of said cause." We have been unable to find this bill of exceptions or any other proceedings in this case between December 30, 1829, and February 2, 1831, the date of this present document.

[3]The next record of these proceedings that we have found is dated March 10, 1831, not February 17, 1831, which would have been "the third Thursday," so the reader will find the story continued under March 10, 1831.

Meanwhile, after we had published Volume III of these *Papers*, Mrs. W. F. Fullerton, Genealogical Research, 624 Oakley Drive, Nashville, Tennessee 37220, found the following document giving the Randolph family version of the case, and sent it to us with a letter dated July 31, 1976. We reproduce it here because it gives one version which appears to explain the lapse of time in prosecution of the case, but, when we get to the proceedings under March 10, 1831, they will give an entirely different explanation of what happened. Now for the Randolph family version.

"On the emigration from Virginia, shortly prior to 1828, the [Randolph] family first passed through East Tennessee, stopping momentarily at Knoxville, then on through Middle Tennessee to Nashville where the family resided for awhile. At that time Henry Randolph, the head of the family, was nearing 70 years of age, and his oldest child, Edward (always called Ned) had charge of the family on their emigration. The latter was a man of high character but he never married. While residing in Nashville, Ned Randolph hired one of their negroes to a man named Robinson [Sterling Clack Robertson]. A dispute arose relative to this negro and a fight ensued between Ned and Robinson in which Robinson stabbed him with a dirk and killed him. Robinson fled to Texas. ..."--Wassell Randolph, "Henry Randolph I (1623-1773) of Henrico County, Virginia, and His Descendants. Preceded by short review of the Randolph family in Early England and elsewhere" (Memphis, Tennessee: Distributed by Cossitt Library, 1952), pp. 81-81. Typescript.

STEPHEN F. AUSTIN TO THE GOVERNOR OF COAHUILA AND TEXAS[1]

[Translated from Spanish]

[Saltillo, February 3, 1831]

Most Excellent Sir:

The official letter from Your Excellency dated November 12 last[2] asking me to make a report as to whether the lands which are being asked for by Messrs. Villeveques in Texas, for colonization, are occupied because they have already been designated for other empresarios, reached me in [San Felipe de] Austin at the time that I was leaving for this city, and I had to bring it here in order to acquire the necessary data from the Secretariat concerning the boundaries of the enterprises already granted, in order to comply more exactly with the said request, as I wrote Your Excellency from the said *villa*.[3] Therefore, having before me the contracts made with various empresarios, as they appear on record in the archive of the Secretariat of the Government, and the map of Texas, it appears that the lands which the aforesaid Messrs. Villeveques are asking for, on the Trinity and Nueces [Neches] Rivers, and which they have designated on the map which they enclose with their request, in blue, are all included in the contracts with Mr. José Viclen [Vehlein] and Company, and Mr. Lorenzo [de] Zavala.

The land which the same gentlemen are asking for, and which they have designated on the same map, in red, is included in the contracts with the Nashville Company, and with Mr. David G. Burnet. There is quite an extensive piece of land situated to the north of the road that goes from Nacogdoches to Natchitoches, which is not occupied by any contract, according to what I have been told, and I find no obstacle to granting it to Messrs. Villeveques in order to be colonized in conformity with the colonization laws. Part of the aforementioned land is situated within the twenty border leagues, and, since they are asking that they be granted two contracts, it can be done, in my opinion, within the following boundaries:

1st. Leaving the Nacogdoches communal lands free, a line shall be run from the said town in a direction between north and west, parallel with the dividing line between Texas and the United States of the North, and twenty leagues distant from the said dividing line, until it intersects the Sulphur River, which is the southern line of the colony of General Arthur G. Wavell, and thence descending the said Sulphur River (known in English by the name of Sulphur Fork) to its mouth in the Red River of Natchitoches, and following the latter downstream to the boundary line, and following the latter toward the south as far as the road that goes from Nacogdoches to Natchitoches, at the point known by the name of Crow's Crossing, or by another name, [Gain]es Crossing, and, from the said crossing, following the said road as far as Nacogdoches, including all the

land inside the twenty border leagues between the said
road and the southern boundary of Wavell's Colony. This
land is designated in yellow on the map which I am enclosing.

2nd. The second contract can be extended under the
land delineated above, and at the northeast corner of the
David G. Burnet Colony, which said corner is fifteen
leagues from Nacogdoches, and from the said corner in a
straight line toward the west to the heights which divide
the waters of the Trinity and Brazos Rivers, and following
the said heights toward the northwest to the southern
boundary of the John Cameron Colony, which said boundary is
twenty leagues from the Red River, and following the said
boundary toward the east to the headwaters of the Sulphur
River, descending the latter until it intersects the western boundary of the land previously delineated for the
first contract, and following the said boundary toward the
south to the point where the first line began, at the
northeast corner of the David G. Burnet Colony. This piece
of land is designated on the said map in green.

It should be observed that part of the land
included in the second demarcation was granted to Empresario
Frost Thorn to colonize, but he has never taken a single
step in the matter, and his contract is going to terminate
in the month of April next because its time has run out.

It should also be noted that the dividing line

between Texas and the United States of the North has not been surveyed, and that there are doubts about whether it will fall below or above the mouth of the Sulphur River.

The lands which I have designated are a good quality, so I am told, and they abound in good timber, springs, and permanent streams, and they have the advantages of several outlets to the coast: one through the port of Galveston, and through the Neches and Angelina rivers, which are navigable, when they are on a rise, to within ten leagues of Nacogdoches; another from the same port through the Trinity River, which is also navigable, and another through [New] Orleans and the Red River up to Natchitoches.

This is all that I can say on the matter in reply to the aforesaid official letter from Your Excellency, and I am reporting it to Your Excellency and returning the map for your information and guidance.

[Stephen F. Austin]

[To the Governor of Coahuila and Texas]

---

[1]Barker, *Austin Papers*, II, 592-593.

[2]This letter has not been found in the Austin Papers, either published or unpublished.

[3]See Stephen F. Austin to Governor Eça y Músquiz, December 14, 1830.

STEPHEN F. AUSTIN'S APPLICATION FOR A COLONIZATION

CONTRACT FOR HIMSELF AND SAMUEL M. WILLIAMS[1]

[Translated from Spanish]

[February 4, 1831]

973   34

SELLO TERCERO   [Seal:]   PARA EL BIENIO DE
                    HACIENDA DEL ESTADO
DOS REALES.   LIBRE DE   1830 Y 1831.
                    COAHUILA Y TEJAS.

Most Excellent Mr. Governor:

I, Citizen Stephen F. Austin, Deputy in the Honorable Con-

gress of the State, with all due respect, wish to inform

Your Excellency that, having dedicated the last ten years

to the work of planting new settlements in the wilderness

of Texas, I have had the satisfaction of seeing them pro-

gress and flourish under the protection and auspices of

the liberal and free Government of the State. But, despite

the advances already made, it is quite necessary not to

relax our efforts to increase the population, particularly

in the interior of Texas, where the wild Indians take ref-

uge, and from whence they come forth to make war on the

new colonies, and along the entire frontier. Therefore,

moved by these considerations, and knowing that it is the

desire of the Government to promote an increase in popula-

tion in the region indicated, I offer to dedicate my practical knowledge to the matter, in order to introduce and establish eight hundred families in the interior of Texas, together with a companion who is a Citizen of the State with eight years of residence, and who has had seven years of experience in colonization, as Secretary of my Colony, with the advantages of knowing three languages: Spanish, French, and English. The companion to whom I refer is Citizen Samuel M. Williams.

As a consequence of what has been set forth above, and by virtue of the enclosed power of attorney which the said Don Samuel has granted to me,[2] I ask Your Excellency to be so good as to grant a colonization contract to Stephen F. Austin and Samuel M. Williams as *empresarios*, to introduce and establish, in conformity with the colonization laws, eight hundred Mexican and foreign families, eligible to be introduced as colonists under the general laws and the laws of the state, and that the vacant lands within the following limits be designated for said enterprise:

Beginning the line on the left [east] bank of the "arroyo de la baca" [Lavaca River] ten leagues from the coast, and following said *arroyo* upstream to its westernmost headwaters, and from thence in a straight line toward the northwest to the road that goes from Béxar to Nacogdoches, known as the Upper Road, and following said road toward the northeast to the Colorado River, it will go up said river to the mouth of the Salado [Salt] or Colorado [Red] Fork which enters about fifteen leagues [39 miles] above the mouth of the Pecan or Nueces River, and from the said Salt Fork a straight line shall be drawn toward the northeast to the heights that divide the waters of the Brazos and Trinity Rivers, and following the said heights toward the southeast to the principal headwaters of the San Jacinto River, and descending this river to the line of the ten litoral leagues along the coast, the said line shall continue toward the west to the point where the first line began on the Lavaca River.

Any lands which may be selected by the Commissioner of the General Government for the establishment of Tenoxtic- lan [Tenoxtitlan] above the said road from Béxar, on the Brazos River, are excepted from this demarcation.

Parts of the lands designated above are included in the colonization contracts of *Empresario* Stephen F. Austin dated June 4, 1825, and November 20, 1827, and parts are in the contract of Robert Leftwich for the Nashville Company, celebrated on April 15, 1825, which contracts will expire six years after the dates on which they were made, so that I ask that this new contract with the said Stephen F. Austin and Samuel M. Williams become effective on the respective days on which the aforementioned contracts expire, giving it a period of six years, counting from that day, for the respective parties. But, despite the fact

that this new contract will not go into effect until the
days indicated, I ask that it be celebrated now, and that
a certified copy be issued to the interested parties so
that they can proceed immediately to make arrangements and
take the necessary measures preparatory to moving families
from the interior of this Republic and from Europe so as
not to lose any time planting the colony as soon as the
other contracts expire.

Leona Vicario [Saltillo], February 4, 1831.

Most Excellent Sir:

[signed:]   Estevan F. Austin

for himself and as agent of

Samuel M. Williams[3]

[rubric]

Also

I ask that an article be included in the aforementioned
contract, stipulating that no one shall have the
right to select and denounce lands within the designated limits without the knowledge and approval
of the said *Empresarios* Austin and Williams because,
without this, it may happen that, on the arrival
of the families contracted for in Europe or in the
interior of this Republic, the same land designated

and promised to them by the *Empresarios*, in order
to stimulate them to emigrate, may be occupied by
others, thus compromising the *empresarios* and the
Government, delaying and greatly displeasing the
emigrants. Valid.

[signed:] Estevan F. Austin

[rubric] [4]

[*For the reply to this petition, see the*
"Colonization Contract of Austin & Williams,
February 25, 1831."]

---

[1]In 1940 Mrs. McLean and I made a trip to Saltillo
and spent a week copying this document and others from the
Spanish originals. At that same time the exact location
and description of this file was as follows: Saltillo,
Secretaría de Gobierno, Archivo, Legajo 25, Expediente
1061, but, when we went back to check the documents on
July 11, 1967, the originals had disappeared. Fortunately,
however, we still have our copy in longhand, and there is
a photostatic copy in The University of Texas at Austin
Library, Barker Texas History Center, under "Saltillo
Archives," Volume XXX, pp. 174-184. The present translation was made by Malcolm D. McLean from the original Spanish manuscript, which was very generously made available
by J. P. Bryan, Jr., No. 3 Shadowlawn, Houston, Texas,
77005, while he was attending the annual meeting of the
Collectors' Institute at UT Arlington on November 6, 1976.
We are happy to publish it here for the Austin family,
since Dr. Barker omitted it from the published *Austin*
Papers; in fact, he did not even list it among the unpublished Austin Papers.

[2]Notice that in this document, dated February 4,
1831, Austin says that he is enclosing the power of attorney, but, in the letter which Austin wrote Williams the
next day, he says he has not been able to find it.

[3]All of these last three lines appear to be in the
handwriting of Stephen F. Austin, but the main body of the

document was written by a third party, neither Austin nor Williams.

[4]The rubric used here under the name of Austin looks very similar to the one used above for the name of Williams.

ON THE NEXT TWO PAGES WE HAVE GRAPHIC EXAMPLES OF ONE OF THE MOST IMPORTANT MOMENTS IN THE COLONIZATION OF TEXAS: WHEN STEPHEN F. AUSTIN APPLIED FOR A COLONIZATION CONTRACT INCLUDING THE AREA ASSIGNED TO ROBERT LEFTWICH, *BEFORE LEFTWICH'S CONTRACT HAD EXPIRED*. LATER AUSTIN WROTE: "I AM OF THE OPINION THAT THE UPPER COLONY WILL TOTALLY RUIN ME ...CURSED BE THE HOUR I EVER THOUGHT OF APPLYING FOR THAT UPPER COLONY."

ON THE LEFTHAND PAGE WE HAVE A FACSIMILE OF THE ORIGINAL DOCUMENT, WHICH WAS MADE AVAILABLE FOR COPYING ON NOVEMBER 6, 1976, BY J. P. BRYAN, JR., NO. 3 SHADOWLAWN, HOUSTON, TEXAS 77005. IT MEASURES 12.5 INCHES LONG BY 8 INCHES WIDE, BUT THE ILLUSTRATION HERE HAS BEEN REDUCED TO ABOUT TWO-THIRDS OF THE ORIGINAL SIZE.

THE FACSIMILE ON THE RIGHTHAND PAGE COMES FROM THE PHOTOSTAT MADE MANY YEARS AGO FROM THE ORIGINAL DOCUMENT ON FILE IN THE STATE ARCHIVES IN SALTILLO. THESE PHOTOSTATS ARE IN THE "SALTILLO ARCHIVES," VOLUME XXX, PP. 174-184, BARKER TEXAS HISTORY CENTER, THE UNIVERSITY OF TEXAS AT AUSTIN.

> ACCORDING TO A ROBERTSON FAMILY TRADITION,
> THIS PAGE CONTAINS A PECULIAR BLOT WHICH,
> WHEN STUDIED IN THE PROPER LIGHT, SHOWS TWO
> LITTLE DEVILS WITH PITCHFORKS MAKING HAY IN
> THE PUBLIC DOMAIN, BUT UNFORTUNATELY, THE
> TRADITION ADDS, THESE PHANTOM FIGURES REVEAL
> THEMSELVES ONLY TO THE PURE IN HEART.

de familias del interior de esta republica y de
europa afin de no perder tiempo en planear
la Colonia luego que se concluyan los otros
Contratos

Leonavicano 4 de Febrero de 1931.

Exmo. Sor.

Estevan F. Austin
para si, y como apoderado de
Samuel M. Williams

Otrosi
Pida que se ponga un art. en el mencionado Contrato que nin-
guno tendra el derecho de escoger y denunciar
tierras dentro de los limites designados sin co-
nocimiento y aprobacion de los dichos Contratan-
tes Austin y Williams por que sin ellos
succeden que a la llegada de las familias contra-
tadas de europa ó del interior de esta republica
el mismo terreno designado y prometido á
ellas por los Empresarios afin de estimular-
las a emigrar seria ocupado por otros asi-
Comprometiendo a los Empresarios y al Govi
erno Contrario y seguro notable de parte de los emigrados = Vale
Estevan F. Austin Con-

STEPHEN F. AUSTIN TO SAMUEL M. WILLIAMS[1]

Leona Vicario [Saltillo], February 5, 1831

Dr. Sir,

In my letter to Johnson I have said all there is to say, about public matters-- We get on slowly, but I think I shall succeed in the main point, which is the Judiciary. I have been fortunate so far, in keeping a harmonious understanding with all, and shall endeavor to continue it-- The petitions for land will all be dispatched next week. The office has been searched for your petition, it cannot be found--[2] This morning I told the secretary that I would present another petition as your agent,[3] he said that he would look once more, and if the other could not be found that I could present a new one, and the Gov[erno]r has promised that it shall be *immediately* dispatched--[4] So that you may consider the thing as certain-- Those who asked for large quantities will get what ought to satisfy them, and if they had confined themselves to reasonable bounds at first, their petitions would have been granted long since--

Father Muldoon leaves tomorrow for Monterrey, he appears to be a true *Austinian* and I think he is sincere for he has obtained a large *bite*[5] of land from the Gov[er-nor] and looks to Texas as his only home, and final resting place.

Chambers has been *bedevilled* here, by delays of
one sort or another, and is not yet dispatched by the tri-
bunal and probably will not be for a month to come.[6] The
obstacle to his admission as a lawyer now is, the want of
his *certificate of baptism*. Tomorrow he presents a petition to Congress to dispence with that requisite, and he
will then be exam[ine]d by the judges--I think he will be
a usefull man in Texas--

Matters are doubtfull in Mexico [meaning Mexico
City]. The partisans of Pedraza are beginning to make a
great noise and you need not be much surprised if he
should come on by land through Texas--if so treat him with
all possible respect and attention, for he is justly
entitled to it-- It is said that [Manuel de Mier y] Teran
is going to Texas soon-- My confidence in him is still
unimpaired, I believe he is the best among them all-- A
number of the first men in Mexico have obtained 11 League
Grants in Texas--

There is a rumor here which I do not like, which is
that [Lorenzo de] Zavala is on the way to Texas, and Teran
is going to repel him by force--I know not where the rumor
came from--I hope it is not so for I do not wish to see the
civil war of the Mexicans introduced into Texas-- Say nothing about it, for it is only vague rumor.

I wrote you from Monclova--from here by José Luis

Carabajal by whom I sent the white horse, also by the last mail-- You have acknowledged the recpt. of mine from Béxar and Rio Grande.   I mention the others that you may know if any miscarry--

I am happy to hear of the safe arrival of Mr. Dwyer and family and others from Alabama which you inform me of in your last letter.   The plan of sending the certificates[7] by Grayson was a very good one.   I wish you to write to him, that I say he has a league of land in Texas,[8] and that he must hurry back to improve it, & bring a wife and *one hundred good families for neighbors*-- You see by Tonys [Anthony Butler's] letter that there are some snakes in the grass round San Felipe.   I have a *notion* who they are, perhaps I am mistaken-- You know that I have been very cautious in shewing his letters--others have done it, & criticized them and it is all charged upon me.

Remember me to Sarah [Mrs. Samuel M. Williams] & Eliza [Williams, Samuel's sister] & all friends.

S. F. Austin

You say nothing about the)
)
progress of the Storehouse)

I enclose Johnson's letter to you [*i.e.*, the letter I wrote Johnson] least it should miscarry.   You must make him pay his portion of the postage.[9]

[Addressed:] Al Ciudnno [Ciudadano, Citizen]

Samuel M. Williams Administrador de correos [Postmaster]

en [San Felipe de] Austin

---

[1]Transcribed directly from the original in the Samuel May Williams Papers, Rosenberg Library, Galveston, Texas. This document was published in Barker, *Austin Papers*, II, 594-595, but the footnotes which appear below were written by Malcolm D. McLean.

[2]On April 6, 1830, Samuel M. Williams had applied to J. Antonio Padilla, General Commissioner, for seven additional leagues of land, but Ramón Músquiz, the Political Chief, did not approve the petition until February 9, 1831, four days after Austin wrote this letter, so the petition that Austin expected to find in Leona Vicario must have still been in Béxar, waiting for Músquiz to endorse it, when Austin went by the office in Leona Vicario to look for it. Meanwhile, on January 3, 1831, while Austin was en route to Saltillo (Leona Vicario), he had written Williams as follows: "After my arrival at Saltillo I think I can get your petition granted ...."--Barker, *Austin Papers*, II, 571-572. This shows us that it was not until after Austin discovered that the Williams petition was missing that he had the inspiration of presenting an entirely different petition, for both himself and Williams.

This brings us to the realization that the document reproduced above, dated February 4, 1831, and purporting to be a joint application by both Austin and Williams, *for a colonization contract*, was an entirely different document from the petition filed by Williams alone on April 6, 1830, *for seven leagues of land*.--See McLean, *Papers*, III, 492-493.

[3]As a matter of fact, Austin had already produced "a new one" on the day before he wrote this letter, and the day before he told the secretary that he would present another petition as the agent of Williams. See "Stephen F. Austin's Application for a Colonization Contract for Himself and Samuel M. Williams," February 4, 1831.

[4]Austin underscored the word *immediately* to convey to Williams the idea that Williams would not possibly have time to issue a new power of attorney and transmit it by horseback from San Felipe de Austin to Leona Vicario. In his letter of March 12, 1831, Austin urged Williams to go back and read over his letters by the last two mails because, he said, "more is meant there than is plainly expressed."--Barker, *Austin Papers*, II, 611-613.

[5]Austin underlined the word "bite" to convey the idea that the transaction was really a bribe (mordida). At the time when Austin wrote this letter, Father Miguel Muldoon had not officially received any land in his own name, but during the course of the next year he received a total of eleven leagues, distributed as follows:

May 14, 1831. 2 leagues from Commissioner Arciniega in present Wharton County.

May 23, 1831. 2 leagues from Commissioner Arciniega in present Fayette County.

December 15, 1831. 2 leagues in Austin's Third Colony in present Galveston County.

February 28, 1832. 5 leagues from Commissioner Arciniega: 2 of which were in Fayette County, and the other three were in Lavaca County.
--Taylor, *The Spanish Archives* ..., p. 216.

[6]It took considerably longer than a month. The decree excusing Thomas Jefferson Chambers from taking the examination, and permitting him to practice law in the State of Coahuila and Texas, was not passed until January 8, 1834. The complete text will be reproduced under that date.

[7]See "Printed Form for Admitting Austin Colonists." entered under January 15, 1831.

[8]Peter Wm. Grayson received 1 league of land in Austin's Third Colony, in present Matagorda County, on July 22, 1831, some five months after this letter was written.--Taylor, *The Spanish Archives* ..., p. 191.

[9]In those days in Mexico it was customary for the person *receiving* the letter to pay the postage. It was not until February 21, 1856, when Guillermo Prieto was Postmaster General, that Mexico established the system of prepaid postage.--Malcolm D. McLean, *Vida y obra de Guillermo Prieto* (México, D.F.: El Colegio de México, 1960), p. 26.

RAMÓN MÚSQUIZ TO ANTONIO ELOSÚA[1]

[Translated from Spanish]

[February 9, 1831]

Office of the Chief of the)
)
Béxar Department _____)

I have been informed of the contents of the official letter from the Most Excellent Commandant General Inspector of these States dated December 20 of last year,[2]
which your Lordship was pleased to enclose for me with
yours dated January 19 last, which, in brief, orders that
the foreigner Sterling Robertson be informed of the suspension of the colonization enterprise for which the North
American families which he had brought in were destined,
and that this office be informed of this measure so that
it may dictate the proper measures to the effect that the
Law of April 6 of last year should be enforced. In obedi-
ence thereto I beg Your Lordship to be so good as to issue
an order to the Citizen Commandant of the Tenoxtitlan Detachment, so that he can arrange for the said Robertson
and the families accompanying him to return to the country
from which they came, placing them for this purpose at the
disposition of the Military Commandant of the town of Nacogdoches so that they may be transferred without fail to the
opposite bank of the Sabine River, calling upon the Citizen
Alcalde of that town for such help as he may need, and in
this connection I shall send him the corresponding order

by the next mail.

God and Liberty. Béxar, February 9, 1831.

Ramón Músquiz

[Rubric]

To the Principal Commandant,)
)
Colonel Don Antonio Elosúa__)

---

[1]Volume 54, pp. 285-285 verso, Spanish Archives, General Land Office, Austin, Texas.

[2]See Manuel de Mier y Terán to Antonio Elosúa, December 20, 1830.

HOSEA H. LEAGUE TO SAMUEL M. WILLIAMS[1]

[February 9, 1831]

Samuel M. Williams Esqr.

Dear Sir, I Sent to Mr. Jacks Room a few days Since for my Partidas[2] and was informed that you had it. If So I wish you would Send it to me by the bearer and also my Lex Moreatoria[3] I loaned you last Spring, and also a Coppy of a letter to Sterling C. Robinson [Robertson], which I requested you to Exhibit to Col. [Stephen F.] Austin, and afterwards to return it to me, and oblige yours &c

H. H. Leag[ue]

February 9th, 1831.

[Addressed:] Samuel M. Williams Esqr.

[Endorsed:] 1831 H. H. League Feb. 9th, Asking for return of books loaned & &

---

[1]Item 23-0568, Samuel M. Williams Papers, Rosenberg Library, Galveston, Texas.

[2]"*Las Partidas*. In Spanish law. The name of the code of laws, more fully described as "*Las Siete Partidas*," ("the seven parts," from the number of its divisions,) which was compiled under the direction of Alphonso X., about the year 1250.

"Its sources were the customary law of all the provinces, the canon law as there administered, and (chiefly) the Roman law. This work has always been regarded as of the highest authority in Spain and in those countries and states which have derived their jurisprudence from Spain."

--Henry Campbell Black, *Black's Law Dictionary: Definitions of the Terms and Phrases of American English Jurisprudence, Ancient and Modern* (Revised Fourth Edition, St. Paul, Minn.: West Publishing Co., 1968), p. 1024.

[3]Probably *Lex Mercatoria*. "The law-merchant. That system of laws which is adopted by all commercial nations, and constitutes a part of the law of the land. It is part of the common law. ..."--*Ibid.*, p. 1056.

ANTONIO ELOSÚA TO THE MILITARY COMMANDANT OF TENOXTITLAN[1]

[Translated from Spanish]

Office of the Military Commandant)   [February 11, 1831]
)
of Coahuila and Texas _____)

The Citizen Political Chief of this Department, in an official letter dated the 9th of the present month, has been pleased to write me as follows:

"I have been informed of the contents of the official letter from the Most Excellent Commandant General Inspector," etc.

I am transcribing it for you for your information and so that you can take care of the enforcement of the orders of the said Political Chief.

God and Liberty. Béxar, February 11, 1831.

[Antonio Elosúa]

To the Military Commandant of Tenoxtitlan.

---

[1]BA Roll 138, Frame 0704.

RAMÓN MÚSQUIZ TO THE GOVERNOR OF COAHUILA AND TEXAS[1]

[Translated from Spanish]

Office of the Chief of the Department   [February 13, 1831]

    No. 27

Most Excellent Sir:

    By the communication from the Most Excellent Commandant General of these States, dated December 30 of the past year, which Your Excellency was pleased to enclose for me with your superior order of January 22 last, I have been informed that approval has been given, by the Supreme General Government, as a consequence of the provisions of the Law of April 6 last, for the new settlements of Mexican families and soldiers at the mouth of the Lavaca River, at the head of Galveston Bay, and at the point which has been given the name of Tenoxtitlan on the Brazos River, which are going to be founded at the expense of the Federal Government, and about the commission which in that connection Your Excellency has been pleased to confer upon me, with the authority to delegate the responsibility to persons whom I consider reliable, in order to proceed to the formal setting up of these establishments and to designate the lands which they are to occupy, according to the number of families of settlers, in conformity with the explanations contained in the said superior order.

    Since I am interested in setting up these useful and appropriate establishments quickly, I will, on the

first opportunity which presents itself, reach an agreement
with the Most Excellent Commandant General, giving him
notice of the aforesaid commission, so that he may be
pleased to tell me the number of families which are to be
located at each one of the three settlements which he has
promoted, in order to proceed to designate the lands which
they may need, suggesting to him that this office is
inclined to delegate the commission to persons whom it considers reliable, and from whom, when necessary, one may
require the responsibility set forth in Article 8 of Law
No. 128. [See text under April 10, 1830.]

Of the points designated for the aforesaid establishments, the one on the Lavaca corresponds to the colonists contracted for by Empresarios Stephen F. Austin,
James Power, and James Wilson; the one on Galveston Bay,
to Don José Vehlein and Company, and the one named Tenoxtitlan, to Don Robert Leftwich, transferred to the Nashville Company. The rights which, according to law, these
empresarios have to the lands which in their contracts may
be occupied by the Mexicans, I understand are reduced to
the premium which has been offered to them with respect to
the number of families which they may introduce; if there
are any other rights, I beg Your Excellency to be so kind
as to tell me about them so that I may be prepared to face
any demands which of necessity the said *empresarios* are
going to make.

This is quite a distinction which Your Excellency has seen fit to confer upon me in appointing me as your commissioner for the formation of new settlements of Mexicans, and I wish most respectfully to express my gratitude to Your Excellency. Despite the fact that this assignment is superior to my limited capacity, I will not omit any kind of sacrifice in order to discharge it properly, in keeping with my desires for the welfare of the State.

God, etc., Béxar, February 13, 1831. Most Excellent Sir, etc.   [Ramón Músquiz]

Extract:

He replies that he has received the communication from the Most Excellent Commandant General of these States dated December 30 of the past year, relative to the new settlements of Mexicans which the Supreme Government of the Union has approved to be established at the points which he mentions, and the news of the commission conferred upon this office in order to proceed to their formal establishment. He announces that, at the proper time, he will get in touch with this superior office, and he inquires as to what rights the *empresarios* have with regard to the lands included in their contracts which may be occupied by these settlements.

---

[1]Volume 53, pp. 102-102 verso, Spanish Archives, General Land Office, Austin, Texas.

THE COMMISSAR OF BÉXAR TO THE COMMISSAR OF MONTERREY[1]

[Translated from Spanish]

[February 14, 1831]

I am remitting to you the enclosed certificate of payment corresponding to the 204 pesos furnished by the subcommissariat under your supervision to Sergeant Juan Antonio del Moral, of the First Permanent Company of Tamaulipas, and Doña María del Refugio Sanches, wife of Captain Severo Ruiz of the Álamo de Parras Company.

God and Liberty. Béxar, February 14, 1831.

To the Citizen Commissar of Monterrey.

---

[1]BA Roll 135, Frames 0244-0245.

ANTONIO ELOSÚA TO MANUEL DE MIER Y TERÁN[1]

[Translated from Spanish]

Office of the Principal Commandant)   [February 15, 1831]
)
of Coahuila and Texas _____)   No. 471.

Most Excellent Sir:

I am respectfully enclosing for Your Excellency the case

drawn up against Private José María Vidal, of the Álamo

Company, who deserted for the second time, so that Your

Excellency, in view thereof, can decide what should be

done.

God and Liberty. Béxar, February 15, 1831.

[Antonio Elosúa]

To the Most Excellent Commandant General.

He encloses, for a superior decision, the case

drawn up against a Private who deserted for the second

time from the Álamo Company.

---

[1]BA Roll 138, Frame 0808.

FRANCISCO RUIZ TO ANTONIO ELOSÚA[1]

[Translated from Spanish]

Álamo de Parras   [February 15, 1831]

Presidial Company

I have in my possession the depositions of Privates Tomás Lazo and Manuel Tarín, who deserted from the Company under my command, which Colonel Citizen José de las Piedras sent to Your Lordship with his official letter of January 17 last, which you were pleased to insert for me in yours dated the first of the current month. I shall endeavor to see that they are continued as soon as *Alférez* Don Santiago Navayra returns, and the said official forwards the afore-mentioned deserters to me. I am reporting this to Your Lordship by way of reply.

God and Liberty. Tenoxtitlan, February 15, 1831.

Francisco Ruiz

[rubric]

To the Principal Commandant   )
)
of Coahuila and Texas,   )
)
Citizen Colonel Antonio Elosúa)

---

[1]BA Roll 138, Frame 0799.

FRANCISCO RUIZ TO ANTONIO ELOSÚA[1]

[Translated from Spanish]

Álamo de Parras   [February 15, 1831]

Presidial Company

I am informed by the superior official letter from Your
Lordship dated January 13 last, in which you were pleased
to forward to me the official letter from the Most Excellent Commandant General Inspector of these States, about
the exposition which General Miguel Barragán has addressed
to the Congress of the Union, proposing measures for making peace, of which he himself has circulated copies to
the authorities of the states, and the other observations
which His Excellency makes in the said official letter,
all of which, as far as I am concerned, will be punctually
complied with.

          God and Liberty. Tenoxtitlan, February 15, 1831.

                                        Francisco Ruiz

                                          [rubric]

To the Principal Commandant   )
)
of Coahuila and Texas,   )
)
Citizen Colonel Antonio Elosúa)

_____

[1]BA Roll 138, Frames 0800-0801.

FRANCISCO RUIZ TO ANTONIO ELOSÚA[1]

[Translated from Spanish]

Álamo de Parras   [February 15, 1831]

Presidial Company

I have been informed, by the official letter from Your

Lordship dated January 18 last, in which you were pleased

to insert for me the official letter from the Most Excel-

lent Commandant General Inspector of these States dated

December 29 last, of what His Excellency wrote to Citizen

Colonel Juan Davis Bradburn to the effect that, assuming

that it is a good location, he is to establish himself at

the place which he has selected, giving it the name of

"Anáhuac," and all the other information contained therein.

I am reporting this to Your Lordship by way of reply.

    God and Liberty. Tenoxtitlan, February 15, 1831.

                                        Francisco Ruiz

                                           [rubric]

To the Principal Commandant   )
)
of Coahuila and Texas,   )
)
Citizen Colonel Antonio Elosúa   )

---

[1]BA Roll 138, Frames 0802-0803.

FRANCISCO RUIZ TO SAMUEL M. WILLIAMS[1]

[Translated from Spanish]

[Tenoxtitlan, February 15, 1831]

Mr. Samuel M. Williams:

My most beloved and fine friend:

This very day it is snowing so hard that, since my house is just a shack, it is getting wet everywhere, and consequently I shall limit myself to telling you that I had the honor of meeting the Mr. Juan Moirey [John H. Money][2] whom you recommended to me in your fine letter of January 17 last, and to offer you my respects.

I regret to tell you that by the last mail I received an order not to permit the establishment at this post of any North American families, in view of the Law of April 6 of last year.[3] Consequently the colony or enterprise which Mr. Esterglin [Sterling] Robertson has under his supervision, or for which he is the agent, has been suspended, in other words, the enterprise of the Nesvil [Nashville] or Tenesí [Tennessee] Company. I have no doubt that it would be a good idea for them to take up this matter with the Government.

It is very cold, and I cannot write any more; therefore I shall close, giving my very expressive greetings to your wife and family. I remain your invariable friend who loves you and attentively kisses your hand.

Francisco Ruiz [rubric]

P.S.

The bearer will give you three *reales* [bits] for the postage on the letter that you sent on to me.

---

[1]Item 23-0571, Samuel May Williams Papers, Rosenberg Library, Galveston, Texas.

[2]Apparently this was John H. Money, who, although he was not allowed to settle in the Nashville Colony, as a member of the Robertson-Thomson party, was admitted the following month as one of Austin's colonists. On March 31, 1831, he received 1/4 league of land in Austin's Third Colony in present Washington County.--Virginia H. Taylor, *The Spanish Archives* ..., p. 214.

[3]See Antonio Elosúa to Francisco Ruiz, January 18, 1831.

RAMÓN MÚSQUIZ TO SAMUEL M. WILLIAMS[1]

[Translated from Spanish]

Office of the Chief, etc.   [February 16, 1831]

I am enclosing for you a copy of the order which,

under date of December 20 of the past year, the Most Excel-

lent Commander General Inspector of these States sent to

the Principal Commandant of this Department, who, under

date of January 19 last, forwarded it to this office for

our information and guidance, to the effect that, due to

the fact that the Law of April 6 of the aforesaid year of

1830 has suspended colonization, I should make said fact

known to the agent of the Nashville Company, Sterling Rob-

ertson, and the families who are accompanying him, who are

not to be admitted to colonize on the said lands, in view

of the fact that all the remaining colonization enterprises

are to be suspended, which on this date have not been estab-

lished, in order that you, by means of the press, may give

it the necessary publicity so that it will come to the

attention of all the *empresarios* who have not yet begun

their colonies, and to all other individuals who may try

to come into the Republic for this purpose.

God, etc. Béxar, February 16, 1831.

To the Citizen Commissar   )   R[amón] M[úsquiz]
of the *Villa* of [San Felipe)
de] Austin, Samuel Williams)

---

[1]Volume 54, pp. 297-297 verso, Spanish Archives,
General Land Office, Austin, Texas.

RAMÓN MÚSQUIZ TO THE ALCALDE OF NACOGDOCHES[1]

[Translated from Spanish]

[February 16, 1831]

Office of the Chief of the

Béxar Department

Under date of the 9th of the current month I wrote the Principal Commandant of this Department as follows:

[Here he quotes Músquiz to Elosúa, February 9, 1831. See copy above.]

I am transcribing it for you for your information, and so that, whenever the families mentioned in the aforesaid enclosure arrive at that post and the Military Commandant orders that they be transported to the other side of the Sabine River, you will lend him whatever assistance he may need in order to do it, in order to comply in this manner with the Law of April 6 of the past year of 1830 which prohibits colonization by North Americans.

God and Liberty. Béxar, February 16, 1831.

Ramón Músquiz

To the Citizen Constitutional Alcalde)
)
of the Town of Nacogdoches _____)

---

[1] Volume 55, pp. 217-218, "Nacogdoches Archives," The University of Texas Library, Austin. The original is reported to be in the Texas State Library, Austin.

ANTONIO ELOSÚA TO SEVERO RUIZ[1]

[Translated from Spanish]

Office of the Principal Commandant)   [February 16, 1831]
)
of Coahuila and Texas   _____)

     I received, with your official letter dated January 28 last, the papers in the case drawn up against Private José María Vidal, who had deserted for the second time from that Company under your command, and with same I have reported the matter to the Most Excellent Commandant General. I am reporting this to you by way of reply.

     God. and Liberty. Béxar, February 16, 1831.

                        [Antonio Elosúa]

To Captain Citizen Severo Ruiz.

---

[1]BA Roll 138, Frame 0848.

ANTONIO ELOSÚA TO SEVERO RUIZ[1]

[Translated from Spanish]

Office of the Principal Commandant)   [February 16, 1831]
)
of Coahuila and Texas_____)

By your official letter dated January 30 last, I have been informed of the purpose for which *Alférez* Citizen Santiago Navayra has come to this city, and he will return to that post as soon as possible.

God and Liberty. Béxar, February 16, 1831.

[Antonio Elosúa]

To Captain Citizen Severo Ruiz.

---

[1]BA Roll 138, Frame 0354.

MANUEL MENCHACA TO ANTONIO ELOSÚA[1]

[Translated from Spanish]

[February 16, 1831]

Antonio Curbier, a Private in the First Permanent Company of Tamaulipas, whom, by order of Your Lordship, I am trying, has appointed as his new defender, Citizen *Alférez* Juan Tello, of the Álamo Company. This notice is contained in the sealed official letter which I am enclosing for Your Lordship so that, if it meets with your approval, you will be so good as to give the proper order so that the said officer, in case he accepts said appointment, can come to this City to take the customary oath, in order to commence the cross-examinations which he is to witness.

God and Liberty. Béxar, February 16, 1831.

Manuel Menchaca

[rubric]

To the Principal Commandant)
)
of this State _____)

---

[1]BA Roll 138, Frames 0835-0836.

ANTONIO ELOSÚA TO JUAN NEPOMUCENO TELLO[1]

[Translated from Spanish]

Office of the Principal Commandant)   [February 16, 1831]
)
of Coahuila and Texas _____)

Alferez Citizen Manuel Menchaca, in an official letter dated today, writes me as follows:

"Antonio Curbier, a Private in the First Permanent Company of Tamaulipas, whom, by order of Your Lordship, I am trying," etc.

I am transcribing it for you in order that you can set out immediately for this City to perform your commission, after giving proper notice to the Military Commandant of that post and to the Commandant of the Company to which you belong.

God and Liberty. Béxar, February 16, 1831.

[Antonio Elosúa]

To *Alférez* Citizen Juan Nepomuceno Tello.

---

[1]BA Roll 138, Frame 0847.

FRANCISCO RUIZ TO ANTONIO ELOSÚA[1]

[Translated from Spanish]

Office of the Military Commandant)   [February 16, 1831]
)
of Tenoxtitlan _____)   No. 54.

We have on file in this Military Headquarters the superior order which, with a note dated January 13 last, Your Lordship was pleased to address to me relative to the preservation of discipline and the good reputation of the Mexican Army, with all the other information contained therein, and consequently it has been made known in this garrison to the individuals of same, as ordered by the Most Excellent Commandant General and Inspector of these States, for its due compliance, and I am reporting this fact to Your Lordship by way of reply.

God and Liberty. Tenoxtitlan, February 16, 1831.

Francisco Ruiz

[rubric]

To the Principal Commandant   )
)
of Coahuila and Texas,   )
)
Citizen Colonel Antonio Elosúa)

---

[1]BA Roll 138, Frame 0821-0822.

FRANCISCO RUIZ TO ANTONIO ELOSÚA[1]

[Translated from Spanish]

Office of the Military Commandant)   [February 16, 1831]
)
of Tenoxtitlan_____)   No. 55.

We have on file in this Military Headquarters the superior

official letter from Your Lordship dated January 13 last,

in which you were pleased to insert for me the official let-

ter from the Most Excellent Commandant General Inspector of

these States which speaks of the exposition which General

Miguel Barragán addressed to the Supreme Congress of the

Union, with the other matters referred to in the said supe-

rior official letter, all of which will be observed exactly

and duly complied with, and I am writing you this by way of

reply.

God and Liberty. Tenoxtitlan, February 16, 1831.

Francisco Ruiz

[rubric]

To the Principal Commandant of Coahuila)
)
and Texas, Citizen Antonio Elosúa_____)

---

[1]BA Roll 138, Frames 0823-0824.

When Francisco Ruiz ordered the arrest of Severo
Ruiz on February 7, 1831, and relieved him of his command
as Captain of the Álamo Company, there was no other officer
available to replace him, so Francisco had to take on the
additional duties as Captain while still serving as Military Commandant of Tenoxtitlan. Therefore we notice that
during this period he writes almost identical letters, both

addressed to Antonio Elosúa: one in Francisco's capacity as
Captain of the Company, such as the one we have already
seen under February 15, 1831, in which he headed his communication: "Álamo de Parras Presidial Company," and Francisco continued Severo's practice of not numbering the letters; the other letter was headed "Office of the Military
Commandant of Tenoxtitlan," and these letters were numbered in the series started by Francisco as soon as he
arrived on the Brazos. In the cases where the wording
varies, we shall reproduce both versions; where the wording is identical, we shall give the text of the first and
make a cross-reference to the second.

FRANCISCO RUIZ TO ANTONIO ELOSÚA[1]

[Translated from Spanish]

Office of the Military Commandant)   [February 16, 1831]
)
of Tenoxtitlan   )   No. 56.

By the superior official letter from Your Lordship dated

January 13 last, in which you were pleased to insert for

me the official letter from the Most Excellent Commandant

General and Inspector of these States, dated December 9

last, I have been informed that in the copies of the Army

Regulations I should copy the order dated June 30, 1817,

which is recorded in the 4th volume of Colón, published in

that same year, with the annotation that it replaces arti-

cles 64 and 65 of the 8th treatise, title 10, of said Regu-

lations, and consequently I shall make this known to the

individuals concerned, for their due compliance, with the

understanding that in this garrison we do not have the vol-

ume of the edition referred to.[2] I am writing this to Your

Lordship by way of making an attentive reply to your afore-

mentioned superior official letter relating thereto.

God and Liberty. Tenoxtitlan, February 16, 1831.

Francisco Ruiz

[rubric]

To the Principal Commandant   )
)
of Coahuila and Texas,   )
)
Citizen Colonel Antonio Elosúa)

----

[1]BA Roll 138, Frames 0825-0826. The copy of this same letter that Francisco Ruiz sent to Elosúa in his capacity as Captain of the Álamo Company appears in Frames 0827-0828.

[2]See Felix Colón de Larriátegui, *Juzgados Militares de España y sus Indias. Por don Felix Colón de Larriátegui* ..., 3rd ed., corr. y aum. (Madrid: Impr. de Repullés, 1817. 4 vols. It is interesting to know that the Spanish law of 1817 was still supposed to be in force on the Brazos River in Texas ten years after Mexico won its independence from Spain.

FRANCISCO RUIZ TO ANTONIO ELOSÚA[1]

[Translated from Spanish]

Office of the Military Commandant)   [February 16, 1831]
)
of Tenoxtitlan_____)   No. 58.

      By the superior official letter from Your Lordship
dated January 18 last, in which you were pleased to tran-
scribe for me the one from the Most Excellent Commandant
General Inspector of these States dated December 20, last
I have been informed that I should give the foreigner
Sterling Robertson to understand that colonization has been
suspended by the Law of April 6 of last year, and I will
comply punctually with what I have been ordered to do, as
soon as the said Robertson, whose whereabouts is unknown
to me, presents himself. I will also comply with everything else contained in your aforecited superior official
letter which I am happy to answer at this time.

      God and Liberty. Tenoxtitlan, February 16, 1831.

                          Francisco Ruiz

                             [rubric]

To the Principal Commandant   )
)
Citizen Colonel Antonio Elosúa)

      [Endorsed in English:] B. Receipt. The Military
Comdt. of Tenoxtitlan to the Principl. Comdt. of Texas at
Béxar, relative the orders of the Comdt. Genl. of Eastn.
Internl States to notify Sterling C. Robertson of the

expiration of the Nashville Compys. Colonization Contract and its suspension by the Provisions of the Law of 6 April 1830.--datd. 16. Feby/31.

Rec'd from the Sec'y of State, Austin, 13th Octr. 1846.

Geo: Fisher

Sp: Clk. G.L. Of.

---

[1]Volume 54, pp. 289-289 verso, Spanish Archives, General Land Office, Austin, Texas.

FRANCISCO RUIZ TO ANTONIO ELOSÚA[1]

[Translated from Spanish]

Office of the Military Commandant)   [February 16, 1831]
)
of Tenoxtitlan_____)   No. 59.

By the superior official letter from Your Lordship dated January 18 last, in which you were pleased to insert for me the one from the Most Excellent Commandant General Inspector of these States dated December 31 last, I have been informed not to permit at this point the establishment of Sterling Robertson nor any other North American family, and that I am to find out the names of those who came in headed in this direction, all of which will be duly fulfilled according to your aforecited superior official letter, which I have the pleasure of answering at this time.

God and Liberty. Tenoxtitlan, February 16, 1831.

Francisco Ruiz

[rubric]

To the Principal Commandant   )
)
Citizen Colonel Antonio Elosua)

     [Endorsed in English:] D. Receipt   The Military
Comdt of Tenoxtitlan to the Principl. Comdt, of Texas at
Béxar of the order of the Comdt. Genl. of the Eastn. Interl.
States, to oppose the establishment of Sterling C. Robert-
son, or any other foreign families (North American) also to
ascertain the names of those who have come in. dated 16th
Feby 1831.
     Rec'd from the Sec'y of State   Austin 13th Octr.
1846

                                        Geo: Fisher
                                        Sp: Clk. G. L. Of.

_____

     [1]Volume 54, pp. 288-288 verso, Spanish Archives,
General Land Office, Austin, Texas.

McLean, PAPERS CONCERNING ROBERTSON'S COLONY IN TEXAS, Volume V

528

FRANCISCO RUIZ TO ANTONIO ELOSÚA[1]

[Translated from Spanish]

[February 16, 1831]

By the official letter from Your Lordship dated January 19 last, I am informed of the official letter which on that same date you addressed to the Commandant of the Álamo Company relative to the funds that *Alférez* Francisco Porras conducted for the said Company and the Picket from Béxar, and I am notifying Your Lordship of this fact by way of reply.

God and Liberty. Tenoxtitlan, February 16, 1831.

Francisco Ruiz

[rubric]

To the Principal Commandant,)
)
Citizen Antonio Elosúa _____)

---

[1]BA Roll 138, Frame 0829.

FRANCISCO RUIZ TO ANTONIO ELOSÚA[1]

[Translated from Spanish]

[February 16, 1831]

With the superior official letter from Your Lordship dated January 19 last I received the documents in the case drawn up against Lieutenant Francisco Castañeda so that I can elevate it to the level of a formal trial under the terms prescribed to me. Francisco Porras, First *Alférez* of the First Permanent Company of Tamaulipas, who is to serve as Secretary in said case, has presented himself to me for that purpose.

Likewise I have been informed that, since Severo Ruiz, Captain of the Álamo Company, must be relieved of his command of same, due to charges which have resulted against him in the aforementioned case, and that, since at present there is no other officer available to replace him, I am to take over the command of said Company, and that I am to receive it with all the proper formalities, as ordered, all of which will be punctually complied with insofar as it lies within my power to do so, and I am reporting this to Your Lordship as an attentive reply to your said superior official letter.

God and Liberty. Tenoxtitlan, February 16, 1831.

Francisco Ruiz

[rubric]

To the Principal Commandant,)
)
Citizen Colonel Antonio Elosúa)

---

[1]BA Roll 138, Frames 0830-0831.

MANUEL DE MIER Y TERÁN TO THE MINISTER

OF INTERIOR AND EXTERIOR RELATIONS[1]

[Translated from Spanish]

Office of the Commandant General   [February 17, 1831]
of the Eastern Interior States

To the Second Section,
Department of the Interior

[Marginal summary:] He answers the superior order which
has to do with permitting Mr. Antonio Esnaurrizar to take
possession of eleven leagues of land in Texas.

Most Excellent Sir:

          The points designated by me up to now for military

posts in the Department of Texas are those in the vicinity

of the Lavaca River, Galveston (toward the mouth of the

Trinity River), and Tenoxtitlan (at the Brazos River Cross-

ing on the Upper Road from Béxar to Nacogdoches), but

there are already claims on these same places, resulting

from the fact that the twenty thousand leagues over which

the said Department extends have been distributed among

enterprises projected by North American colonies. As can

be seen from the enclosed copy, the Government of the

State of Coahuila and Texas no longer has any more lands

to dispose of, but, nevertheless, in view of the fact

that the Law of April 6 [1830] suspends the contracts

which have not gone into effect, Mr. Antonio Esnaurrizar

may find a place for the eleven leagues which Your
Excellency has been pleased to mention, in your superior
note of the 24th of the past month, among the lands which
are going to be left vacant and, supposing that his colony
is going to be composed of Mexican nationals, his interests
will be conciliated with those of the Nation by making his
location in the vicinity of Tenoxtitlan.

God and Liberty. Matamoros, February 17, 1831.

Manuel de Mier

y Terán

[rubric]

To the Most Excellent Secretary of
Interior and Exterior Relations

---

[1]México. Secretaría de Fomento. Colonización.
Legajo IV, 1823-1835, Expediente 26, p. 176. Typescript in
The University of Texas Archives. This *expediente*, which
begins on p. 166 of that volume, started out as a petition
to establish a colony on the banks of the Sabine River.
However, according to Taylor, *The Spanish Archives*..., p.
183, Antonio María Esnaurizar finally received 11 leagues
of land on November 10, 1831, but they were located even
farther west, being distributed as follows: 8 1/2 leagues
in Guadalupe County, 1 in Comal County, and 3/4 of a league
in Hays County. (That actually adds up to 11.25 leagues--
a difference of only 1,107 acres--but who are we to question
a lady's arithmetic?)

LEANDRO AGUILAR TO THE COMMISSAR OF BÉXAR[1]

[Translated from Spanish]

Office of the Subaltern   [February 17, 1831]

Commissar of Monterrey.

Four months have already passed now since I sent you the receipts from the wife of Captain Severo Ruiz, corresponding to the months of October, November, and December of the past year, and one for the end of January of the present year, totaling one hundred and twenty pesos, for which I have not, to this date, received the customary certificate so that I can credit it properly on my books in this office. Likewise I have not received certificates for the five receipts which I have also sent to you from Sergeant Juan Antonio del Moral, of the First Permanent Company of Tamaulipas, corresponding to the months of August, September, October, November, and December last, totaling one hundred and forty-two pesos and four reals. Trusting in your efficiency, I am hoping that you will be so good as to enclose the aforementioned certificates for me by return mail because I need them to balance my books in this office at the end of the fiscal year, which is drawing near, and so that these documents will not be left outstanding when they should be recorded in the respective books.

I have the honor of communicating this information to you in this manner, and to assure you of my esteem and consideration.

God and Liberty.   Monterrey, February 17, 1831.

Leandro Aguilar

[rubric]

To the Citizen Commissar of Béxar.

---

[1]BA Roll 138, Frames 0851-0852.

RAMÓN MÚSQUIZ TO MANUEL DE MIER Y TERÁN[1]

[Translated from Spanish]

General Don Manuel de Mier y Terán:

Béxar, February 18, 1831

My very dear sir and respected friend:

As you probably know, and as I am reporting to you officially now, the Governor of the State, on being urged by you with respect to the new settlements of Mexicans which you have promoted and begun with the detachments located at the mouth of the Lavaca, at Galveston, and at Tenoxtitlan, has commissioned this office with the power to delegate the responsibility to persons whom it considers reliable. Of those whom you presented to the Government, I know Don Rafael Chovel[1], and surely he will be the commissioner for Lavaca. I have already proposed to him this assignment or one as surveyor for that town, and I am awaiting his reply in order to proceed to make the respective appointment. For Galveston I have formed the idea that it should be the Chief who is going to be appointed for the new District of Nacogdoches on the recommendation of this office. I hope that the individual upon whom this assignment is to be conferred will be of the best quality, and for Tenoxtitlan I have no opinion, although it is very well deserved by Lieutenant Colonel Don Francisco Ruiz who, if it appears all right to you, could be the commissioner for that post, although he has the handicap of being an outsider, and for this reason I have hesitated to comply completely with your desires. The suitability and extreme efficiency which characterize this gentleman give me confidence to absolve the scruple which I have had. If I issued the commissions to persons who are under the jurisdiction of somebody else, I would find myself deprived of the power of exercising my authority, especially with reference to Law No. 128, [of April 10, 1830] of which I am enclosing a copy for you.

The Commandant of Galveston, Colonel Davis [*i.e.*, Juan Davis Bradburn] has placed obstacles in the way of Citizen José F. Madero, who was commissioned by the Governor of the State to give possession to the foreigners on the San Jacinto and Trinity who obtained permission from the General Government to be legally established, saying that to do so would be contrary to the Law of April 6 of last year. I notified Madero of this development, and he reached an agreement with Mr. [Juan] Davis [Bradburn] whereby Bradburn allowed the commissioner to comply with his duty, and, although this decision should quiet him down, I thought it prudent to issue the instructions contained in the enclosed copy as the most efficient means of putting an end to the question. The provisional demarcation which I made of the land for the new settlement of Mexicans you will see in the contract referred to in my instructions, of which I suppose you must have a copy.

I am in doubt as to who is to pay the fees for the commissioner, those of the surveyor, and for the stamped paper used in placing settlers in possession of land in the new settlements.

I beg you to be so kind as to give me your opinion concerning this matter, and please pardon me for writing such a long letter this time. I remain your most affectionate and attentive servant who kisses your hand.

[Ramón Músquiz]

---

[1]Volume 53, pp. 104-104 verso, Spanish Archives, General Land Office, Austin, Texas.

JORGE DE CEVALLOS TO ANTONIO ELOSÚA[1]

[Translated from Spanish]

[February 18, 1831]

I received the superior order from Your Lordship dated the 21st of last month, in which you were pleased to instruct me to accept the appointment as defender of Private Luciano Flores, and for that purpose I set out from Tenoxtitlan for this City and I will comply with your said order, which I am now attentively answering.

God and Liberty. Béxar, February 18, 1831.

Jorge de Cevallos

[rubric]

To the Principal Commandant of Coahuila)
)
and Texas, Colonel Antonio Elosúa_____)

---

[1]BA Roll 138, Frames 0860-0861.

MANUEL DE MIER Y TERÁN TO ANTONIO ELOSÚA[1]

[Translated from Spanish]

Office of the Commandant General   [February 19, 1831]
Inspector of the Eastern Interior States.

If the Political Chief of that Department [Ramón Músquiz] will be so good as to look after the conservation and education of the creatures [papooses] that were taken prisoners, as mentioned by His Lordship in his official letter dated the 12th of the present month, the original of which Your Lordship sent to me with your official letter dated the 21st of same, No. 499, they can remain in the possession of the persons who have asked permission to keep them, so that their pious intentions can be carried out.

God and Liberty. Matamoros, February 19, 1831.

M. Mier y Terán

[rubric]

To the Principal Commandant)
)
of Coahuiltexas_____)

---

[1]BA Roll 138, Frame 0868.

FRANCISCO RUIZ TO SAMUEL M. WILLIAMS[1]

[Translated from Spanish]

Tenoxtitlan, February 19, 1831

Mr. Samuel M. Williams:

My fine and appreciated friend: With singular appreciation I received your favor of the 19th of the current month informing me of the news which you have received from our good friend Don Stephen [F. Austin], and the other things which you were pleased to communicate to me. I appreciate it very much, and I am glad for our aforementioned friend. According to what they write me, it seems that Mexico will settle down, God willing. Many of the officials on Guerrero's side, they tell me, are presenting themselves to be pardoned, and such news gives us a good hope that everything will return to order. Let us, therefore, hope for such a desirable time.

With regret I again inform you, as I said in my last letter dated the [15th] of the present month, that I have received an order not to permit any North American family to remain or settle here, and furthermore, not to permit anybody to come in after the Decree of April 6 of the past year, and, knowing that Mr. [John H.] Money has come in later from Tennessee, I am sorry. I find myself in the very hard position of not being able to permit them to stay at this point, and therefore I beg you to be so good as to

communicate this unfavorable news to him so that no harm
will result to him for having come. Likewise I hope that
he will pardon me, but as a military man and a subordinate
I must obey. In the same manner, I hope that you, my dear
friend, will pardon me. Put yourself in my place and tell
yourself what you would do in a similar situation. I do
not doubt that you will absolve me, and that you will rest
assured that the time will come when I can prove that I am
very much your friend and that I desire to serve you.

I am tired of my fate and I want, in order to see
if it will improve, to be discharged from military service
and live tranquilly, even though it may be in the wilderness, and for that purpose I hope you will not forget to
select me a piece of land, or, as our aforesaid friend
would say, please notify me when the commissioner for that
colony arrives so that I can send my concession and such
documents as he may require in order to make the survey.[2]

Please remember me to your wife, and do not hesitate to call on your friend who loves you and kisses your
hand.

Francisco Ruiz

P.S.   [rubric]

The bearer will hand you the three reales that I owe you
for postage last time.

[Addressed:] To Mr. Samuel M. Williams in the
Villa of [San Felipe] de Austin.

[Endorsed:] Fran[cisco] Ruiz Feb. 19, 1831.

---

[1]Xerox copy of Item 23-0583, Samuel May Williams Papers, Rosenberg Library, Galveston, Texas.

[2]Francisco Ruiz received 9 leagues of land from Commissioner Luke Lesassier on August 31, 1833, distributed as follows: 4 in present Robertson County, 2 in Brazos County, 2 in Milam County, and 1 in Burleson County. On March 16, 1834, he received 2 leagues from Commissioner Juan Nepomuceno Seguín in present Karnes County.--Taylor, *The Spanish Archives* ..., p. 235.

STEPHEN F. AUSTIN TO SAMUEL M. WILLIAMS[1]

[From Williams Papers, Rosenberg Library, Galveston, Texas]

Saltillo Feb. 19. 1831.

S M. Williams. Dr Sir

Yours of 25 Jany is recd and the letters enclosed except the one from my sister which I hope you will send by next mail as I am very anxious to see it.

I am much pleased with the new arrangement of the pap[er][2] tho I do not like the motto--*Mexico es mi patria*, would do better, for it will be as much as to say to people abroad "we have a country and are proud of it, and we are ready and willing to defend her rights," and it will remind our *home folks* whom they belong to. I recommend that [the] motto I have suggested be adopted, or something like it.

That paper must be conducted with great prudence, you have no idea there, what importance is attached, even to trifles, coming from the *Austinians*. That little establishment[3] badly as it has been conducted, has been of great service to [Texas] and has had an agency in warding off some blows that were meditated against that country, for it has in some degree tended to correct some very erronious opinions as to the character of the new settlements and their feelings towards the Govt.

Last spring the idea was very general in Mexico that Texas was the Botany Bay of the U.S. and that the Govt. of the North was secretly encouraging the emigration of bad

men and vagabonds, who were destitute of principle, for the
purpose of enciting them to rebel against this Govt. and
produce confusion on the frontier, which would have been a
pretext to enter the country and put things to rights as
Jackson entered Florida etc. This Govt. now believes that
the settlers of *my colony* at least, are men of principle
who will respect their oaths of fidelity, and will never
forget that they have recd fortunes from this Govt. and
favors which no other Govt ever extended to any people.
The suspicions against the U.S. Govt. are also all removed.
But what is deemed to be the dignity of this Govt. will not
suffer it to move the repeal of the law of 6 April unless
some prominent reason can be given for so doing. I wish
the people of Texas to give such a reason by proofs of fidelity and attachment to Mexico and the best way of mani-
festing these proofs is through the news paper-- Let it be
what its title [*The Mexican Citizen*] professes. A *Mexican*
defends everything that is mexican--but in genl terms, without being in favor or against political parties.

The parties of this country are not clearly defined
and have not that definite and fixed character, nor perma-
nency of purpose which parties generally have in other
countries. Thus, since the to[t]al overthrow and imprisonment of Guerrero, a new party has sprung up composed of
Guerreroists and *Pedrassistas*, a most unnatural connection,

for the former expelled the latter by the revolution of
Acordada, and it seems as tho they had now united to put
down the present administration--that effected, the Guerreroists will perhaps enter the lists with Pedraza for the
supremacy. If we enter into such a scramble we shall be
like children in a mob, and as likely to be trodden upon
by friends as by foes. Hence it is that situated as we
are, it is dangerous to be classed as belonging to any
party. Our neutrality injures neither, for our weight is
of not sufficient importance to injure or benefit either
materially, and it may gain us the good will of both, or
what is of just as much importance to us, both will let us
alone.

You are well aware that in my intercourse with this
govt. I have followed a few fixed rules from which I have
never deviated since 1821 when I first entered the country.
In the first place I came with pure intentions. I bid an
everlasting farewell to my native country, and adopted this,
and in so doing I determined to fulfil rigidly all the
duties and obligations of a *Mexican citizen*--I have endeavored to keep all the officers with whom I was in direct
communication in a good humor, and to make friends of them.
I have excused and even invented plausable reasons to justify or explain away all the political errors of my adopted
countrymen. I have been silent as to all their defects,
and lavish of praise where there was the least pretext for

bestowing it, but at the same time decisive and unbending where a constitutional or vested right of vital importance was directly attacked. Rights of minor consideration I have paid no attention to, for bad feeling might be engendered about *trifles*, that would jeapordize an important interest. To sum up all I have endeavored to do my duty as a *Mexican citizen*.

My native countrymen are blunt republicans, and do not always reflect sufficiently, and some of them have accused me of debility, want of firmness temporizing etc. It was my duty to steer my precious bark (the Colony) through all the shoals and quicks[ands] regardless of the curses and ridicule of the passengers. I knew what I was about--*they* did not.

The law of 6 April was founded in error and unjust suspicions, but to have said so, would have been very impolitic, and highly injurious, for it would have wounded *self love*, *pride* etc. (dangerous things to touch among any people) and it would have strengthened the suspicions which produced the law for everything said against it would have been taken as evidence of disaffection. For these reasons in the remarks which were made in the *Texas*[Gazette] in June, July etc the policy of the Govt. was rather defended than condemned, and circumstances were stated to shew that there were reasons for that measure which justified it. This gratified the *self love* of its authors on the one hand (a great point gained) and they were very much surprised on the other to see that the very people who were most injured by the measure, were the first to excuse and defend it. This caused inquiries to be made through various channels, as to the real characters of the settlers and their feelings towards the Govt. and the result has been very favourable as to my colony. This at once explains the reasons why so many more favors have been extended to that colony than to any other. The people at large know of no favors they have received, neither do they know, nor can they appreciate what I have done for them for the past ten years, but *you* and *I* know that emigration to that colony could have been stopped, and that all ports could have been closed, or a George Fisher with a guard at each. These things ought to convince every reflecting man in that Colony that this Govt. will reward and properly appreciate all those who *do their duty as Mexican citizens*, and who obey the laws and set their faces against confusion and illegal proceedings.

The foregoing remarks are made as an introduction for what is to follow--you will soon find yourselves in an awkward and rather delicate situation in that Colony, and I thought it might shed some light upon the path which you ought to take, to explain fully the rules and policy I have uniformly pursued.

There are two points of collision in prospective

in that country, both of them, East of my Colony. One is

between Madero and Teran--The other between Zavala and

Teran--or rather between the latter and a company who have

contracted to settle Zavalas, Vielen [Joseph Vehlein] and

Burnetts grants--the Settlers are to be Germans, Swiss

french etc.,--all Europeans--have nothing to do with these

collisions--do as I have frequently been compelled to do--

play the turtle, head and feet within your own shell--some

of the people may curse and abuse--no matter--they abused

me the best friend they ever had. Better break all the

timber[4] in Texas, than to break *Boss*[5] [Teran,] for the for-

mer is plenty and can be replaced, but the lat[t]er being

a fine texture is not to be found everyday. That colony is

the heart of Texas; keep all sound there, and we shall gain

the confidence of the Govt. and save the Country, but if

you go to the extremities to try and cure diseases, you

interfere with the head doctor, which he will take very

ill (for all doctors are jealous of their prerogatives),

and besides there will be danger of introducing disease

into the *heart*, by infection.

[Hand pointing:] Whether the Genl Govt. has author-

ity to annul Zavala's grant or not is no question for *us*

to interfere with, neither have we anything to do with

Madero's commission etc. those are matters between the

interested parties and the Govt. with which my colony ought

to have nothing to do, in any shape manner or form. My

colony has cleared away the rude asperities of the wilder-
ness--made Texas known--given it a station in geography--a
place, and a distinguished one, in the class of *desirable
countries*, and has demonstrated its value, by developing
its resources. In doing *this*, it has done enough to aid
others who now wish to settle in that country, and they
ought not to expect that we will unite with them in proj-
ects for forcing their way against the will of the Govt. or
that we are to make common cause of their quarrels and collisions, and if they do expect it I hope they will be
deceived, hope! I know they will, for there is too much
sound common sense and too much honest patriotism in the
people of Austins colony for them to be misled, or to devi-
ate from the line of their duty as Mexican Citizens, and
besides they have a *great deal* to loose, the others have
much to gain but *nothing* to loose. [Hand pointing.]

But while, on the one hand, you avoid suffering
yourselves to be made parties to the collisions which I
have alluded to, against the Govt, also try on the other,
not to take any active, or open, or any part at all in
them against the new settlers-- Be mere lookers on--say
nothing--give no opinions--no advice--take no part--have
nothing to do with the matter at all--refer them to the
Govt. but if Genl Teran issues any orders *obey them*. He is
our main stay. You may rely upon it and he is worthy of

our confidence and support. Don't let the paper be made
the vehicle for venting the spleen or abuse of Madero or
anybody else, make it a *Dignified Calm Judicious "Mexican
Citizen"* adopt the motto I have proposed and adhere to its
principles rigidly--all will come round right--many of the
most influential men of all parties, in office, and out, in
the City of Mexico and elsewhere have procured grants in
Texas and more are dayly making. *All these* are true friends
to the *real* prosperity of that country. We can make them
our friends by adopting the policy I have indicated, or
rather by following the policy I have always followed.

You can submit this letter to the Congress[6] or to
as many of my friends as you think prudent, and should any
serious difficulty arrise and you should think that it
would do any good to make my opinions known, you can have
it done so far as *Congress* may judge prudent and correct,
by means of an editorial article--that plan would do better
than to make any extracts [f]rom this letter.

Padre Muldoon left some days since--he wrote me
from Monterrey that he had recd his appointment of *Cura de
Austin* from the Provisor, and I presume will soon be with
you--his councils will be of service to you, and the colony,
for I believe he has the true interests of that colony much
at heart--he has some vanity, and I think a very benevolent
heart, and pure intentions. I told him that Texas might

be made a Bishoprick of in a few years, if we could get rid
of the 13 article of our State Constitution,[7] and the 11
Article[8] of the law of 6 April. I am very much pleased
with him, as a man, and much better as a *Padre*.

I have spun out a long thread and it is time to
break off, which I will do by requesting you to remember
me affcy. to Mrs. W. and Mrs. S. and to Luke [Lesassier],
Willy [R.M. Williamson], Jack [one of three brothers--
William H., Spencer, or Patrick C.], [Oliver] Jones, [F.W.]
Johnson etc.,[9] and take good care of my nephew Moses Austin
Bryan, besides being the grandson and bearing the name of
the man who was the first author of all our fortunes in
that country, he is the son of a very favourite sister of
mine.

Hasta Cada Rato

S. F. Austin.

N. B. If times get very bad and public opinion
should seem to waver, it might be well to publish the paragraph marked thus--[hands pointing] as an extract from me--
tho all this left *totally* to the wisdom of *congress*.

---

[1]Barker, *Austin Papers*, II, 599-604.

[2][Dr. Barker's note:] This was The Mexican Citizen,
edited by R. M. Williamson. There are four numbers of this
paper in the Wagner Collection of Yale University, but no
other copies are known.

[3][Dr. Barker's note:] The Texas Gazette.

[4]The word *timber* is used here to refer to Francisco Madero since *madero* means *log* in Spanish. Madero had been appointed General Land Commissioner of Texas on September 27, 1830, by Governor José María Letona to succeed Juan Antonio Padilla. Madero reached Texas on January 14, 1831, and gave notice of his plans to begin issuing titles in the Trinity River area. When Juan Davis Bradburn learned of Madero's intentions, he ordered the commissioner and his surveyor, José María Carbajal, arrested, claiming that their actions were in violation of the Law of April 6, 1830.--*Handbook of Texas*, II, 127.

[5][Dr. Barker's note:] Austin uses this term frequently during this period. It evidently refers to a person, but the context is never clear enough to identify him with certainty. Terán, as commissioner of colonization and general commandant, is a likely guess. [Added by McLean:] It was more likely to have been Ramón Músquiz, the political chief [or Boss] of the Department. Músquiz was later accused of being a secret partner in the Austin & Williams contract.

[6]Evidently a group of advisers, probably including Luke Lesassier, R. M. Williamson, and F. W. Johnson, and perhaps others.

[7][Dr. Barker's note:] The article excluding slavery.

[8][Dr. Barker's note:] The article prohibiting settlement of immigrants from the United States in Texas.

[9]Notice that three of these names (Oliver Jones, Luke Lesassier, and Robert M. Williamson) correspond to three of the persons mentioned by Hosea H. League in his letter of November 11, 1830, as those who were so intent upon persecuting him, and a fourth name, ironically enough, is that of William H. Jack, the person to whom League wrote the letter.

PROCLAMATION BY JOSÉ MARÍA SALINAS,

ALCALDE OF BÉXAR[1]

[Translated from Spanish]

Office of the Political Chief   [February 20, 1831]

of the Department of Béxar.

The Most Excellent Governor of the State of [Coahuila and Texas] has been pleased to send me the following decree:

"The following decree has been communicated to me by the Secretariat of State and Foreign Relations.=The Most Excellent Vice President of the United Mexican States has been pleased to send me the following decree.=The Vice President of the United Mexican States, exercising the supreme executive power, to the inhabitants of the Republic, be it known: That the General Congress has decreed the following.=The General Congress will close its present extraordinary sessions on the 30th day of the present month.= Juan Nepomuceno Acosta,[2] Senator President.=Andrés Quintana Roo, Deputy President.=José María Marín, Senator Secretary. =Manuel Miranda, Deputy Secretary.=Therefore I order that this be printed, published, and circulated, and that it be duly obeyed. Palace of the Federal Government in Mexico City, December 29, 1830.=Anastacio Bustamante.=To Don Lucas Alamán.=And I am communicating it to you for your information and guidance.=God and Liberty. Mexico City, December

29,1830.=[signed:] Alamán.=And I am forwarding it to Your
Lordship for your information and guidance.=God and Liberty.
=Leona Vicario [Saltillo], January 10, 1831.=[signed:]
[José María] Viesca.=Santiago del Valle, Secretary.=To the
Political Chief of the Department of Béxar."

And I am transcribing it for you, for your information and guidance.

God and Liberty. Béxar, February 12, 1831.

Ramón Músquiz

[rubric]

To the Citizen Alcalde)
)
of this City._____)

And in order that it may come to the attention of
everybody and be punctually and duly complied with, I
order that it be published as a proclamation [*i.e.*, be read
by the town crier] for such purposes as may be appropriate.
Meeting Hall of San Fernando de Béxar, February 20, 1831.

José María Salinas

[rubric]

Ignacio Arocha

Secretary [rubric]

---

[1]BA Roll 138, Frames 0893-0894. One reason that
this document is included here is to show how long it took

official news to travel from Mexico City to the Texas frontier. In this case, it took from December 29, 1830, to
February 20, 1831, for the decree to reach San Antonio,
Texas, more than two months, and it no doubt took at least
two more weeks for it to reach Tenoxtitlan and Nacogdoches,
since the mail was carried only once every two weeks
between San Antonio and Nacogdoches.

[2]The second reason for including this document is
because it shows that Juan Nepomuceno Acosta, who received
a grant of eleven leagues of land in Texas on November 21,
1833, had served as President of the Senate of the Mexican
National Congress in 1830, thus proving the statement that
Stephen F. Austin made in his letter of February 19, 1831,
that "many of the most influential men of all parties, in
office, and out, in the City of Mexico and elsewhere have
procured grants in Texas and more are daily making. ..."
The land that Acosta received from Commissioner Vicente
Aldrete was located as follows: 5 leagues in present Lime-
stone County, 3 in Freestone, and 3 in Anderson.--Taylor,
The Spanish Archives..., p. 151. We are particularly
pleased to be able to add this information about Juan Nepomuceno Acosta because there is no article about him in
The Handbook of Texas or the *Diccionario Porrúa*.

SANTIAGO NAVAYRA TO ANTONIO ELOSÚA[1]

[Translated from Spanish]

[February 20, 1831]

As a consequence of the appointment which Your Lordship
was pleased to confer upon me, commissioning me for the
construction of the fortification which is going to be
built at Tenoxtitlan, according to an order which was communicated to me to that effect by the Commandant of that
post, Lieutenant Colonel Francisco Ruiz, dated October 8
last, I made an agreement with that Chief to go to the
Villa of [San Felipe de] Austin in search of an expert who
could enlighten me about the costs which the said work
would involve, so that, in view thereof, I could draw up
the budget requested in the order of the Most Excellent
Commandant General, but, either because of the different
language spoken by the inhabitants of [San Felipe de]
Austin, and for that reason the difficulty which I encountered here in understanding them, and making them understood, or because of the absolute lack, in all these towns,
of an engineer, architect, or even a stone mason trained
in such works, it has not been possible for me to gather,
even after exhausting every possible resource, the data
which without a doubt are indispensable in order to calcu-
late the aforementioned budget, and I have only acquired
the two attached lists of information which, after having

them translated, I am forwarding to the hands of Your Lordship so that, if you think it appropriate, you can elevate
them to the knowledge of the Most Excellent Commandant General so that His Excellency, since he has at his disposal
all the resources and knowledge needed, may be pleased to
send a qualified person to figure out all the costs which
the aforecited work may demand, with the understanding that,
as far as I am concerned, I will lend all the cooperation
that lies within my limited knowledge concerning the matter,
as well as the greatest efficiency and punctuality, in carrying out his superior orders, as well as those of Your
Lordship, in everything that you may be pleased to impose
upon me. = God and Liberty. Béxar, February 20, 1831.=
[signed:] Santiago Navayra.= To the Principal Commandant,
Colonel Antonio Elosúa.

erMcLean, PAPERS CONCERNING ROBERTSON'S COLONY IN TEXAS, Volume V

557

PRUDENT CALCULATION FOR THE FORMATION

OF THE FORTIFIED HOUSE OF WOOD

[Translated from Spanish]

		Pesos.	R.	G.
52,165.	Feet of wood at 5 pesos	2.608.	2.	".
13,041.	Ditto more at ditto	.652.	".	6.
12,300.	Ditto of boards at ditto.	.615.	".	".
3,850.	Ditto of [shakes ?] at 8 pesos per 100.	.308.	".	".
90,600.	Shingles at 6 pesos per thousand.	.543.	5.	".
1,500.	Pounds nails at 1 real 6 granos	.270.	".	".
	Door latches and locks	.75.	".	".
	For carting the wood and erecting the building	5.000.	".	".
	For the floors	.300.	".	".
	For the roofs	.150.	".	".
	For the roofer	.100.	".	".
	For making the doors and windows	.75.	".	".
	For making the *noria*[2]	.300.	".	".
	For digging the moat	.881.	2.	".
49,000....	Bricks at 20 pesos per thousand	.980.	".	".
	For the tools necessary for constructing the buildings	.500.	".	".
	TOTAL :	13.358.	1.	6.

NOTE.

The outside walls shall be two feet thick, and the inside walls one foot. The necessary things will be built outside of this country [elsewhere], at the lowest possible cost, plus freight, and the work must be very well done.

		Pesos.	R.	G.
66	Men for 100 days at 15 pesos per month	3.808.	1.	8.
13	Officials for 100 days at 40 pesos per month	1.999.	7.	4.
20	Quintals[3] of iron	".400.	".	".
4	Crosscut saws at 10 pesos	". 40.	".	".
2	Handsaws at 12 pesos	". 24.	".	".
	Other items that are needed, such as picks,) shovels, and similar articles	)".500.	".	".
	Nails, doorlocks, hinges	".345.	".	".
30	Oxen at 25 pesos	".750.	".	".
10	Oxcarts at 30 pesos	".300.	".	".
15,000	Pounds of meat	".450.	".	".
200	*fanegas* [about 316 bushels] of corn at 3 pesos	".600.	".	".
500	Pounds of coffee	".115.	".	".

		Pesos.	R.	G.
500	Pounds of sugar	". 50.	".	".
300	" " salt	". 18.	".	".
	TOTAL:	9.400.	1.	".

Things that will be left over when the building is done:

30 Oxen at 25 pesos	750.)			
60 Axes at 2 pesos	132.)			
10 Broadaxes at 4 pesos . . .	40.)			
4 Crosscut saws at 10 pesos . .	40.) .. 1.286.	".	".	
2 Handsaws at 12 pesos . . .	24.)			
Other tools, picks, shovels,	)			
and similar items . . .	300.)			

TOTAL:	8.114.	1.	".

One foreman for 100 days . . .	.384.	6.	".
TOTAL:	8.498.	7.	".

This list was drawn up by an expert in Austin's Colony, which is near
Tenoxtitlan. Béxar, February 20, 1831.= [signed:] Santiago Navayra.

A Copy.

PRUDENT CALCULATION FOR BUILDING THE FORTIFIED

HOUSE OF BRICK AT TENOXTITLAN

80   workmen in one day will mold and stack 16,0[00]
bricks, on the assumption that five workmen will
be capable of making 1,000 daily, from which calculation in six months [working 26 days a month]
they would complete   2,496,000

If the workmen were capable, skillful, or fast in
making them, we could knock off at least 2 months.

		Pesos.	R.	G.
80	workmen at the rate of 5 pesos per month for 6 months	2.400.	".	".
50	Ditto to burn them and to furnish the brick-) layers with them and the mortar, etc., for 6) months at 5 pesos . . . .)	1.500.	".	".
25	workmen [at 5 pesos] for 3 months to burn the necessary amount of lime	".375.	".	".
15,000	feet of boards, flooring, and the other things that must be made by laborers	.400.	".	".
20	quintals of iron and 400 pounds of nails . .	.300.	".	".
3	*Waguines* [wagons] and the oxen to pull them .	.750.	".	".
	Services or salaries of a person to direct the making of the bricks, and the bricklayers, and the rest	7.498.	".	".
	For the Carpenters and Blacksmiths	".750.	".	".
	For a wooden stockade on the wall of the moat, and for digging the said moat	1.500.	".	".
	For the competent number of utensils . . .	".500.	".	".
	For expenses, contingencies, or extraordinary things which it is impossible to calculate exactly or to put them in any one class . .	4.000.	".	".
	TOTAL:	19.973.	".	".

Estimate

For the outside walls of the moat, terrapleining the bul-
    warks and the esplanades, the wall of the patio, and
    for the stables, estimated . . . . 1.351.400.
For two bulwarks and the esplanades . . . . ".431.100.
For the exterior walls of the different stables, for the
    powder magazine, *azoteas* [flat roofs] of the stables,
    and for the terraplein of the patio and the *noria* . .".634.000.
                                              2.416.500.

    For this quantity of bricks it will take at least 3,000 *fanegas*
(7,731 bushels) of lime. For beams, one hundred thousand feet of
lumber. For boards (thick and thin), ten thousand feet. Iron for
the work, 2,000 pounds, and 400 pounds of nails.

    This list was drawn up in the *Villa* of [San Felipe de] Austin
by an architect whose name I do not know, to whom I was introduced
for that purpose by the Commissar Citizen Guillermo Guilemes [Samuel
May Williams]. Béxar, February 20, 1831.= [signed] Santiago Navayra.

    A Copy.

---

[1]BA Roll 138, Frames 0884-0887. For the background
of this project, see McLean, *Papers*, IV, 339-343, 486-487,
and the following documents in the present volume: Francisco Ruiz to Antonio Elosúa, November 14, 1830; Antonio
Elosúa to Rafael Chowell, November 16, 1830; Antonio Elosúa
to Manuel de Mier y Terán, December 9, 1830; Francisco
Ruiz to Antonio Elosúa, December 13, 1830, and Francisco
Ruiz to Samuel M. Williams, December 26, 1830.

[2]A *noria* was a
device consisting of a
series of buckets on a
wheel, originally used
in Spain and the Orient
for raising water, like
this:

noria

--Miguel de Toro y Gis-
bert, *Pequeño Larousse
Ilustrado* (Paris:
Editorial Larousse,
1964), p. 724.

[3]A *quintal* was equal to 101.44 pounds in Mexico--
J. Villasana Haggard and Malcolm Dallas McLean, *Handbook
for Translators of Spanish Historical Documents* (Oklahoma
City: Photoprinted by Semco Color Press, 1941), p. 83.
Consequently 20 quintals would have been equal to about
2,028.8 pounds.

FRANCISCO RUIZ TO ANTONIO ELOSÚA[1]

[Translated from Spanish]

Álamo de Parras   [February 24, 1831]

Presidial Company.

As a consequence of the superior official letter of Your
Lordship which, under date of January 19 last, you were
pleased to send to the Captain of the Álamo Company, which
is under my command, relative to the forwarding of dispatches of Officials to the Commissariat of that City,
Alférez Juan Nepomuceno Tello is going to that City with
no other purpose than to present, in the said Commissariat,
the dispatches corresponding to the Captain and Officials
of the said Company, and he is going commissioned for that
purpose, with the understanding that he has been instructed
to pick up there the dispatches of Lieutenant Francisco
Castañeda for the same purpose. I wish to add that he is
not carrying the dispatch of *Alférez* Jorge Cevallos because
this official is absent, and I will see that it is forwarded at the proper time, just as soon as he returns. All
of which I have the honor of reporting to Your Lordship
for your superior information.

God and Liberty. Tenoxtitlan, February 24, 1831.

Francisco Ruiz

[rubric]

To the Principal Commandant,)
)
Citizen Colonel Antonio Elosúa)

---

[1]BA Roll 138, Frames 0945-0946.

THE AUSTIN & WILLIAMS CONTRACT[1]

[Translated from Spanish]

[February 25, 1831]

174

No. 1061   P. 970   [Deleted:] N. 27.

Year of 1831

[Deleted:] No. 594

Leg. No. 45. *Expediente* concerning Citizen Stephen F. Austin
and Samuel M. Will[i]ams settling eight hundred
Mexican and foreign families in the vacancies
that may be left in the enterprises which have
previously been contracted for by the former
[*i.e.* Stephen F. Austin] and in the enterprise
contracted for by Robert Leftwitch [Leftwich]
for the Nashville Company.

February 25.
    [1]831.

On this date permission was granted to Don Stephen F. Austin
and Don Samuel M. Will[i]ams to colonize with 800
families the vacancies left over from the enterprises which he [Stephen F. Austin] has contracted
for previously, designating the limits to which he
must be restricted as expressed in the contract.

Ends on page 979.

[*Along the lefthand margin of the UT-Austin photostat of this page there is a note which reads:
"The originals are spotted up to 983."*]

[*The next item in this file is the document
which purports to be a certified copy of
the power of attorney issued by Samuel M.
Williams to Stephen F. Austin on December
17, 1830. See copy under that date.*]

[*Then comes Stephen F. Austin's application
for a colonization contract for himself and
Samuel M. Williams, February 4, 1831, which
we have already included above, under that
date.*]

182

SELLO TERCERO   PARA EL BIENIO DE

                          [seal]

DOS REALES.   1830 Y 1831.

Conditions with which the Supreme Government of the State

admits the project proposed by Citizen Stephen F. Austin,

for himself and as agent of Samuel M. Will[i]ams, in order

to colonize with eight hundred Mexican and foreign families,

on the land which he requests in the preceding petition:

Article 1.   The present project is admitted by the Govern-

             ment of the State insofar as it is in conform-

             ity with the Colonization Law issued by the

             Honorable Congress on March 24, 1825, and con-

             sequently there is designated for the *empresa-

             rios*, within the following limits, the land on

             which they are to plant the colony which they

             are offering. The said measurement shall begin

             on the left bank of the Lavaca River, withdraw-

             ing ten leagues from the coast, following said

             River upstream to its westernmost head-

             waters; from thence a straight line shall be

             drawn to the Northwest until it touches the

             road that goes from Béxar to Nacogdoches, known

             with the name of the Upper Road, and following

this in a Northeasterly direction to the Colorado River, ascending the right bank of said
River to the mouth of the Salt or Red Fork,
which enters about fifteen leagues [39 miles]
above the mouth of the Pecan or Nueces River;
from the said Salt Fork a straight line shall
be drawn to the Northeast to the heights which
divide the waters of the Brazos and Trinity
Rivers; following the said heights toward the
Southeast to the principal headwaters of the
San Jacinto River and, descending this River
to the line of the ten littoral [coastal]
leagues, the said line shall continue toward
the West to the point where the present demarcation began.

Article 2.   Although in the preceding demarcation is found
included the part of the lands contracted with
the Government by the *empresarios* Stephen F.
Austin and Robert Leftwich, for the Nashville
Company, this fact has not been an obstacle to
celebrating the present contract, due to the
fact that Austin agrees to it, with reference
to the part that affects him, and for Leftwich
there will expire, on April 15 of the present
year, the term that was granted to him for that

purpose when he celebrated his contract, and up to now he has not complied with even a part thereof.

Article 3. With reference to the land designated, the *empresarios*

978   183

are hereby obligated to introduce and establish, at their own expense, eight hundred Mexican and foreign families, in conformity with whatever may be stipulated, both by the general laws of the Republic and by the special laws of the State.

Article 4. All the possessions which, with their corresponding titles, may be found within the limits designated in Article 1, shall be respected by colonists of this enterprise, it being the responsibility of the *empresarios* to comply with this obligation.

Article 5. The State retains for itself the right of ownership over all the surplus lands that will be left over from this project, after the land

which, according to the laws, corresponds to
the *empresarios* and colonizing families, has
been distributed to them.

Article 6.   In conformity with Article 8 of the said Colonization Law, the *empresarios* are hereby obligated to introduce the eight hundred families
contracted for within a period of six years,
beginning on April 15 of the present year,[2]
under penalty of losing the rights and favors
which are granted to them by the said law.

Article 7.   It is the obligation of the *empresarios* not to
introduce, nor to permit in their colony, men
of bad conduct or those who have committed atro-
cious crimes, and to see that no person shall
carry on trade in firearms and ammunition with
the tribes of wild Indians in exchange for
horses or mules.

Article 8.   Whenever there is a sufficient number of men,
the National Local Militia shall be organized
and regulated in conformity with the laws governing the matter.

Article 9.   This colony shall be regulated by the individual whom this Government shall appoint for the

issuing of the respective land titles, and he

shall observe the laws of colonization that

are in force in the State, as well as the

General Colonization Law of August 18, 1824,

and the instructions for

979   184

SELLO TERCERO   PARA EL BIENIO DE

[seal]

DOS REALES.   1830 Y 1831.

commissioners which the Honorable Congress has

approved, being particularly careful not to

give any possession whatsoever, within the

designated limits, to persons who have not

been approved by the *empresarios*.

Article 10. Official communications, instruments, and other

public documents drawn up in the colony shall

be written in the Spanish language.

Article 11. For everything else not expressed in these

articles, the *empresarios* and the new colony

shall be subject to the Federal Constitution

and laws, and to the Constitution and the special laws of the State.

And the Most Excellent Governor and Citizen Stephen F. Austin, for himself and as agent of Samuel M. Will[i]ams, being in agreement with the articles of the present contract, do hereby obligate themselves respectively to comply reciprocally with same, before me, the undersigned Secretary of the Office of Government, and they signed it so that it might be a matter of record. And, after an order was issued that a certified copy of the entire *expediente* should be given to the party representing the *empresarios*, in order that it may serve them for their protection and as a title in due form, the original has been filed in the Secretariat under my supervision, for the proper purposes. City of Leona Vicario [Saltillo], February 25, 1831.-Interlined=*de camino*. =Valid.

J. M. Viesca   Estevan F. Austin

[rubric]   [rubric]

Santiago del Valle,

Secretary

[rubric][3]

---

[1]In 1940 Mrs. McLean and I made a trip to Saltillo
and spent a week copying these documents and others from
the Spanish originals. At that time the exact location
and description of this file was as follows: Saltillo, Secretaría de Gobierno, Archivo, Legajo 45, Expediente 1061,
but, when we went back to check the documents on July 11,
1967, the originals had disappeared.

Fortunately, however, we still have our copy in
longhand, and there is a photostatic copy in the Barker
Texas History Center, the University of Texas at Austin, in
the "Saltillo Archives, 1688-1876," Volume XXX, pp. 174-180,
182-184. Due to an error in numbering, there is no page
numbered 181.

This present translation is being made from the UT-
Austin photostats, and we are being very careful to indicate the original pagination, with the various page numbers,
seals, and other special markings so that the originals can
be readily identified whenever they turn up. Although this
was the most gigantic of all the colonization contracts in
Texas, Dr. Barker omitted the text from the published *Austin
Papers*, and we have not been able to find it printed anywhere else, in either Spanish or English, so that is why we
are so happy to be able to make it available to researchers
here, in its entirety.

[2]The Austin & Williams Contract was scheduled to
start on April 15, 1831, because that was the date on which
Robert Leftwich's contract was due to expire. See McLean,
Papers, II, 296-301. The fact that Austin went ahead and
got the State Government of Coahuila and Texas to issue his
contract on February 25, 1831, nearly two months *before* the
Leftwich contract had expired, later led to charges that
the Austin & Williams Contract was made in bad faith, on
the basis of incorrect information supplied to the Mexican
officials by Stephen F. Austin.

[3]The UT-Austin photostat ends at this point, but,
when Mrs. McLean and I saw the original in Saltillo in 1940,

this page had the following endorsement:

> Poder.
>
> Del Ciud° Samuel M. Williams
> á favor del Ciud°Estevan F.
> Austin.
>
> dros. satisfechos

The document made available by J. P. Bryan, Jr., on November 6, 1976, also had this same manuscript endorsement.

In the "Translations of Empresario Contracts," pp. 190-191, Spanish Archives of the General Land Office, Austin, Texas there is a different English translation of the Austin & Williams Contract with this additional information at the end: "A Copy of the original file of documents in the archives of the State Department in my charge, from which this was taken by order of His Excellency the Governor. Leona Vicario, June 30th, 1831. Signed Santiago del Valle Secretary.

"The foregoing is a correct translation of a certified copy in Spanish on file in this office. General Land Office of the Republic of Texas, City of Austin April 20th, 1840.-- The words--"within the limits above described"--"especial" --" & the new Colony"--interlined before signing.

> "Thomas G. Western
>
> "Translator pr. Contract"

In the Harllee Papers of the Robertson Colony Collection, in the University of Texas at Arlington, there is still another English translation which ends as follows:

"General Land Office)
State of Texas_____)

I, E. Sterling C. Robertson, Spanish Clerk of said office, bonded and sworn. Certify the foregoing to be a correct translation of the original contract on file in this office. Given under my hand at the City of Austin on the 25th day of August A. D. 1848.

> "E. Sterling C. Robertson
>
> "Sp. Clk. G. L. Off.

"Made for my own use)
       Sterling"

PICTURES   OF   THE   PARTNERS

AUSTIN & WILLIAMS

APPEAR ON THE

NEXT   TWO

PAGES.

STEPHEN F. AUSTIN.

STEPHEN FULLER AUSTIN (1793-1836)
AUTHOR OF THE COLONIZATION PLAN
THAT SWALLOWED UP THE UPPER COLONY.

--D. W. C. Baker, *A Texas Scrapbook*
...(New York: A. S. Barnes & Company
1875), frontispiece.

SAMUEL MAY WILLIAMS (1795-1858),
AUSTIN'S PARTNER IN THE AUSTIN
& WILLIAMS CONTRACT

--*Photograph Courtesy of the
Rosenberg Library, Galveston.*

THE 1835 EDITION OF AUSTIN'S MAP

On the opposite page we have an excerpt showing the Austin
& Williams Grant as depicted on the "MAP OF TEXAS with
Parts of the Adjoining States. COMPILED BY STEPHEN F.
AUSTIN. PUBLISHED by H. S. TANNER. PHILADELPHIA. Note.
The Latitude and Longitude of Saltillo, Monterey, Laredo,
Béxar, Nacogdoches and the Point where the boundary line
leaves the Sabine are from the observations of GENERAL
TERAN OF THE MEXICAN ARMY. 1835."

Notice that there is no line showing that the colony stops
ten leagues (or 26 miles) from the coast, as specified in
the contract.

When the line reaches the westernmost headwaters of the
Lavaca River, it does not continue in a straight line *northwest*, as called for in the contract, it runs due *north*.

On reaching the mouth of the Salt or Red (Colorado) Fork
of the Colorado River, the line does not run *northeast*;
it runs due *north* to a point above the Tahcajunova River,
then follows what must have been an Indian trail, veering
first north then south, in a generally easterly direction,
to the Cross Timbers.

At that point it makes no attempt to follow the watershed
between the Brazos and Trinity Rivers, down to the headwaters of the San Jacinto River. When the line does appear,
it moves east from the headwaters of the San Jacinto, to
follow the watershed between the San Jacinto and the Trinity.

For the foregoing reasons we choose to refer the reader to
the map we have used as the frontispiece of this volume.
There the all-enveloping nature of the Austin & Williams
Contract is clearly depicted.

49

ÁLAMO DE PARRAS PRESIDIAL COMPANY[1]

[Translated from Spanish]

[March 1, 1831]

Budget showing the amounts due the individuals of said Company in the present month, after deducting for invalids and pensions.

Officers.	Pesos	R.	G.	Pesos	R.	G.
1 Captain--------------------#.	117.	6.	0.			
1 Lieutenant----------------#.	62.	6.	6.			
1 First *Alférez*-------------#.	47.	0.	10.	.266.	7.	6.
1 Second Ditto-------------#.	39.	2.	2.			

Enlisted Men.						
1 Sergeant------------------#.	29.	1.	0.			
1 Bugler--------------------#.	11.	5.	6.			
6 Corporals at 24ps. 2rrs. 2gs. #.	145.	5.	0.	1.176.	1.	3.
51 Privates at 19ps. 3rrs. 3gs. -#.	989.	5.	9.			

Invalids Added.						
1 Private-------------------#.	8.	0.	0.			
Gratifications.				. 48.	3.	7.
For the men-----------------#.	40.	3.	7.			

Rewards for Constancy.						
1 at 90 rrs.----------------#.	11.	2.	0.			
1 at 9 rrs.----------------#.	1.	1.	0.	. 14.	5.	0.
3 at 6 rrs.----------------#.	2.	2.	0.			
			#	1.506.	1.	4.

Credit for Additions.

Credit to the deserter Manuel
Tarín, who was apprehended on
January 12 last, and for one
month and twenty days--------#. 31. 7. 3.

Ditto for the deserter Tomás
Lazo, who presented himself
on the 16th of the said month
of January, and for one month
and sixteen days he earned---#. 29. 3. 3.

Ditto for Private Homobono
Carabajal, who transferred
to this Company on the 21st
day of said month of January,
and for one month and eleven
days he earned--------------#. 26.   2. 3.
                                          # 1.593. 6. 1.

Deduct for Losses.

Deduct from this total 30
pesos that are being enjoyed
in Monterrey by the family
of the Captain of said Company pertaining to the
present month---------------   . 30. 0. 0.
        Carried Forward----------------------# 1.563. 6. 1.

                                          Pesos   R. G.

        Brought Forward----------------------# 1.563. 6. 1.

Add to this total the pay of
Chaplain Juan Nepomuceno Ayala,
who is serving as an attaché
in this Company----------------------------# . 40. 0. 0.
                        Net Assets---# 1.603. 6. 1.

        Tenoxtitlan, March 1, 1831.

            As the one in charge of the Paymaster's Office:

O.K.   Francisco Mesa

[Francisco] Ruiz   [rubric]

        [rubric]

_____

[1]BA Roll 139, Frames 0060-0062.

FRANCISCO RUIZ TO ANTONIO ELOSÚA[1]

[Translated from Spanish]

[March 1, 1831]

Office of the Military Commandant   No. 60

of Tenoxtitlan

      With the greatest interest I have endeavored to find out the names of the North Americans who with Sterling Robertson entered the country headed in this direction, and, although I have not omitted any measure within my reach to accomplish the desired end, I have only succeeded in acquiring a simple note written in English,[2] and I have not been able to understand it well up to now for lack of an interpreter. I am enclosing it with the regret that I have not been able to find a single individual at this post who could translate it into Spanish, in compliance with the superior official letter concerning that subject which you were pleased to send me under date of January 18 last,[3] which I am now answering, adding that, if in the future I should be able to obtain another more detailed report, I will notify Your Lordship of that fact at that time for your information.

      God and Liberty. Tenoxtitlan, March 1, 1831.

Francisco Ruiz

[rubric]

To the Principal Commandant)
of Texas, Citizen Colonel)
Antonio Elosúa_____)

Endorsed in English: E. Communication Mily.

Comdt. of *"Tenoxtitlan"* to the Principl. Comdt. in Tejas

at Bejar, in answer to the order to ascertain the names of

families which immigrated into Tejas with Sterling C.

Robertson. "names not ascertained" dated. 1 Mrch 1831

Rec'd from the Secy of State Austin 13th Oct.

1846.

Geo: Fisher

Sp: Clk. G. L. Of.

---

[1]Volume 54, pp. 290-290 verso, Spanish Archives, General Land Office, Austin, Texas.

[2]Forwarded with Ramón Músquiz to the Alcalde of the *Villa* of [San Felipe de] Austin, March 29, 1831.

[3]See Antonio Elosúa to Francisco Ruiz, January 18, 1831.

MANUEL DE LOS SANTOS COY TO RAMÓN MÚSQUIZ[1]

[Translated from Spanish]

Nacogdoches Court   [March 1, 1831]

No. 26.

As soon as we received, in the ordinary correspondence, the superior communication from the Most Excellent Governor of the State, dated December 31 of last year,[2] which Your Lordship was pleased to insert for me under date of January 28 of this year, it was given the proper publicity in the form of a proclamation, and not through the press, because the individual who owns it does not speak the Mexican language, for the one who used to do it withdrew.

I find myself facing a great difficulty with this same measure with regard to the sales of lands of Mexicans to foreigners; that is to say, not only concerning the contracts, and the colonization enterprises, but as to whether one is to understand that it also includes those who have been favored by the Government with one to eleven leagues. I hope that Your Lordship will be so good as to clear up this matter for me, so that I won't be left responsible, as judge, in case such an interpretation has been authorized.

God and Liberty. Nacogdoches, March 1, 1831.

Manuel de los Santos Coy

[rubric]

To the Political Chief of)
)
the Department of Béxar.)

---

[1]BA Roll 139, Frames 0110-0111.

[2]See José María Viesca to Ramón Músquiz, December 31, 1830.

THE COMMISSAR OF BÉXAR TO SEVERO RUIZ[1]

[Translated from Spanish]

[March 3, 1831]

In duplicate I have received the budget for the company under your command corresponding to the month of February, which you were pleased to enclose for me with your official letter dated the 1st of the same month [February 1, 1831].

God and Liberty. March 3, 1831.

To the Captain of the Álamo de Parras Company,)
)
Don Severo Ruiz_____)

---

[1]BA Roll 135, Frame 0246.

THE COMMISSAR OF BÉXAR TO FRANCISCO RUIZ[1]

[Translated from Spanish]

[March 3, 1831]

I am returning to you, after having made a proper record thereof, the three cedulas which previously, for that purpose, you were pleased to enclose for me with your official letter dated February 15 last, which I have the honor of answering.

God, etc. Béxar, March 3, 1831.

To Lieutenant Colonel and Commandant)
)
of the Álamo de Parras Company,   )
)
Don Francisco Ruiz_____)

---

[1]BA Roll 135, Frame 0246.

FRANCISCO RUIZ TO ANTONIO ELOSÚA[1]

[Translated from Spanish]

Álamo de Parras   [March 3, 1831]

Presidial Company

We have on file, in this Company under my command, the

superior official letter from Your Lordship dated January

18 last, in which you were pleased to insert for me the

official letter from the Most Excellent Commandant General

Inspector of these States, dated December 29 last relative

to the seniority that must be counted in the position of

regular lieutenant colonel after having obtained that

office, and I am notifying Your Lordship of this fact by

way of making an attentive reply.

        God and Liberty. Tenoxtitlan, March 3, 1831.

                                        Francisco Ruiz

                                        [rubric]

To the Principal Commandant   )
)
Citizen Colonel Antonio Elosúa)

---

[1]BA Roll 139, Frame 0184.

        The next day (March 4, 1831), Francisco Ruiz wrote
another letter to Antonio Elosúa, this time speaking as the
Military Commandant of Tenoxtitlan, and he repeated the
text of this letter verbatim.--BA Roll 139, Frames 0208-
0209.

LEANDRO AGUILAR TO ANTONIO ELOSÚA[1]

[Translated from Spanish]

Subcommissariat of Monterrey.   [March 3, 1831]

For the purposes indicated in the order from the
Most Excellent Commandant General of these States, dated
October 11 last, which Your Lordship was pleased to insert
for me on January 12 of the current year, I have received
the Tahuacano Indian that was forwarded by Your Lordship
to this Commissariat, and I have been informed that Your
Lordship did not do likewise with the other three who were
destined for this capital, for the reasons which Your Lordship was pleased to explain to me in the official letter of
the aforementioned date, which I have the honor of answering.

God and Liberty. Monterrey, March 3, 1831.

Leandro Aguilar

[rubric]

To Colonel Antonio Elosúa,)
)
Principal Commandant of the)
)
State of Coahuila and Texas.) Béxar.

---

[1]BA Roll 139, Frames 0178-0179.

FRANCISCO RUIZ TO ANTONIO ELOSÚA[1]

[Translated from Spanish]

[March 4, 1831]

Office of the Military Commandant   No. 62

of Tenoxtitlan

     With singular appreciation I received the superior

official letter from Your Lordship dated February 11 last

in which you were pleased to insert for me the one from the

Political Chief of this Department dated the 9th of the

same month[2] relative to the expulsion of Sterling Robert-

son and the North American families who with him entered

the country headed in this direction, and, in view of the

contents thereof, I should tell you that the families refer-

red to therein did not arrive at this post, due to the fact

that they had been ordered to begin their departure, as I

informed Your Lordship in my official letter of November

13 last,[3] and those who came the closest to this post, as

soon as I received the order not to permit their establish-

ment, I made them countermarch. For this reason none of

them exist in the immediate vicinity of this establishment.

I wish to add that the fatal condition of the horses at

this garrison does not permit us, as we should like to do,

to go out and look for the aforesaid families, either in

Austin's Colony or in any other direction that they may

have gone. On the other hand, in my opinion, since they

never arrived at this post, as I have already stated, and

since we do not know how many there were or who they were,
it would be difficult to get them together, no matter how
hard we might try here, for the only way we could find out
where they are would be through the colonists, for I do
not even know where Robertson himself is, all of which I
regret to report to Your Lordship in reply to your aforecited superior official letter.

God and Liberty. Tenoxtitlan, March 4, 1831.

Francisco Ruiz

[rubric]

To the Principal Commandant   )
of Coahuila and Texas, Citizen)
Colonel Antonio Elosúa_____)

[Endorsed in English:] F. Receipt, the Mility.
Comdt. of Tenoxtitlan to the Principl. Comdt. of Texas, at
Bejar, of the order of the Political Chief of Texas, relative to the expulsion of Sterling C. Robertson from Texas,
& families that came with him.--4. Mrch/831.

Rec'd from the Sec'y of State Austin 13th Octr
1846.   Geo: Fisher

Sp. Clk. G. L. Of.

---

[1]Volume 54, pp. 291-291 verso, Spanish Archives,
General Land Office, Austin, Texas.

[2]See Ramón Músquiz to Antonio Elosúa, February 9,
1831.

[3]See Francisco Ruiz to Antonio Elosúa, November 13,
1830.

JOSÉ FRANCISCO MADERO TO SAMUEL M. WILLIAMS[1]

[Translated from Spanish]

Atascosito, March 4, 1831

Mr. Samuel Williams:

My esteemed Friend and Sir:

Via Nacogdoches I have received a letter from my *compadre* Don Víctor [Blanco] in which he tells me to talk to you about his land matter and the lands of the people in Mexico City,[2] and, since I have an interest in seeing that my *compadre* is served satisfactorily, I am taking the liberty of reminding you of what I told you in that *Villa*, which is as follows: the greater part of the eleven leagues of my aforementioned *compadre* I should like very much to locate in that colony [*i.e.*, the Austin & Williams Colony], for which purpose I have already obtained the approval of Mr. Austin.

In view of the above I hope that you, by means of your knowledge, will designate there the lands which you believe are the best, and, in view of the fact that they are already surveyed, you will send me, at the first opportunity, the writ of petition and the surveyors' field notes in order to be able to issue the titles and in this way begin to comply with the request of our good friend Blanco.

I have been quite sick on account of my teeth; therefore I am not saying anything about military matters. For the present I wish to conclude by sending my best regards to your *señoritas*, wife and sister (whose feet I kiss), and, without forgetting my regards for my companion Arciniega, I remain your attentive Friend and obedient Servant who kisses your hand.

J. Francisco

Madero [rubric]

I want to [remind] my companion and you not to forget my request [and to send the documents] by the messenger boy when he returns, and have him to bring the papers, [newspapers?]. On another occasion I will send the ones that I have here, for now I have the toothache too bad to read.

[Endorsed:] J. F Madero Mar 4 1831.

---

[1]Item No. 23-0589, Samuel May Williams Papers, Rosenberg Library, Galveston, Texas.

[2]See Madero to Williams, March 15, 1831.

FRANCISCO RUIZ TO SAMUEL M. WILLIAMS[1]

[Translated from Spanish]

Tenoxtitlan, March 5, 1831

My very fine and ever beloved friend:

By your favor of February 23 last, which I received
with extreme pleasure, I see that every day you are giving
me more proofs of your generosity, and my gratitude is
increasing. I wish to give you my most expressive and
repeated thanks for everything contained therein, for my
spirit has been left, if not completely, somewhat tranquil.
Now to take up another subject.

In my mail last time I was expecting documents concerning the concession of land, and I did not get them. I
do not know why. If they should send them to me in due
course, I shall forward them to you, and then I shall say
something to you on the subject, but I want to thank you
now thousands of times for the many favors which you have
done me, and which you offer to do for me. I desire an
occasion in order to be able, or one which will furnish me
a way, to repay you for so much affection.

By the same mail I have received a number of matters connected with my work which are keeping me busy all
the time and do not allow me to write as much as I should
like to. I want to thank you for the news relative to our
good friend Don Stephen [F. Austin] and political matters,
which I hope will continue in the manner which we desire.

Please be so kind as to give my regards to Don Miguel Arciniega, with expressions of affection.

Please remember me to your wife and give her my most attentive and expressive greetings, together with the rest of the family, and, as for yourself, please receive the invariable affection which is professed for you by one who assures you that he is your friend who loves you very much and who kisses your hand.

Francisco Ruiz

[rubric]

P.S.

The bearer of this letter will hand you the three reales for postage due on the last mail and three more reales so that you will please frank a letter for postage to Béxar which will be delivered to you by the same soldier. Valid.

[Addressed:] To Mr. Samuel M. Williams in the *Villa* [of San Felipe] de Austin.

Postage paid with 6 reales.

[Endorsed:] Francisco Ruiz Tenoxtitlan [saying] that he will remit land titles as soon as he receives them, etc.

---

[1]Item 23-0591, Samuel M. Williams Papers, Rosenberg Library, Galveston, Texas.

STEPHEN F. AUSTIN TO SAMUEL M. WILLIAMS[1]

[From Williams Papers, Rosenberg Library, Galveston, Texas]

Saltillo March 5, 1831

Dr. Sir.

I recd nothing from you or anyone from Texas by the last mail--your last letter Jany. 25. I am really uneasy that I got nothing by the last mail. I wrote you on the 19 of last month a long letter, also to Luke [Lesassier] and Rhoads Fisher and Hunter, which I hope you have recd. My principal object here is to try and prevent harm--if I succeed in that I shall do a great deal--this you can say to the Ay[untamien]to to whom I intended to have written by this mail, but will write a long letter by next [mail].

[I have] sent some papers to Dn Ramon [Músquiz] [with the] request to send them to you, they [v]omit *fire* against the present administration. The death of Guerrero appears to have given new vigor, and a vindictive rage to the fallen party. Bustam[an]te can truly say, as Calvits negro did the night his drunken master shot him *"I have taken my head in my hand."* But, how many storms have passed away with a simple *valgame Dios*. Thank God Texas is beyond the reach of these internal hurricanes and I hope they never will reach there, tho this depends mainly on the people of that country. *Keep harmony and Union among yourselves*--and all is safe.

Private--I wrote by last mail that your petition

was granted[2]--since then I have recd the testimonio [certi-fied copy][3] and will send it and all the others by Fernando Rodrigues who starts in a few days for Bexar.

The power of attorney is effected in union with myself[4]--the lower line is ten leagues from the West[5]--the upper on the heads of the Brazos and Colorado: I wish the [B]*oss* [Terán?], to take a part in this--if he will, all is safe.[6] I am operating on a pritty large scale, for a taci-turn and noisless man, but I have no other object in view that [than] the genl prosperity of *us all*[7] and particularly of this nation and government. Keep all this to yourself: The fate of Texas, in some respects depends on the month of *May* next--untill then look back and take council from the past a[nd keep] all quiet--you can shew [parts of?] the letter to Luke if you think prop[er but] to no one else and he must not mention or breathe it to anyone.[8]

Remember me affectionately to Sarah and Eliza and my little nephew and write me how Stephen is, you say noth-ing of him--I presume he is still at Westalls. Send the enclosed by first opportunity.

S. F. Austin [rubric]

Tell Mancha [that] her son is well and ....

[Addressed:] Sam M. Williams

---

[1]Barker, *Austin Papers*, II, 606-607.
[2]See Austin to Williams, February 5, 1831.

[3]See Austin & Williams Contract, February 25, 1831.

[4]See power of attorney allegedly granted by Samuel M. Williams to Stephen F. Austin, December 17, 1830. It seems strange that Austin should have to tell Williams how the power of attorney was made out when Williams was supposed to have issued the instrument himself. Also note the following instructions in the letter Austin wrote to Williams on March 12, 1831: "... read over my letters by the last two mails more is meant there than is plainly expressed--also one to Luke."--Barker, *Austin Papers*, II, 611-613.

[5]Barker read this word as "west," but it should be "coast."

[6]Apparently Austin had written Mier y Terán on February 8, 1831, and asked him to take a part in the upper Colony.--See Barker, *Austin Papers*, II, 635. Later (on January 8, 1832) he wrote Mier y Terán: "I was hoping that you would take the new colony ...under your protection, as I indicated to you from Saltillo."--*Ibid.*, 734. In view of this evidence there can be no doubt that the *Boss* was Mier y Terán.

[7]The expression *us all* probably refers to the *Congress* or group of advisers identified by Dr. Barker as Luke Lesassier, R. M. Williamson, F. W. Johnson, and perhaps others, and not humanity in general, as the casual reader might be led to believe.

[8]Austin is trying to tell Williams to keep everything quiet about the Austin & Williams Contract until after Robert Leftwich's contract has expired on April 15, 1831.

END OF VOLUME V

We did get to the Upper Colony in this volume, as we had promised, and it looks as though Austin & Williams have established a monopoly on Texas colonization. What actually happened, however, was that they delayed the settlement of Central Texas for at least three years, from 1831 to 1834, because they failed to have a Land Commissioner appointed to issue titles to the Anglo-American families who were actually there during that period. Instead they allowed non-resident Mexican politicians to locate huge eleven-league grants in the area, which later tied up the land titles in litigation for generations, as we shall see in Volume VI.

BIBLIOGRAPHY

BIBLIOGRAPHY

Manuscripts

Bryan, J. P., Jr., Collection, No. 3 Shadowlawn, Houston, Texas 77005.

Robertson Papers at Salado. Documents preserved in the home built in Salado, Bell County, Texas, by Elijah Sterling Clack Robertson, son of Empresario Sterling C. Robertson. In 1939 they were there in the possession of a great-grandson of Empresario Robertson, also named E. S. C. Robertson.

Williams Papers, Samuel May. Rosenberg Library, Galveston, Texas. 77550.

Public Documents

Austin Papers. See Barker.

BA. See Texas. Bexar County. San Antonio. "The Bexar Archives at The University of Texas Archives, Austin."

Barker. *Austin Papers*, II. *Annual Report of the American Historical Association for the Year 1922. In Two Volumes and a Supplemental Volume. Vol. II. The Austin Papers. Edited by Eugene C. Barker.* Washington: United States Government Printing Office, 1928.

Coahuila and Texas. (*Mexican State*). Laws.
     Kimball, J. P. (translator). *Laws and Decrees of the State of Coahuila and Texas* .... Houston: Telegraph Power Press, 1839. For complete entry, see Volume IV, page 601, of these *Papers*.

Coahuila and Texas (*Mexican State*). Secretaría de Gobierno del Estado. Saltillo.

     Legajo 25, *Expediente* 1061. The original documents were missing in Saltillo when we went back to check them on July 11, 1967, but there is a facsimile copy in the "Saltillo Archives," Vol. XXX, pp. 175-176, The University of Texas Archives, Austin.

Colección de constituciones de los Estados Unidos Mexicanos.
3 vols.; México: Imprenta de Galvan á cargo de
Mariano Arévalo calle de Cadena núm. 2, 1828.

Mexico. Fomento. Colonización.

> *Legajo* IV, 1823-1835. Typed transcripts in The
> University of Texas Archives, Austin.

Tennessee. Davidson County. Nashville.

> Circuit Court Minutes, Microfilm Roll 524, Books F-
> G, 1826-1831.

Tennessee. Supreme Court of Errors and Appeals. Nashville.

> "Minute Book of Tennessee State Supreme Court of
> Errors and Appeals, 1831-1834." Department of
> Archives, Fifth Floor, Tennessee State Library and
> Archives, 403 Seventh Avenue North, Nashville,
> Tennessee 37203.

Texas. Bexar County. San Antonio.

> "The Béxar Archives, at The University of Texas
> Archives, Austin," Texas Christian University,
> Fort Worth, Texas 76129, Microfilm 3. Cited as
> "BA":
> Roll 134. September 1, 1830--October 3, 1830.
> " 135. October 4, 1830--November 4, 1830.
> " 136. November 5, 1830--December 12, 1830.
> " 137. December 13, 1830--January 17, 1831.
> " 138. January 18, 1831--February 26, 1831.
> " 139. February 27, 1831--April 10, 1831.
> We are happy to report that on May 30, 1978, The
> UTA Library received Segments Two and Three of the
> microfilms, which it had had on order from UT
> Austin since March 7, 1977. Heretofore we have had
> to borrow the film from the Texas Christian Univer-
> sity Library, which has cooperated most generously.
> Now UTA has all three segments of the Bexar
> Archives on microfilm, with the three pamphlet
> *Guides* that accompany the collection.

Texas. Commission of Control for Texas Centennial Celebra-
tions. Harold Schoen (compiler). *Monuments
Erected by the State of Texas to Commemorate the
Centenary of Texas Independence: the Report of the
Commission of Control for Texas Centennial Celebra-
tions.* Austin: Commission of Control for Texas
Centennial Celebrations, 1938.

Texas. General Land Office. Spanish Archives. Austin.

Volumes 53, 54, and 55.

"Translations of Empresario Contracts."

Taylor, Virginia H. *The Spanish Archives of the General Land Office of Texas.* Austin: The Lone Star Press, 1955.

Texas. Laws.

Gammel, H. P. N. (compiler and arranger). *The Laws of Texas, 1822-1897.* ... 10 vols.; Austin: The Gammel Book Store, 1898. For complete entry, see Volume II, page 656, of these *Papers.*

Texas. Lee County. Historical Survey Committee.

History of Lee County, Texas. Quanah, Texas: Nortex Press, 1974.

Texas. State Library. Archives. Austin.

Nacogdoches Archives. There is also a typed copy of the "Nacogdoches Archives" in The University of Texas Archives, Austin.

Texas. University at Arlington. Library. Special Collection.

Harllee Collection. Documents preserved by the late Mrs. William Curry Harllee, a great-granddaughter of Empresario Sterling C. Robertson. They are now (1978) in the Robertson Colony Collection.

Sutherland Collection. Documents preserved by Mrs. Thomas Shelton Sutherland, Sr., a great-granddaughter of Empresario Sterling C. Robertson. For further details, see Volume IV, page 601, of these *Papers.*

Texas. University at Austin. Library. Archives. The Eugene C. Barker Texas History Center, Sid Richardson Hall, 2.109.

Austin Papers, 1765-1899; 9 feet, 6 inches; Mss., printed, cartographic, pictorial, typescript, photocopy.

Franklin, Benjamin Cromwell. Papers, 1805-1915;
3 feet, 11 inches; Mss., printed, typescript,
photocopy.

Robertson, Sterling Clack. Family Papers, 1824-
1865; 17 items; Mss., photocopy, typescript.

[Note added by McLean: These papers passed down
through Sterling Clack Robertson's son, Elijah
Sterling Clack Robertson, to E. S. C.'s
daughter, Mrs. Cone Johnson (née Eliza Sophia
"Birdie" Robertson, and from her to her niece,
Mrs. William Curry Harllee, who deposited them
for safekeeping at UT Austin.]

United States. Bureau of the Mint. *Medals of the United
States Mint*. Prepared under the direction of the
Honorable Eva Adams, Director of the Mint, by Cap-
tain Kenneth M. Failor, USNR, Consultant to the
Director of the Mint, and Eleanora Hayden, Bureau
of the Mint. Washington, D. C.: U. S. Government
Printing Office, [1969].

Map

"MAP OF TEXAS with Parts of the Adjoining States. COMPILED
BY STEPHEN F. AUSTIN. PUBLISHED by H. S. TANNER.
PHILADELPHIA. Note. The Latitude and Longitude of
Saltillo, Monterey, Laredo, Béxar, Nacogdoches and
the Point where the boundary line leaves the Sabine
are from the observations of GENERAL TERAN OF THE
MEXICAN ARMY. 1835."

The excerpt used in this volume was taken from a
reduced copy of the original furnished by Miss
Winnie Allen.

Newspapers

Arkansas. Little Rock.

Arkansas Gazette. 1830. Microfilm in Amon Carter
Museum of Western Art, Fort Worth, Texas.

Mexico. Mexico City.

*Registro Oficial del Gobierno de los Estados-Unidos
Mexicanos*. 1831. Originals in the Special

Collections of the Library, The University of
Texas at Arlington.

Missouri. St. Louis.

Louisiana Gazette, 1811, 1822. Microfilm in the
Amon Carter Museum of Western Art, Fort Worth,
Texas. Note: In 1811 St. Louis *was* in Louisi-
ana.

Tennessee. Nashville.

The Nashville Republican and State Gazette. 1830.
Microfilm in the Amon Carter Museum of Western
Art, Fort Worth, Texas.

Texas. San Felipe de Austin.

The Texas Gazette. 1830. Microfilm in The Univer-
sity of Texas at Arlington Library, shelved in
B-SS Div. under "Pre-Civil War & Republic of
Texas newspapers," set no. 1, Reel No. 5.

Periodicals

Barker, Eugene C. (ed.). "Descriptions of Texas by Stephen
F. Austin," *Southwestern Historical Quarterly*,
Austin, Texas, Vol. XXVIII, No. 2 (October, 1924),
pp. 98-121.

_____. "Minutes of the Ayuntamiento of San Felipe de
Austin, 1828-1832," VI, *The Southwestern Historical
Quarterly*, Austin, Texas, Vol. XXII, No. 4 (April,
1919), pp. 353-359.

_____. VII. *The Southwestern Historical Quarterly*, Vol.
XXIII, No. 1 (July, 1919), pp. 69-77.

_____. IX. *The Southwestern Historical Quarterly*, Vol.
XXIII, No. 3 (January, 1920), pp. 214-223.

Blount, Edward. "Location of the Old Contraband Trace in
Nacogdoches County," *The Junior Historian of the
Texas State Historical Association*, Austin, Vol.
VI, No. 3 (December, 1945), pp. 7-11.

Horton, L. W. "General Sam Bell Maxey: His Defense of
North Texas and the Indian Territory," *Southwestern Historical Quarterly*, Vol. LXXIV, No. 4 (April,
1971), pp. [507]-524.

Kuykendall, J. H.   "Reminiscences of Early Texans.   A Collection from the Austin Papers ....   4.   Recollections of Barzillai Kuykendall," *The Quarterly of the Texas State Historical Association*, Vol. VI (July, 1902, to April, 1903), pp. 317-319.

McLean, Malcolm Dallas.

　　Articles published in *Texas Parade* magazine, Austin, Texas, in the following order:

　　　　"They Shot Father Hidalgo," May, 1948, pp. 10-11, 27.

　　　　"The Flame of Freedom," June, 1948, pp. 6-7, 43.

　　　　"Mission to Mexico," July, 1948, pp. 20-21.

　　　　"The Meaning of Mañana," August, 1948, pp. 12, 34-35.

　　　　"Leftwich's Grant," October, 1948, pp. 35-36, 38-39.

　　　　"Teha Lanna," November, 1948, pp. 28-29.

　　　　"Austin's Little Colony," December, 1948, pp. 25-26.

　　　　"The Nashville Colony," January, 1949, pp. 12-13.

　　　　"The Awful Extremity," February, 1949, pp. 6-7, 26.

　　　　"Sandy Hair and Silver Spurs," March, 1949, pp. 8, 25.

　　　　"Squatter's Rights," April, 1949, pp. 22-23.

　　　　"Clandestine Passage," May, 1949, pp. 8-9.

　　　　"Tenoxtitlan, Dream Capital of Texas," *Southwestern Historical Quarterly*, Austin, Vol. LXX, No. 1 (July, 1966), pp. [23]-43.

　　　　　　This article had been published originally in *The Burleson County Citizen and The Caldwell News*, Caldwell, Texas, May 7, 21, 28, June 4, 11, 18, 25, July 2 and 23, 1964.

Zuber, William Physic. "Thomson's Clandestine Passage
     around Nacogdoches," *The Quarterly of the Texas
     State Historical Association*, Vol. I, No. 1 (July,
     1897), pp. 68-70.

Books

Academia Española. *Diccionario de la lengua española.*
     Madrid: Talleres Espasa Calpe, S. A., 1936.

Alessio Robles, Vito. *Coahuila y Texas desde la consuma-
     ción de la Independencia hasta el Tratado de Paz de
     Guadalupe Hidalgo.* 2 vols.; México: Talleres Grá-
     ficos de la Nación, 1945-1946.

Baker, DeWitt Clinton. *A Texas Scrap-Book. Made up of the
     History, Biography, and Miscellany of Texas and its
     People.* New York: A. S. Barnes & Company, 1875;
     facsimile reproduction of the original, The Steck
     Company, Austin, Texas, 1935.

Belden, Bauman L. *Indian Peace Medals Issued in the United
     States.* New Milford, Connecticut: M. Flayderman &
     Co., 1966.

Black, Henry Campbell. *Black's Law Dictionary: Definitions
     of the Terms and Phrases of American English Juris-
     prudence, Ancient and Modern.* Revised Fourth
     Edition, St. Paul, Minnesota: West Publishing Co.,
     1968.

Colón de Larriátegui, Félix. *Juzgados Militares de España
     y sus Indias. Por don Felix Colón de Larriátegui
     ....* 3rd ed., 4 vols.; Madrid: Impr. de Repullés,
     1817.

Davis, James D. *History of Memphis ....* Memphis: Hite,
     Crumpton & Kelly, Printers, 1873.

*Diccionario Porrúa de historia, biografía y geografía de
     México.* 3d ed., 2 vols.; México, D. F.: 1970-1971.

Ericson, Carolyn Reeves. *Nacogdoches--Gateway to Texas, A
     Biographical Directory, 1773-1849.* Fort Worth:
     Arrow/Curtis Printing Company, Publishing Division,
     1974.

Greenwood, Val D. *The Researcher's Guide to American Gene-
     alogy. By Val D. Greenwood. With an Introduction*

by Milton Rubicam. Baltimore: Genealogical Publishing Co., Inc., 1973; Fourth Printing, 1977.

Haggard, John Villasana, and Malcolm Dallas McLean. *Handbook for Translators of Spanish Historical Documents. By J. Villasana Haggard, Translator of the Spanish Archives of Texas. Assisted by Malcolm Dallas McLean, Archivist, The San Jacinto Museum of History. Archives Collection, The University of Texas.* Oklahoma City: Photoprinted by Semco Color Press, 1941. Published with funds from the Institute of Latin American Studies, The University of Texas at Austin.

Handbook of Texas. *The Handbook of Texas. Walter Prescott Webb, Editor-in-chief. H. Bailey Carroll, Managing Editor. Llerena Friend, Mary Joe Carroll, Louise Nolen, Editorial Assistants. In Two Volumes. ...* Austin: The Texas State Historical Association, 1952.

_____. *A Supplement. Volume III. Eldon Stephen Branda, Editor. Foreword by Joe B. Frantz. ...* Austin: The Texas State Historical Association. Joe B. Frantz, Director. L. Tuffly Ellis, Associate Director, 1976.

Harllee, William Curry. *Kinfolks* ... (3 vols. and index volume; New Orleans: Searcy & Pfaff, Ltd., 1934-1937). See Volume III, page 545, for complete bibliographical entry.

Henson, Margaret Swett. *Samuel M. Williams, Early Texas Entrepreneur.* College Station: Texas A&M Press, 1976.

Lewis Publishing Company. *A Memorial and Biographical History of McLennan, Falls, Bell and Coryell Counties, Texas. Illustrated. Containing a History of this Important Section of the great State of Texas, from the Earliest Period of its Occupancy to the Present Time, together with Glimpses of its Future Prospects; also Biographical Mention of Many of the Pioneers and Prominent Citizens of the Present Time, and Full-page Portraits of some of the most Eminent Men of this Section. ...* Chicago: The Lewis Publishing Company, 1893.

[Lindley, E. R. (compiler)]. *Biographical Directory of the Texas Conventions and Congresses, 1832-1845.* No place, no publisher, 1941.

McLean, Malcolm Dallas. *Papers Concerning Robertson's Colony in Texas. Compiled and Edited by Malcolm D. McLean. Volume I. 1788-1822. The Texas Association.* Fort Worth: Texas Christian University Press, 1974.

_____. *Volume II. 1823 through September, 1826. Leftwich's Grant.* Fort Worth: Texas Christian University Press, 1975.

_____. *Volume III. October, 1826, through April, 1830. The Nashville Colony.* Fort Worth: Texas Christian University Press, 1976.

_____. *Volume IV. May through October 10, 1830. Tenoxtitlan, Dream Capital of Texas.* Arlington, Texas: The UTA Press, 1977. Note: The entire unsold stock of Volumes I, II, and III was bought from the Texas Christian University Press, so that all the volumes can now be ordered from the UTA Press, Box 19929, The University of Texas at Arlington, Arlington, Texas 76019.

McLean, Malcolm Dallas. *Vida y obra de Guillermo Prieto.* México, D. F.: El Colegio de México, 1960.

Also see Haggard, John Villasana, and Malcolm Dallas McLean.

Prucha, Francis Paul. *Indian Peace Medals in American History.* Madison: The State Historical Society of Wisconsin, 1971.

Randolph, Wassell. "Henry Randolph I (1623-1773) of Henrico County, Virginia, and His Descendants. Preceded by short review of the Randolph family in Early England and elsewhere." Memphis, Tennessee: Distributed by Cossitt Library, 1952. Typescript.

Ray, Worth S. *Austin Colony Pioneers. Including History of Bastrop, Fayette, Grimes, Montgomery and Washington Counties, Texas.* Austin: The Pemberton Press, Jenkins Publishing Company, 1970.

Smithwick, Noah. *The Evolution of a State, or Recollections of Old Texas Days, by Noah Smithwick (Nonagenarian). Compiled by His Daughter, Nanna Smithwick Donaldson.* Austin: Gammel Book Company, 1900; Original Narratives of Texas History and Adventure ... A facsimile reproduction of the original. The Steck Company, Austin, Texas, 1935.

Streeter, Thomas Winthrop. *Bibliography of Texas, 1795-1845*. 3 parts in 5 vols.; Cambridge: Harvard University Press, 1955-1960.

Toro y Gisbert, Miguel de. *Pequeño Larousse Ilustrado*. Paris: Editorial Larousse, 1964.

Winkler, Ernest William (ed.). *Letters and Documents of Early Texians, 1821-1845. In Facsimile. Folio Collection of Original Documents. Selected and Annotated by E. W. Winkler, Bibliographer, The University of Texas Library*. Austin: Published by The Steck Company, 1937.

INDEX

INDEX

Failor, Kenneth M.: 64, 604
Falls County, Texas: 285, 297, 405, 407, 608
Faneuil Hall of Texas: 275
Farías, Eucevio: 370
Farmer, James: 46, 263-264
Fayette County, Tenn.: 374
Fayette County, Texas: 45, 284, 500, 609
Fifth Avenue, New York, N.Y.: 199
Fifth Permanent Batallion: 450-451
Filisola's Grant: 577
First Permanent Company of Tamaulipas: 41, 59, 121, 369, 409, 413, 445, 448, 479, 508, 519-520, 529, 532
Fisher, George (or Jorge): 89, 343, 368, 372, 419, 527, 546, 581, 588
Fisher, Rhoads: 593
"Flame of Freedom": 606
Flayderman & Co., M.: 64, 607
Fletcher, Roy: 466
Fletcher, Thomas H.: 260
Flores, Gaspar: 60, 146, 148, 150
Flores, José: 449
Flores, Luciano: 461, 537
Flores, Nicolás: 449-451
Florida: 543
Florida Territory: 75
Flying Company of Tamaulipas: 41
Fomento: 421
Fonteno, Julián: 441
Ford, William W.: 45-46, 281-282
Fort Anáhuac: see Anáhuac, Texas.
Fort Bend County, Texas: 175
Fort Tenoxtitlan: see Tenoxtitlan.
Fort Worth, Texas: 10, 65, 119, 297, 602, 604-605, 607, 609, Colophon
Fort Worth Linotyping Co.: Colophon
Foster, John T.: 374, 376
Foster, Mr.: 256
France: 66, 347
Franklin Papers, Benjamin Cromwell: 91, 174, 604
Frantz, Joe B.: 608

Fredonian Rebellion: 50, 400
Freestone County, Texas: 554
Friend, Llerena: 608
Frierson, Elias Pullin: 257
Frierson, Samuel D.: 257
Friley, Hiram: 119, 152
Fuente Fernández, Pedro de la: 474
Fuentes, Preciliano: 82-83, 294-295
Fulchear, Churchill: 382
Fullerton, Mrs. W. F.: 10, 481

Gaines (or Crow) Crossing: 484
Galindo, José Ignacio: 297
Gallardo, Juan José: 455
Galván, Damacio (or Damasio): 33, 60, 103, 223
Galván, Imprenta de: 296, 602
Galveston, Texas: 10, 88, 136, 192, 229, 238, 353, 357, 395, 397, 416, 424, 486, 499, 503, 514, 530, 534-535, 541-542, 575, 590, 592-593, 601
Galveston Bay: 360, 473, 505-506, 577
Galveston Bay and Texas Land Company: 358
Galveston County, Texas: 500
Galveston Island: 577
Gammel, Hans Peter Nielson: 474, 603
Gammel Book Company: 609
Gammel Book Store: 474, 603
García de Texada, Antonio: 66
Garza, José Antonio de la: 451
Garza, José Manuel de la: 455
Garza, José María de la: 449
Garza, Father Refugio de la: 40, 290, 293
Garza, Remigio: 79
Garza, Tivurcio de la: 161
Gates, Charles: 217
Genealogical Publishing Co., Inc.: 316, 608
General Land Office of Texas, Austin: 10, 45, 47-48, 69, 125, 134, 165, 184-185, 190, 221, 253, 260-261, 297, 309, 318, 324, 343, 362, 368, 437, 463, 502, 507, 515, 526-527, 536, 572, 581, 588, 603
"General Sam Bell Maxey . . .": 605
George IV, King of Great Brit-

ain: 279, 345
Georgia: 175
Germans: 420, 547
Giles County, Tenn.: 46, 193, 235, 281, 283, 314, 316, 430
Giles County Circuit Court: 315
Gillespie, W. E.: 257
Givens, C. C.: 340
God: 69-79, 81, 83-87, 99-106, 108, 110, 113-114, 117-118, 121-125, 127, 130-132, 134, 137, 146, 148, 150, 154, 156-158, 160-172, 177-180, 182, 184, 186-188, 190, 212-215, 219-221, 223, 225, 228-230, 232-233, 237-238, 240-248, 265, 269-270, 279-280, 287-288, 290-291, 293, 295, 297, 299, 301-303, 306-313, 318, 322, 324-325, 327, 329-334, 341-342, 344-351, 365, 367, 378, 386, 390-393, 396, 401-402, 408-410, 412-417, 421, 433-438, 444, 446, 455-458, 460-461, 463-464, 467-468, 470-472, 475-476, 479, 502, 504, 507-512, 515-522, 524-526, 528-529, 531, 533, 537-539, 552-553, 556, 561, 580, 582-586, 588, 593
Goff, Isaac S.: 258
Goliad (formerly La Bahía): 41, 86, 154, 158, 169, 369, 383, 385, 405, 416, 436, 450, 453, 577
Goliad Ayuntamiento: 80-81, 99, 169
Gómez Pedraza, Manuel: 346, 497, 543-544
Gonzales, Texas: 41, 372, 384-385, 453
Gordon, Robert: 315
Goyens, William: 442
Granados, Laureano: 450
Grande, José de Jesús: 474
Gratification Fund: 244
Gray, Thomas: 372
Grayson: 498
Grayson, Peter Williamson: 500
Great Britain: 279, 345
Greenwood, Val D.: 316, 607
Griffin, Washington: 152
Grillet, Antonio: 441
Grimes County, Texas: 46, 284, 609

579, 586, 604
Montgomery County, Texas: 45, 284, 609
Montreal, Canada: 207
Monuments Erected by the State of Texas ...: 56, 602
Moore, John Henry: 62
Moore, William S.: 258
Moral, Juan del: 121, 413, 508, 532
Morelos, *Villa* of: 163
Morton, William: 145
Morrison, John S.: 442
Morrisson, Moses: 143
Moutom, Manuel: 452
Moya, Onorato: 86, 158
Muldoon, Michael (or Miguel): 496, 500, 549
Munguía, Thomás: 445, 447-448
Músquiz, Padre: 399
Músquiz, Ramón: 33, 42-44, 50-51, 80-83, 99, 112, 137, 146-148, 150, 154, 162, 169, 191, 193, 237, 247-248, 270-272, 294-295, 298-299, 302, 305-308, 317-318, 330, 341, 359, 363, 378, 383, 399, 403, 411-412, 444, 450-451, 455, 462, 464, 468, 499, 501-502, 505, 507, 515-516, 534, 536, 538, 551, 553, 581-583, 588, 593

Nacogdoches: 4, 34, 43-45, 48-49, 53, 76, 83, 94, 97, 101-102, 108, 115-116, 128, 131, 139, 145, 161-162, 182, 184, 196-197, 199-205, 208-209, 220, 229-230, 237-238, 248-249, 254, 256, 268, 279-280, 294-295, 297, 302-303, 305-308, 317, 322, 326, 341, 358-360, 388-389, 416, 433, 436, 438, 441, 443, 453, 455, 464, 484-486, 488, 501, 516, 530, 554, 565, 576, 582, 589, 604, 607
Nacogdoches Archives, Texas State Library: 182, 195, 299, 302, 306, 309, 318, 323, 464, 603
"Nacogdoches Archives," University of Texas at Austin: 182, 302, 318, 323, 443, 516, 603

Nacogdoches County, Texas: 199
Nacogdoches Court: 305, 582
Nacogdoches District: 473, 534
Nacogdoches Garrison: 370
Nacogdoches–Gateway to Texas ...: 297, 607
Nance, Eleanor Hanover (Mrs. Joseph Milton Nance): 10, 93, 95
Nashville, Tennessee: 10, 235, 260, 262, 418, 481-482, 484, 602, 605
Nashville Colony (Grant): 3, 43-45, 55, 194-195, 264, 281, 343, 404, 406, 428, 514, 606, 609
Nashville Company: 34, 42-46, 51, 53-55, 133, 166, 193, 195, 202, 264, 266-267, 283, 298-299, 308, 317, 418, 489, 506, 513, 515, 526, 563, 566
Nashville Grave Yard: 46, 319
Nashville Republican and State Gazette: 119, 605
Natchitoches: 43, 181, 230, 355, 358, 484, 486
National Archives: 10
Naturalization Law, Mexican National: 474
Navarro, Eugenio: 369
Navarro, José Antonio: 450
Navasota River: 577
Navayra, Santiago: 38, 85, 87, 114, 142, 213, 242, 278, 300, 352, 379, 381, 423, 447, 449, 469, 471-472, 510, 518, 555-556, 558, 560
Neches River: 483, 486, 577
Nedderman, Wendel H.: 9
Neff, Pat M.: 56
Nelson, P.: 258
Nesbitt, Robert A.: 10
Nesvil: see Nashville.
New Mexico Territory: 155
New Milford, Connecticut: 64, 607
New Orleans: 43, 48-50, 56, 115, 129, 156, 176, 181, 197, 347, 366, 405, 486, 608
New Spain: 66
New York: 574
New York, N.Y.: 199
New York City: 607
Newcomer, James: 9

Newman's Camp: 145
Newspaper Microfilm Collection: 10
Nicholson, A. O. P.: 257
Nolen, Louise: 608
Noles, Butler: 258
Norcarolina: see North Carolina.
noria (defined): 560
Nortex Press: 466, 603
North Americans: 44, 189, 191, 354, 360, 367-368, 398, 501, 513, 516, 526-527, 530, 539, 580, 587
North Carolina: 75, 314
North Congress, Austin, Texas: 292
North Cooper, Arlington, Texas: Colophon
North Texas: 285, 605
Northwest: 207
Northwest Fur Company: 207
Novara, Mr.: 254, 256
Nueces River: 4
Nuevo León: 121
Nuevo Santander, Colony of: 66
Nuncio Creek: 126
Núñez, Timoteo: 402

Oakley Drive, Nashville, Tenn.: 481
Ocampo, Carlos: 341
O'Connor Foundation, Kathryn: 3
Oelfke, Judy: Colophon
Ohio: 75
Ojayú: see Ohio.
Oklahoma: 359
Oklahoma City: 560, 608
Old Contraband Trace: 199
Old San Antonio Road: 94
Old Smuggler's Road: 199
Old Three Hundred: 153, 175
Olds, James: 442
Opelousas Road: 405
Organized Research Fund: 9
Orient: 560
Original Narratives of Texas History and Adventure: 609
Ortega, José: 105-106, 230
Overton, James: 193
Oyster Creek, Texas: 175

Padilla, Juan Antonio: 82-83, 237, 247, 294-295, 307, 326,

Robertson, Elijah: 314-315

Robertson, Elijah Sterling Clack: 282, 407, 572, 601, 604

Robertson, Eliza Sophia ("Birdie"): see Johnson, Mrs. Cone.

Robertson, Peyton: 46, 319-321

Robertson, Sterling Clack (*Empresario*): 10, 36, 42-47, 53, 55-56, 104, 133, 156, 165-166, 189, 191, 193, 195, 197, 199, 202-204, 221, 235-236, 243, 260-262, 264, 276, 281-284, 299, 308-309, 314-317, 319-321, 342-343, 366-368, 377, 404-407, 428-431, 437, 447, 466, 481-482, 501-502, 513-515, 525-527, 580-581, 587-588, 601, 603

Robertson & Thomson: 43, 46

Robertson Colony Collection: 9, 236, 572, 603, Colophon

Robertson Colony Room: 10

Robertson's Colony: 5, 50, 55, 57, 66, 153, 201-203, 284, 297, 341, 443, 447, 453, 466, 609

Robertson County, Texas: 95, 253, 541

Robertson Papers, Sterling C., Salado, Texas: 407, 601

Robertson Papers, Sterling C., University of Texas at Austin: 282, 284, 429, 604

Robinson, George: 217

Robleau, Pierre: 441

Rocha, Jesús: 330

Rodríguez, Antonio: 86, 158

Rodríguez, Fernando: 55, 450-452, 594

Rodríguez, Ignacio: 60, 103, 451

Roddy, Ephraim: 465-466

Román, José María: 403, 449-451, 455

Romans: 503

Rosales, Matilde S.: 10

Rose, Louis: 442

Rosenberg Library: 10, 88, 136, 192, 353, 357, 395, 397, 424, 499, 503, 514, 541-542, 575, 590, 592-593, 601

Rubicam, Milton: 316, 608

Rueg, H.: 341

Ruiz, Francisco: 34, 38, 40-46, 71, 84-85, 87-88, 93, 113-114, 117, 122-127, 129, 132-136, 156, 165-168, 172, 177-180, 186, 188-192, 198, 213-214, 218-219, 221, 231-233, 242-244, 250, 252-253, 265, 286-287, 300, 310, 317, 324, 331, 344-353, 379, 393-395, 422-423, 433, 435, 437, 446-451, 454, 457, 469-470, 510-514, 521-529, 534, 539-541, 555, 560-561, 579-581, 584-585, 587-588, 591-592

Ruiz, Severo: 41-42, 72-73, 118, 121, 140, 142, 157, 170-171, 212, 245, 252, 265, 278, 311-313, 332, 334, 381, 390-392, 394, 401-402, 408, 413, 445-453, 456, 467, 471-472, 478, 508, 517-518, 522-523, 529, 583

Ruiz, Mrs. Severo (María del Refugio Sánchez): 41, 313, 508, 532

Rumayor, Joaquín: 237

Ruoff, Anna Marie: 359

Sabine River: 34, 46, 358, 419, 501, 516, 531, 576, 604

Sacco, Michel: 441

St. Louis, Missouri: 50, 56, 605

St. Paul, Minn.: 503, 607

Salado, Texas: 407, 601

Salazar, Antonio: 312, 332

Salinas, José Antonio: 33, 411, 450, 468

Salinas, José María: 552-553

Salt (or Red) Fork, Colorado River: 4, 53-54, 489, 566, 576

Saltillo (formerly Leona Vicario), Coahuila: 50-51, 270, 335, 340, 354, 356, 365, 398, 421, 424, 463, 474, 483, 490-491, 493-496, 499, 542, 553, 570-572, 576, 593, 595, 601, 604

"Saltillo Archives," University of Texas Library, Austin: 340, 491, 571, 601

Saltillo Ayuntamiento: 400

Sambrano, José María: 161

Samuel M. Williams, Early Texas Entrepreneur: 359, 608

San Andrés River: see Little River.

San Antonio, Texas: 34, 66, 94, 136, 554, 601-602 (also see Béxar)

San Antonio Crossing of the Brazos: 33, 61

San Antonio de Béxar, *Presidio* of: see Béxar.

San Antonio de Valero Mission: see Alamo (Texas shrine).

San Antonio-Nacogdoches Road: 145, 153

San Antonio River: 577

San Antonio Road: 144, 152, 193-194, 201

San Bernard River: 145, 577

San Felipe de Austin: 34, 38, 41, 43, 45, 48-49, 51-53, 81, 89, 96, 119-120, 128-129, 137-139, 145, 173, 175, 181, 197, 200-201, 205, 210, 216, 222, 232, 254, 256, 269-270, 274, 303-304, 327, 335-338, 340, 352, 357-358, 394, 405, 424-427, 453, 469, 483, 498-499, 515, 540, 549, 555, 560, 577, 581, 592, 605

San Felipe de Austin Ayuntamiento: 80-81, 99, 111-112, 143, 151, 153, 372-373, 382, 387, 398, 400, 439-440

San Fernando de Béxar, *Villa* of: see Béxar.

San Francisco, California: 64

San Gabriel (formerly San Xavier) River: 33, 65

San Jacinto, Battle of: 36

San Jacinto Museum of History: 608

San Jacinto River: 4, 50, 53-54, 144, 358, 397, 473, 489, 535, 566, 576

San Luis Potosí: 102

San Luis Potosí Province: 66

San Marcos River: 168

San Phillipi: see San Felipe de Austin.

San Xavier: see San Gabriel.

Sanches, Nicacio (or Nicasio): 33, 59-60, 146, 148, 150, 383, 390

Sánchez, María del Refugio: see Ruiz, Mrs. Severo.

Sanders, Joel B.: 258

Sandoval, Mariano: 451

"Sandy Hair and Silver Spurs": 606

Santa Bárbara, Chihuahua: 41, 452

COLOPHON

The large type used on the front cover, the spine, and the title page of this volume is a combination of 60-point Craw Clarendon Condensed, 24-point Century Nova, and 12-point Century. The preliminary pages, the index, and the colophon were composed at the Fort Worth Linotyping Company, 610 S. Jennings, Fort Worth, Texas 76104, under the supervision of Walter L. Huzarevich, Jr., using Century Schoolbook 10-point and the matching italics. The tapes were composed by Dahlia Clark and Barbara Mann on an Automix MPM-6 keyboard and printed on a Mergenthaler VIP.

The text of the original documents was typed by Jennifer Jiles, Margaret S. McLean, and Laura Braddy in the temporary quarters of the Robertson Colony Collection, UTA Library 650C, on an IBM Correcting Selectric II typewriter with a Puerto Rican keyboard, using the following typing elements: 10-pitch Courier 72 040, 10-pitch Courier 72 015, 12-pitch Light Italic 032, 12-pitch Light Italic SP-970, and 12-pitch Prestige Elite 72, with Correctable Film Ribbon No. 1 299 095 and Lift-off-Tape No. 1136433.

This year, however, the maintenance contract for our typewriters was changed from IBM to Southwest Office Systems, Inc., 425 North Cooper, Arlington, Texas 76011.

The cards for preparing the index were contributed by Melvin Pierce, Director, Academic Computing Services, The University of Texas at Arlington.

The layout of the book, the paste-up of the pages, the design for the front cover, and the layout of the folder announcing publication of this volume were all done by Judy Oelfke, 2829 W. Cantey, Fort Worth, Texas 76109.

This entire volume was printed by the photo-offset process on Ultima Laid Finish Soft White 60-pound paper by the Davis Brothers Publishing Company, Inc., which moved to its new building at 4500 Speight, Waco, Texas, on November 1, 1977. We particularly wish to thank Robert E. Davis, President, and three members of his staff: Mike Prim, Lane Price, and Bill Shirley.

The hardbound oversewn binding, with gold stamping on blue fabric, and standard white endsheets, was done by the John D. Ellis Bindery, 141 Manufacturing, Dallas, Texas 75207.

This first edition of 1,000 copies is being published on October 17, 1978, to commemorate the 148th anniversary of the date upon which the Álamo Presidial Company arrived at the permanent site of Fort Tenoxtitlan, on the Brazos River in Texas.